I still jog since I started on the morning of the Tennis Festival held on March 30th. I feel like I'm in shape these days. Maybe I'll keep doing it and go for the Honolulu Marathon!

– Takeshi Konomi

D0963008

About Takeshi Konomi

Takeshi Konomi exploded onto the manga scene with the incredible **THE PRINCE OF TENNIS**. His refined art style and sleek character designs proved popular with **Weekly Shonen Jump** readers, and **THE PRINCE OF TENNIS** became the number one sports manga in Japan almost overnight. Its cast of fascinating male tennis players attracted legions of female readers even though it was originally intended to be a boys' comic. The manga continues to be a success in Japan and has inspired a hit anime series, as well as several video games and mountains of merchandise.

THE PRINCE OF TENNIS
VOL. 21
The SHONEN JUMP Manga Edition

STORY AND ART BY
TAKESHI KONOMI

Translation/Joe Yamazaki
Consultant/Michelle Pangilinan
Touch-up Art & Lettering/Vanessa Satone
Design/Sam Elzway
Editors/Joel Enos & Leyla Aker

Editor in Chief, Books/Alvin Lu
Editor in Chief, Magazines/Marc Weidenbaum
VP of Publishing Licensing/Rika Inouye
VP of Sales/Gonzalo Ferreyra
Sr. VP of Marketing/Liza Coppola
Publisher/Hyoe Narita

Printed in the U.S.A.

Published by VIZ Media, LLC
P.O. Box 77010
San Francisco, CA 94107

SHONEN JUMP Manga Edition
10 9 8 7 6 5 4 3 2 1
First printing, September 2007

www.viz.com

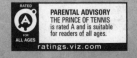

THE WORLD'S
MOST POPULAR MANGA

www.shonenjump.com

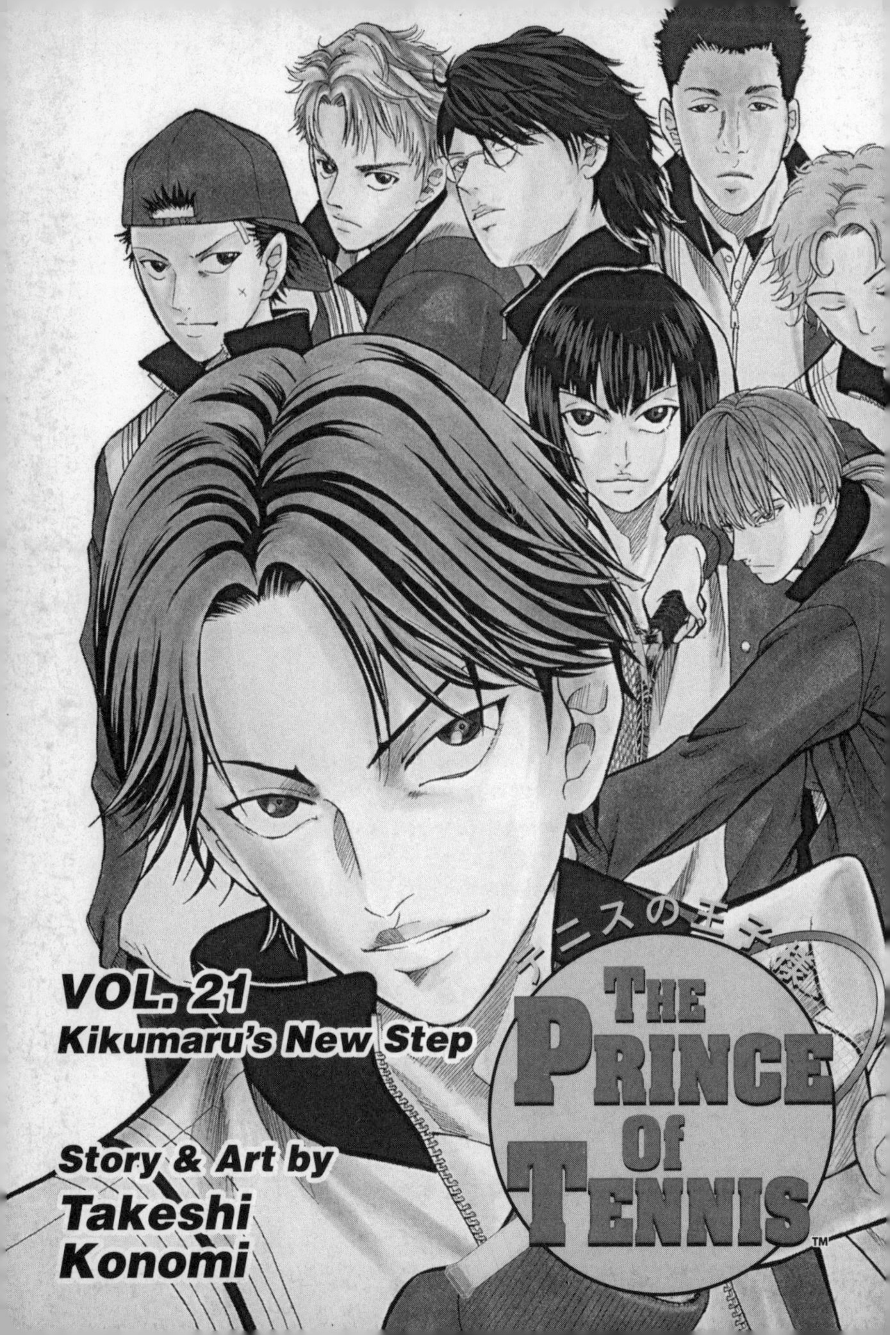

THE PRINCE OF TENNIS™

VOL. 21
Kikumaru's New Step

Story & Art by
Takeshi Konomi

ENNIS CLUB

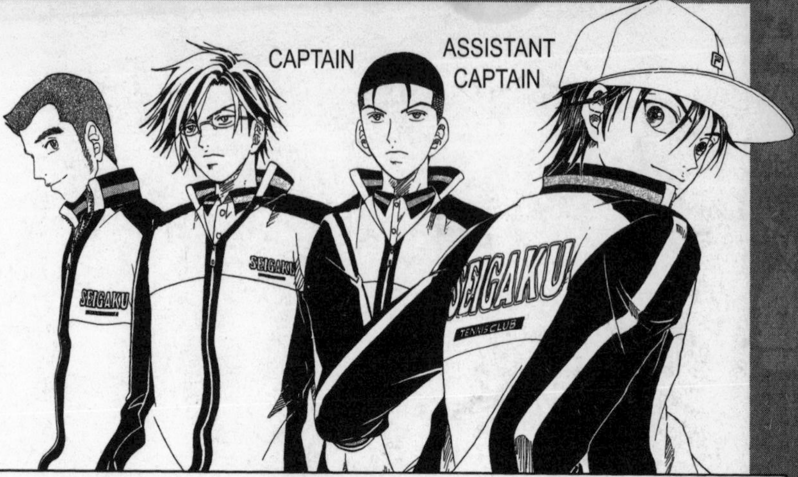
CAPTAIN
ASSISTANT CAPTAIN

• TAKASHI KAWAMURA • KUNIMITSU TEZUKA • SHUICHIRO OISHI • RYOMA ECHIZEN •

Seishun Academy student Ryoma Echizen is a tennis prodigy with wins in four consecutive U.S. Junior tournaments under his belt. Then he became a starter as a 7th grader and led his team to the District Preliminaries! Despite a few mishaps, Seishun won the District Prelims and City Tournament, and even earned a ticket to the Kanto Tournament.

The Kanto Tournament begins and Seishun's first-round opponent is last year's Nationals runner-up, Hyotei. Seishun is victorious, but Kunimitsu injures his shoulder. He leaves the team to seek treatment in Kyushu. Without him, the Seishun team strengthens their team unity and defeats their next opponent, Midoriyama! With their ticket to the Nationals already in hand, they now must face Chiba's Rokkaku in the semis! Seishun strikes first, winning the No. 2 Doubles match, but...

STORY &

HARACTERS

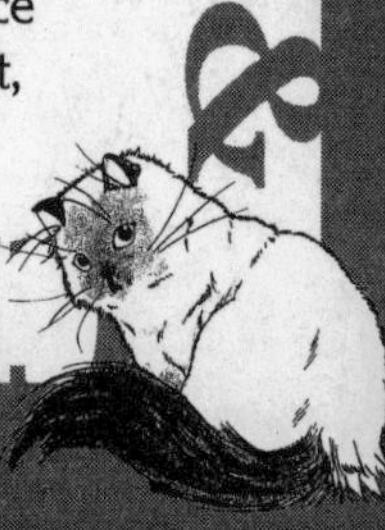

SEIGAKU T

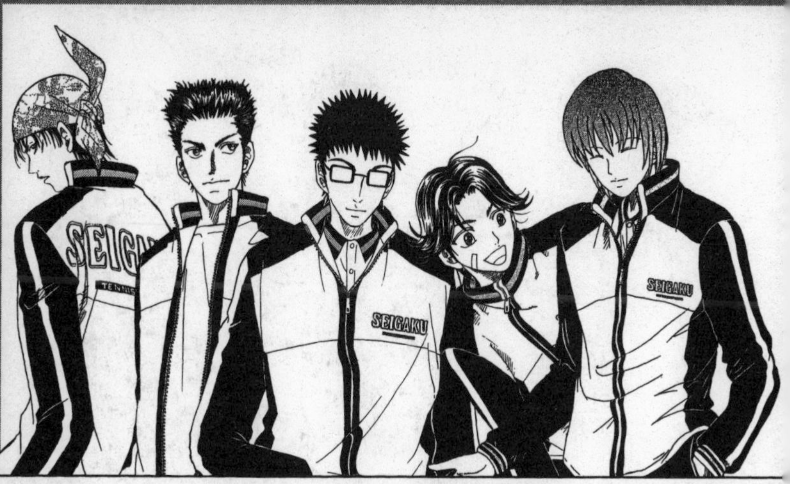

• KAORU KAIDO • TAKESHI MOMOSHIRO • SADAHARU INUI • EIJI KIKUMARU • SHUSUKE FUJI •

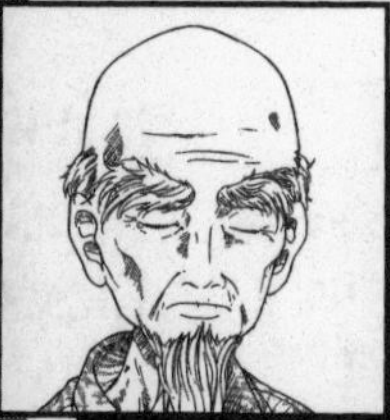

ROKKAKU JUNIOR HIGH SCHOOL TENNIS COACH

OJI

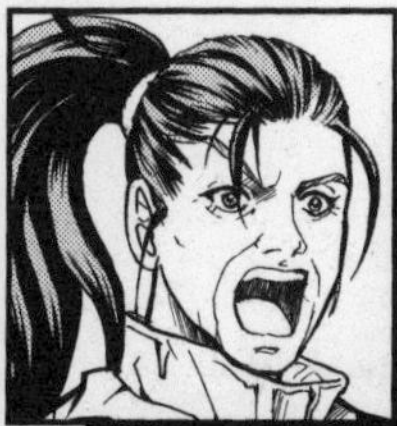

SEISHUN ACADEMY TENNIS COACH

SUMIRE RYUZAKI

THE PRINCE OF TENNIS

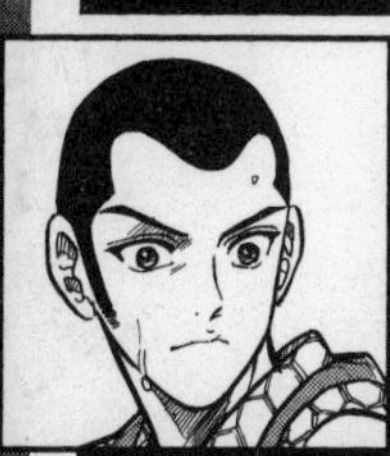

ROKKAKU JUNIOR HIGH SCHOOL

KENTARO AOI

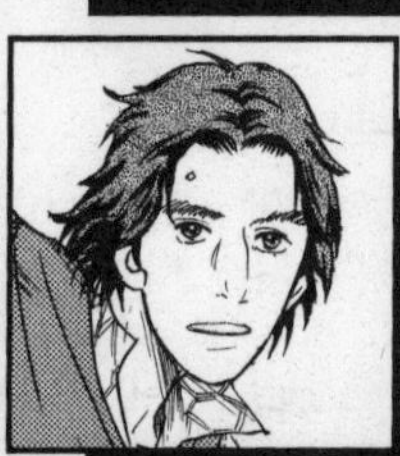

ROKKAKU JUNIOR HIGH SCHOOL

MAREHIKO ITSUKI

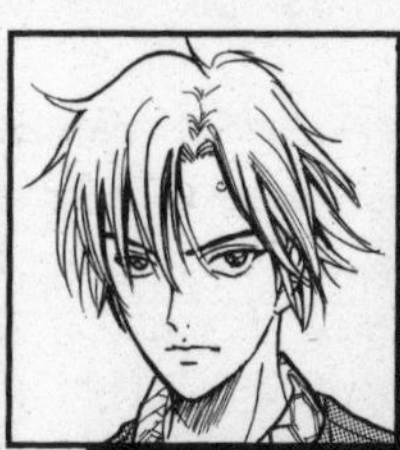

ROKKAKU JUNIOR HIGH SCHOOL

KOJIRO SAEKI

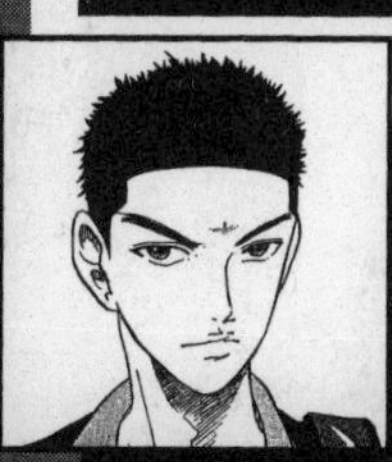

FUDOMINE

KIPPEI TACHIBANA

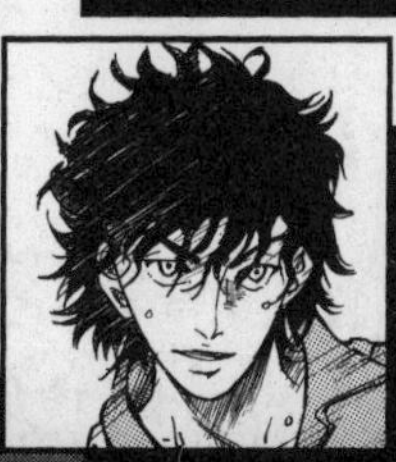

RIKKAI

AKAYA KIRIHARA

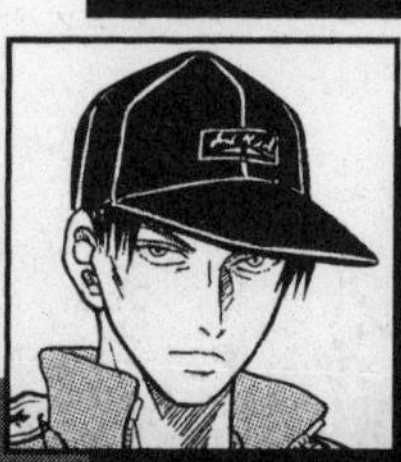

RIKKAI

GENICHIRO SANADA

CONTENTS

Vol. 21
Kikumaru's New Step

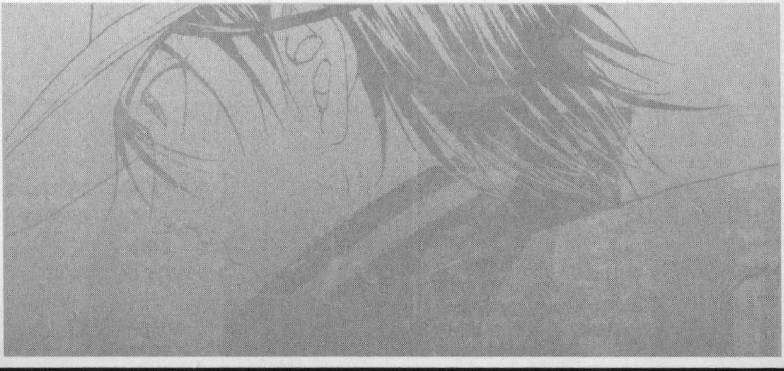

GENIUS 177: PINCH

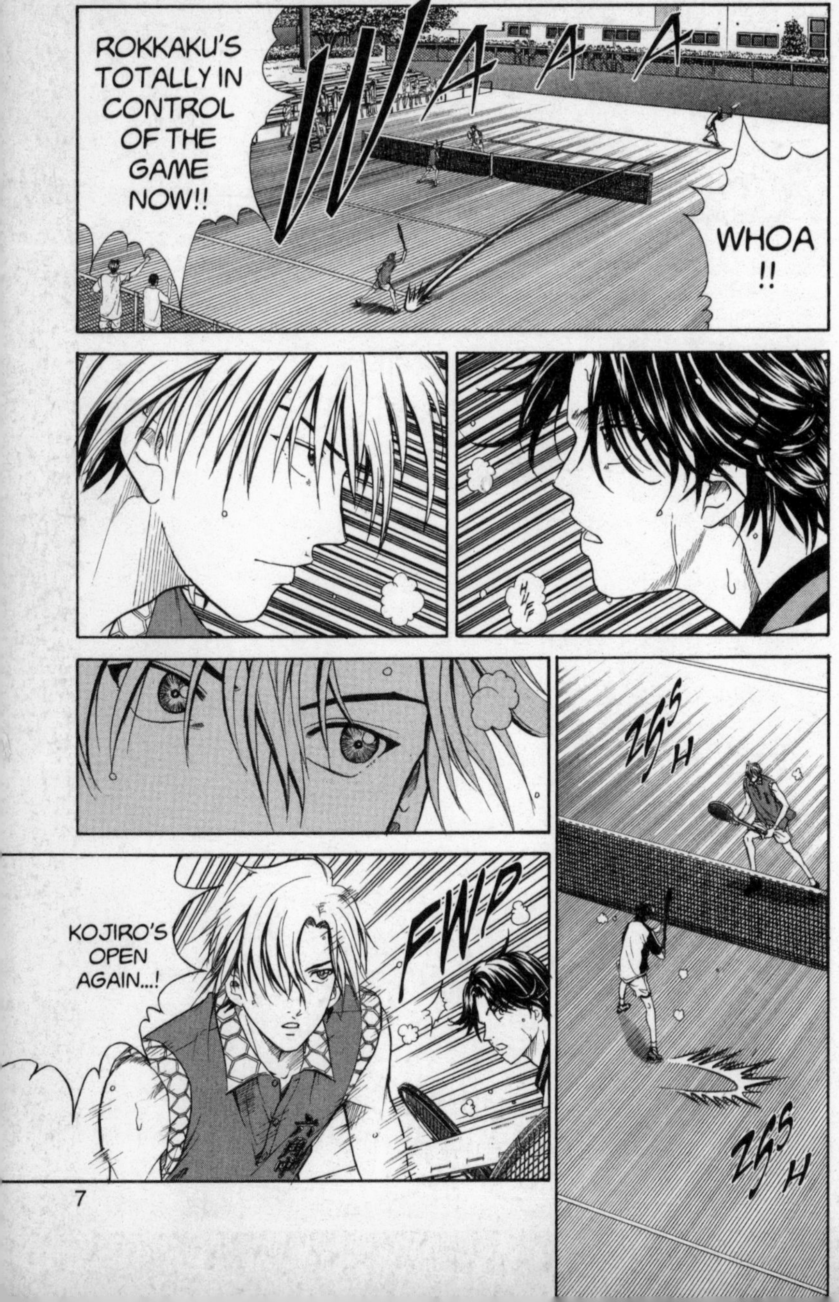

WAAA
WHOA !!
ROKKAKU'S TOTALLY IN CONTROL OF THE GAME NOW!!
HUFF
ZSSH
FWP
KOJIRO'S OPEN AGAIN...!
ZSSH

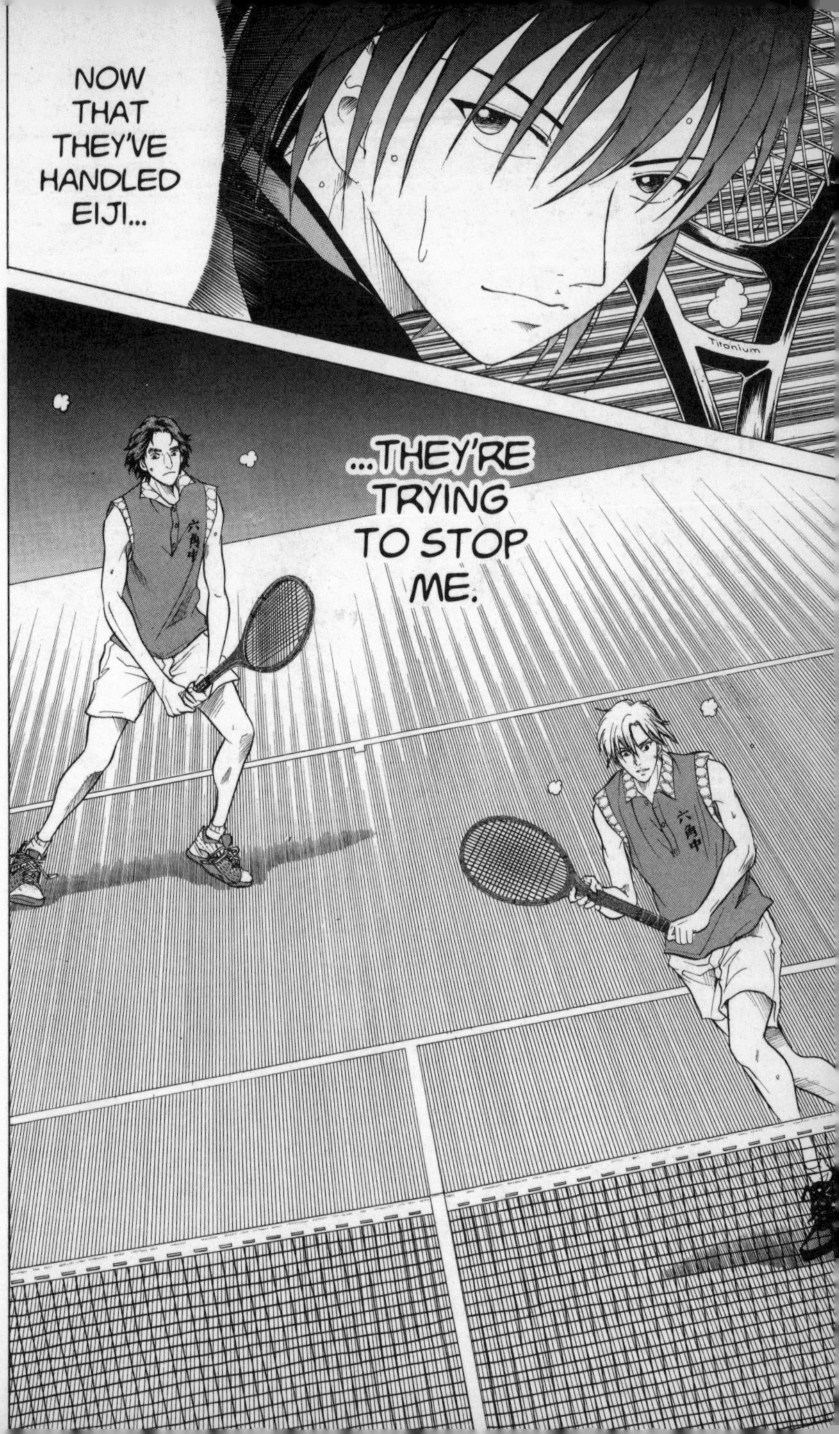
NOW THAT THEY'VE HANDLED EIJI...
...THEY'RE TRYING TO STOP ME.
Titanium

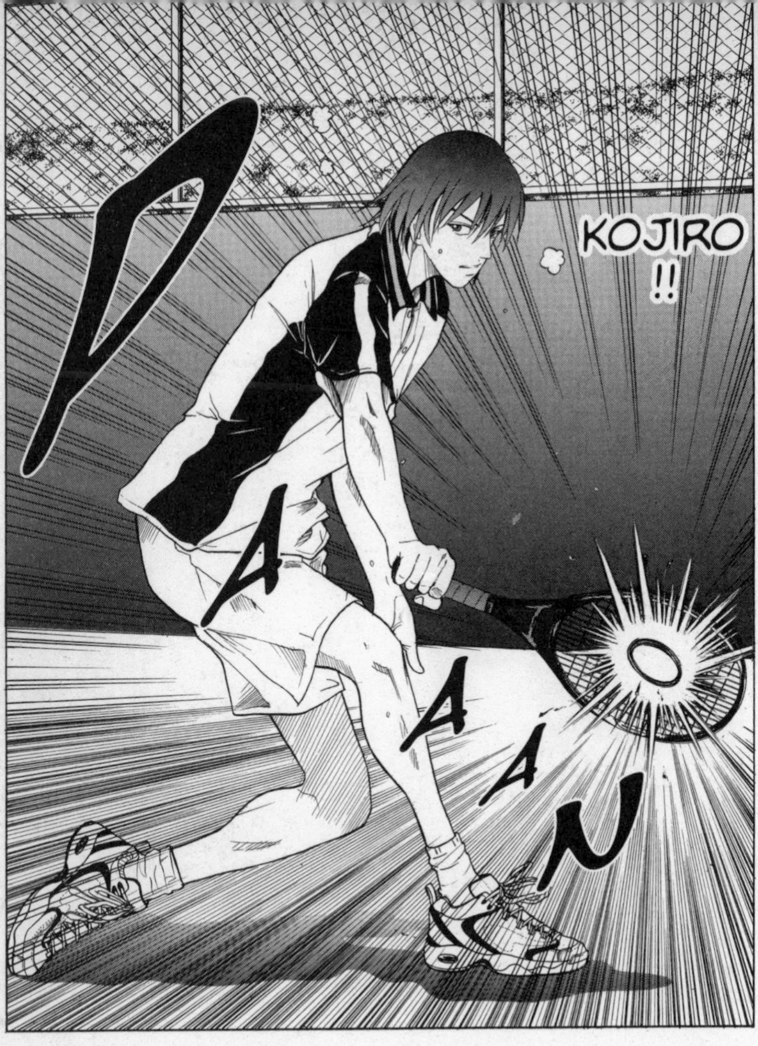
KOJIRO !!
PAAAAN

GENIUS 177: PINCH

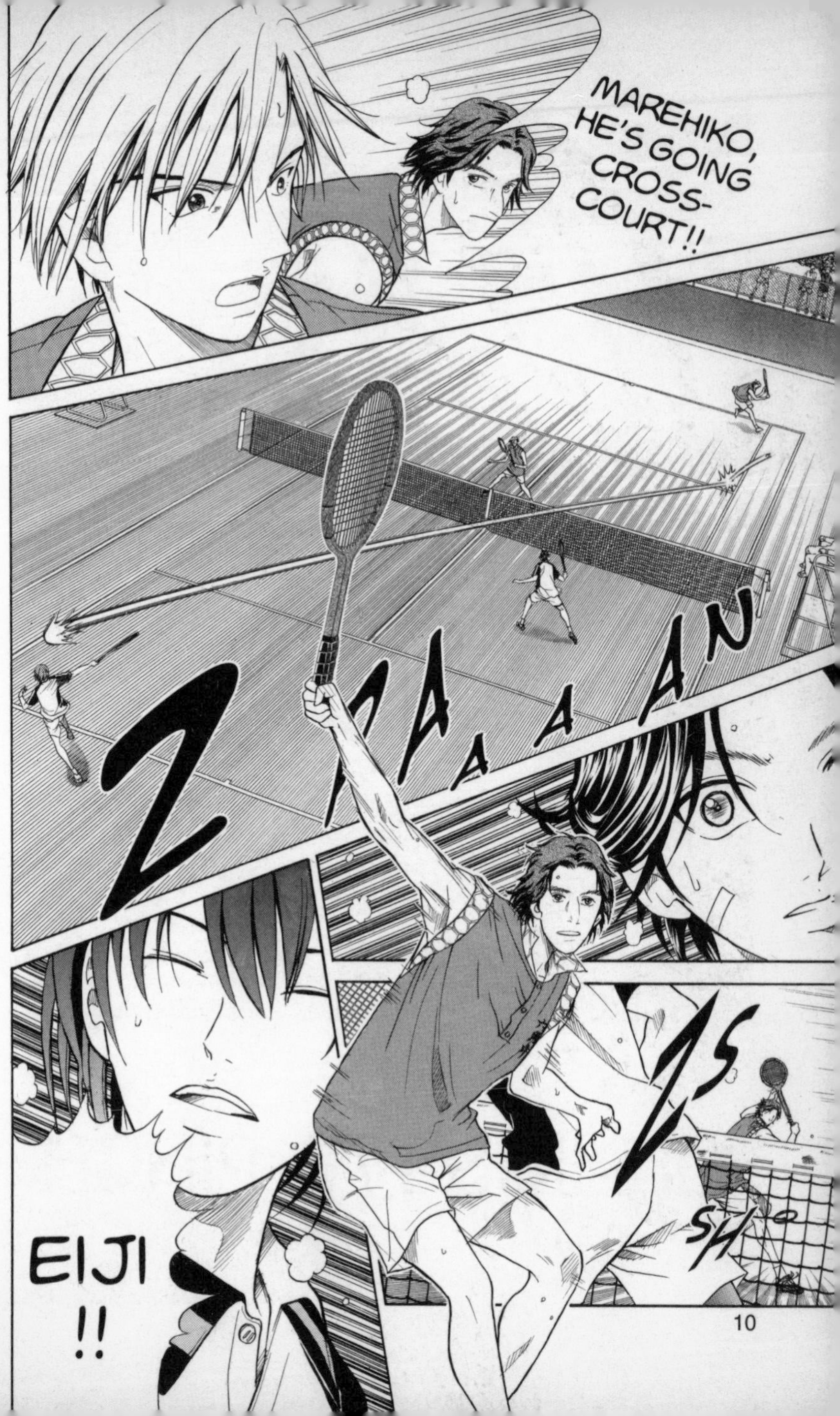
MAREHIKO, HE'S GOING CROSS-COURT!!
ZPAAAAAN
SH
EIJI !!

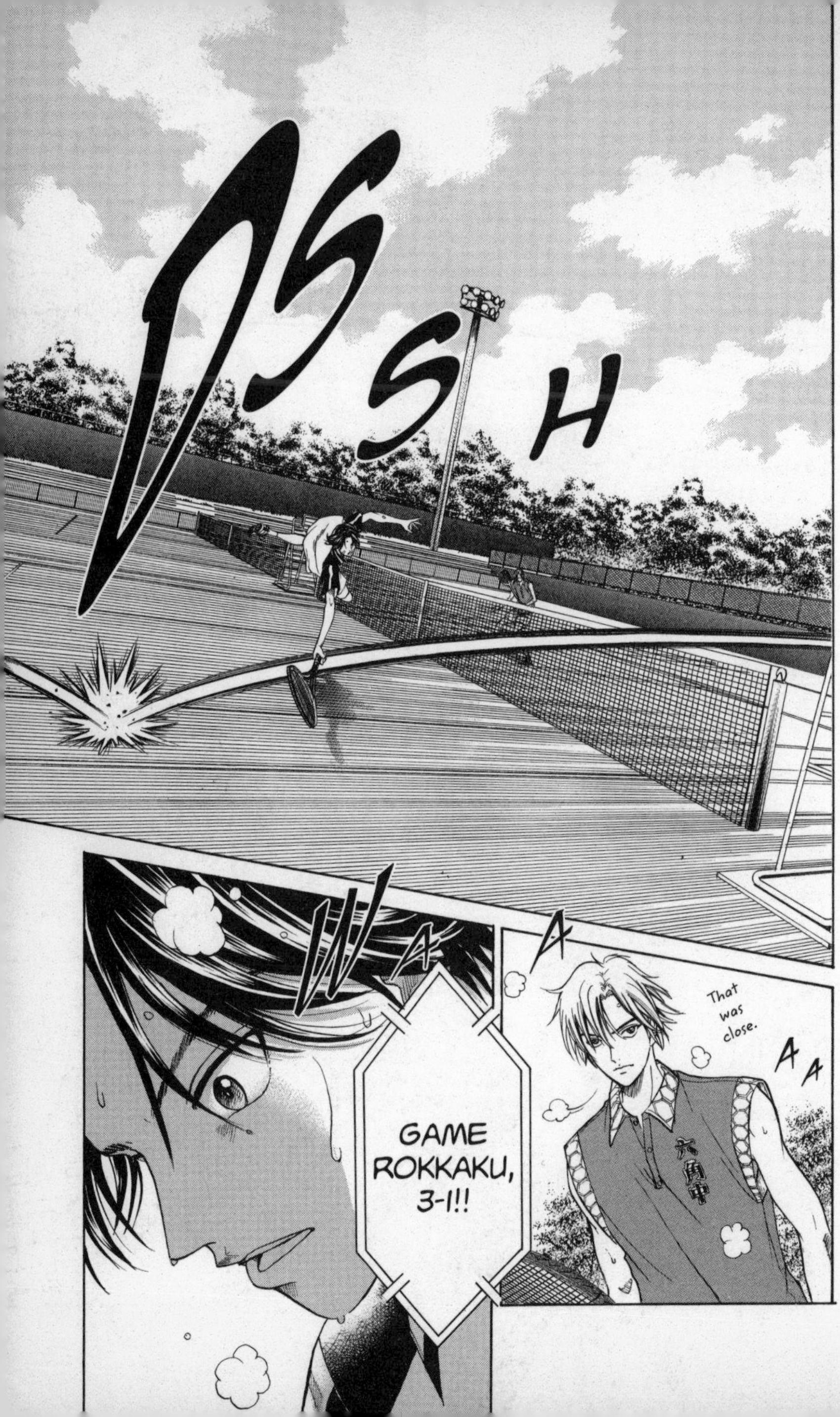

DSSH
WAAAA
GAME ROKKAKU, 3-1!!
That was close.

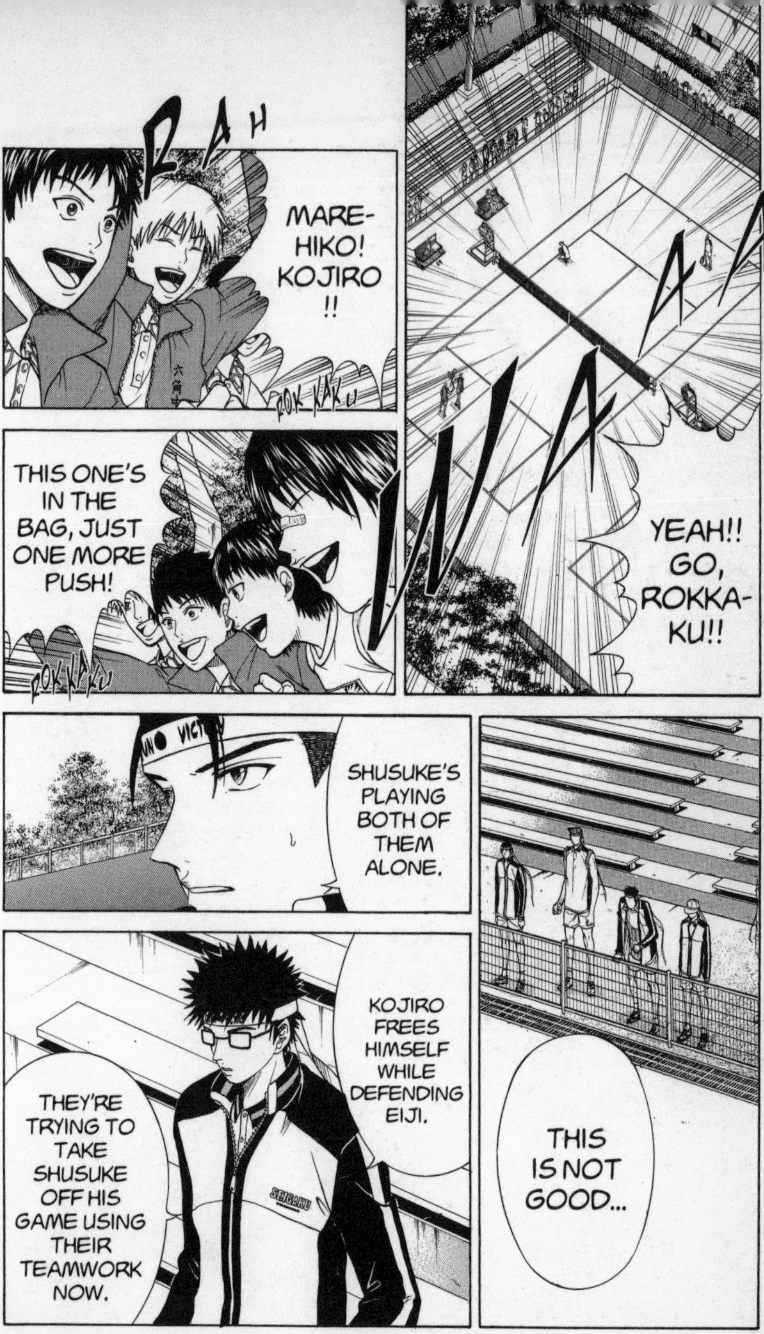
WAAAA
YEAH!! GO, ROKKAKU!!
RAH
MARE-HIKO! KOJIRO !!
ROKKAKU
THIS ONE'S IN THE BAG, JUST ONE MORE PUSH!
ROKKAKU
THIS IS NOT GOOD...
SHUSUKE'S PLAYING BOTH OF THEM ALONE.
KOJIRO FREES HIMSELF WHILE DEFENDING EIJI.
THEY'RE TRYING TO TAKE SHUSUKE OFF HIS GAME USING THEIR TEAMWORK NOW.

READ THIS WAY

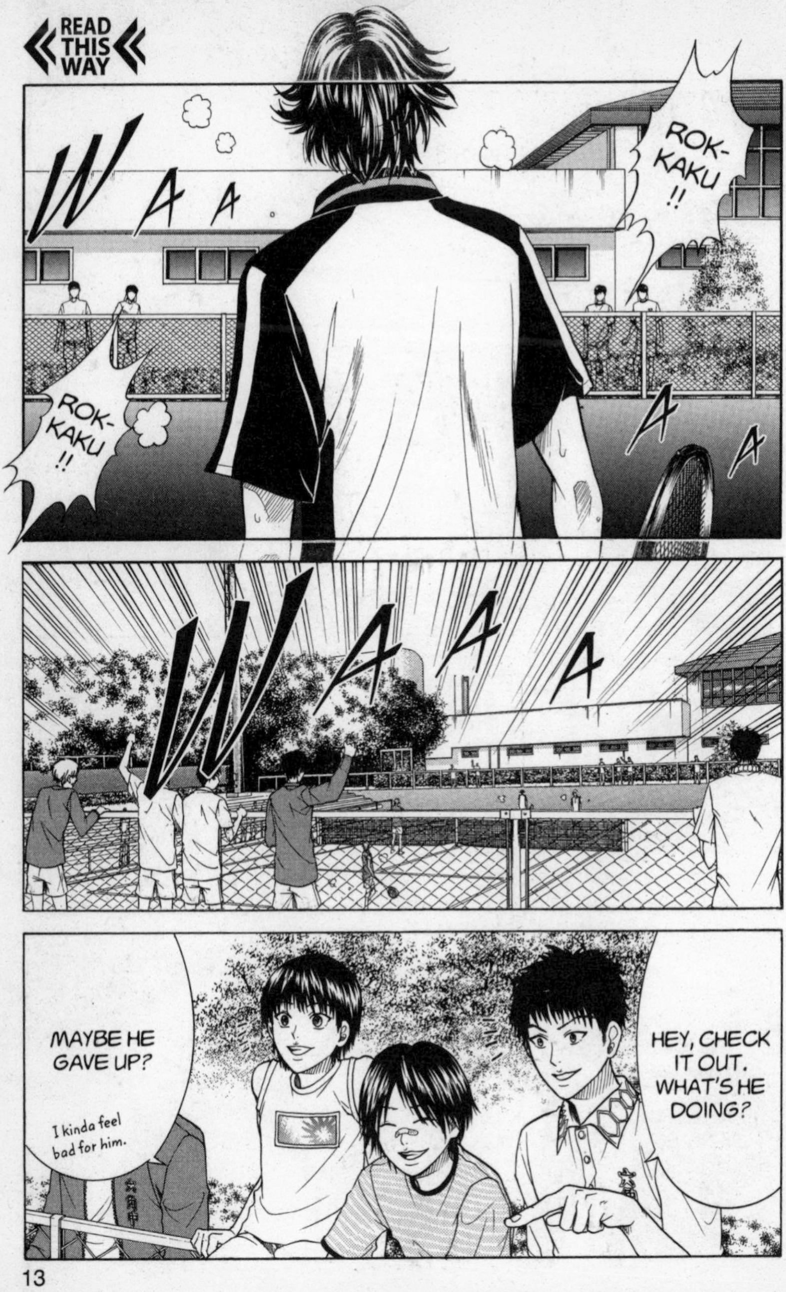
WAAA
ROKKAKU!!
ROKKAKU!!
AA
WAAA
HEY, CHECK IT OUT. WHAT'S HE DOING?
MAYBE HE GAVE UP?
I kinda feel bad for him.

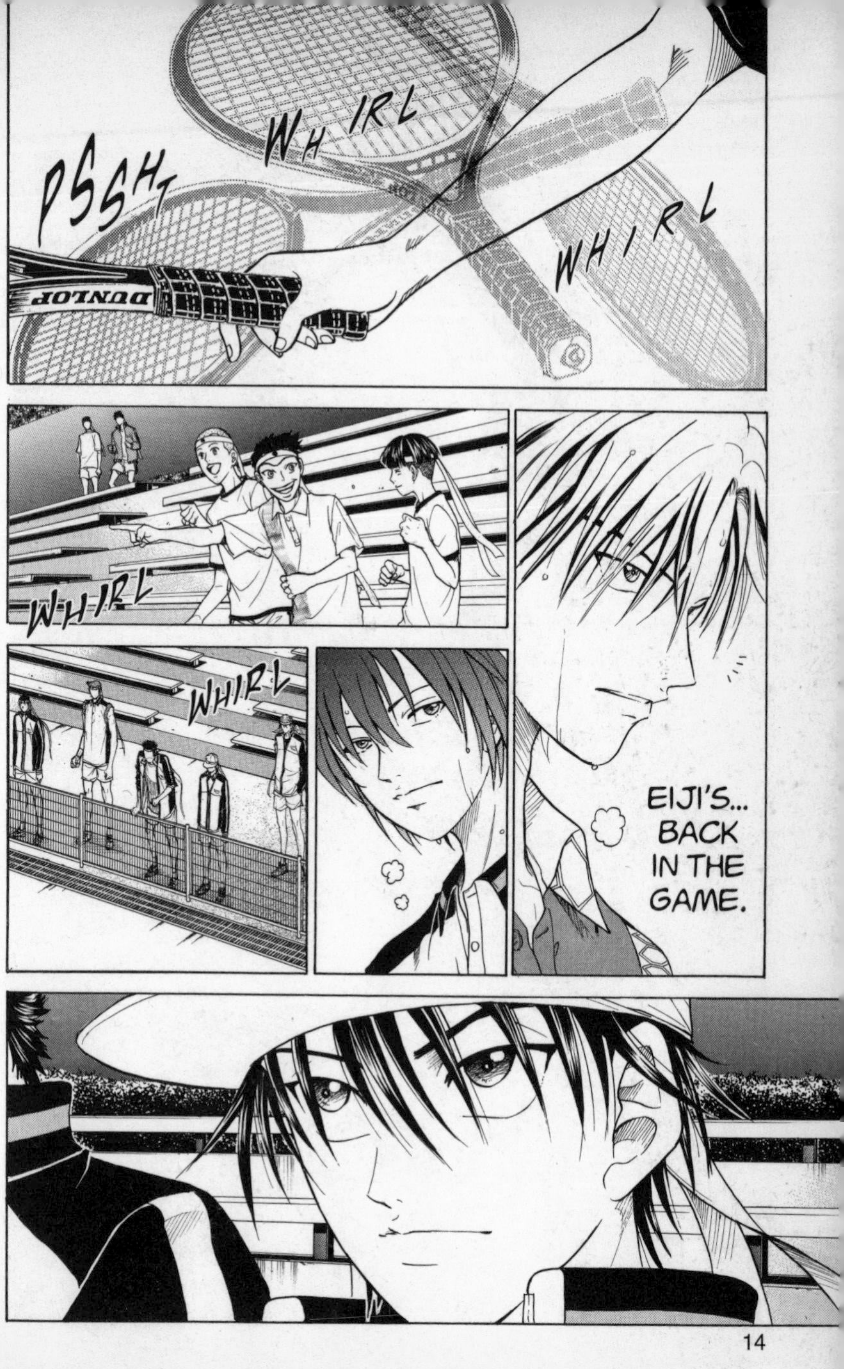
WHIRL
PSSHT
WHIRL
EIJI'S... BACK IN THE GAME.
WHIRL
WHIRL

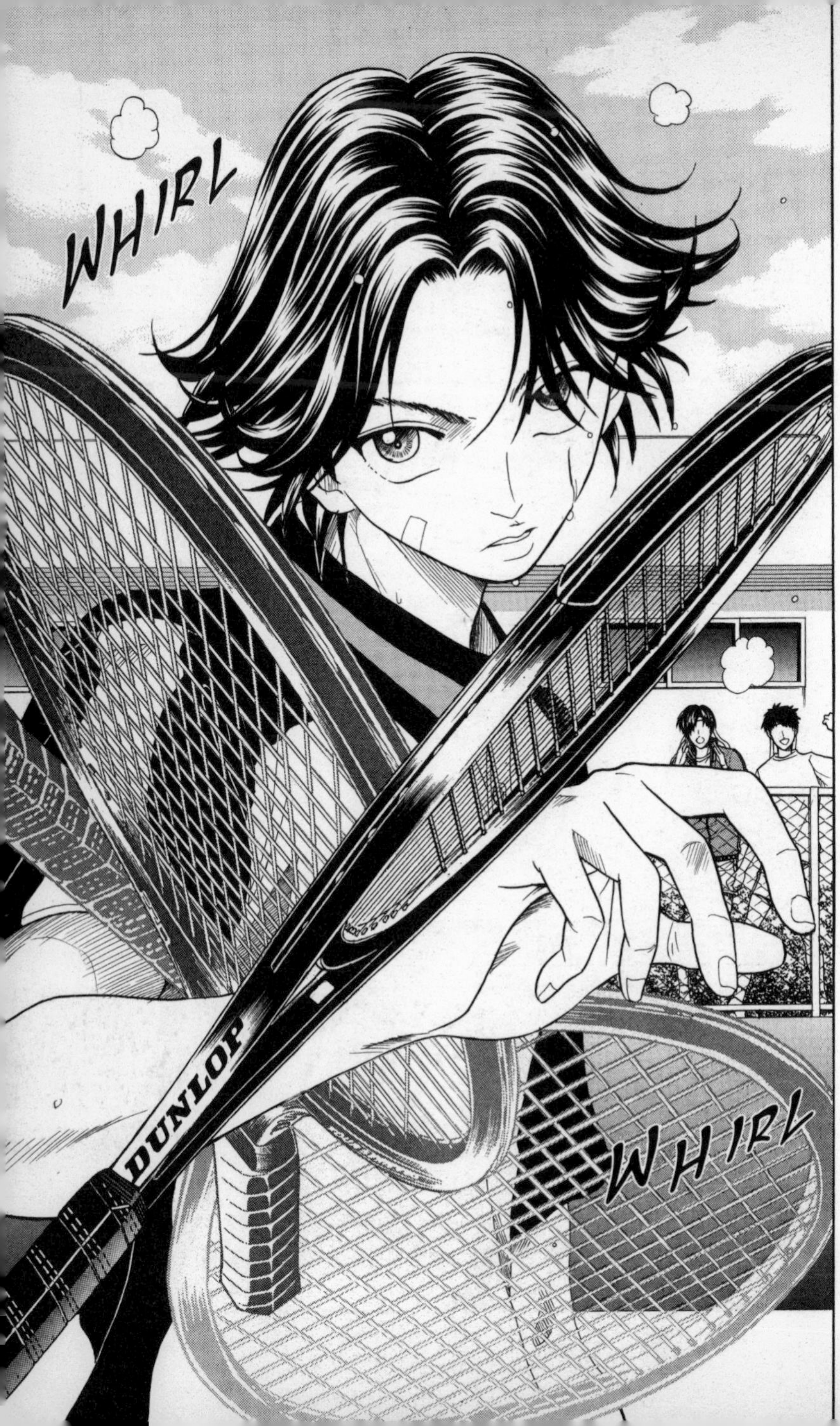
WHIRL
DUNLOP
WHIRL

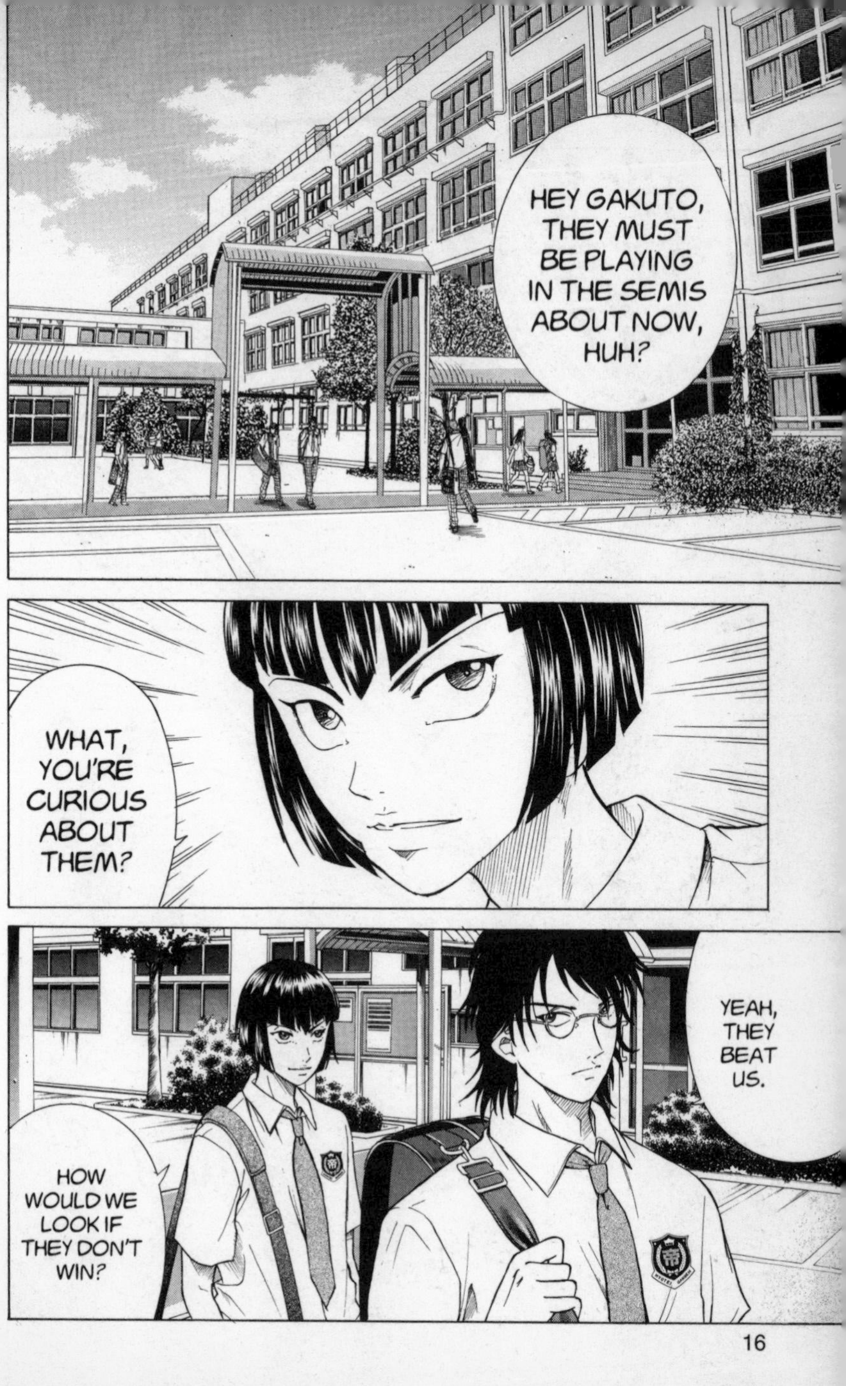
HEY GAKUTO, THEY MUST BE PLAYING IN THE SEMIS ABOUT NOW, HUH?
WHAT, YOU'RE CURIOUS ABOUT THEM?
YEAH, THEY BEAT US.
HOW WOULD WE LOOK IF THEY DON'T WIN?

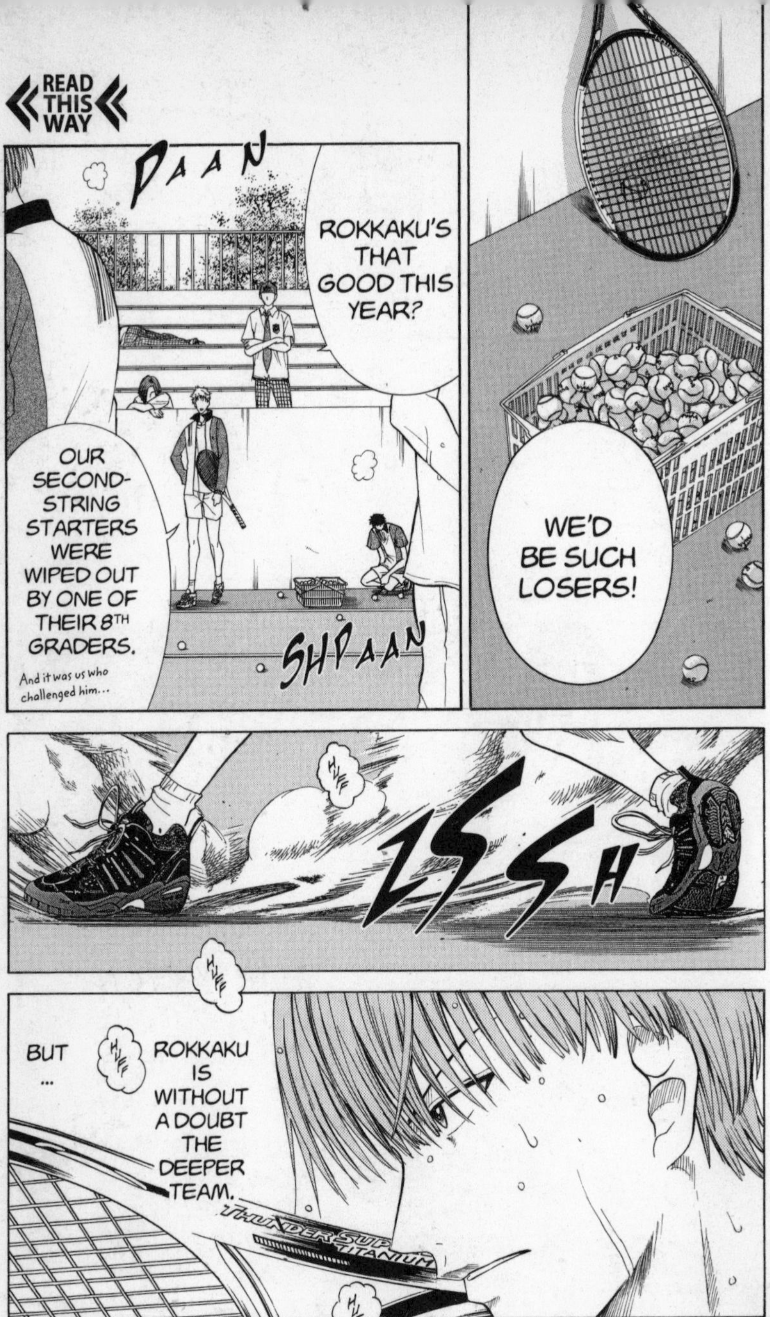
READ THIS WAY
WE'D BE SUCH LOSERS!
ROKKAKU'S THAT GOOD THIS YEAR?
DAAN
OUR SECOND-STRING STARTERS WERE WIPED OUT BY ONE OF THEIR 8TH GRADERS.
And it was us who challenged him...
SHPAAN
HUFF
ZSSH
HUFF
BUT ...
HUFF
ROKKAKU IS WITHOUT A DOUBT THE DEEPER TEAM.
THUNDER SUP
TITANIUM
HUFF

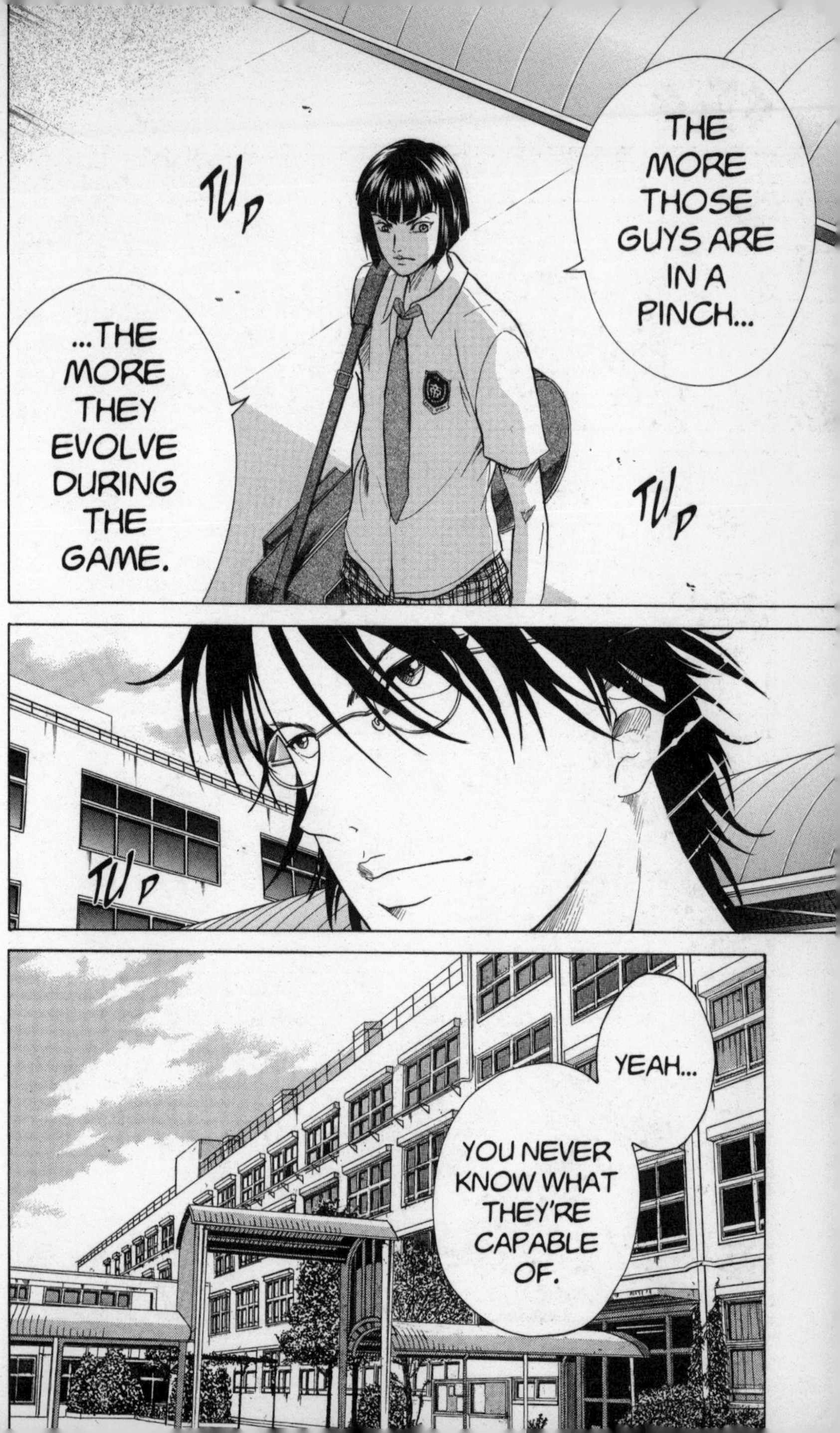
THE MORE THOSE GUYS ARE IN A PINCH...
TUP
...THE MORE THEY EVOLVE DURING THE GAME.
TUP
TUP
YEAH...
YOU NEVER KNOW WHAT THEY'RE CAPABLE OF.

READ THIS WAY

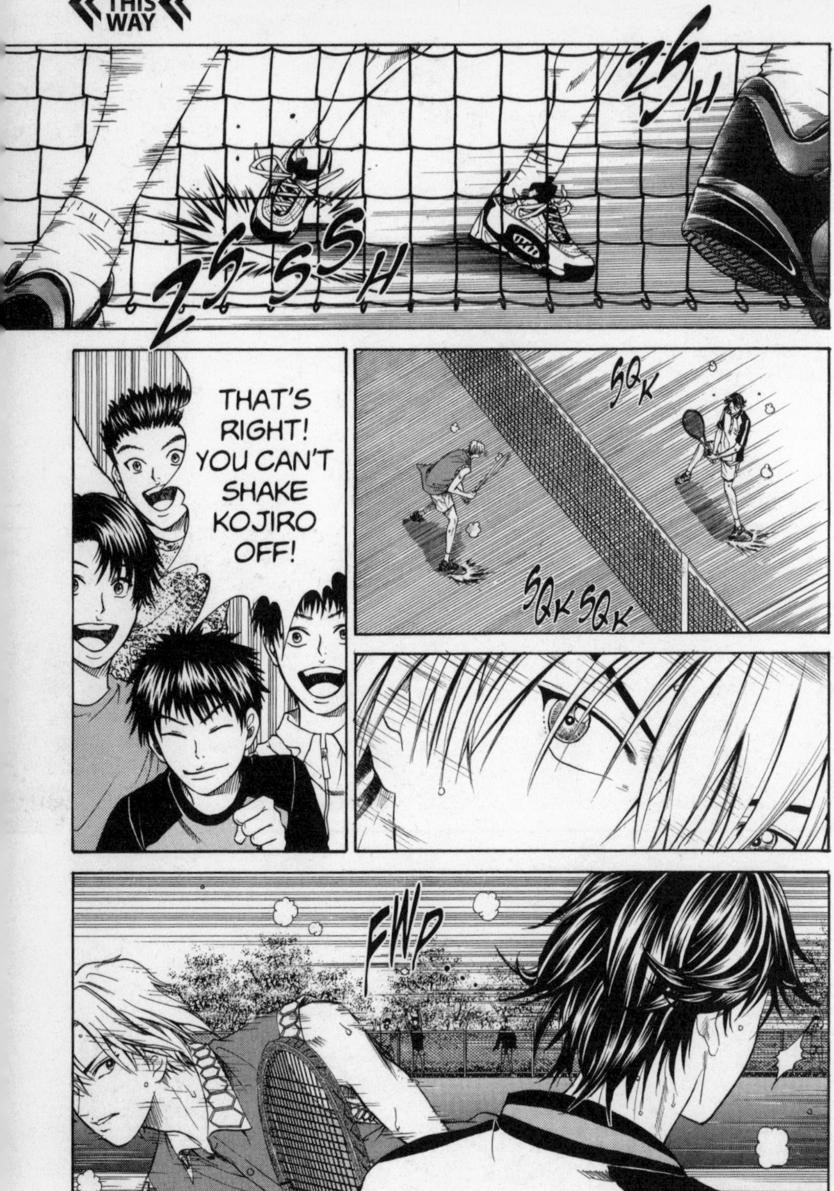
ZSSH
ZSSSSH
SQK
SQK SQK
THAT'S RIGHT! YOU CAN'T SHAKE KOJIRO OFF!
FWP

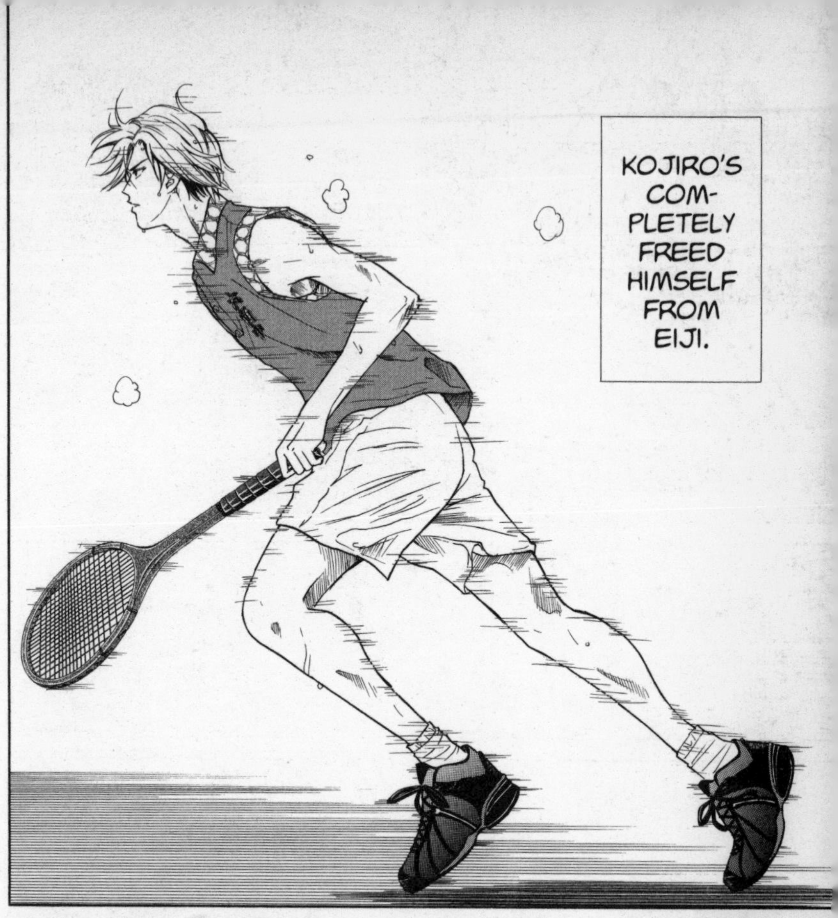
KOJIRO'S COM-PLETELY FREED HIMSELF FROM EIJI.

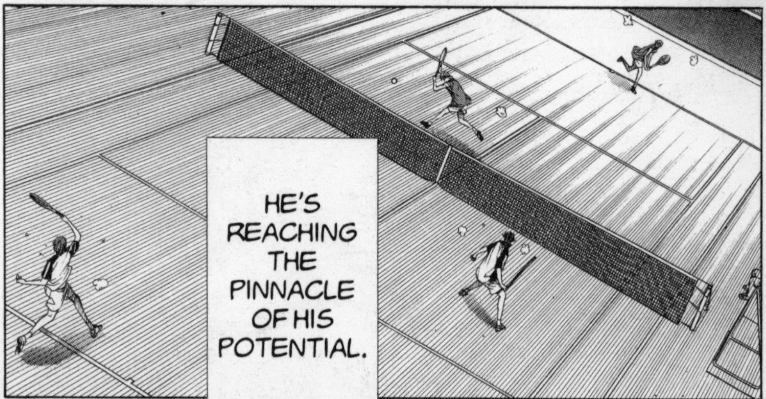
HE'S REACHING THE PINNACLE OF HIS POTENTIAL.

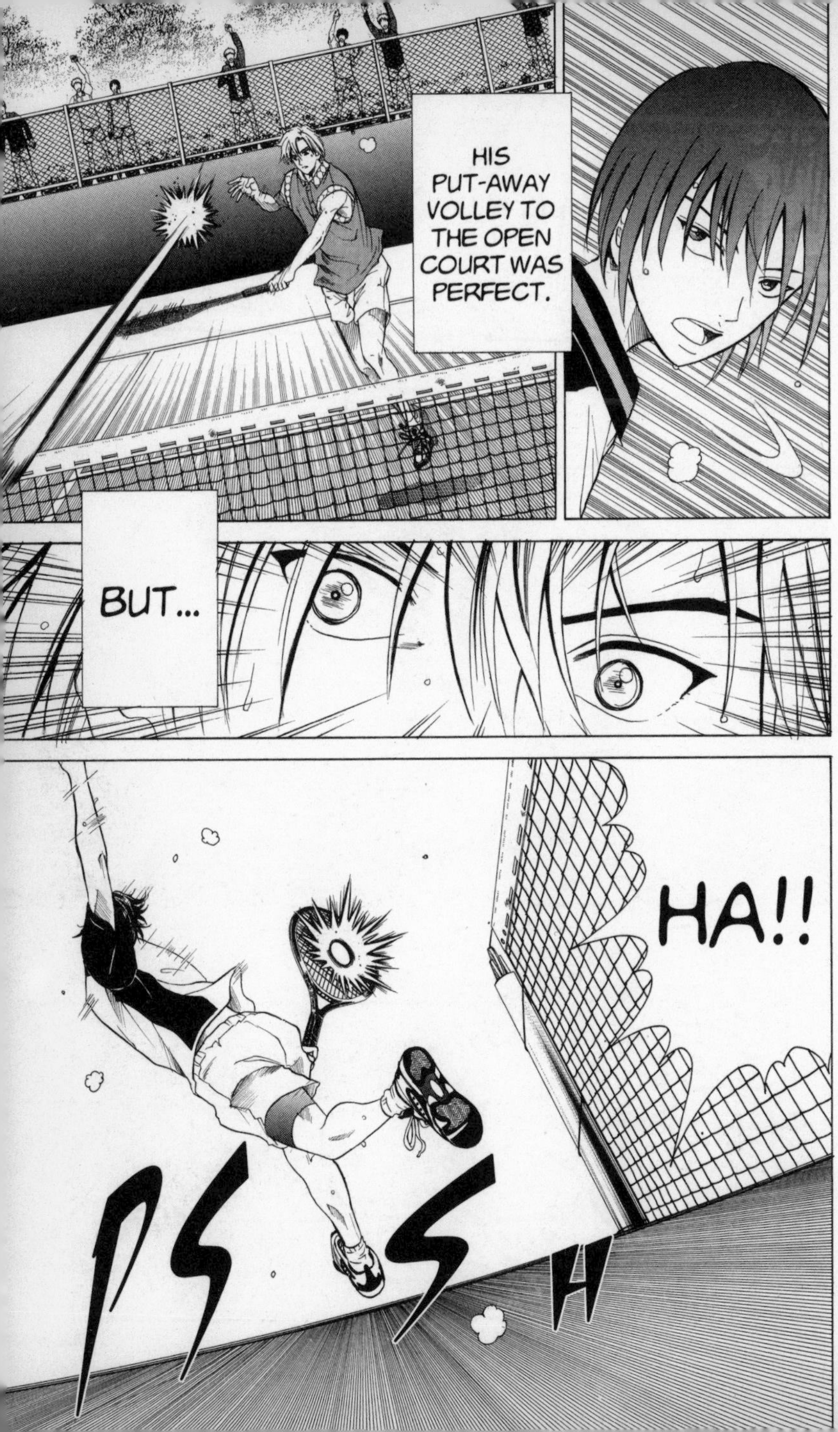

HIS PUT-AWAY VOLLEY TO THE OPEN COURT WAS PERFECT.
BUT...
HA!!
PSSH

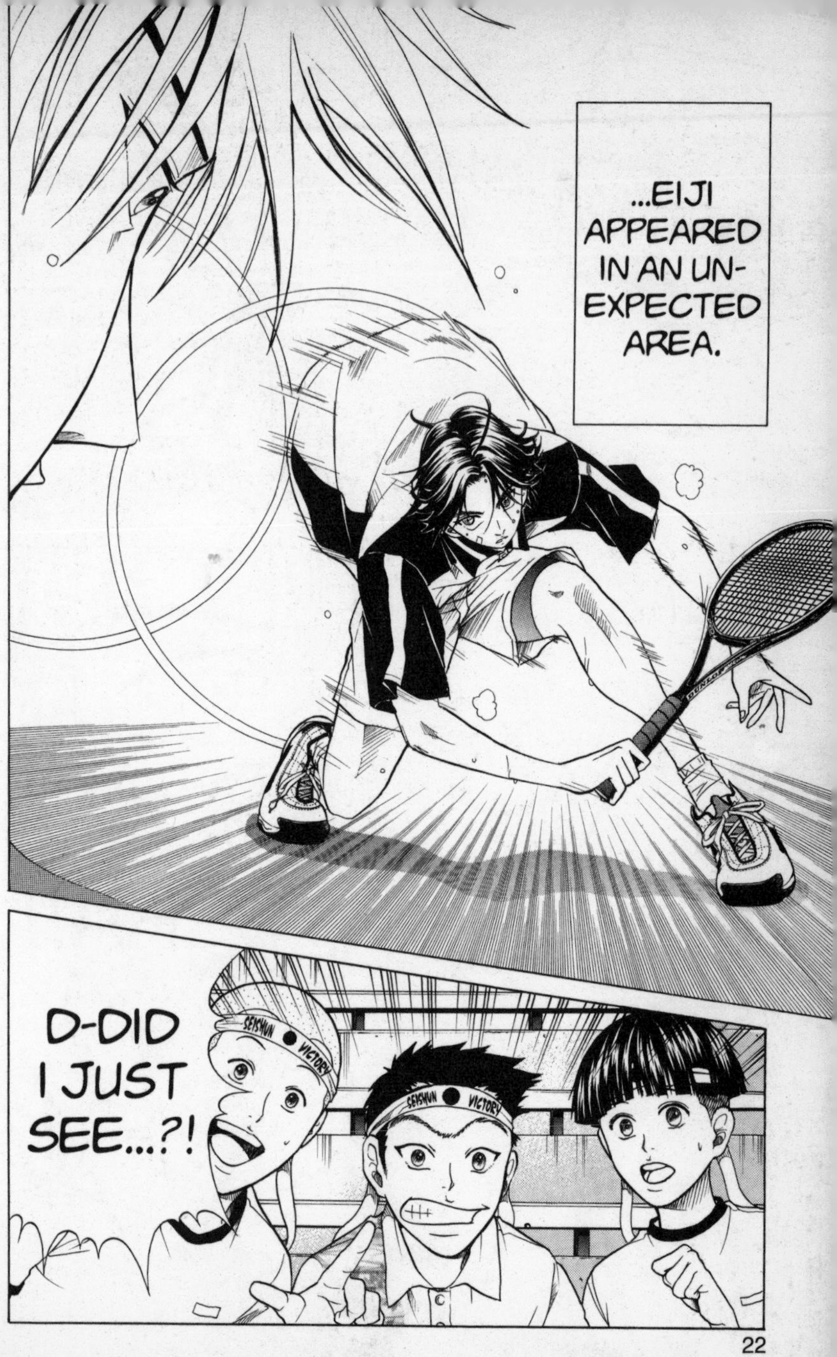
...EIJI APPEARED IN AN UN-EXPECTED AREA.
DUNLOP
SEISHUN VICTORY
D-DID I JUST SEE...?!
SEISHUN VICTORY

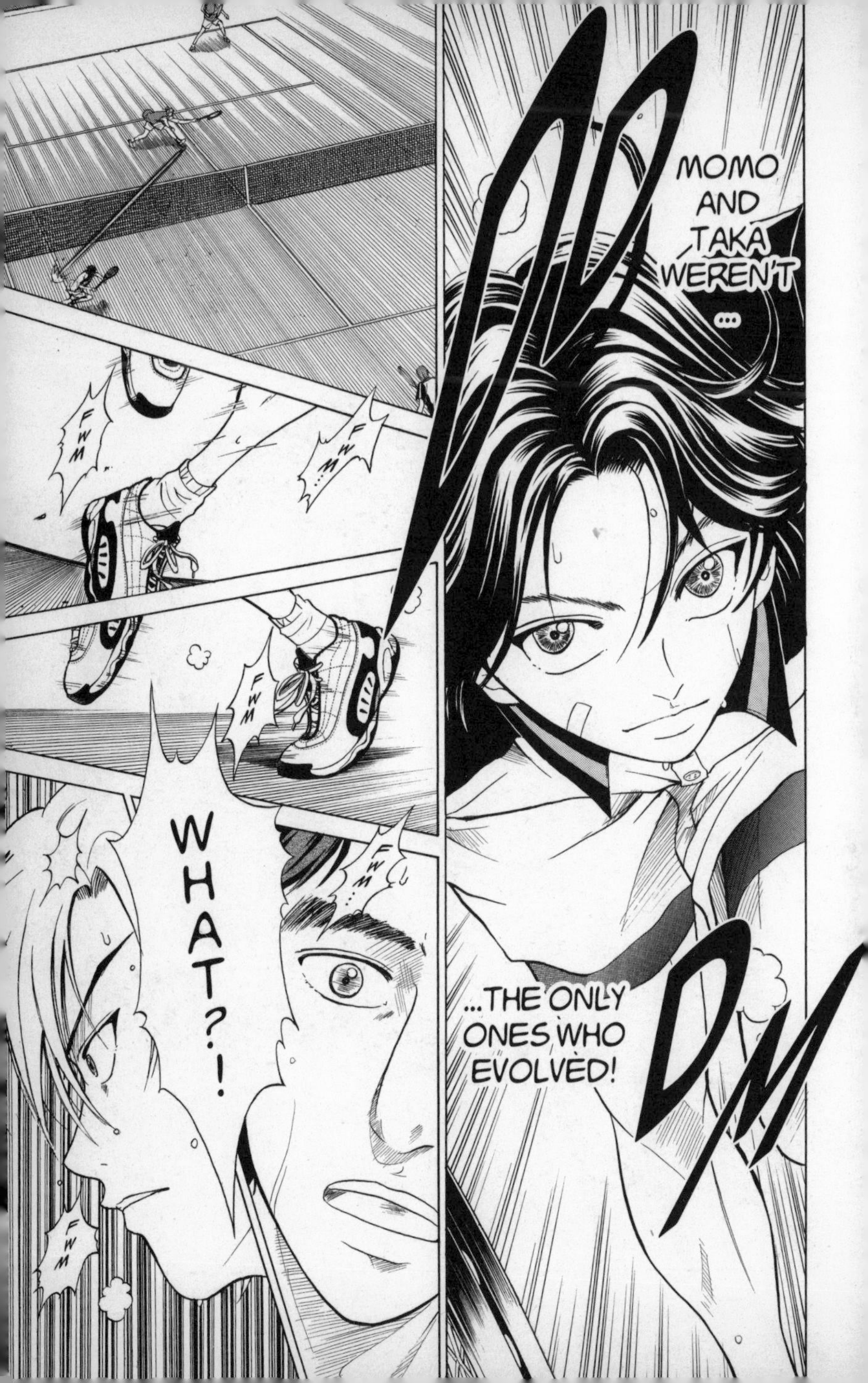
MOMO AND TAKA WEREN'T ...
...THE ONLY ONES WHO EVOLVED!
FWM
FWM...
FWM
FWM...
WHAT?!
FWM

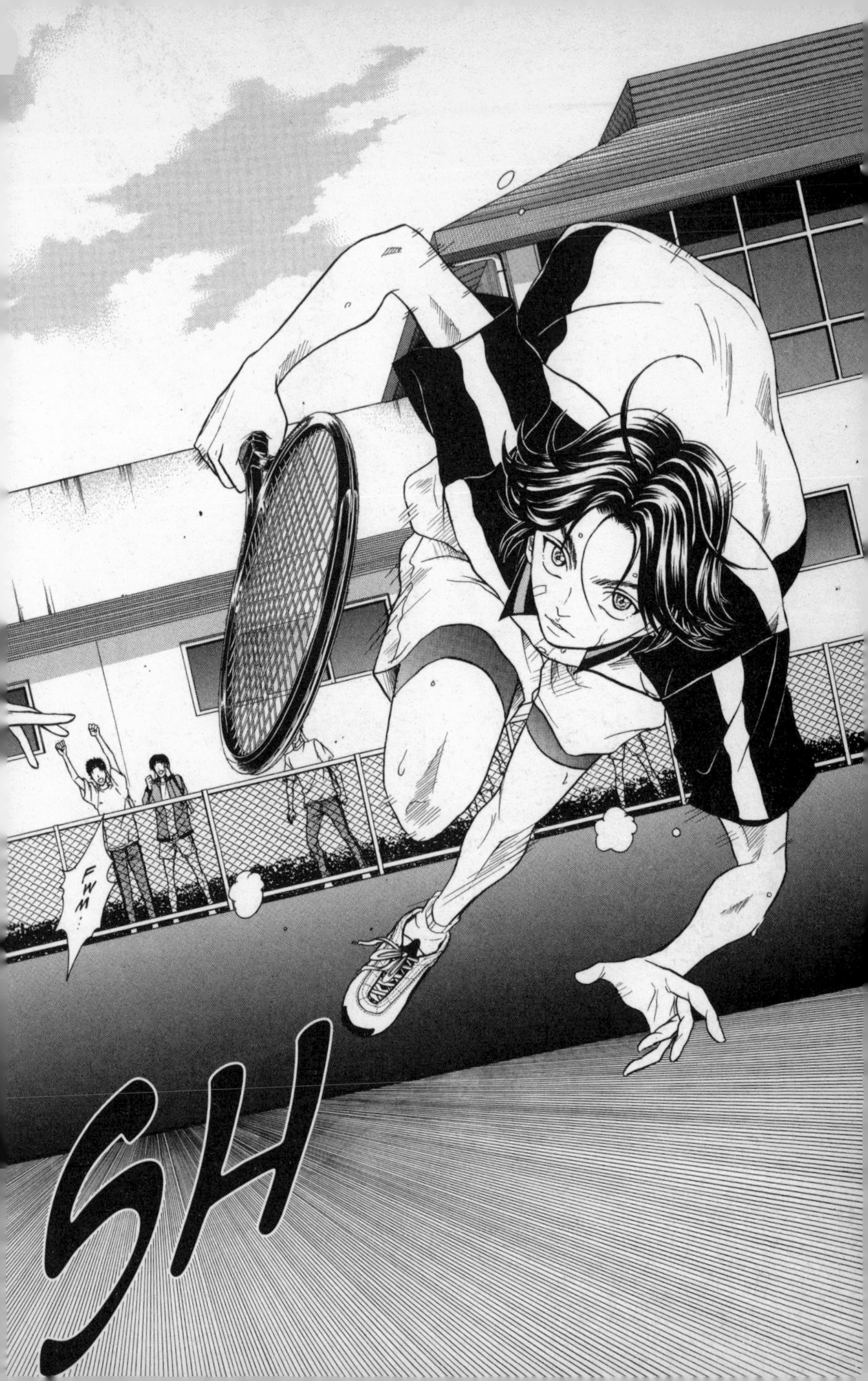
FWM...
SH

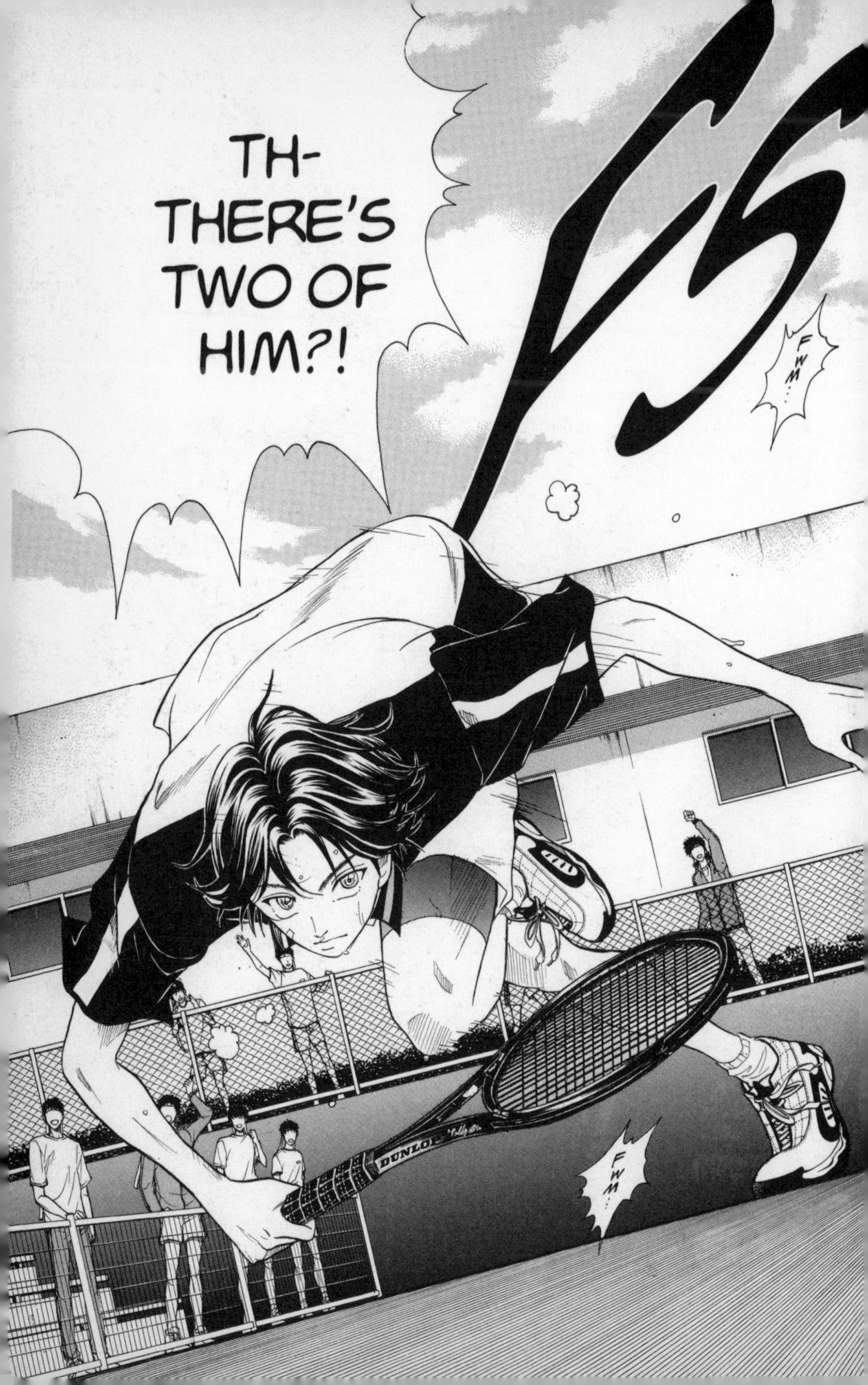
TH-
THERE'S
TWO OF
HIM?!
FWM...
FWM...

テニスの王子様

THE PRINCE OF TENNIS™

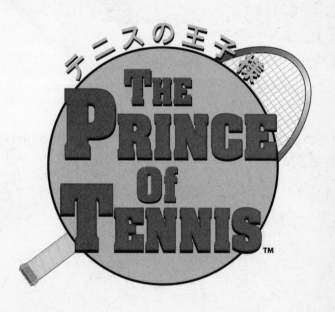

GENIUS 178: KIKUMARU'S NEW STEP

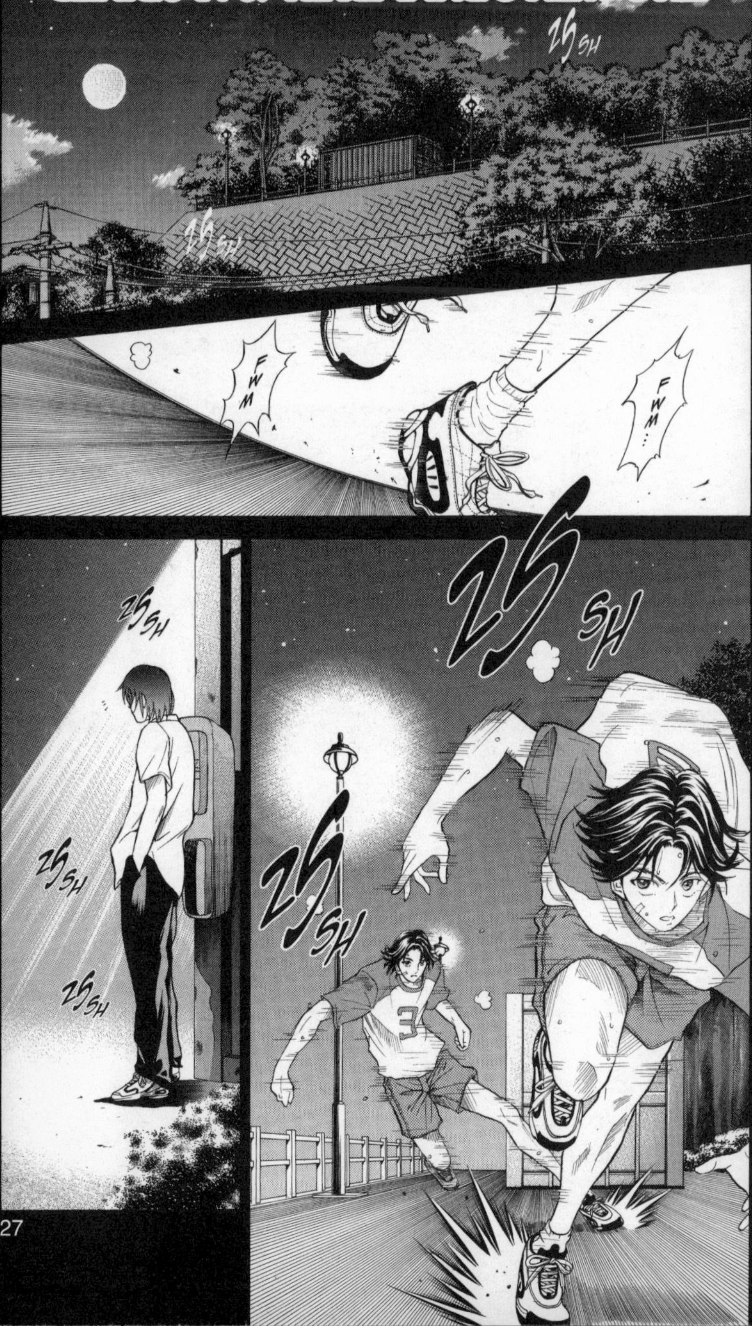

ZSSH
ZSSH
FWM
FWM...
ZSSH
ZSSH
ZSSH
ZSSH
ZSSH
ZSSH

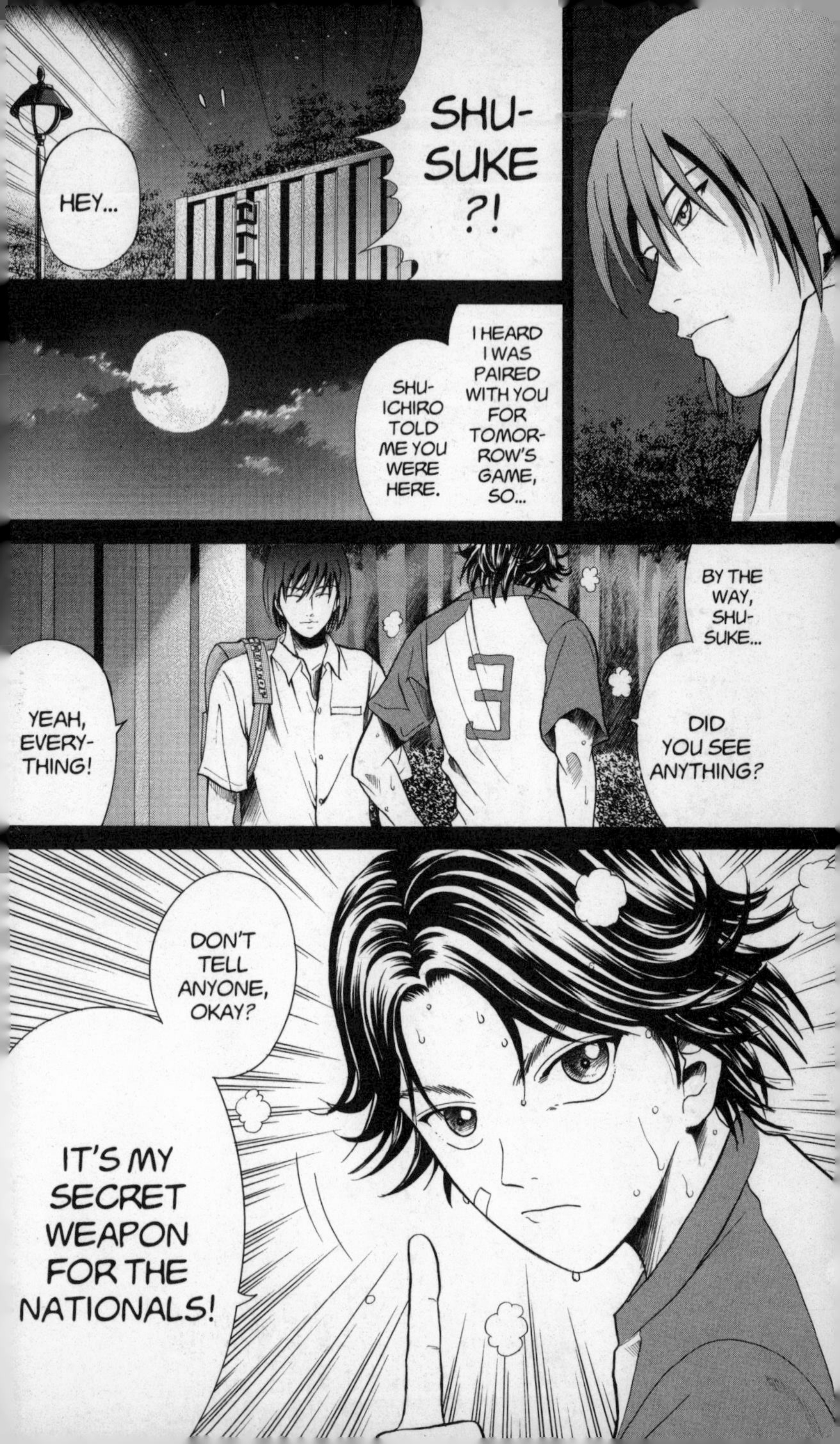
SHU-SUKE?!
HEY...
I HEARD I WAS PAIRED WITH YOU FOR TOMORROW'S GAME, SO...
SHUICHIRO TOLD ME YOU WERE HERE.
BY THE WAY, SHUSUKE...
DID YOU SEE ANYTHING?
YEAH, EVERYTHING!
DON'T TELL ANYONE, OKAY?
IT'S MY SECRET WEAPON FOR THE NATIONALS!

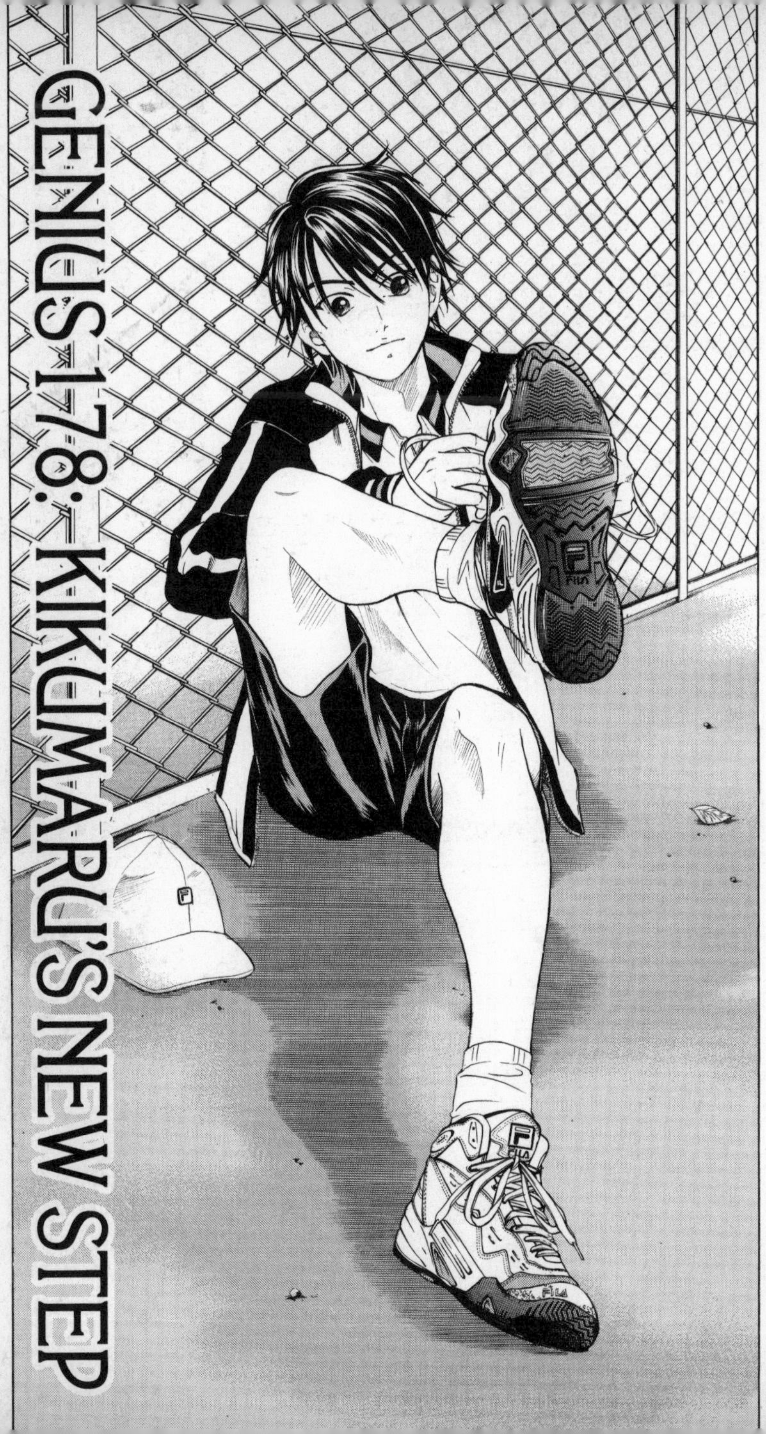
GENIUS 178: KIKUMARU'S NEW STEP

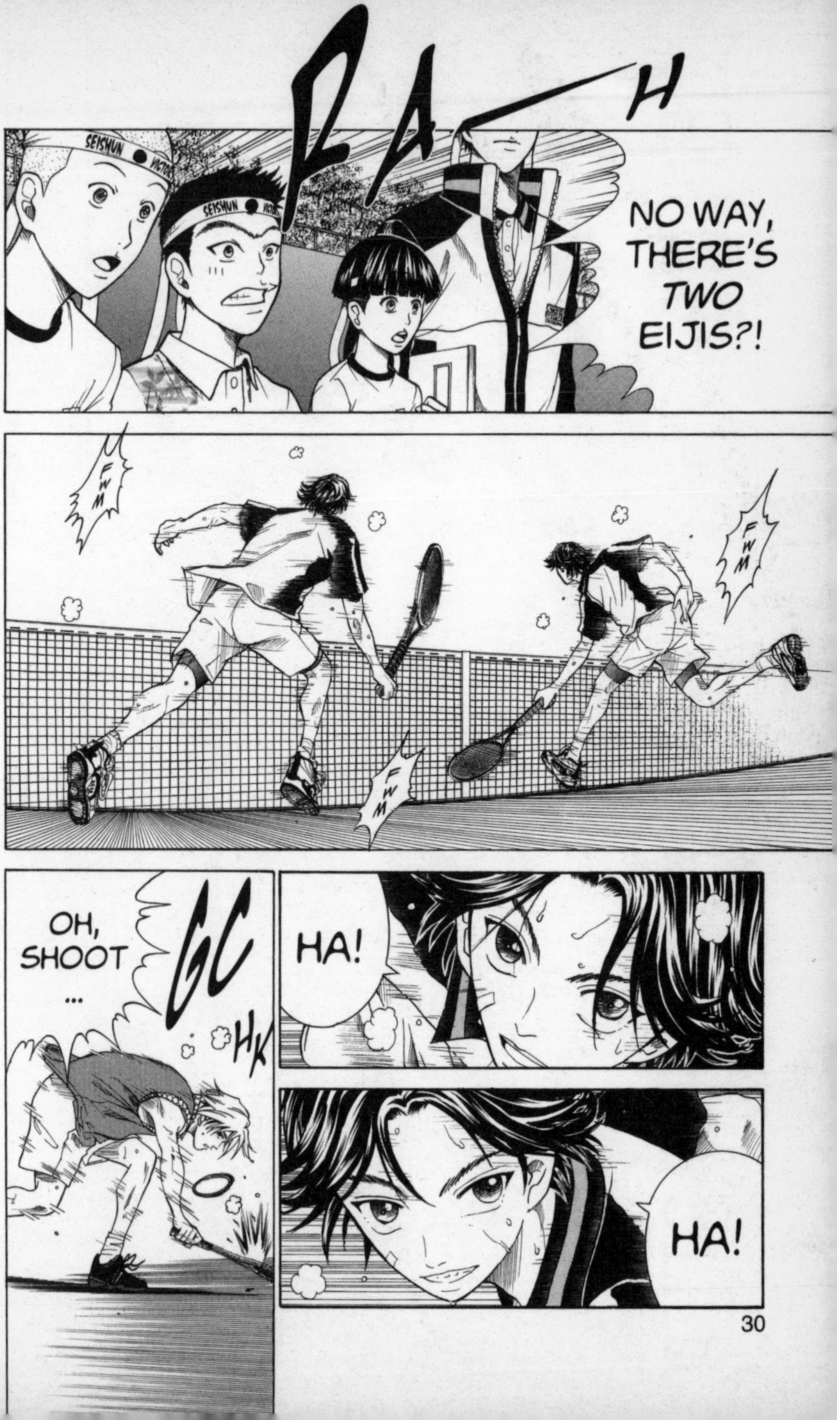
PAH
NO WAY, THERE'S TWO EIJIS?!
FWM
FWM
FWM
HA!
HA!
OH, SHOOT ...
GCHK

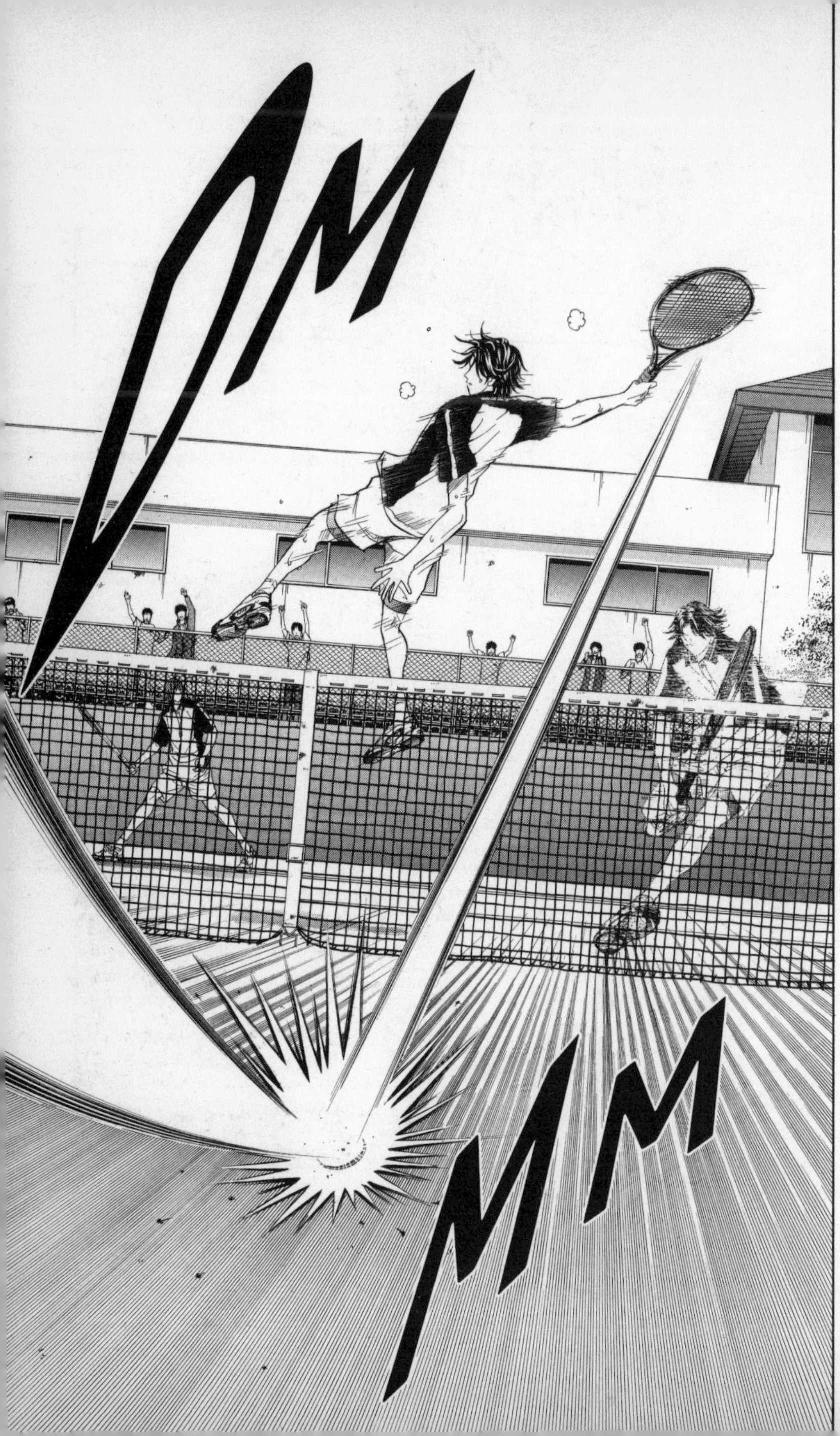

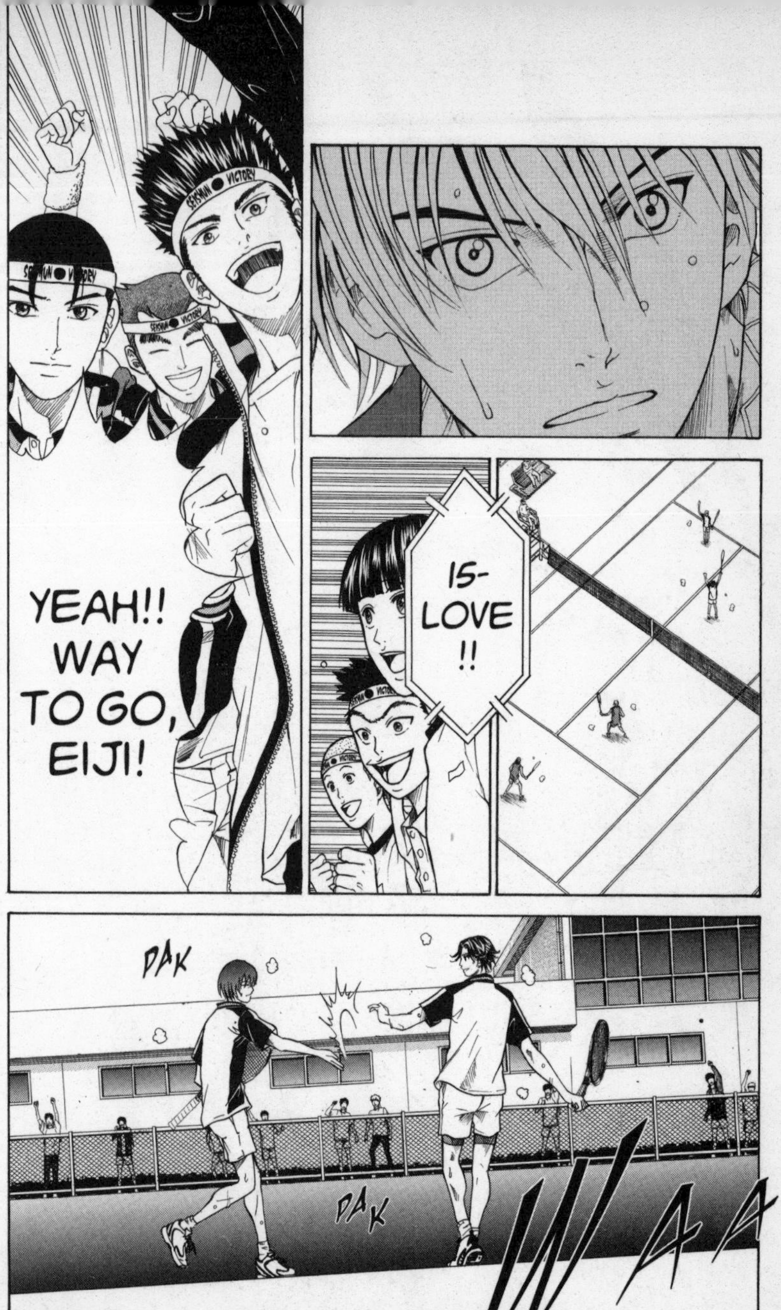
15-
LOVE
!!
YEAH!!
WAY
TO GO,
EIJI!
DAK
DAK
WAAA

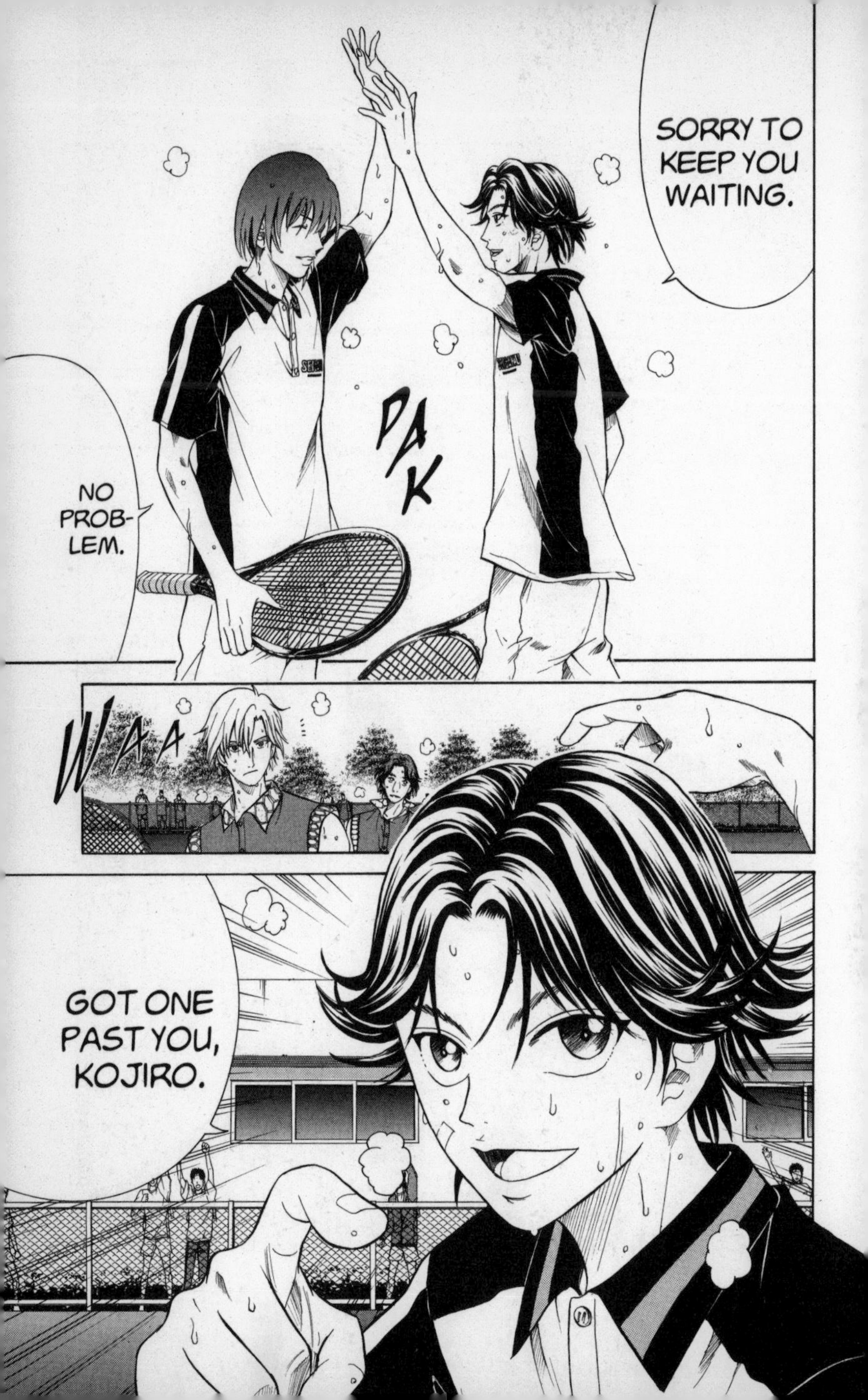

SORRY TO KEEP YOU WAITING.
DAK
NO PROB-LEM.
WAA
GOT ONE PAST YOU, KOJIRO.

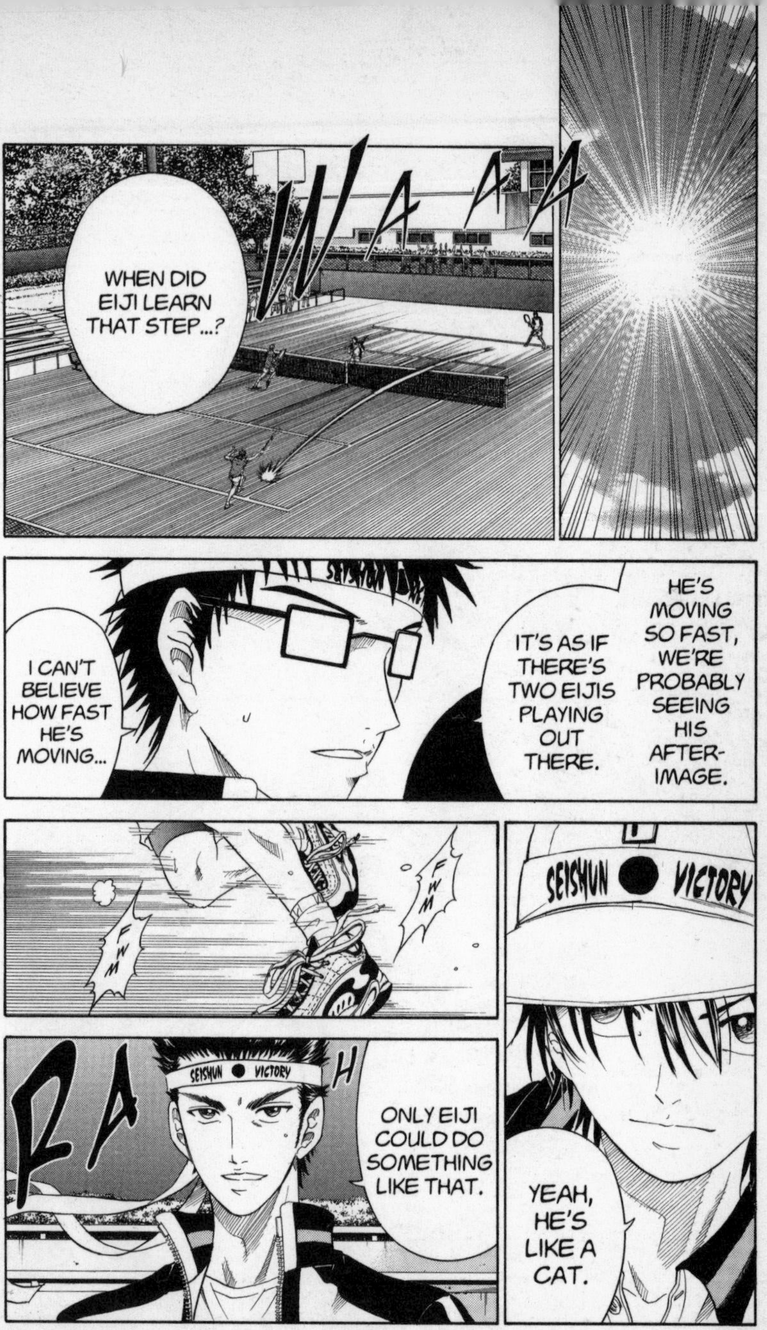
WAAA
WHEN DID EIJI LEARN THAT STEP...?
HE'S MOVING SO FAST, WE'RE PROBABLY SEEING HIS AFTER-IMAGE.
IT'S AS IF THERE'S TWO EIJIS PLAYING OUT THERE.
I CAN'T BELIEVE HOW FAST HE'S MOVING...
FWM
FWM
SEISHUN VICTORY
RAH
SEISHUN VICTORY
ONLY EIJI COULD DO SOMETHING LIKE THAT.
YEAH, HE'S LIKE A CAT.

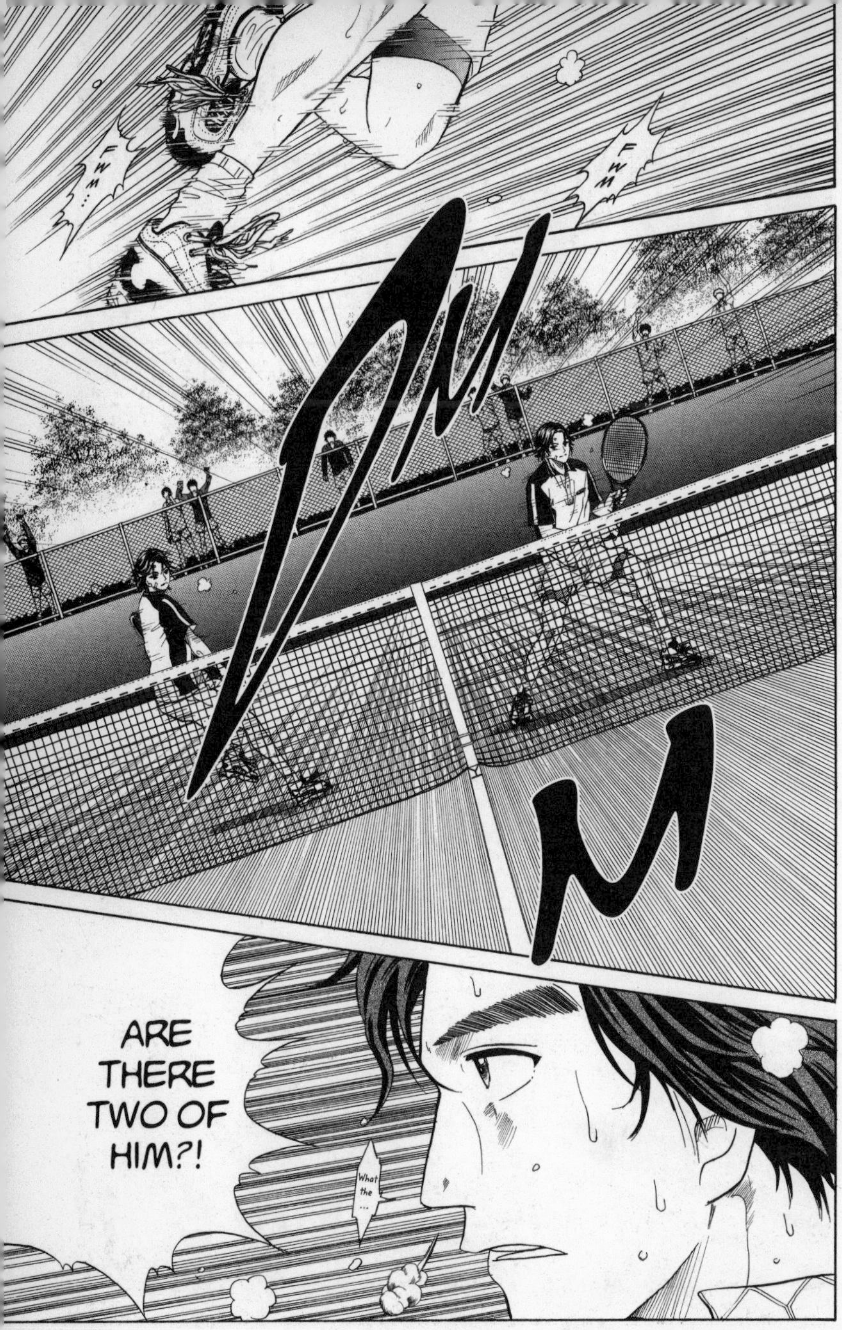
FWM...
FWM
FWM
ARE THERE TWO OF HIM?!
What the ...

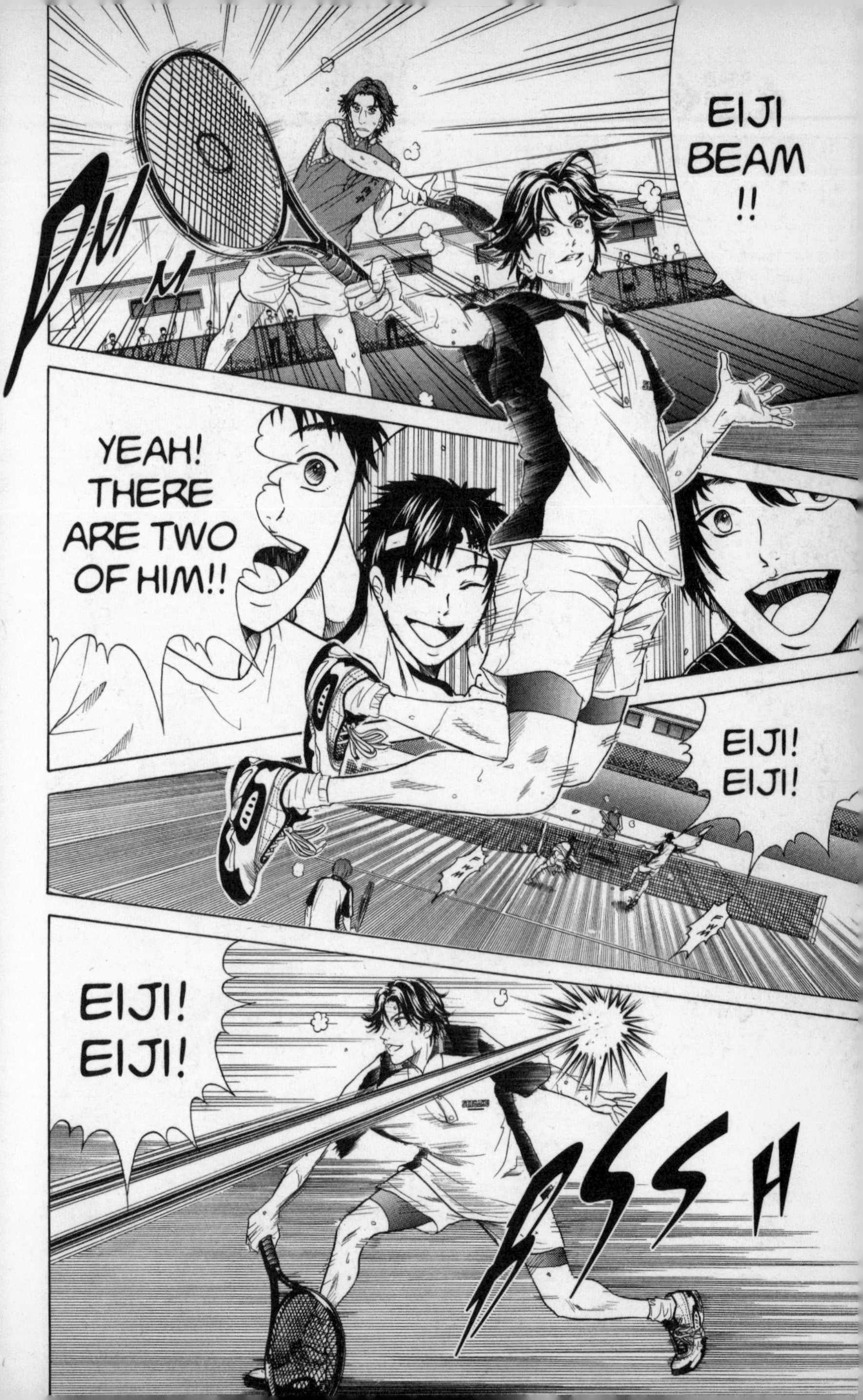
EIJI BEAM !!
DMM
YEAH! THERE ARE TWO OF HIM!!
EIJI! EIJI!
EIJI! EIJI!
WSSSH

READ THIS WAY

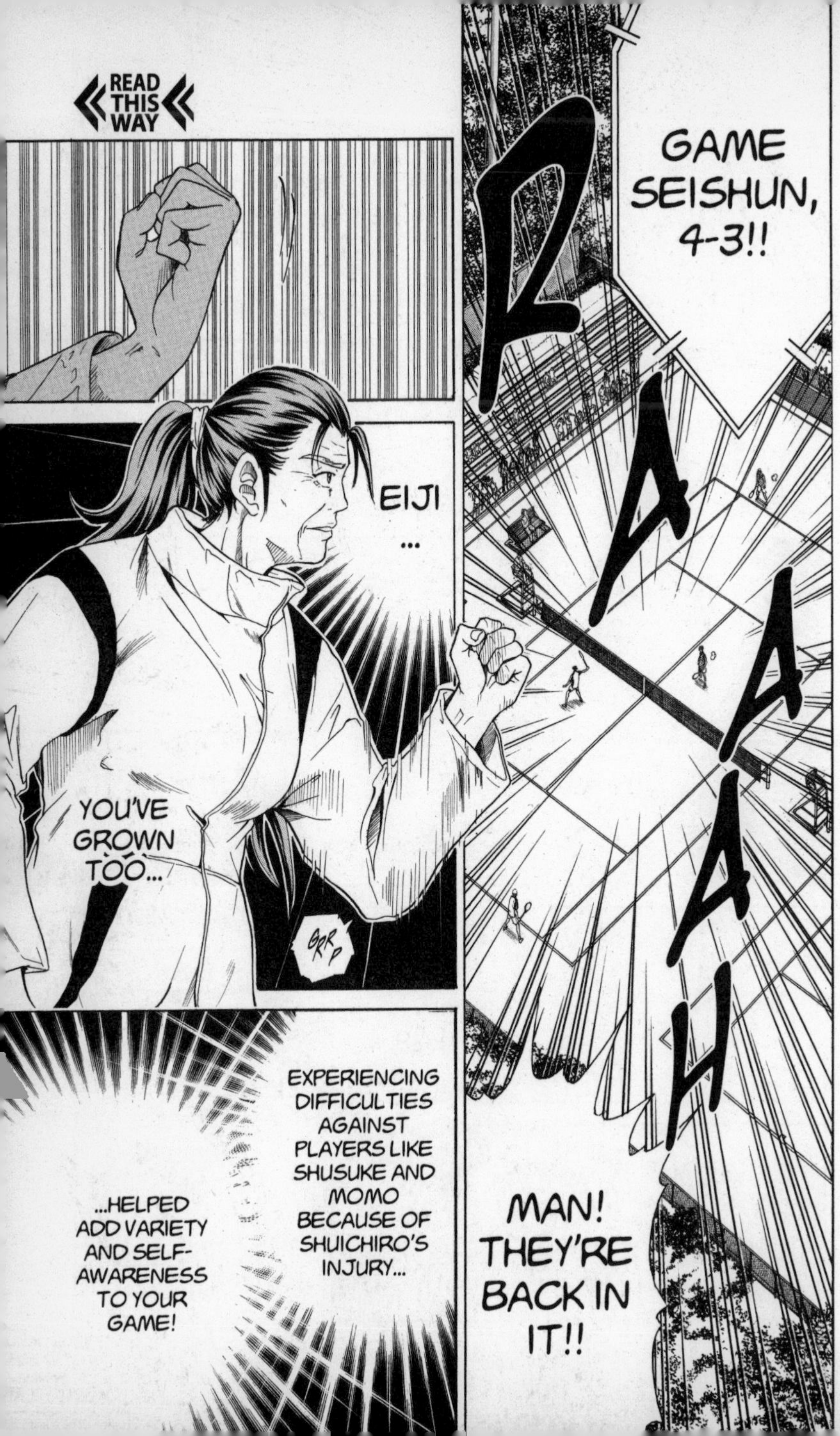
GAME SEISHUN, 4-3!!
RAAAAAH
MAN! THEY'RE BACK IN IT!!
EIJI ...
YOU'VE GROWN TOO...
GRRP
EXPERIENCING DIFFICULTIES AGAINST PLAYERS LIKE SHUSUKE AND MOMO BECAUSE OF SHUICHIRO'S INJURY...
...HELPED ADD VARIETY AND SELF-AWARENESS TO YOUR GAME!

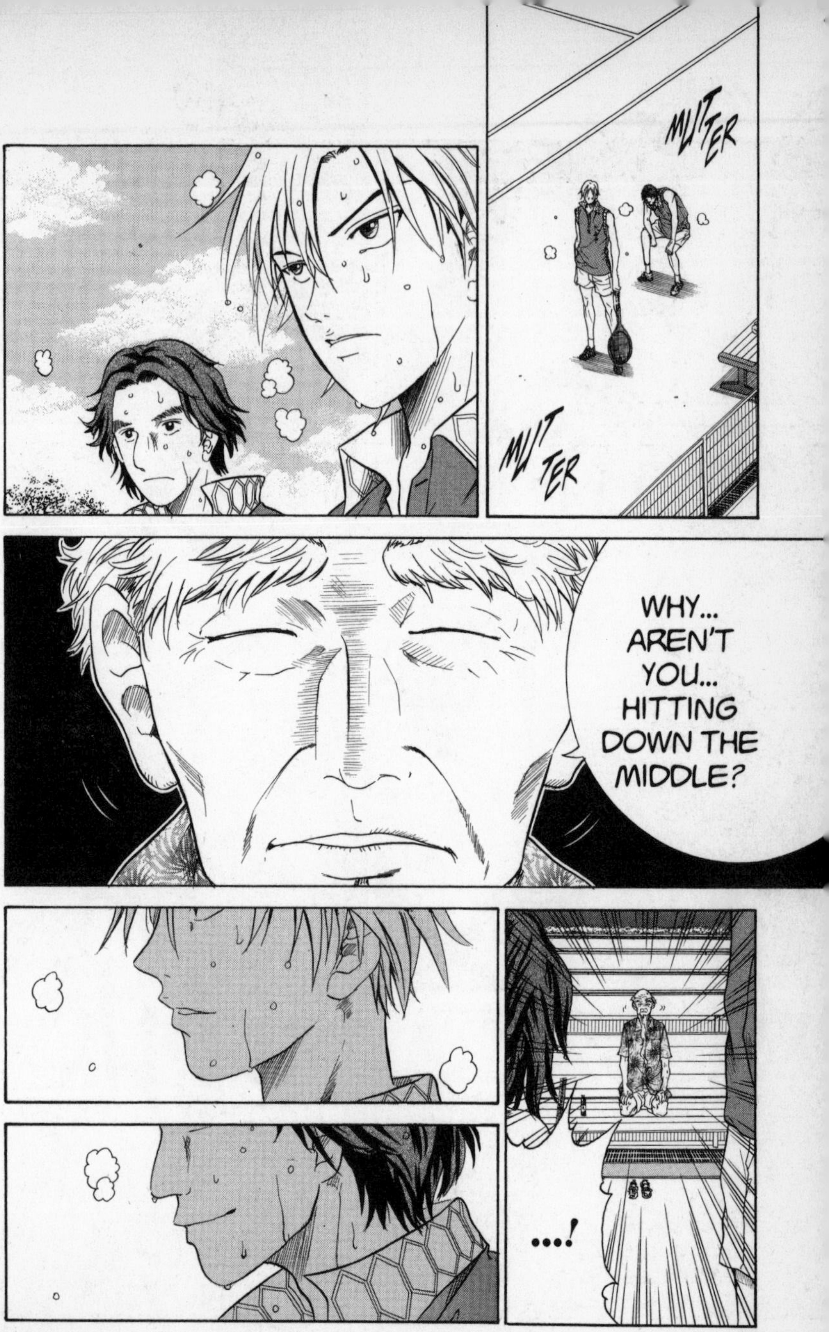
MUTTER
MUTTER
WHY... AREN'T YOU... HITTING DOWN THE MIDDLE?
...!

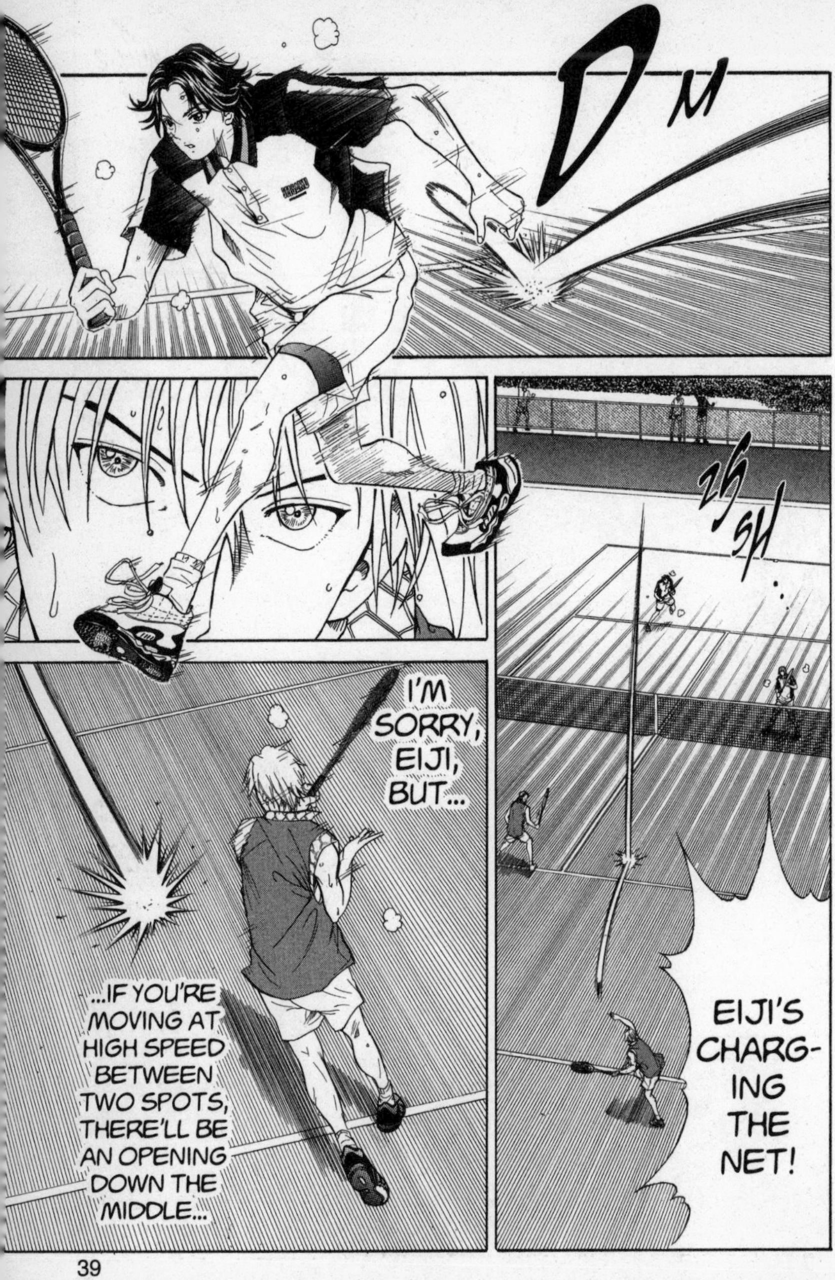
DM
EIJI'S CHARGING THE NET!
I'M SORRY, EIJI, BUT...
...IF YOU'RE MOVING AT HIGH SPEED BETWEEN TWO SPOTS, THERE'LL BE AN OPENING DOWN THE MIDDLE...

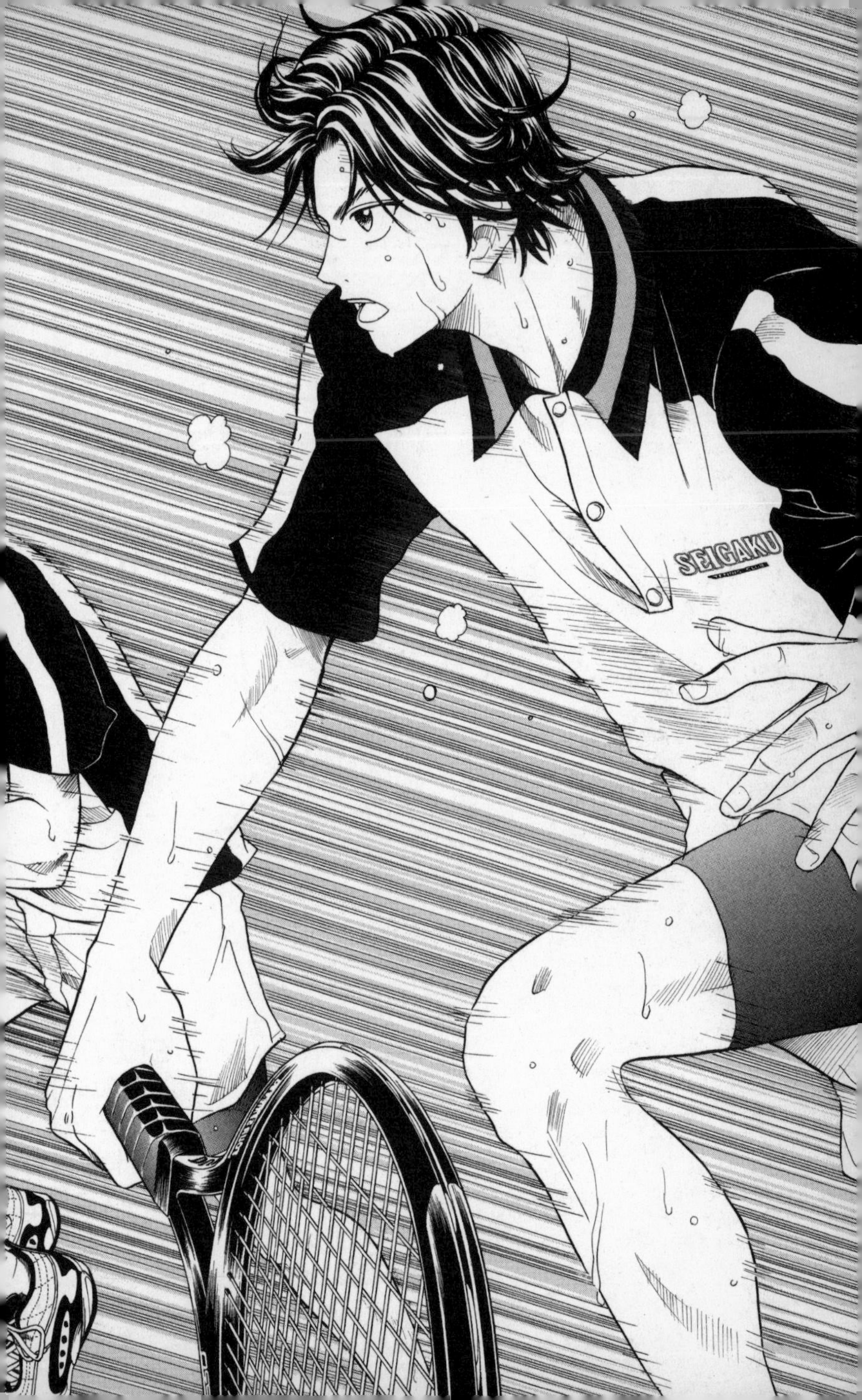
SEIGAKU

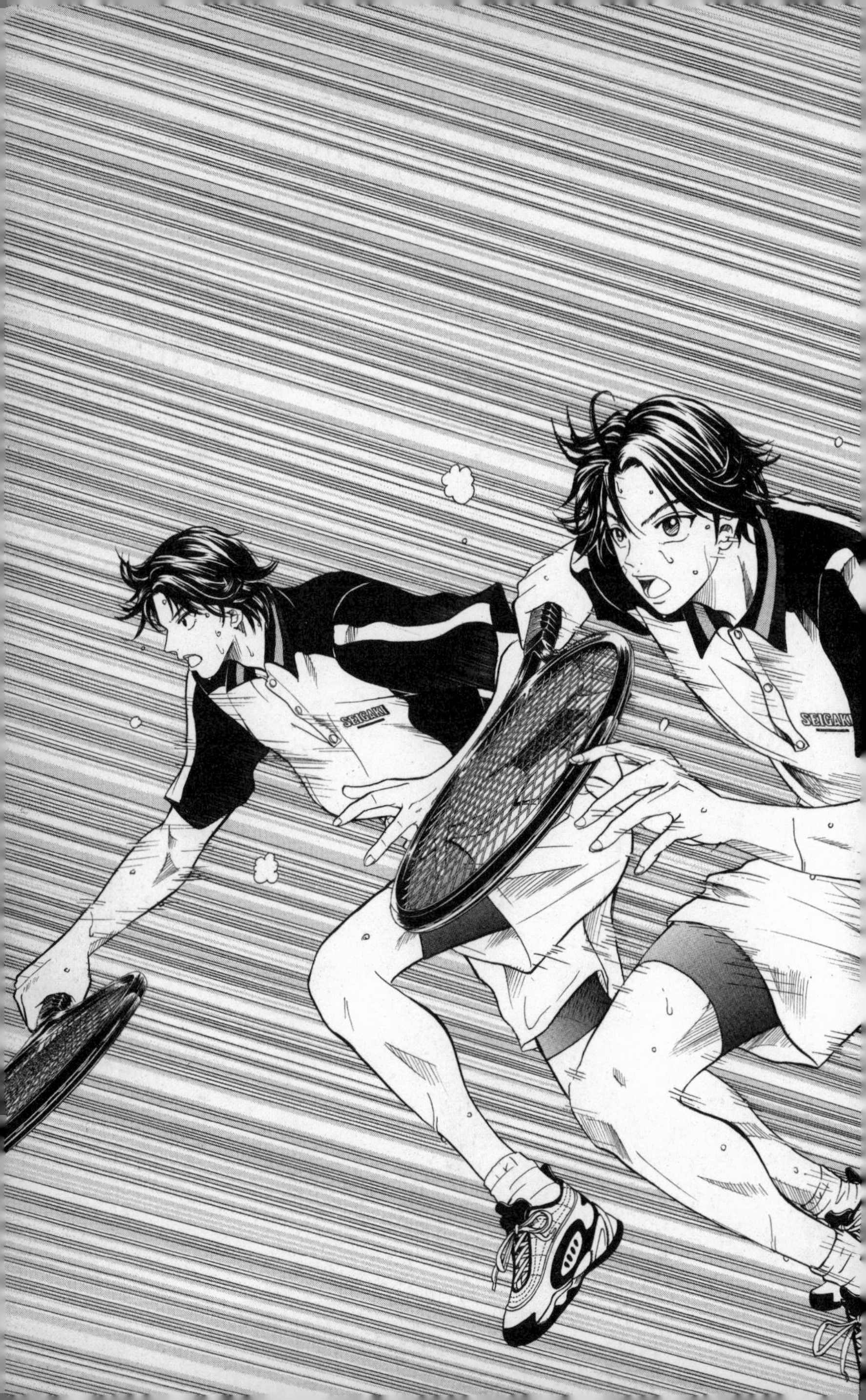
SEIGAKU
SEIGAKU

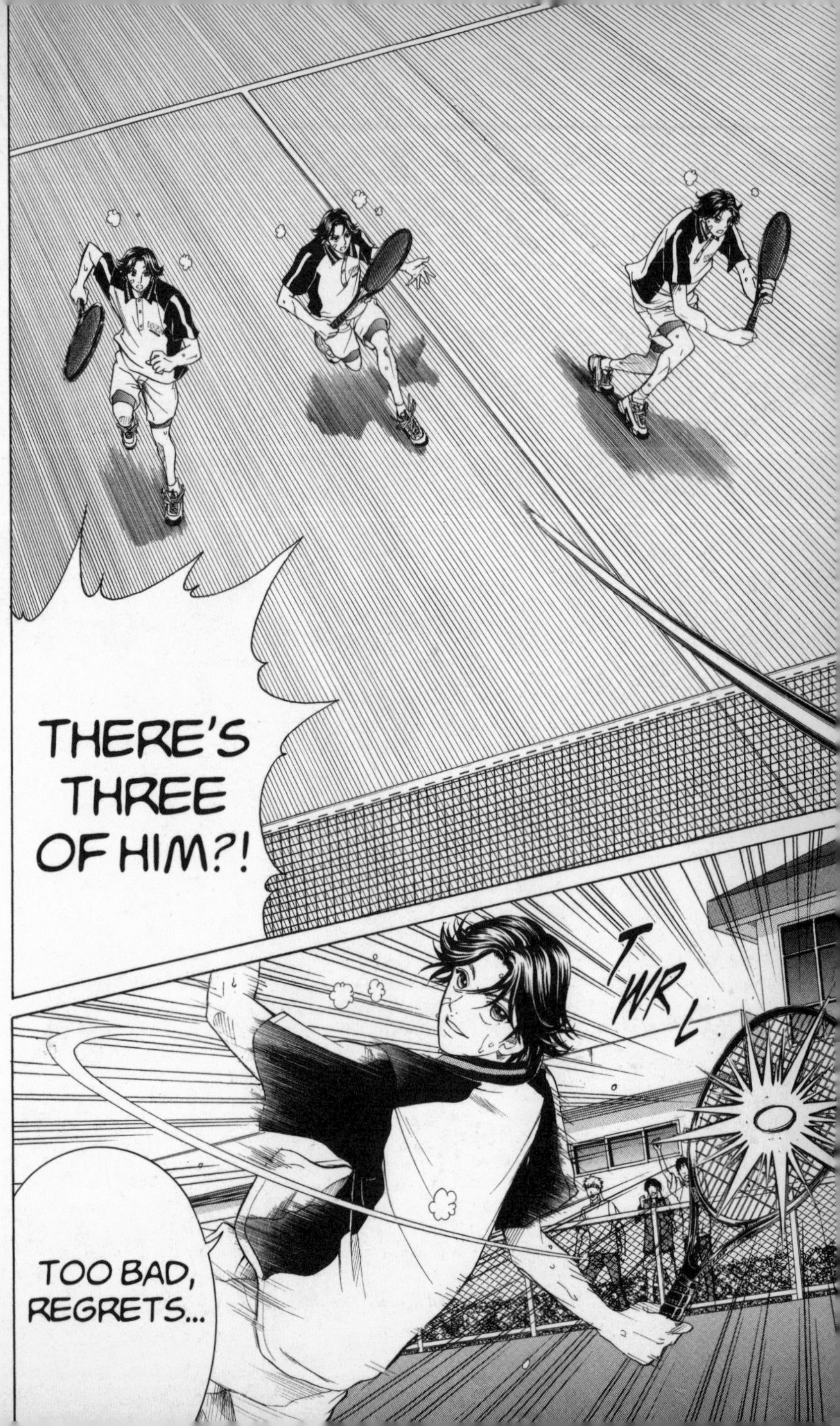
THERE'S THREE OF HIM?!
TWRL
TOO BAD, REGRETS...

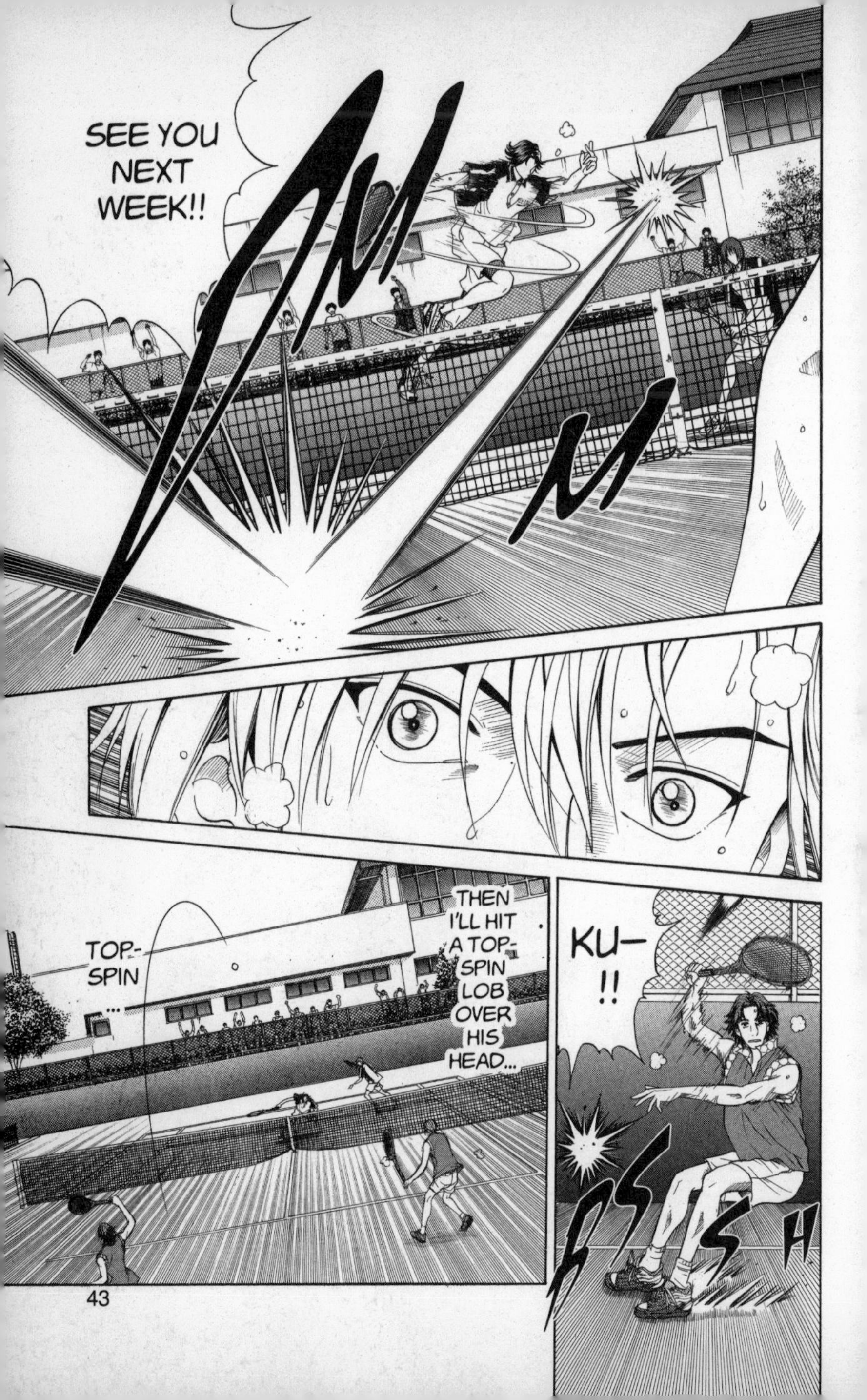
SEE YOU NEXT WEEK!!
KU-!!
THEN I'LL HIT A TOP-SPIN LOB OVER HIS HEAD...
TOP-SPIN...

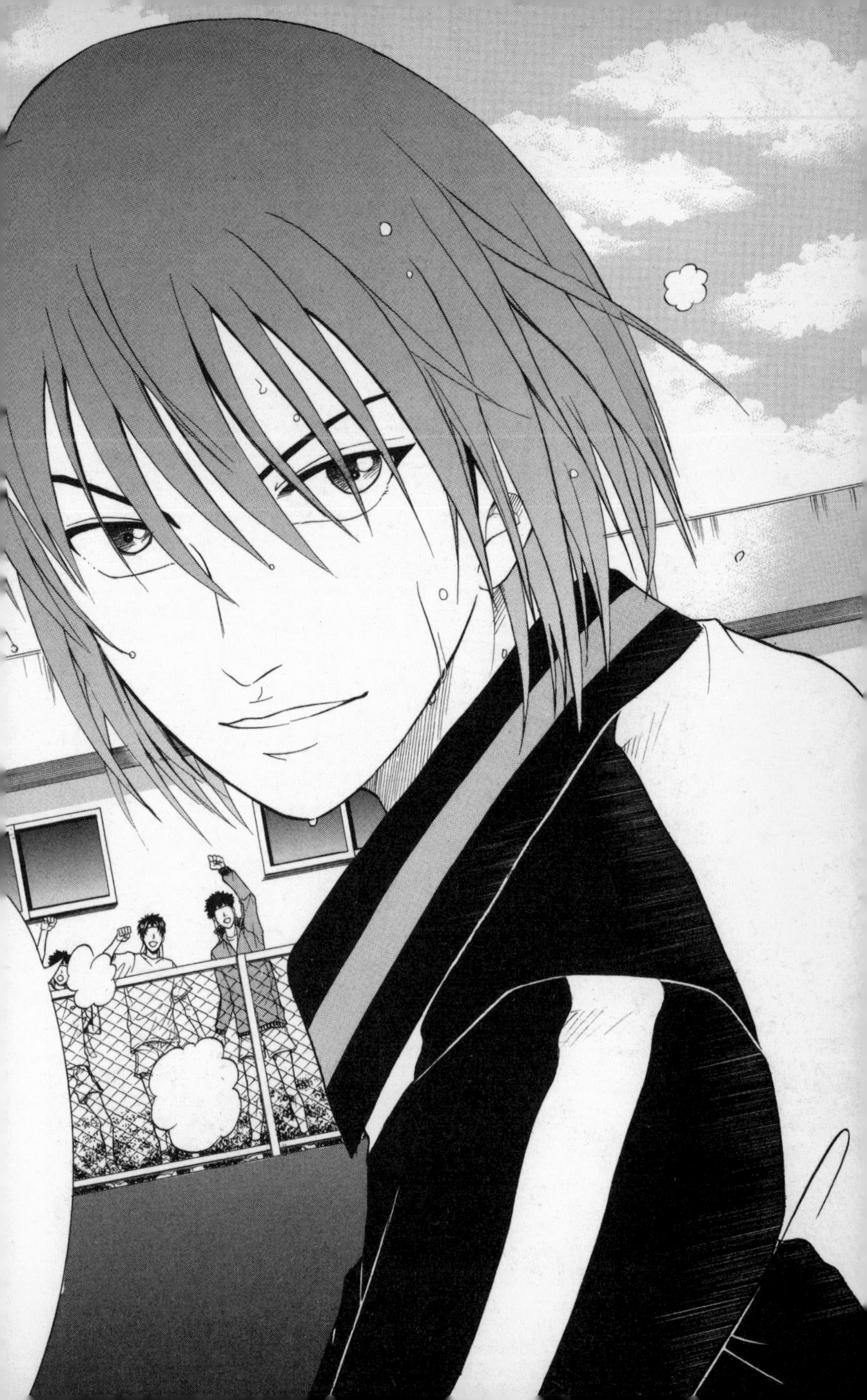

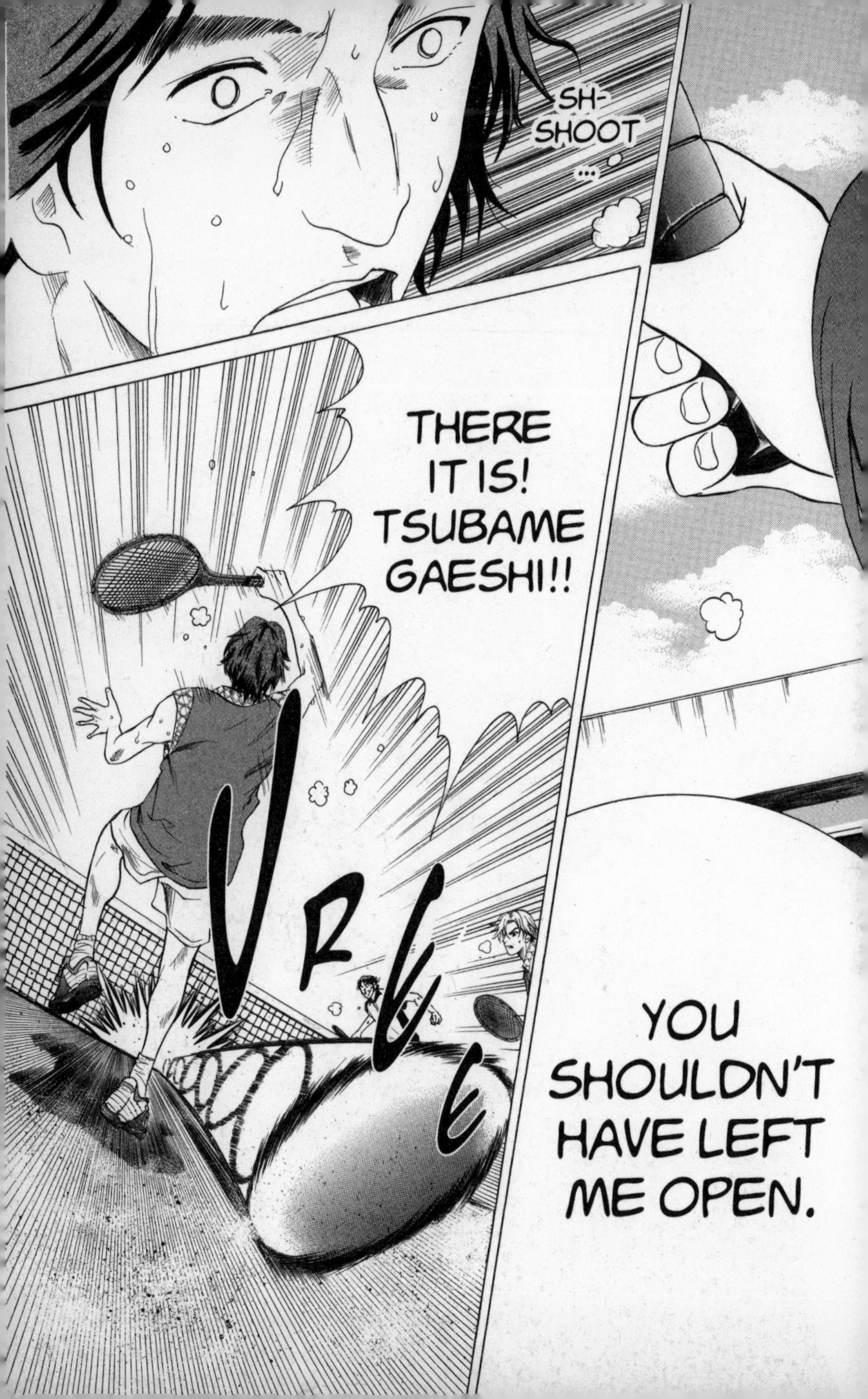
SH-SHOOT ...
THERE IT IS! TSUBAME GAESHI!!
YOU SHOULDN'T HAVE LEFT ME OPEN.

テニスの王子様

THE PRINCE OF TENNIS™

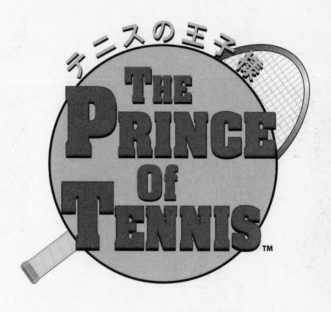

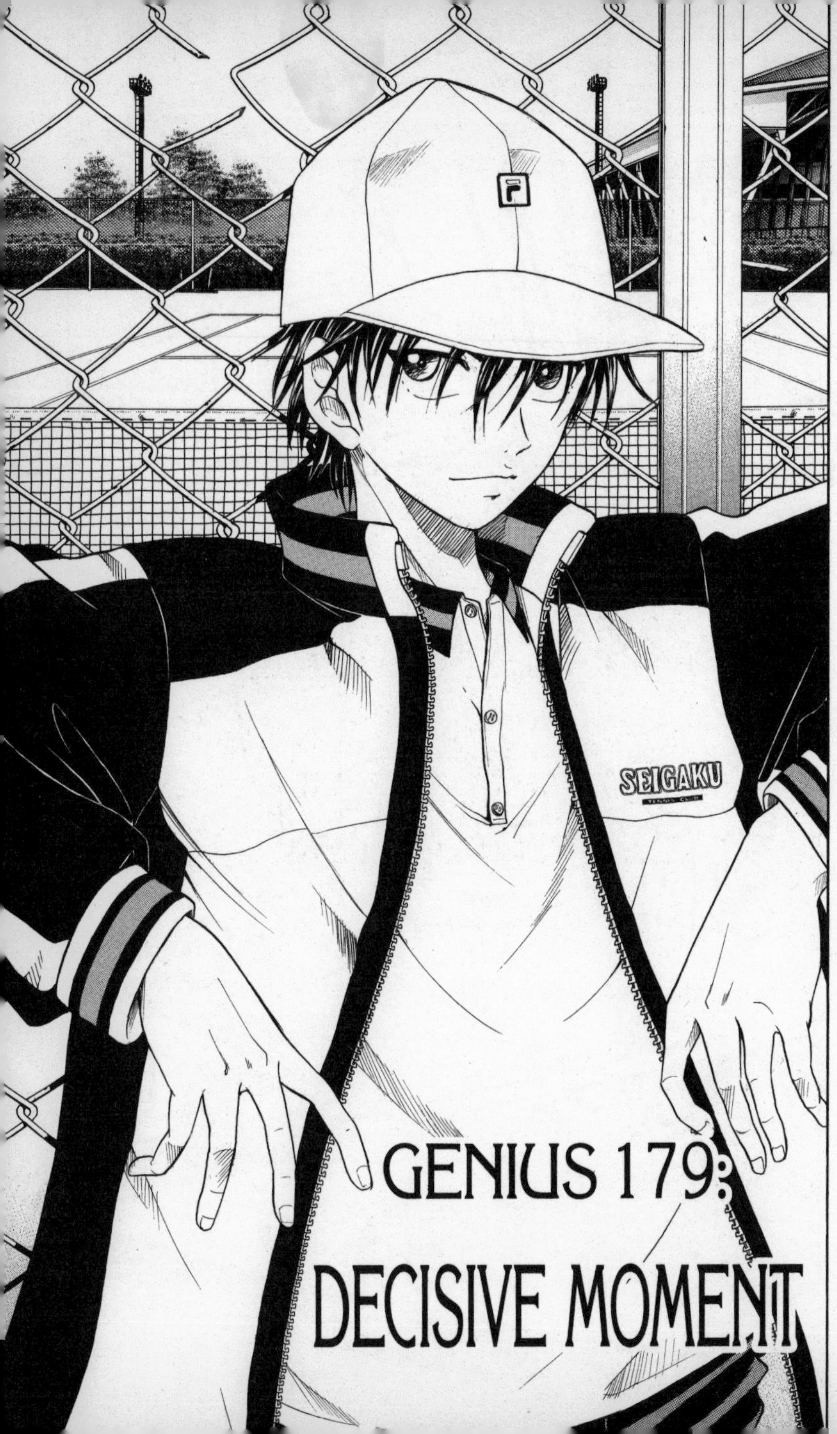
SEIGAKU
GENIUS 179:
DECISIVE MOMENT

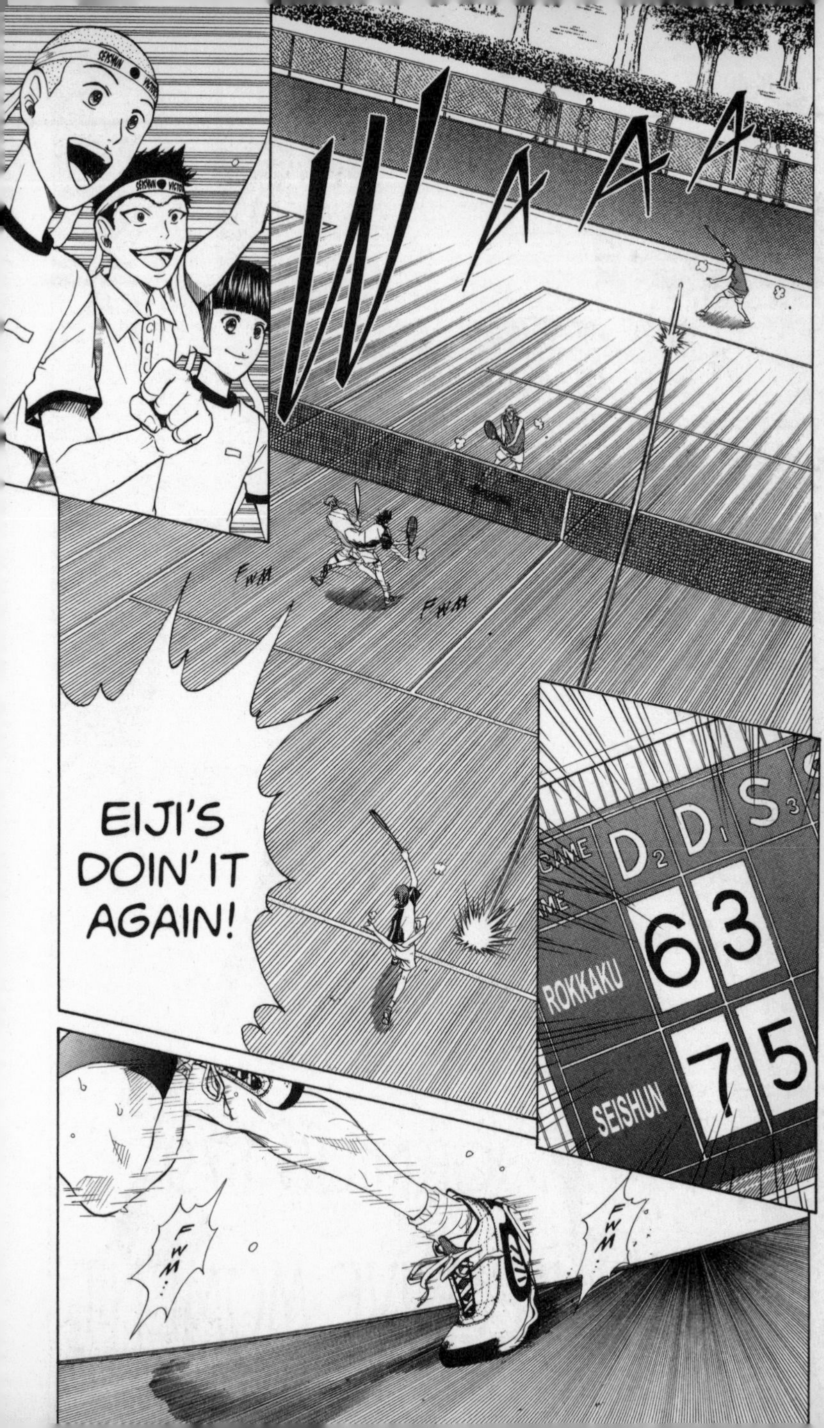

WAAA
FWM
FWM
EIJI'S DOIN' IT AGAIN!
D2 D1 S3
ROKKAKU 6 3
SEISHUN 7 5
FWM...
FWM...

READ THIS WAY

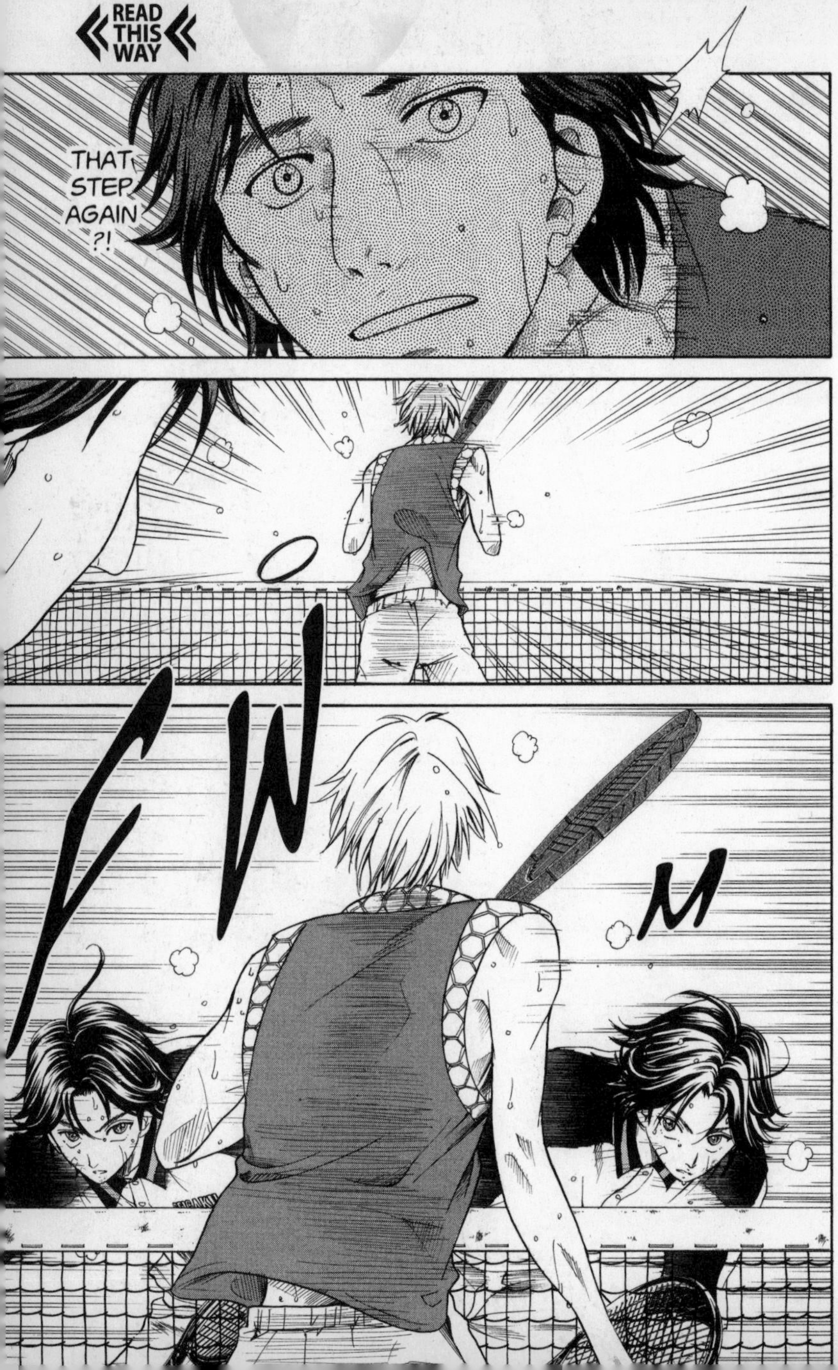
THAT STEP AGAIN?!
FWM

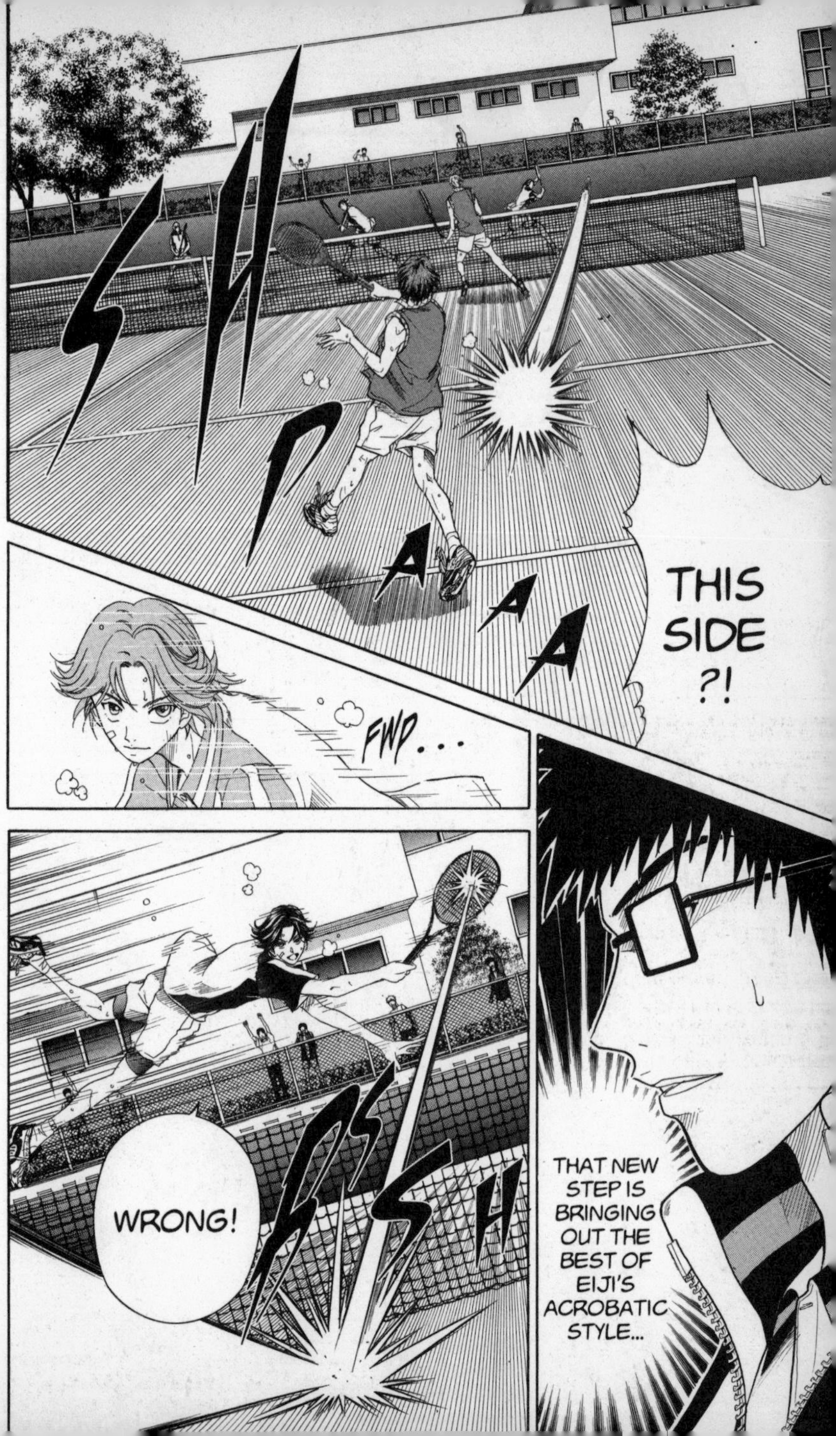
SHP
AAA
THIS SIDE ?!
FWP...
THAT NEW STEP IS BRINGING OUT THE BEST OF EIJI'S ACROBATIC STYLE...
WRONG!
KSSH

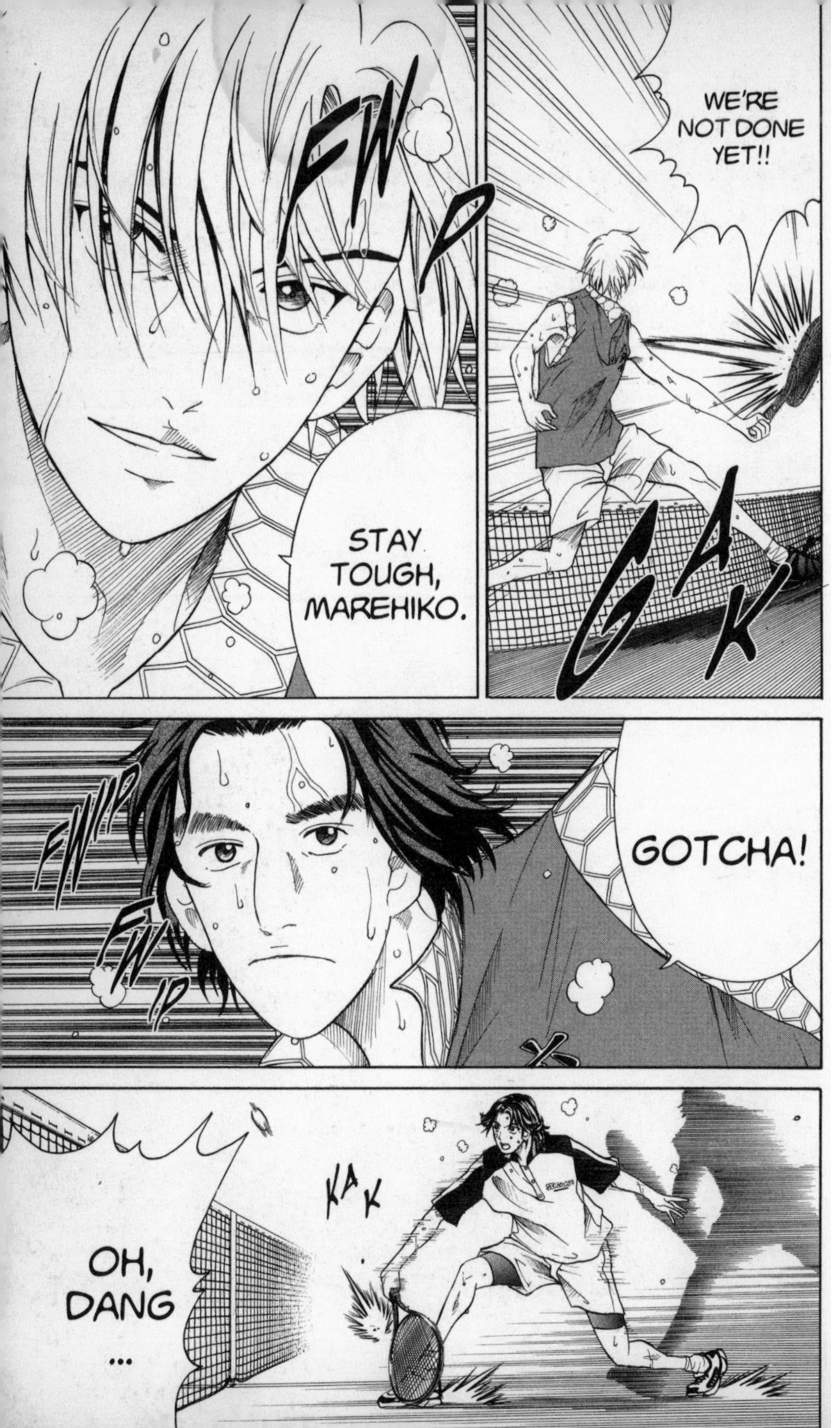
WE'RE NOT DONE YET!!
GAK
FWIP
STAY TOUGH, MAREHIKO.
GOTCHA!
FWIP
FWIP
KAK
OH, DANG ...

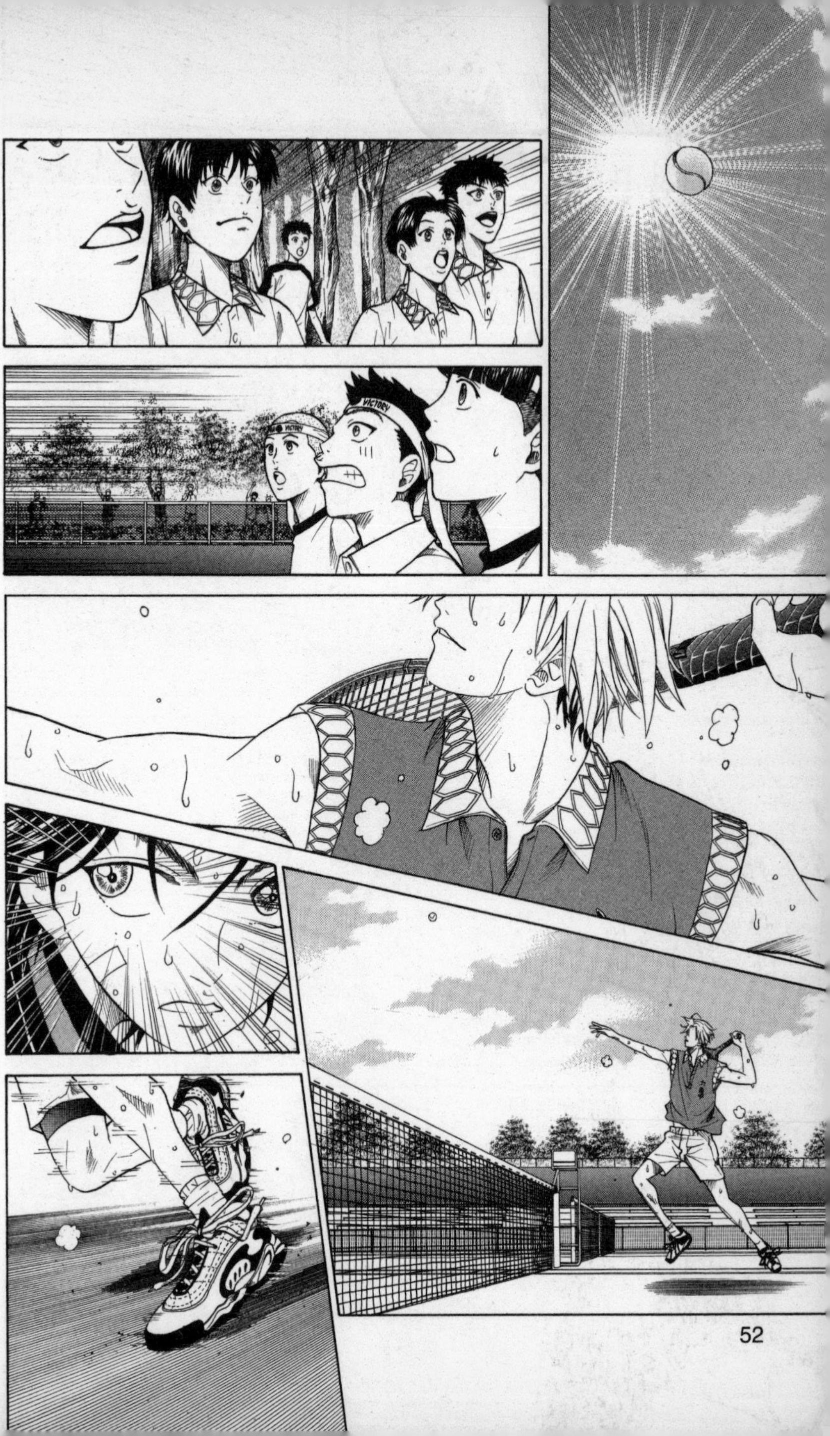
VICTORY

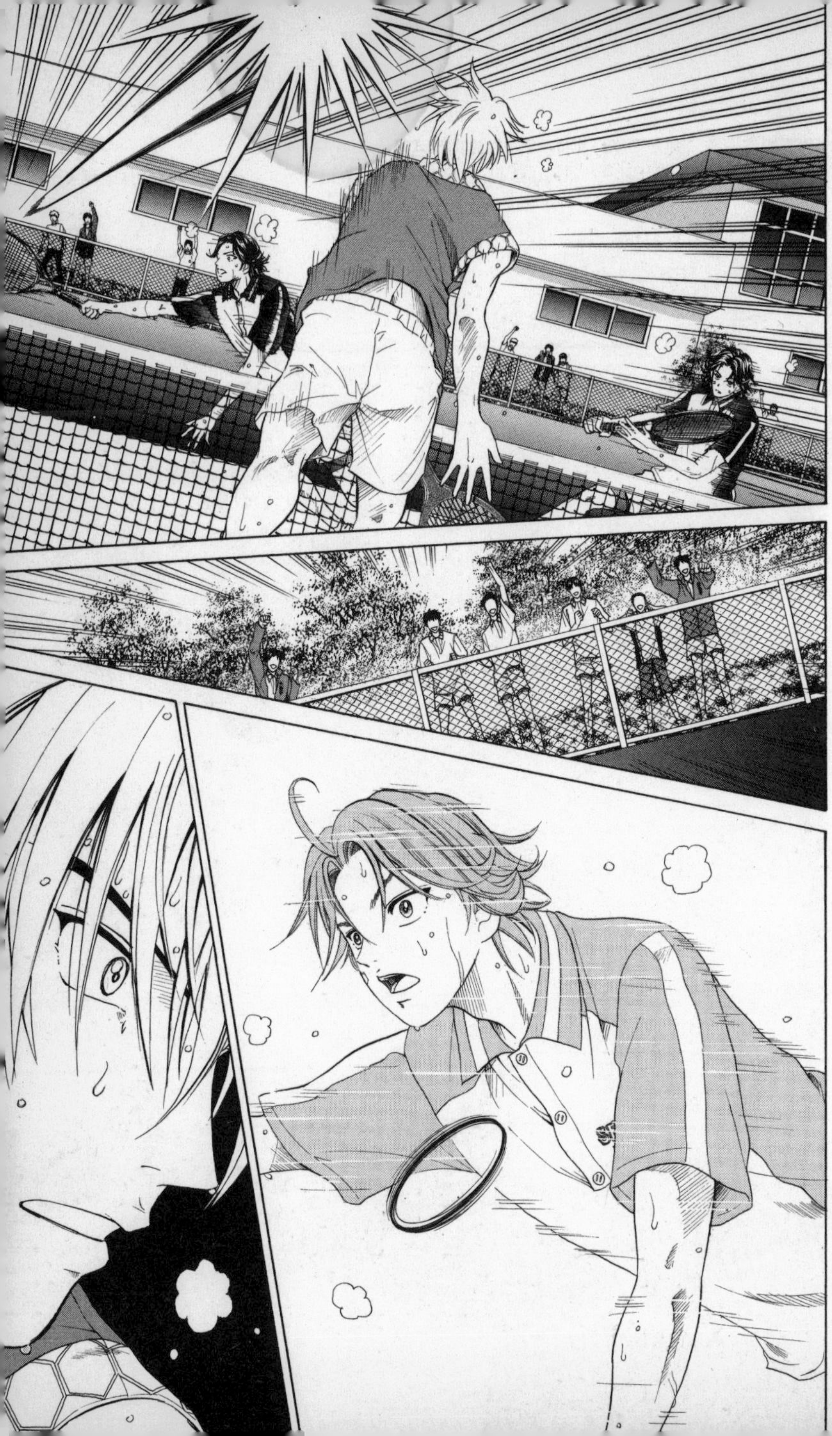

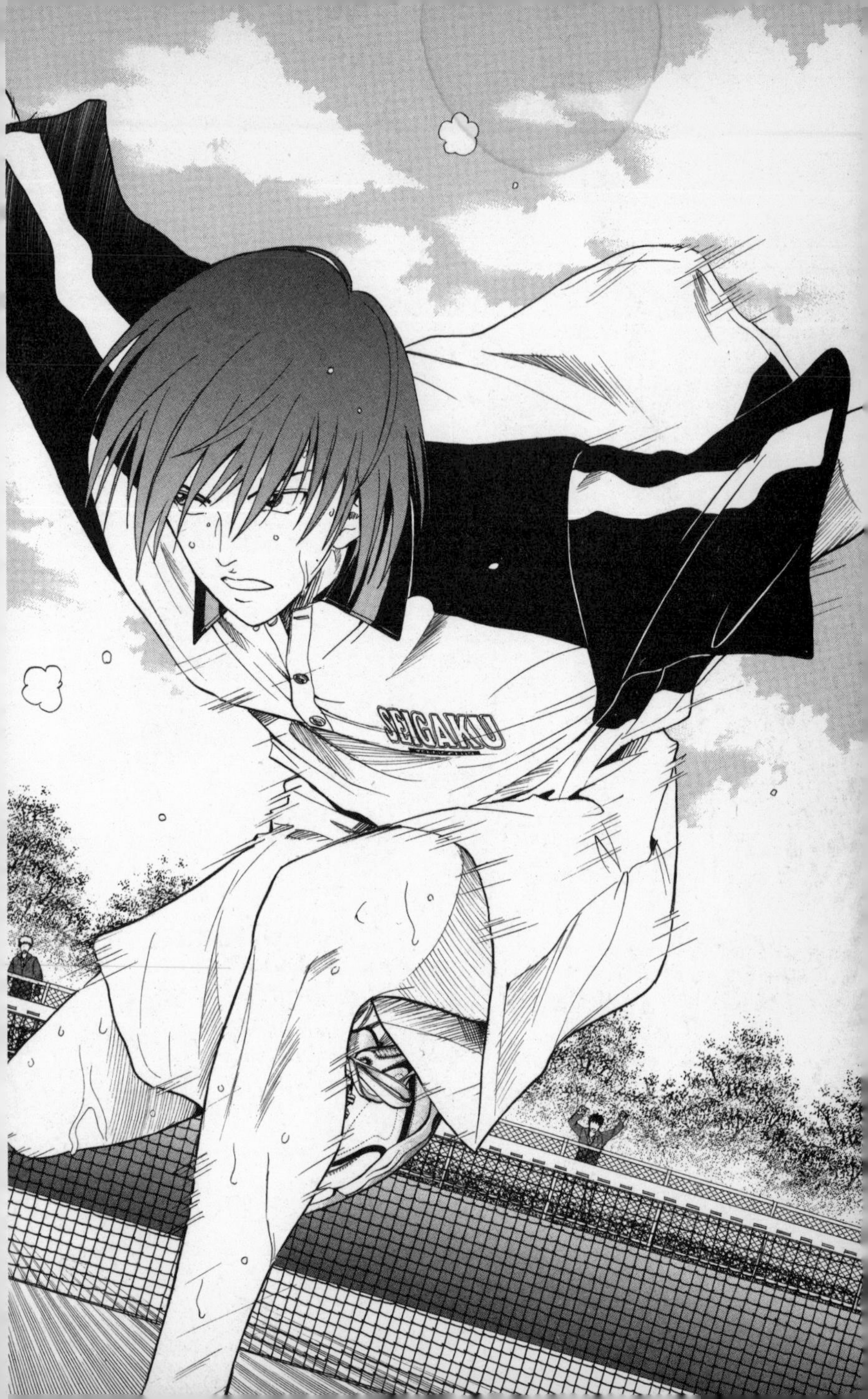
SEIGAKU

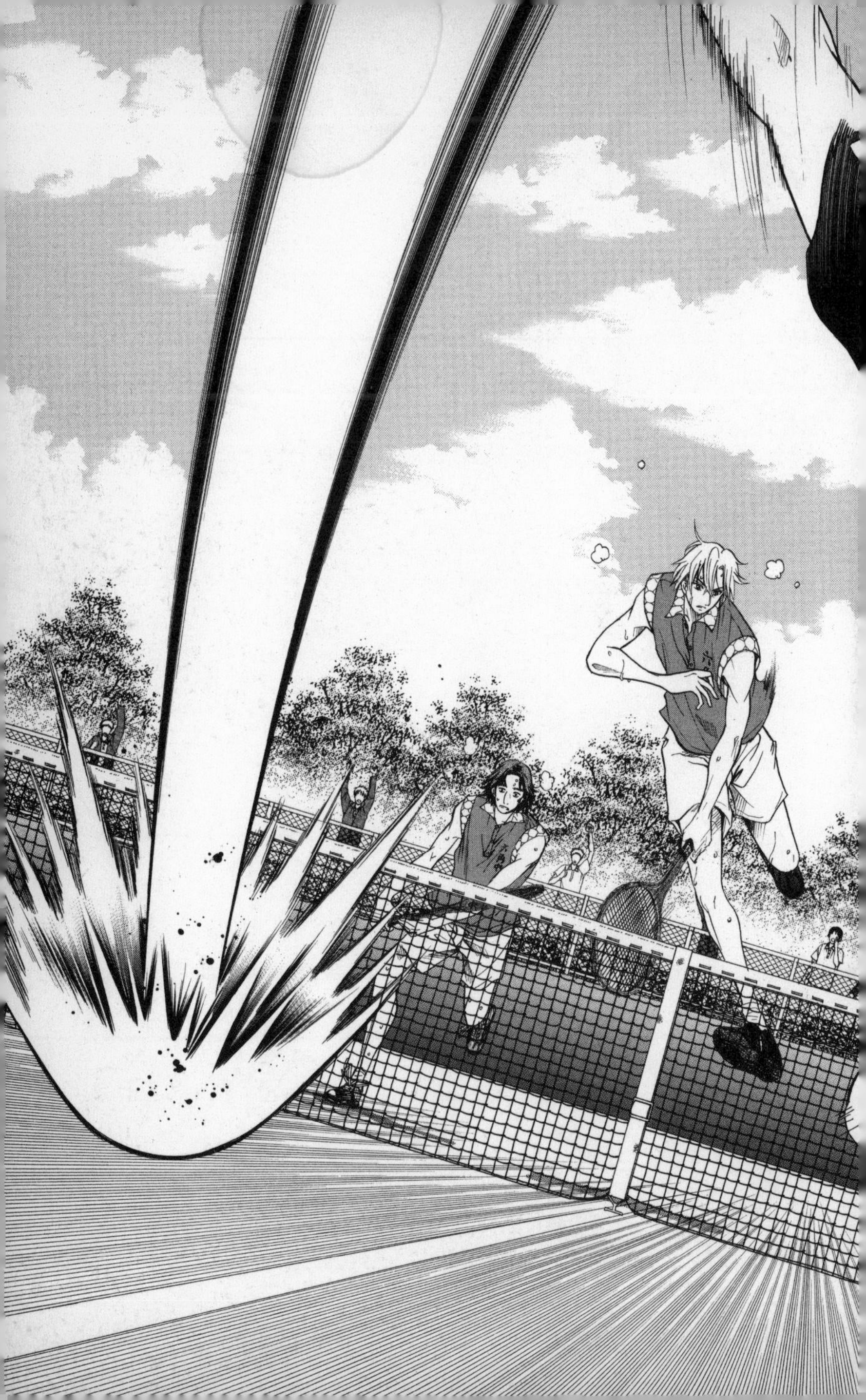

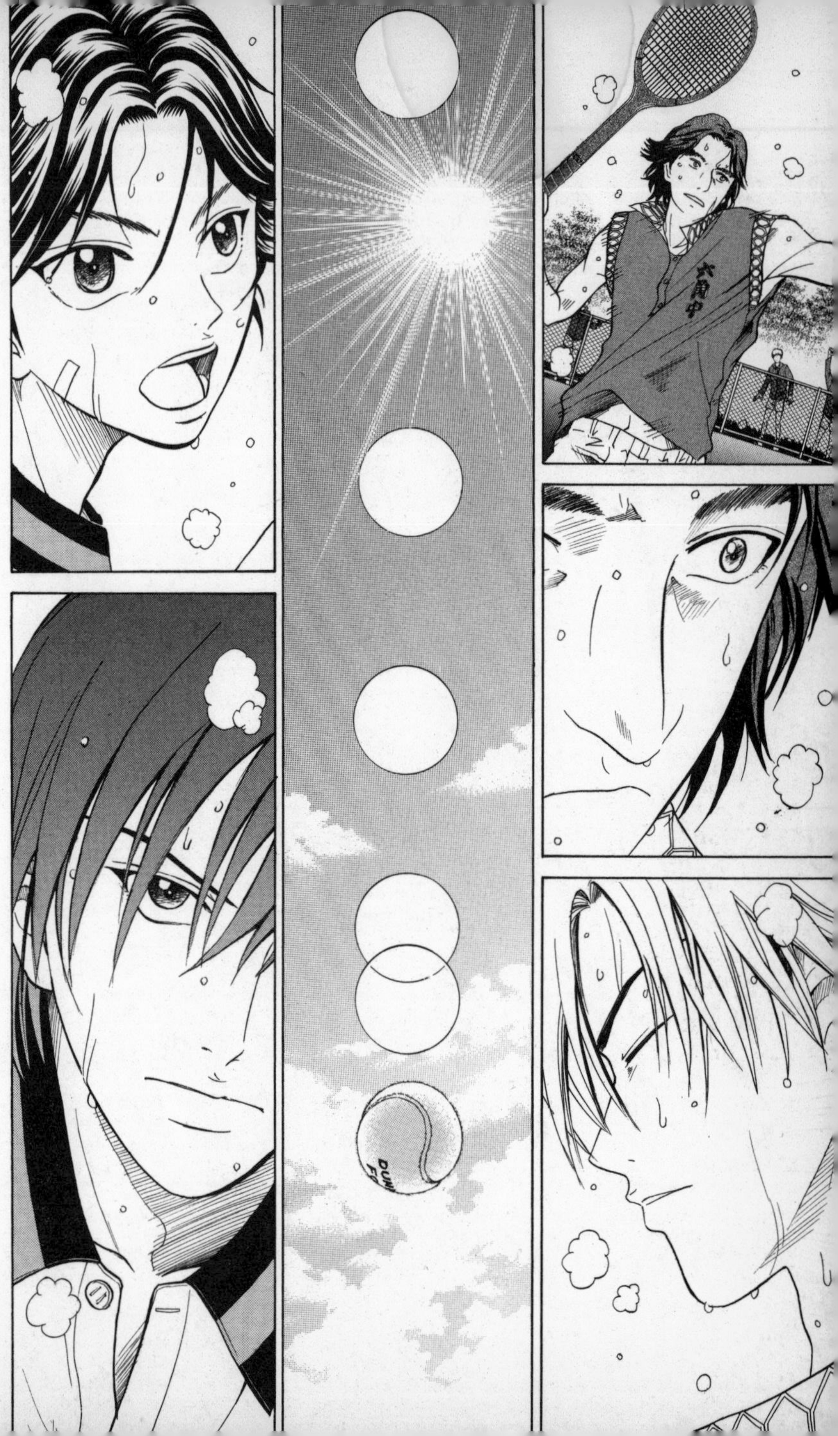

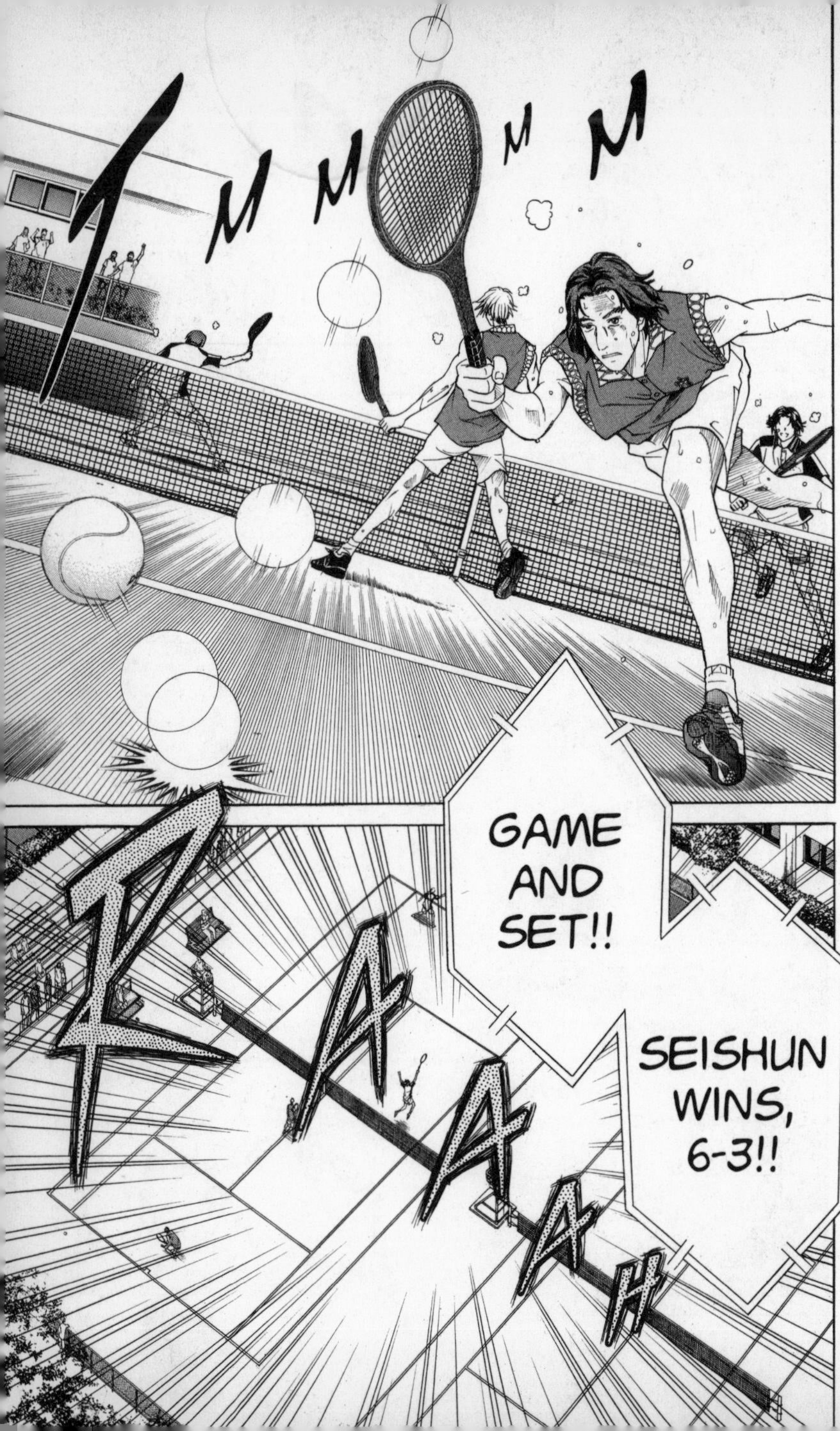
GAME AND SET!!
SEISHUN WINS, 6-3!!

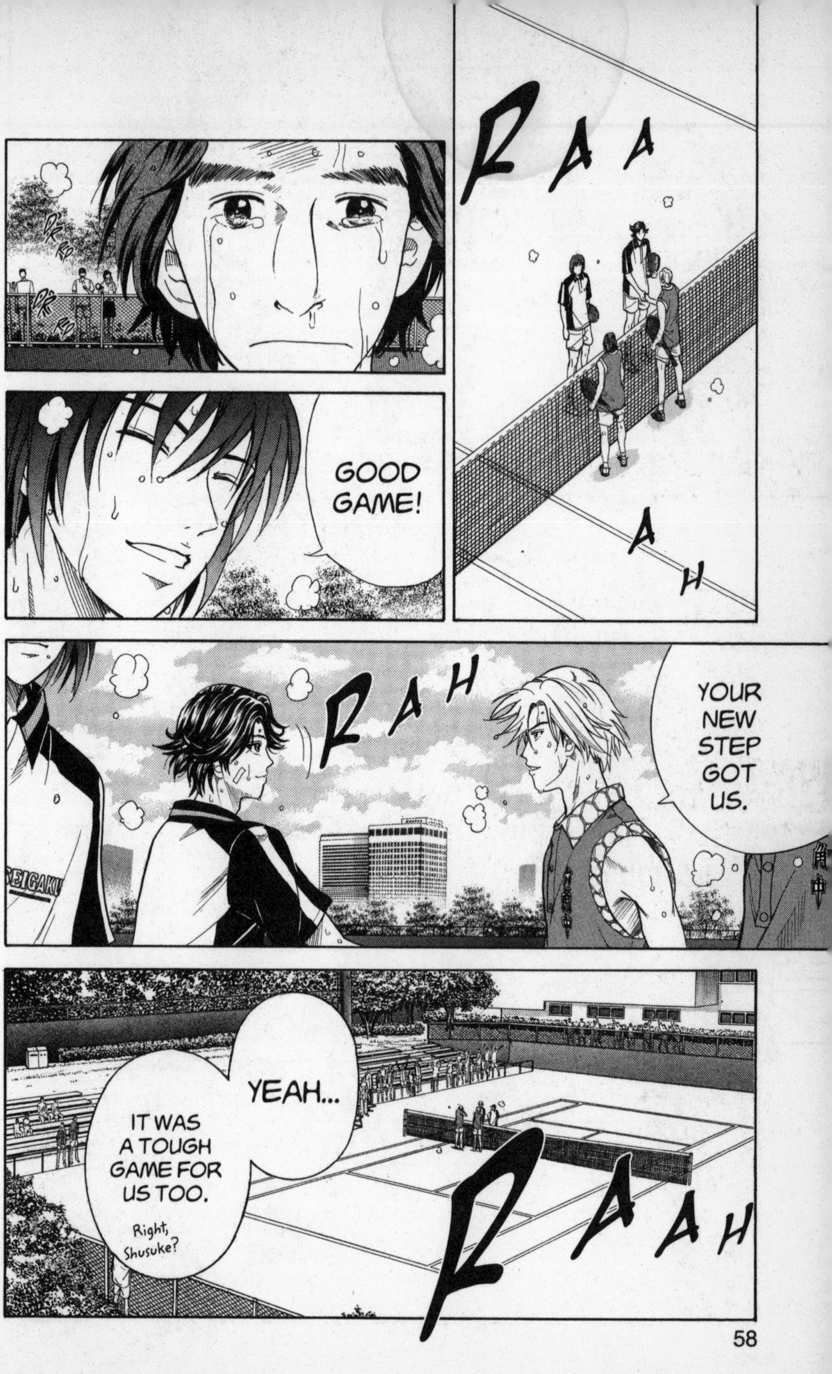
RAAA
AH
GOOD GAME!
YOUR NEW STEP GOT US.
RAH
YEAH...
IT WAS A TOUGH GAME FOR US TOO.
Right, Shusuke?
RAAH

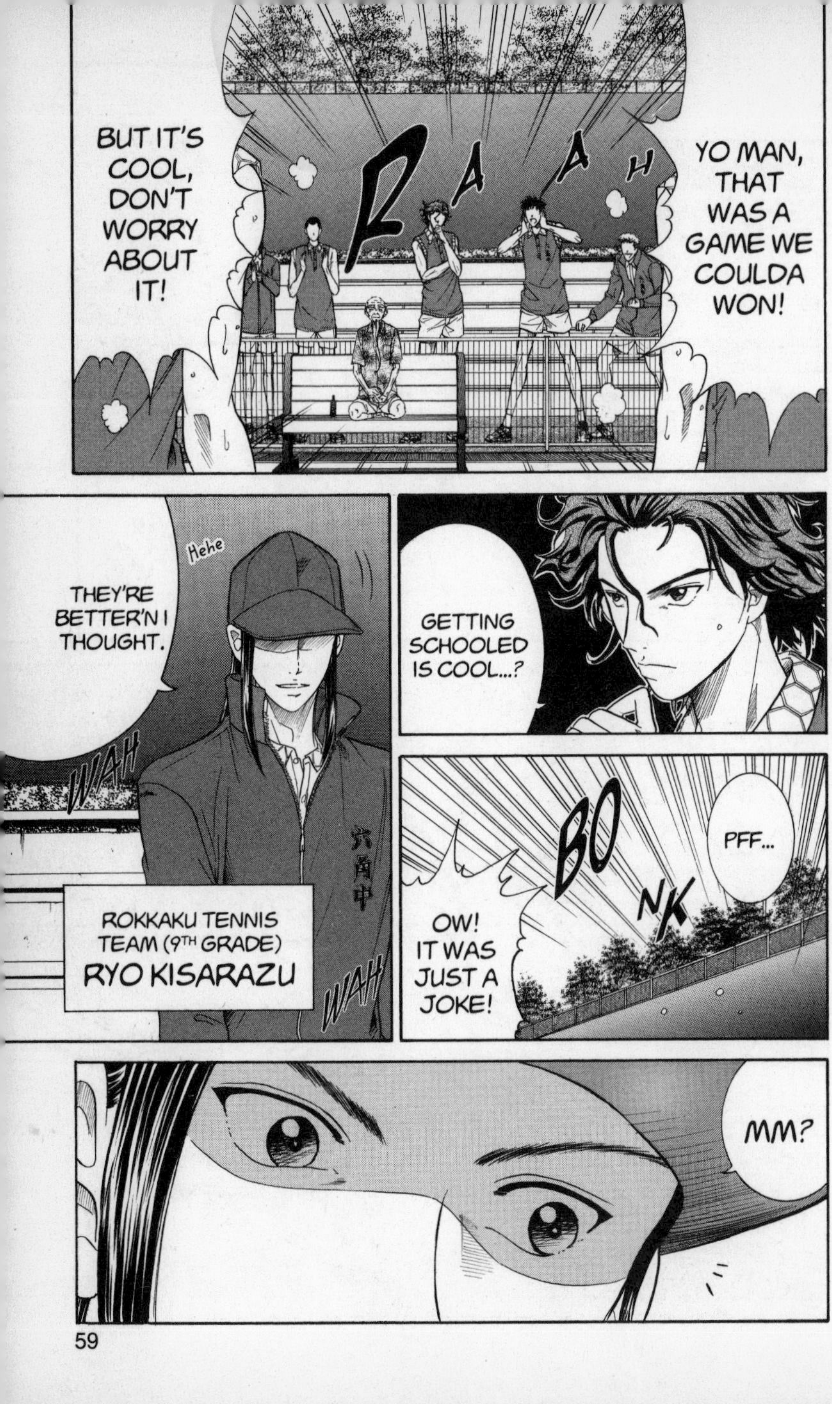

YO MAN, THAT WAS A GAME WE COULDA WON!
RAAH
BUT IT'S COOL, DON'T WORRY ABOUT IT!
GETTING SCHOOLED IS COOL...?
PFF...
BONK
OW! IT WAS JUST A JOKE!
Hehe
THEY'RE BETTER'N I THOUGHT.
WAH
WAH
六角中
ROKKAKU TENNIS TEAM (9TH GRADE)
RYO KISARAZU
MM?

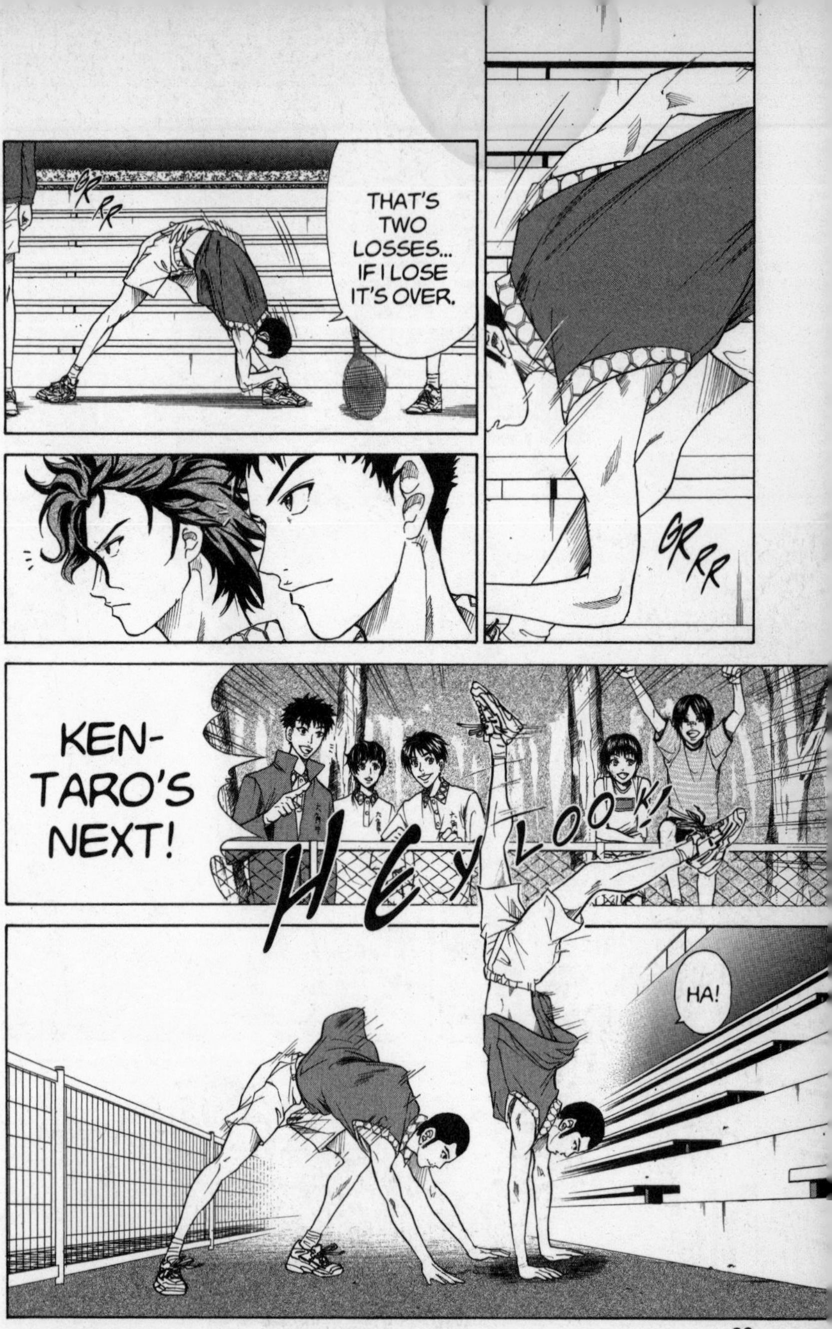
GRRR
GR-R-R
THAT'S TWO LOSSES... IF I LOSE IT'S OVER.
KEN-TARO'S NEXT!
HEY LOOK!
HA!

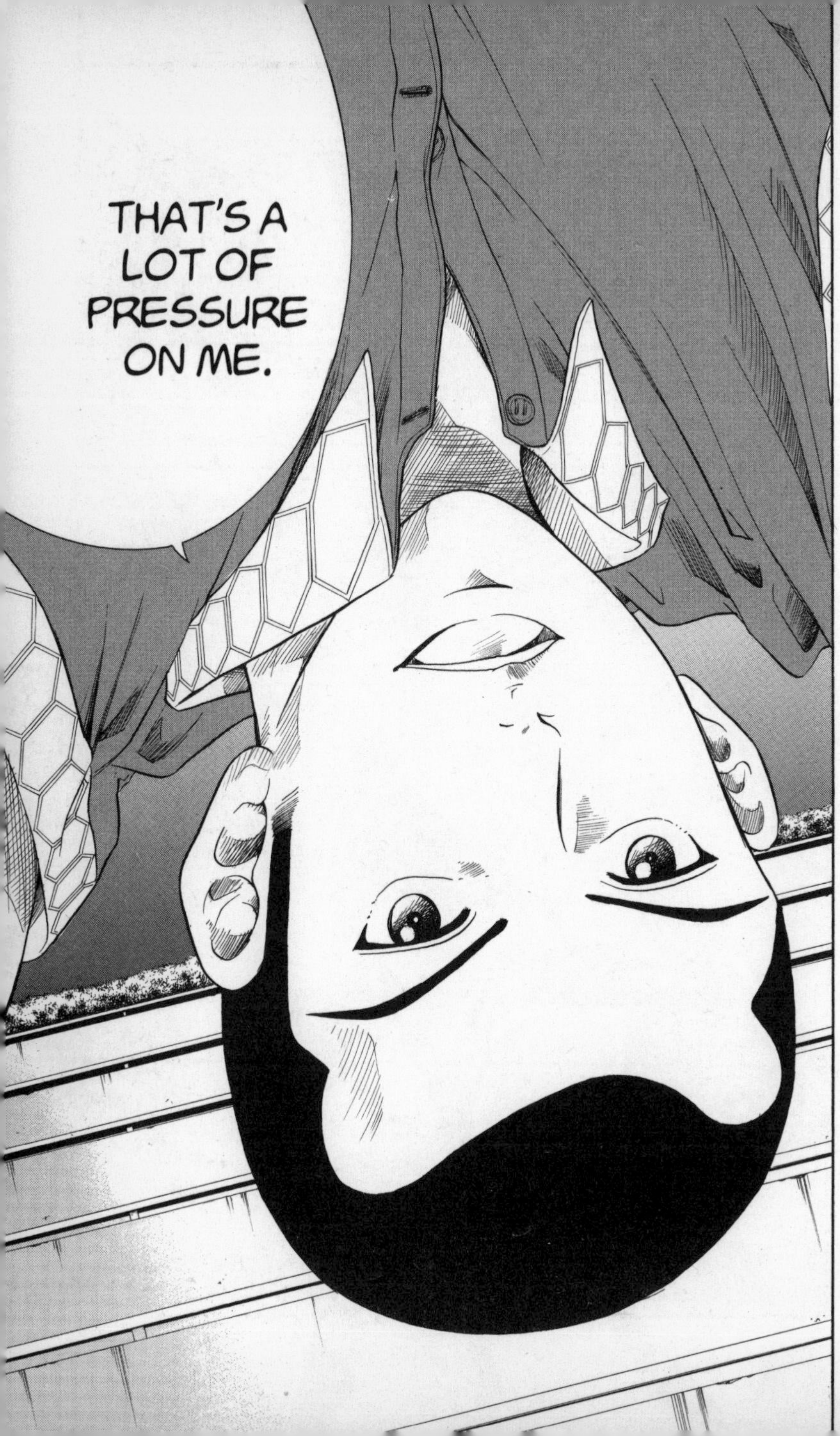
THAT'S A LOT OF PRESSURE ON ME.

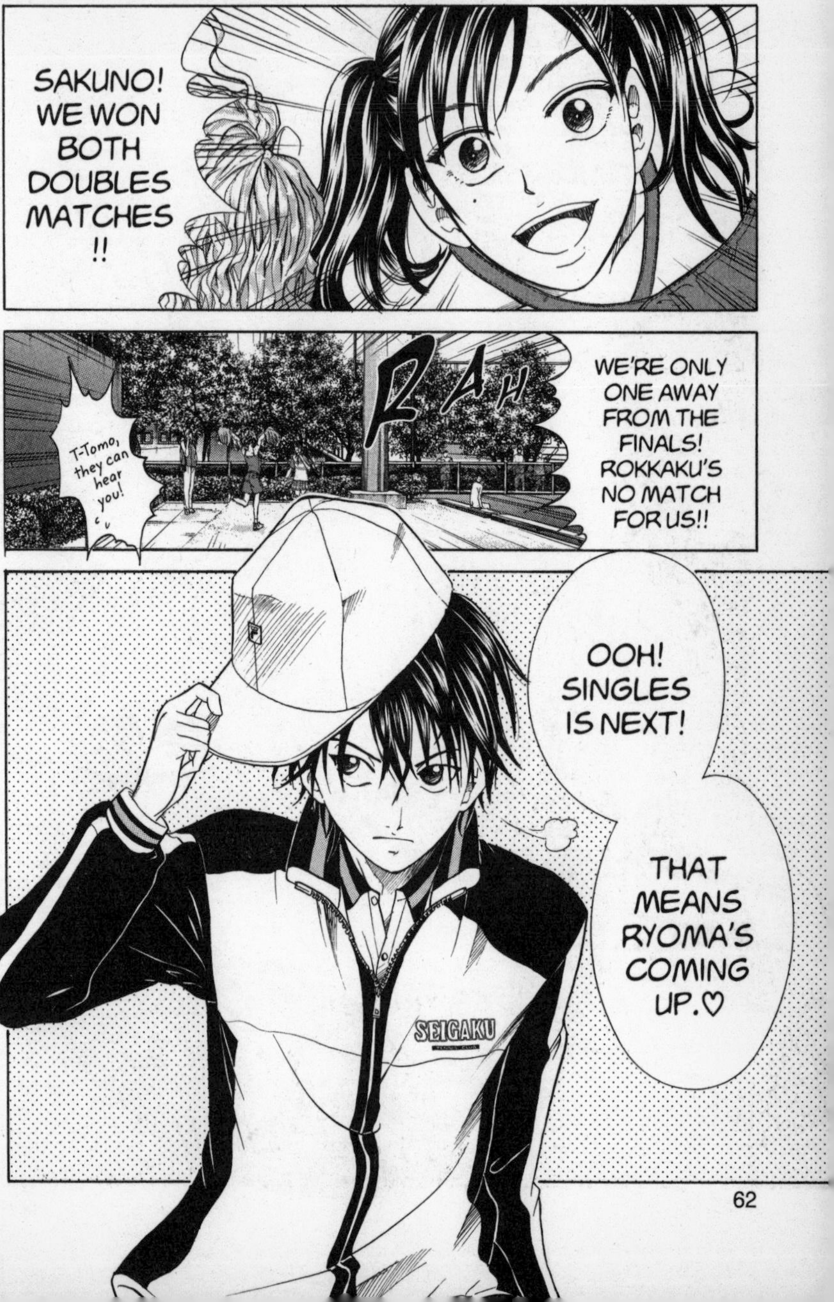
SAKUNO! WE WON BOTH DOUBLES MATCHES !!
WE'RE ONLY ONE AWAY FROM THE FINALS! ROKKAKU'S NO MATCH FOR US!!
RAH
T-Tomo, they can hear you!
OOH! SINGLES IS NEXT!
THAT MEANS RYOMA'S COMING UP.♡
SEIGAKU

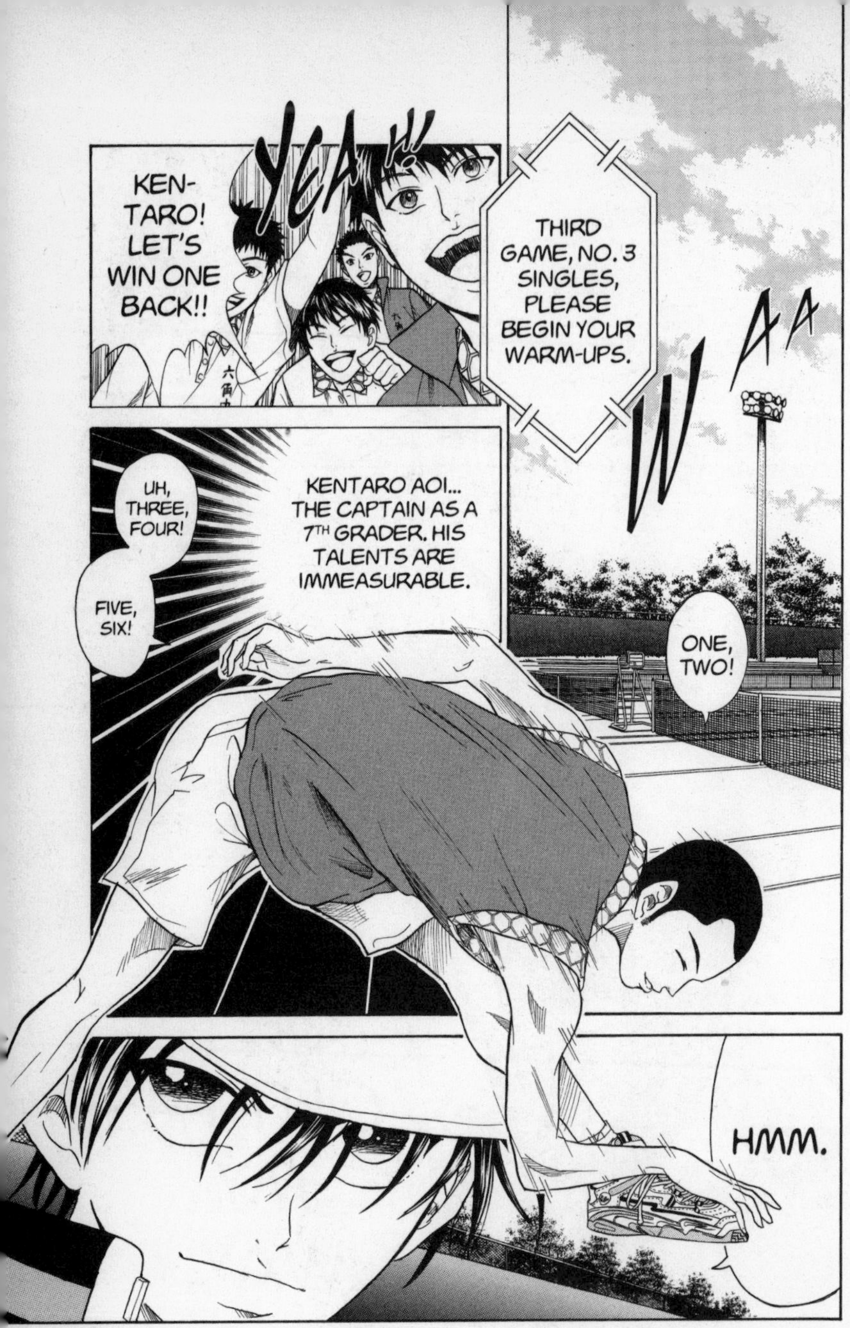
THIRD GAME, NO. 3 SINGLES, PLEASE BEGIN YOUR WARM-UPS.
WAA
YEAH!!
KEN-TARO! LET'S WIN ONE BACK!!
ONE, TWO!
KENTARO AOI... THE CAPTAIN AS A 7TH GRADER. HIS TALENTS ARE IMMEASURABLE.
UH, THREE, FOUR!
FIVE, SIX!
HMM.

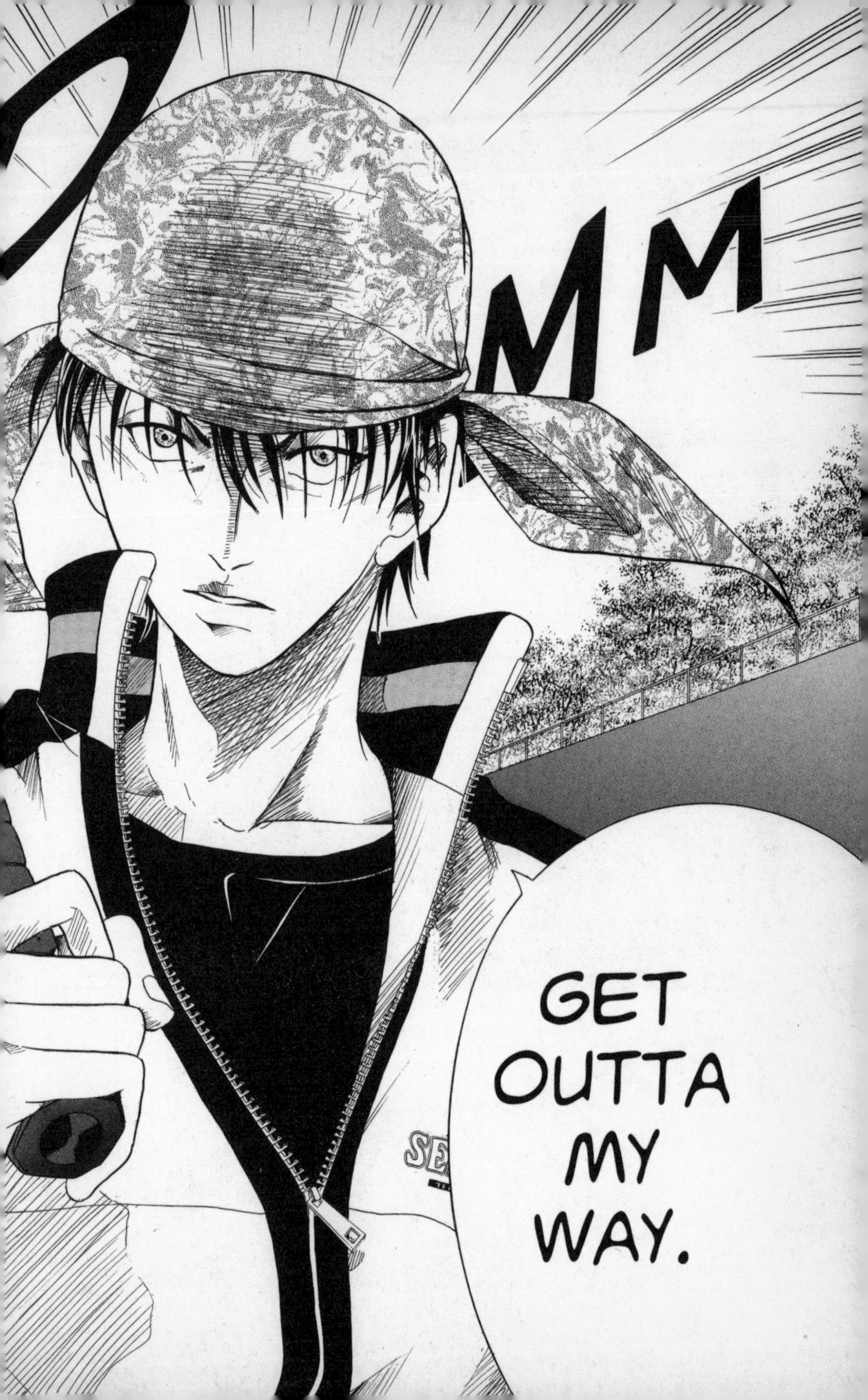
MM
GET OUTTA MY WAY.

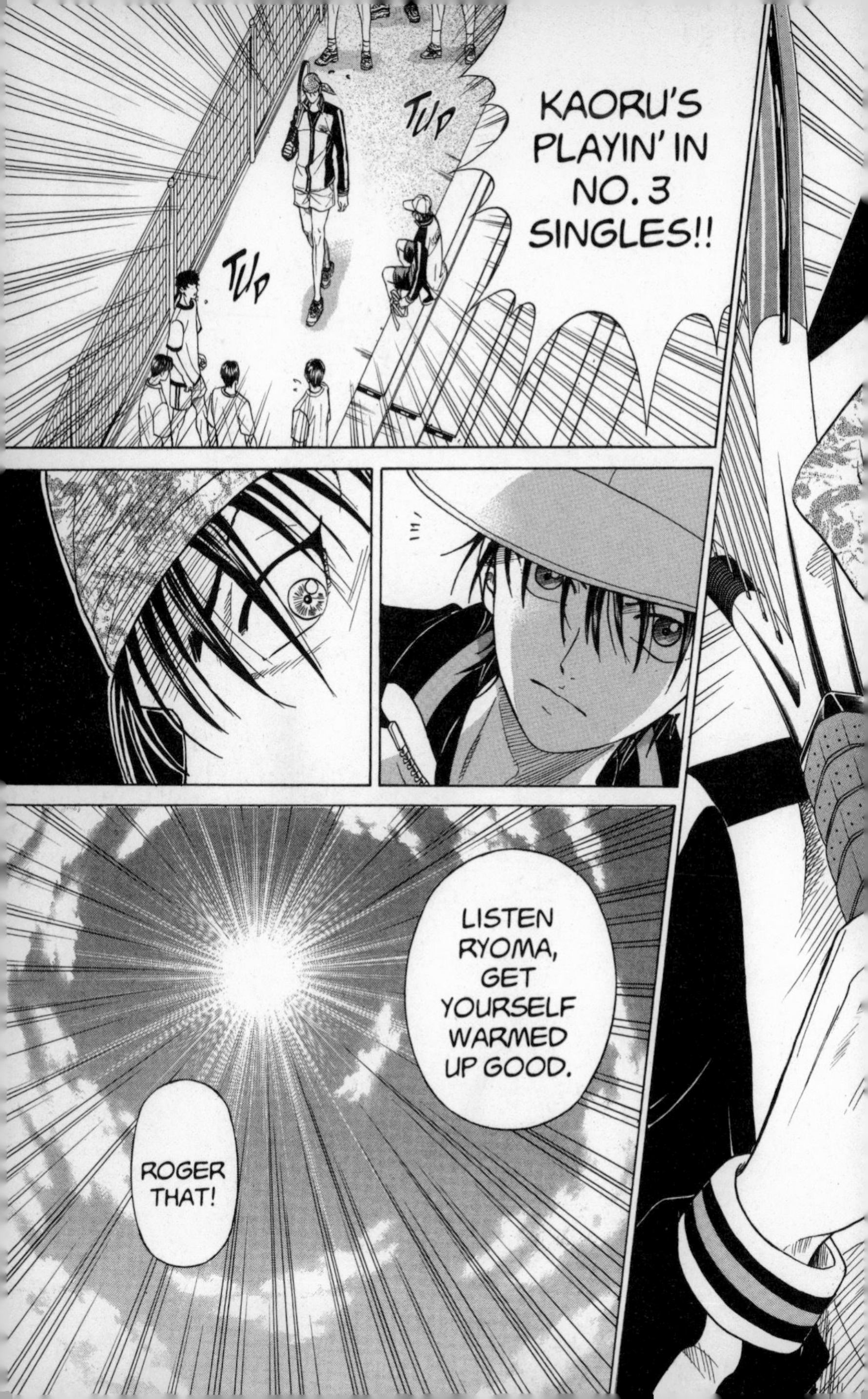
KAORU'S PLAYIN' IN NO. 3 SINGLES!!
TUP
TUP
LISTEN RYOMA, GET YOURSELF WARMED UP GOOD.
ROGER THAT!

テニスの王子様

THE PRINCE OF TENNIS™

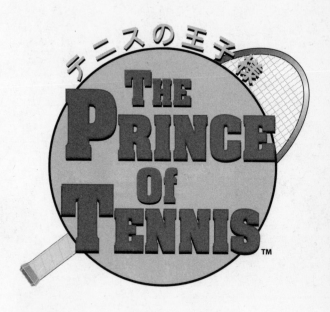

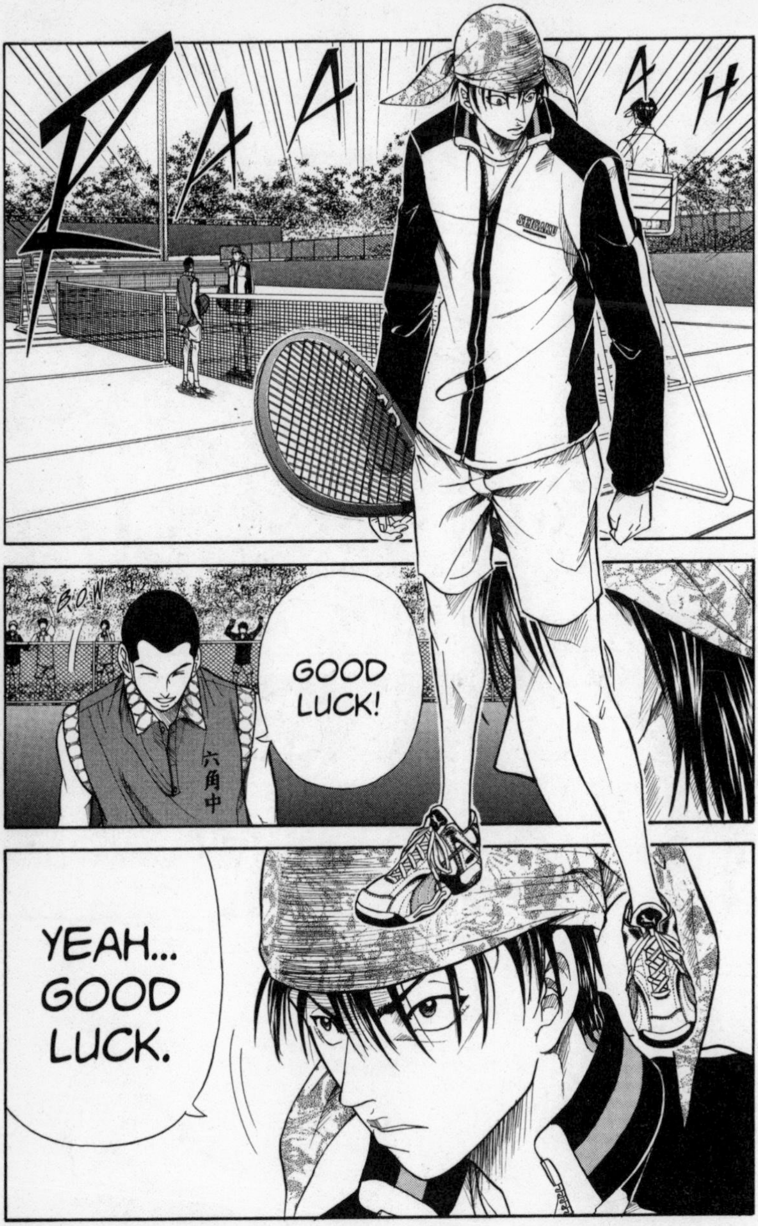
ZAAAH
BOW
GOOD LUCK!
六角中
YEAH... GOOD LUCK.

GENIUS 180: PRESSURE

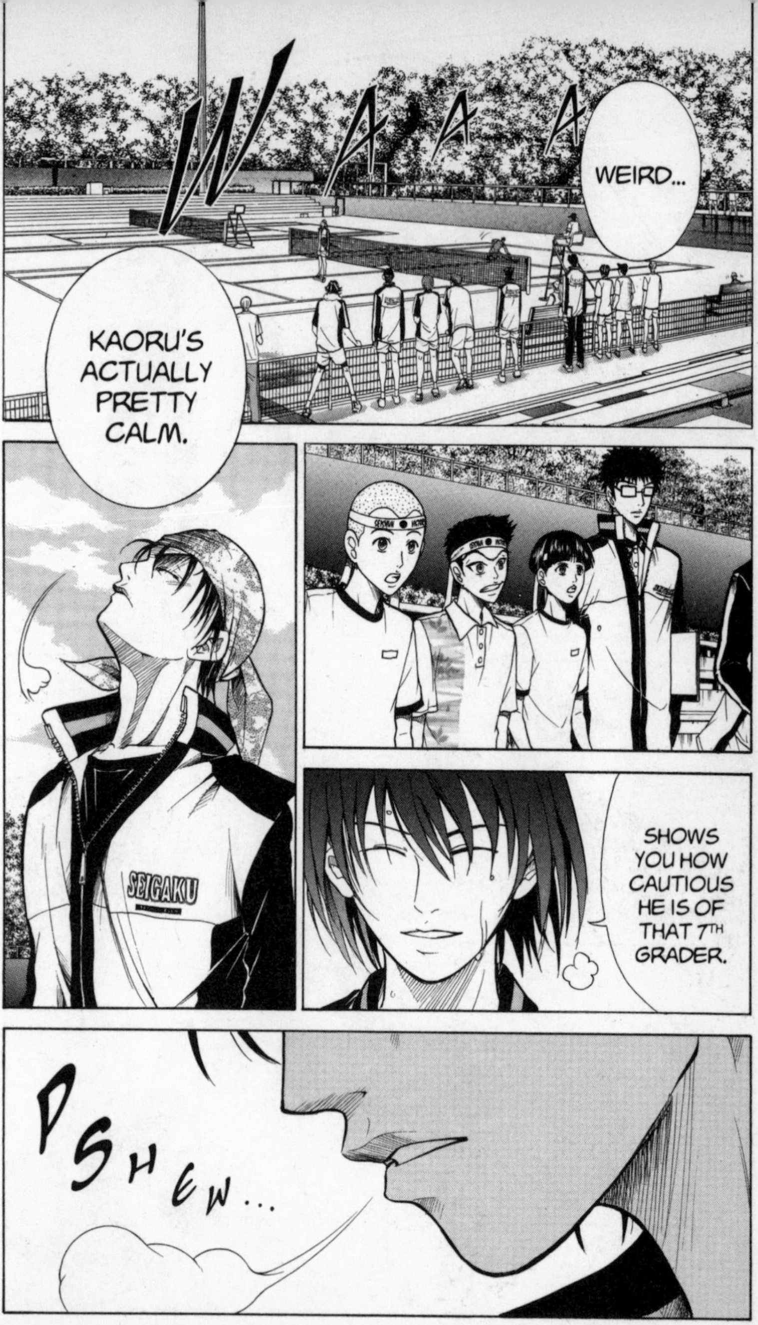
WAAA
WEIRD...
KAORU'S ACTUALLY PRETTY CALM.
SHOWS YOU HOW CAUTIOUS HE IS OF THAT 7TH GRADER.
PSHEW...

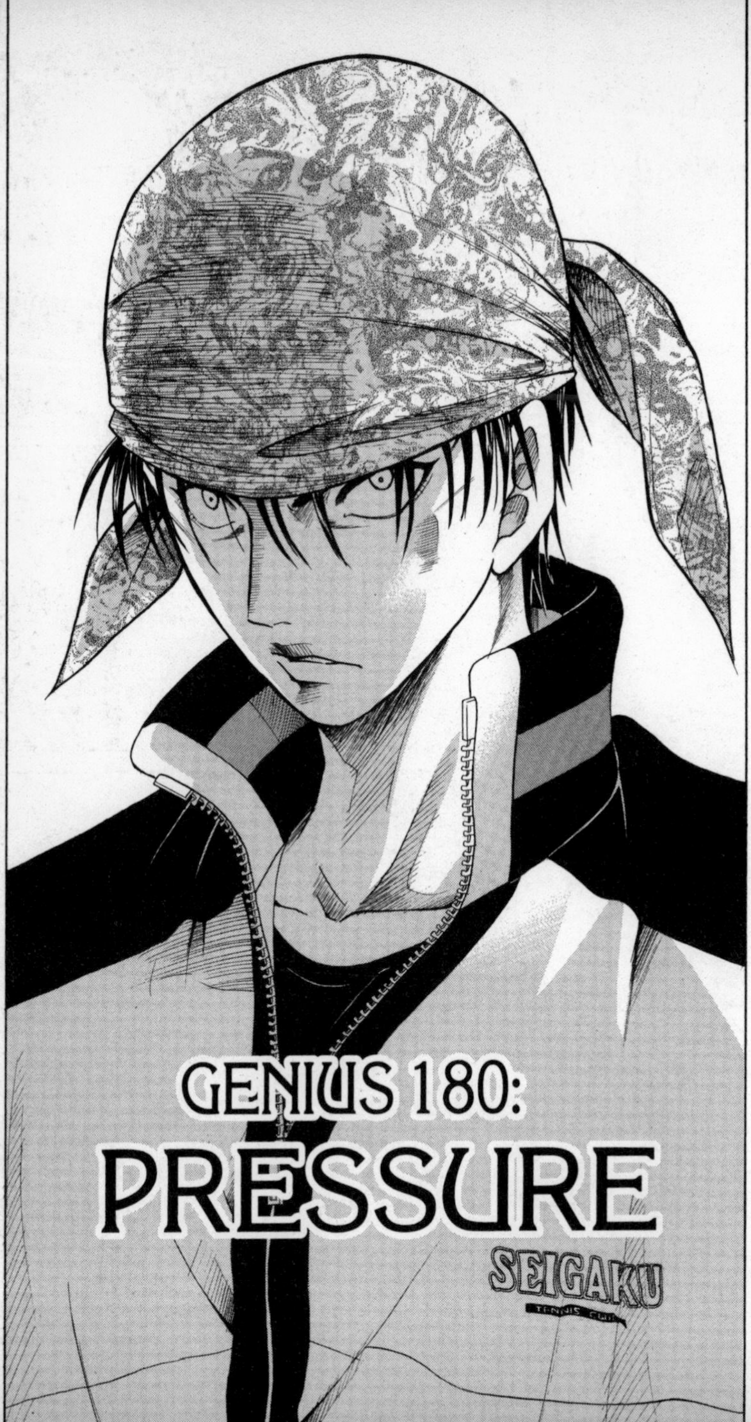
GENIUS 180:
PRESSURE
SEIGAKU

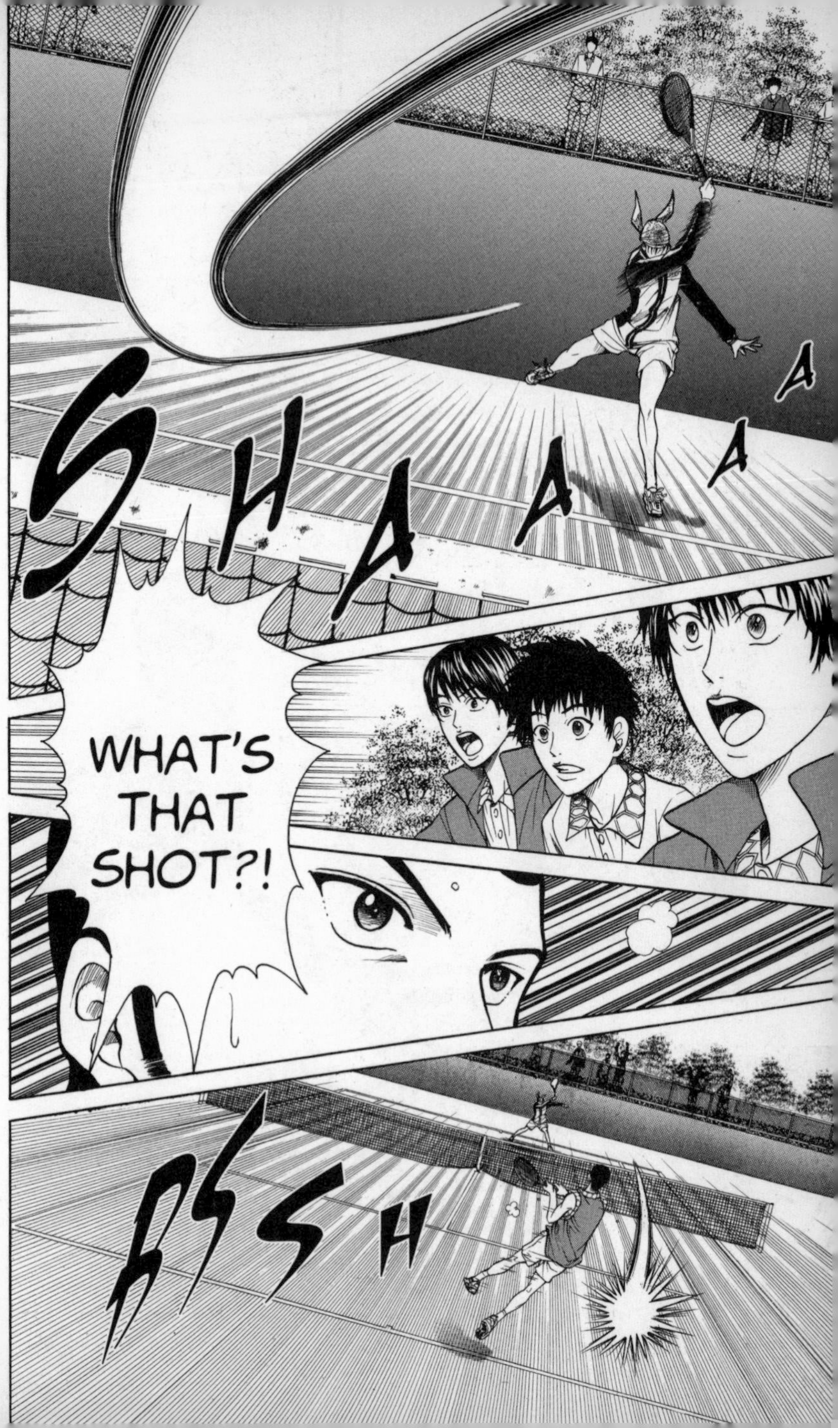
SHAAAAA
WHAT'S THAT SHOT?!
BSSH

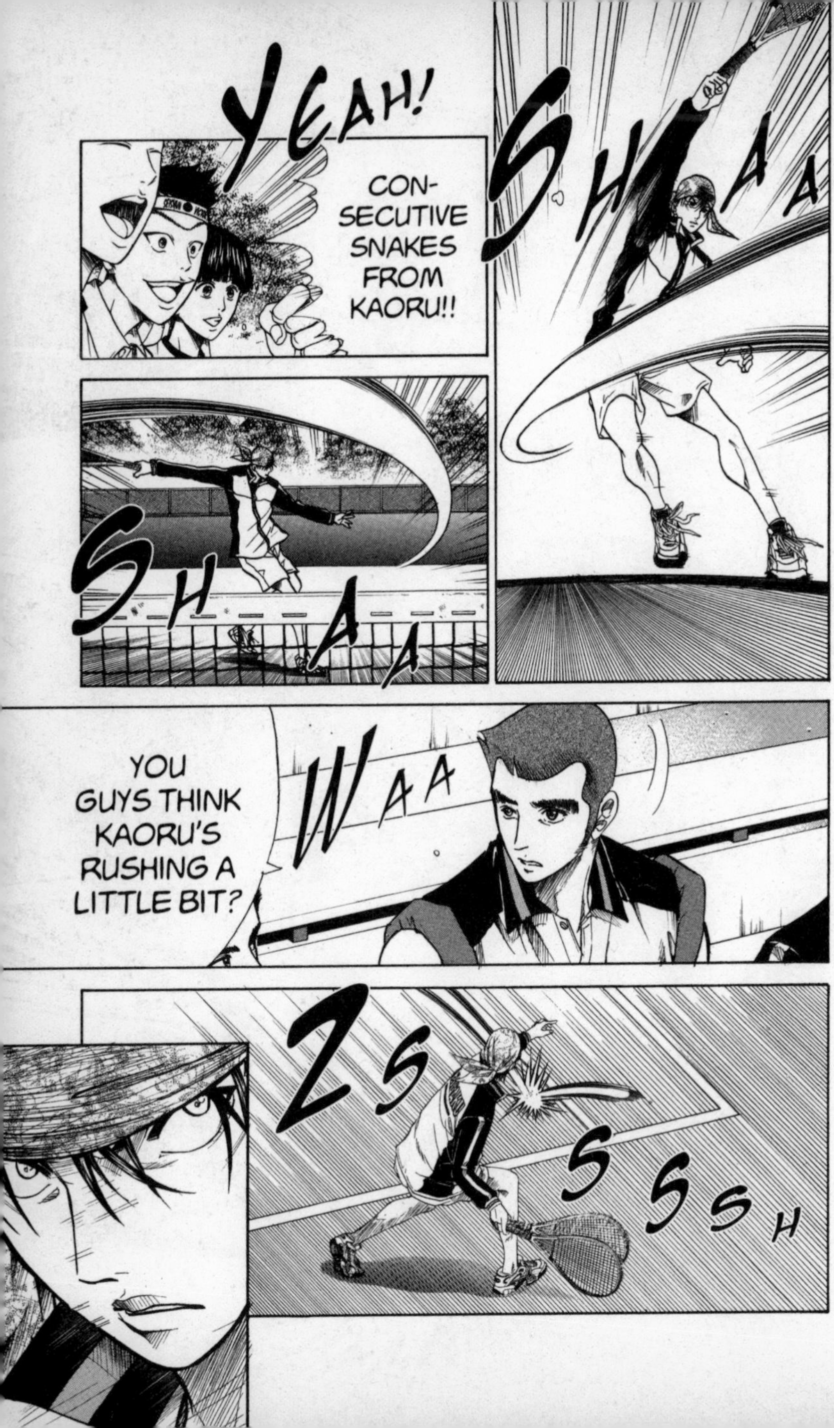
SHAA
YEAH!
CON-SECUTIVE SNAKES FROM KAORU!!
SHAA
WAA
YOU GUYS THINK KAORU'S RUSHING A LITTLE BIT?
ZSSSSH

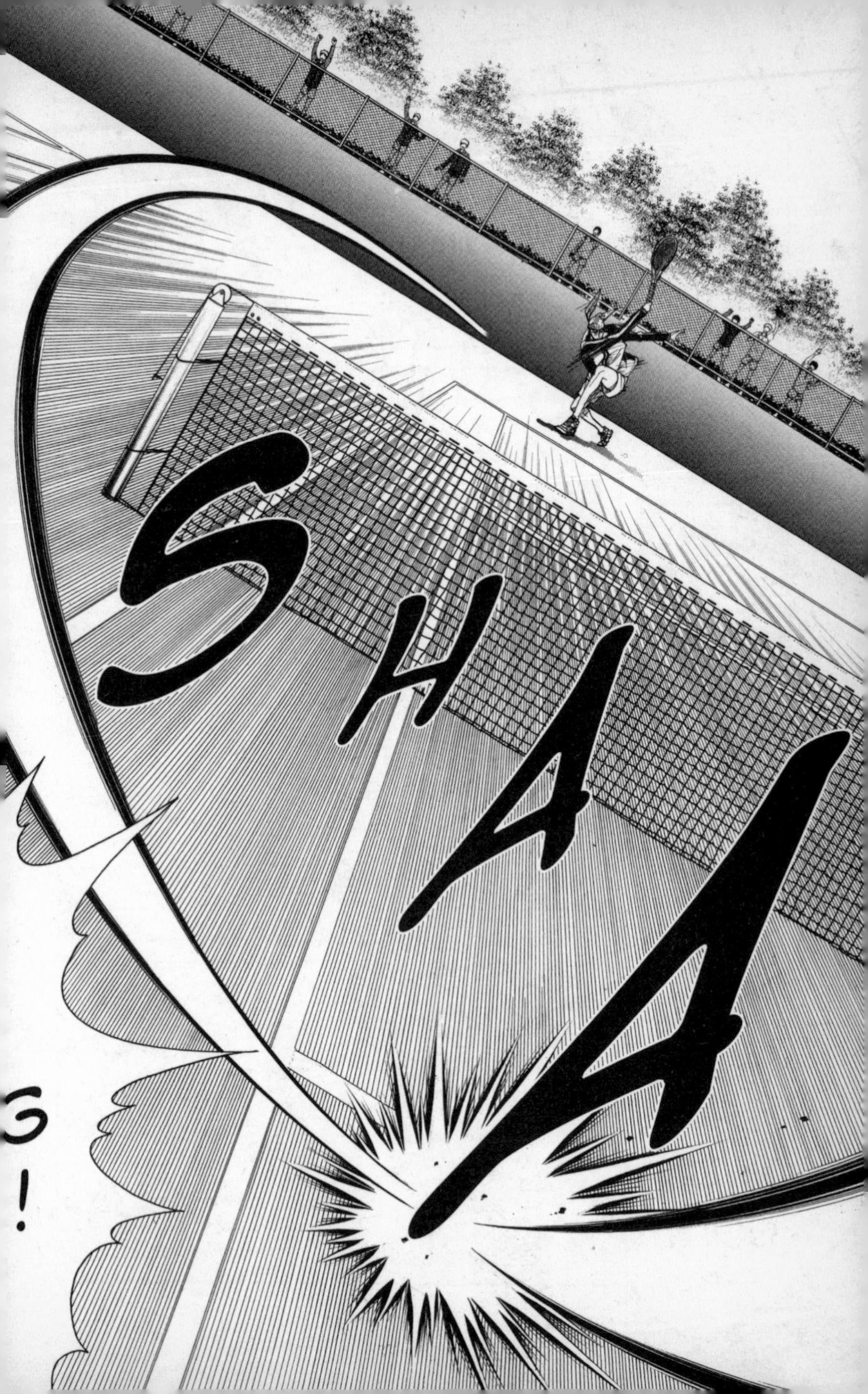
SHAA
S!

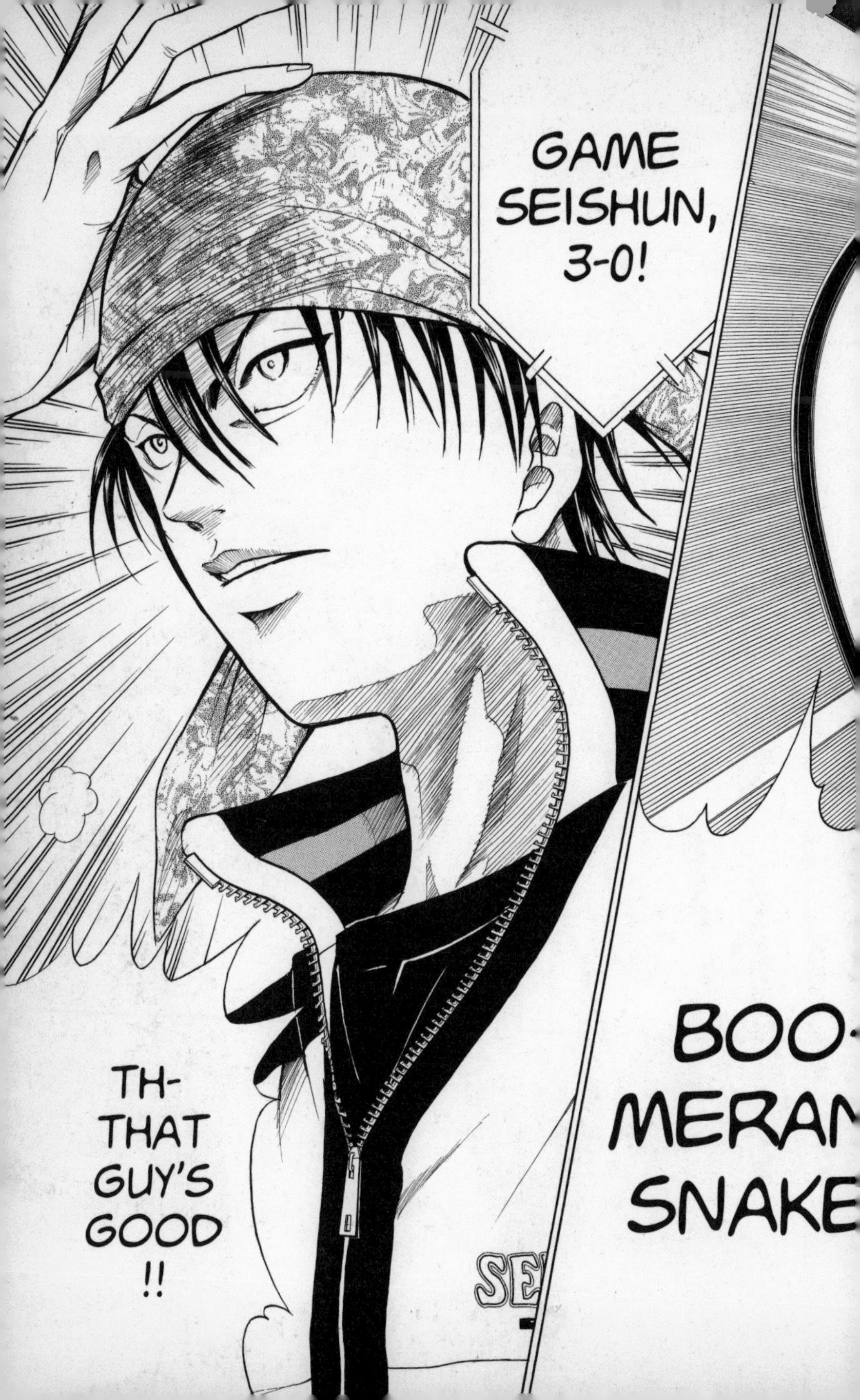
GAME SEISHUN, 3-0!
BOO- MERAN SNAKE
TH- THAT GUY'S GOOD !!

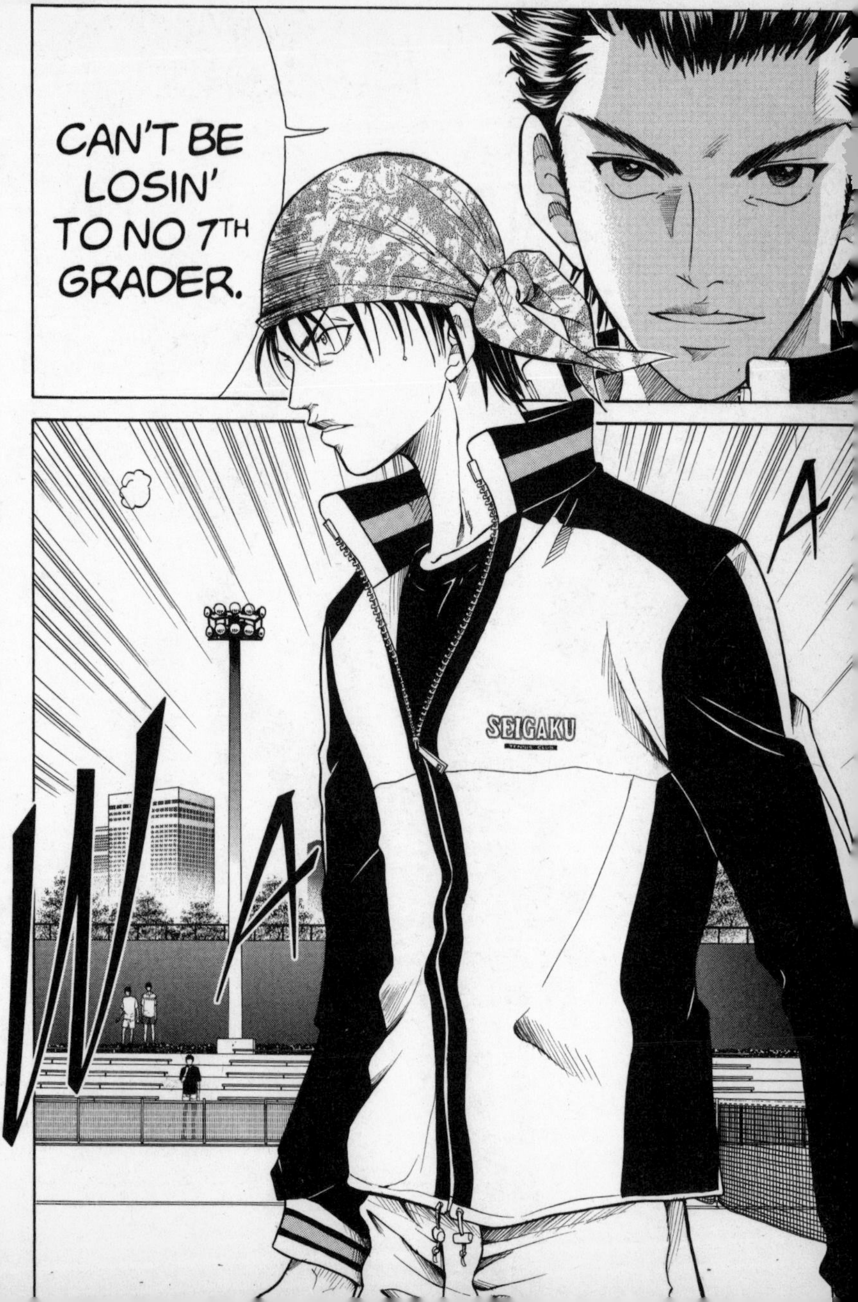

CAN'T BE LOSIN' TO NO 7TH GRADER.
WA
A
SEIGAKU

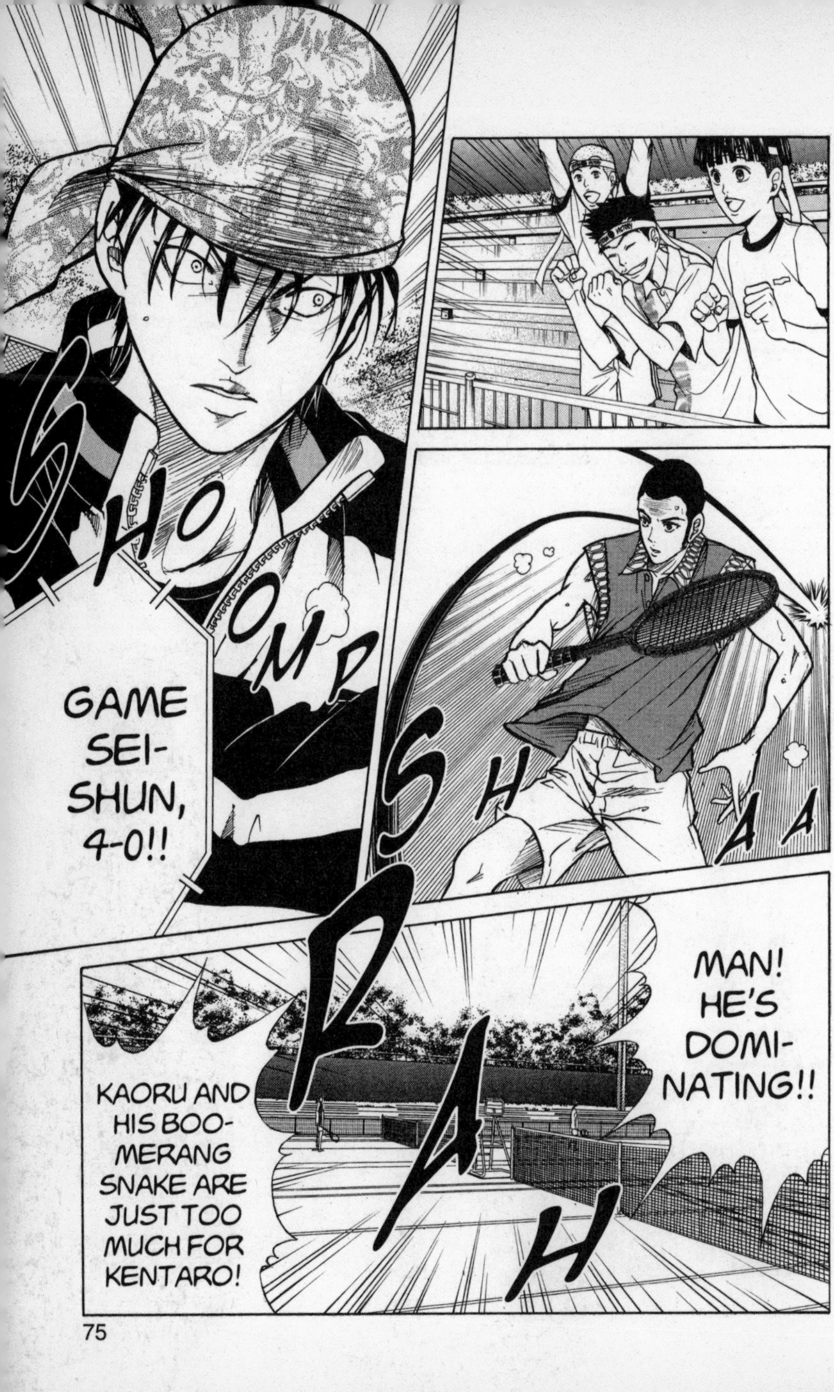
SHOMP
GAME SEI-SHUN, 4-0!!
SHAA
MAN! HE'S DOMINATING!!
KAORU AND HIS BOOMERANG SNAKE ARE JUST TOO MUCH FOR KENTARO!

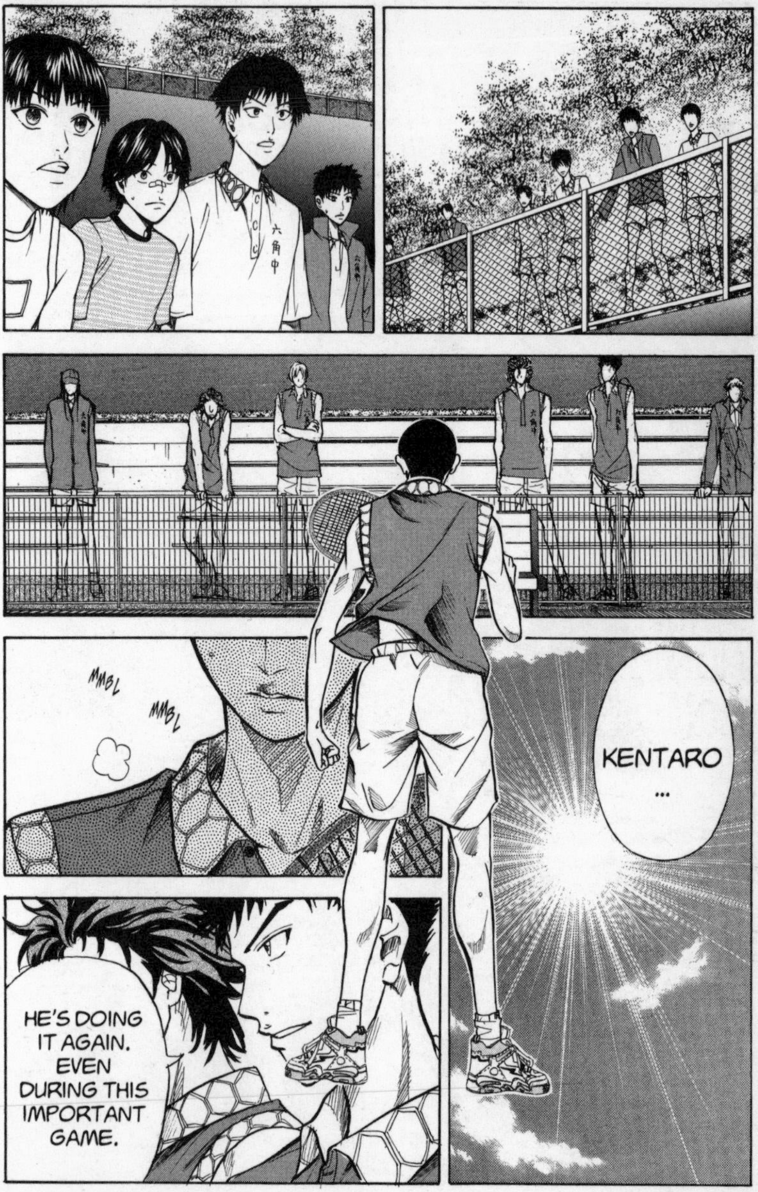
KENTARO ...
MMBL
MMBL
HE'S DOING IT AGAIN. EVEN DURING THIS IMPORTANT GAME.

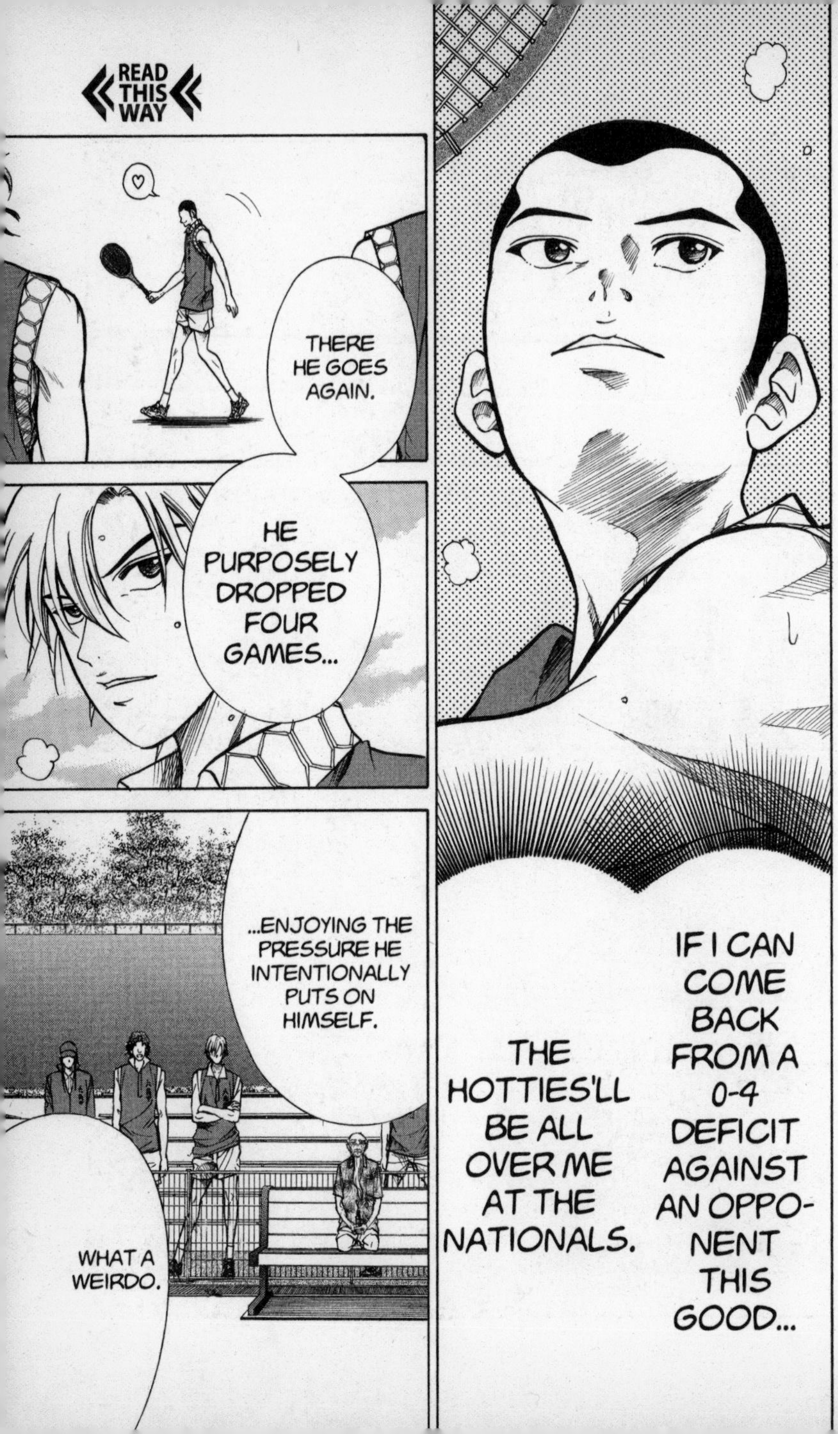
READ THIS WAY
IF I CAN COME BACK FROM A 0-4 DEFICIT AGAINST AN OPPONENT THIS GOOD...
THE HOTTIES'LL BE ALL OVER ME AT THE NATIONALS.
THERE HE GOES AGAIN.
HE PURPOSELY DROPPED FOUR GAMES...
...ENJOYING THE PRESSURE HE INTENTIONALLY PUTS ON HIMSELF.
WHAT A WEIRDO.

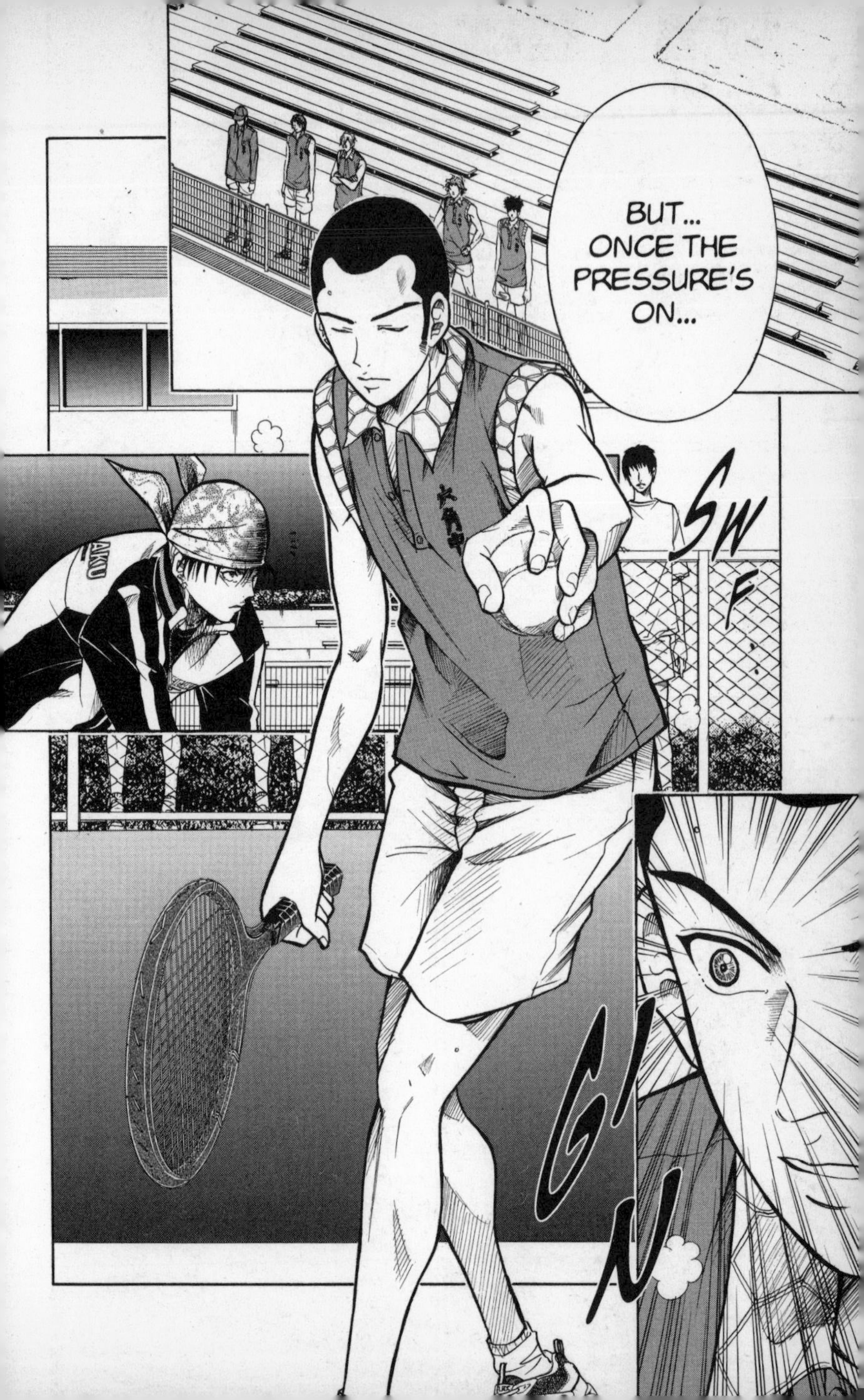
BUT... ONCE THE PRESSURE'S ON...
SWF
GIN

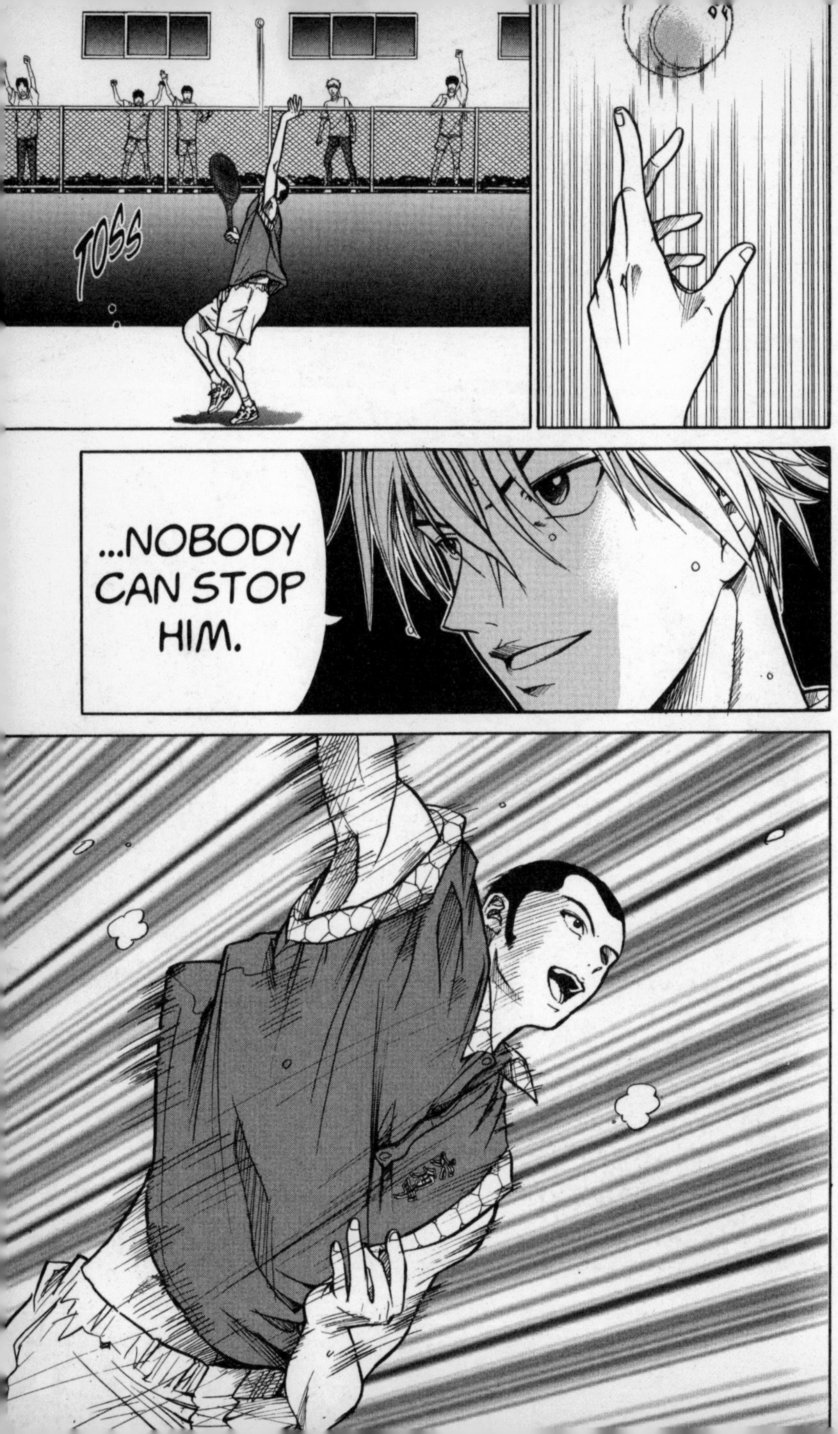
TOSS
...NOBODY CAN STOP HIM.

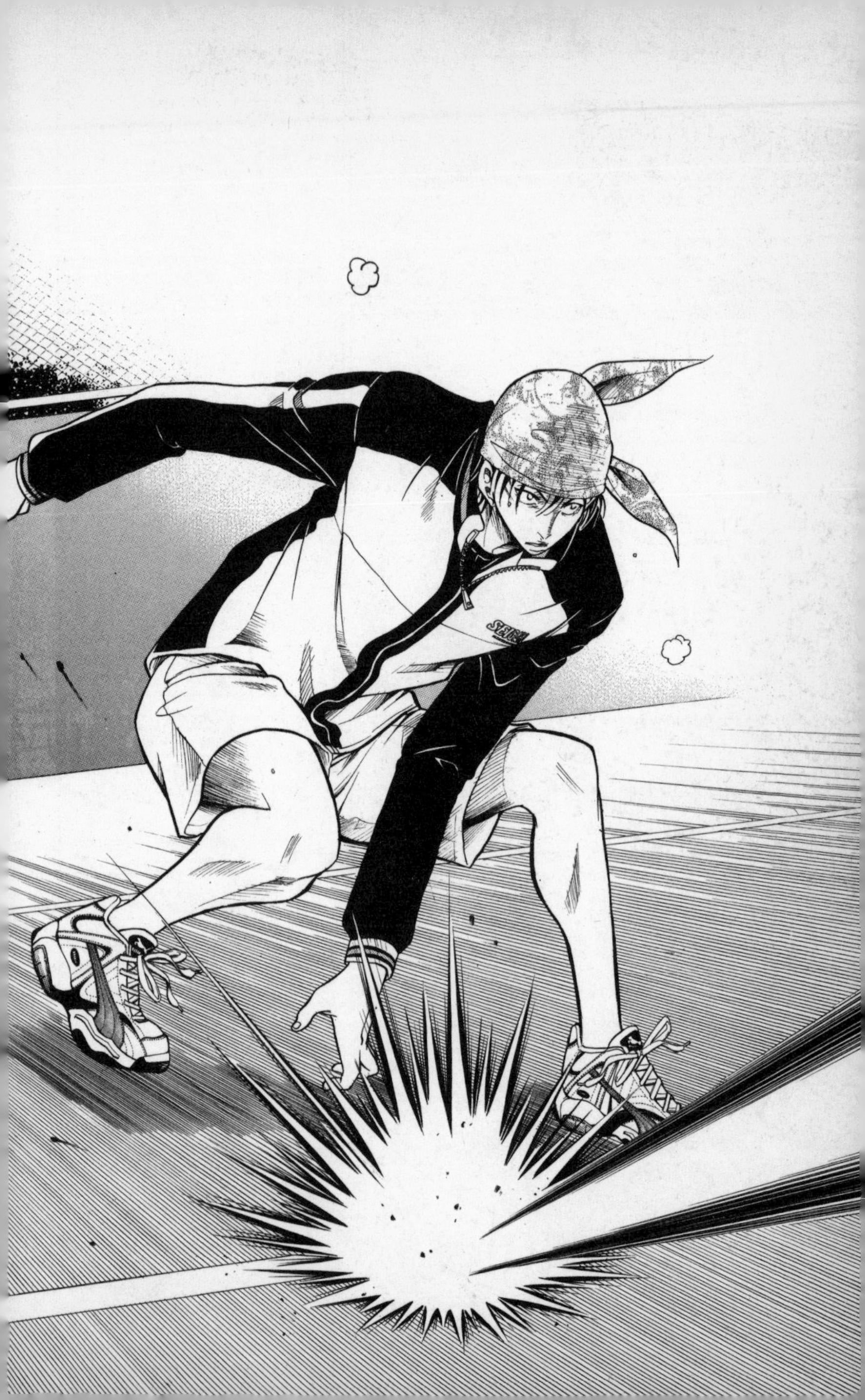

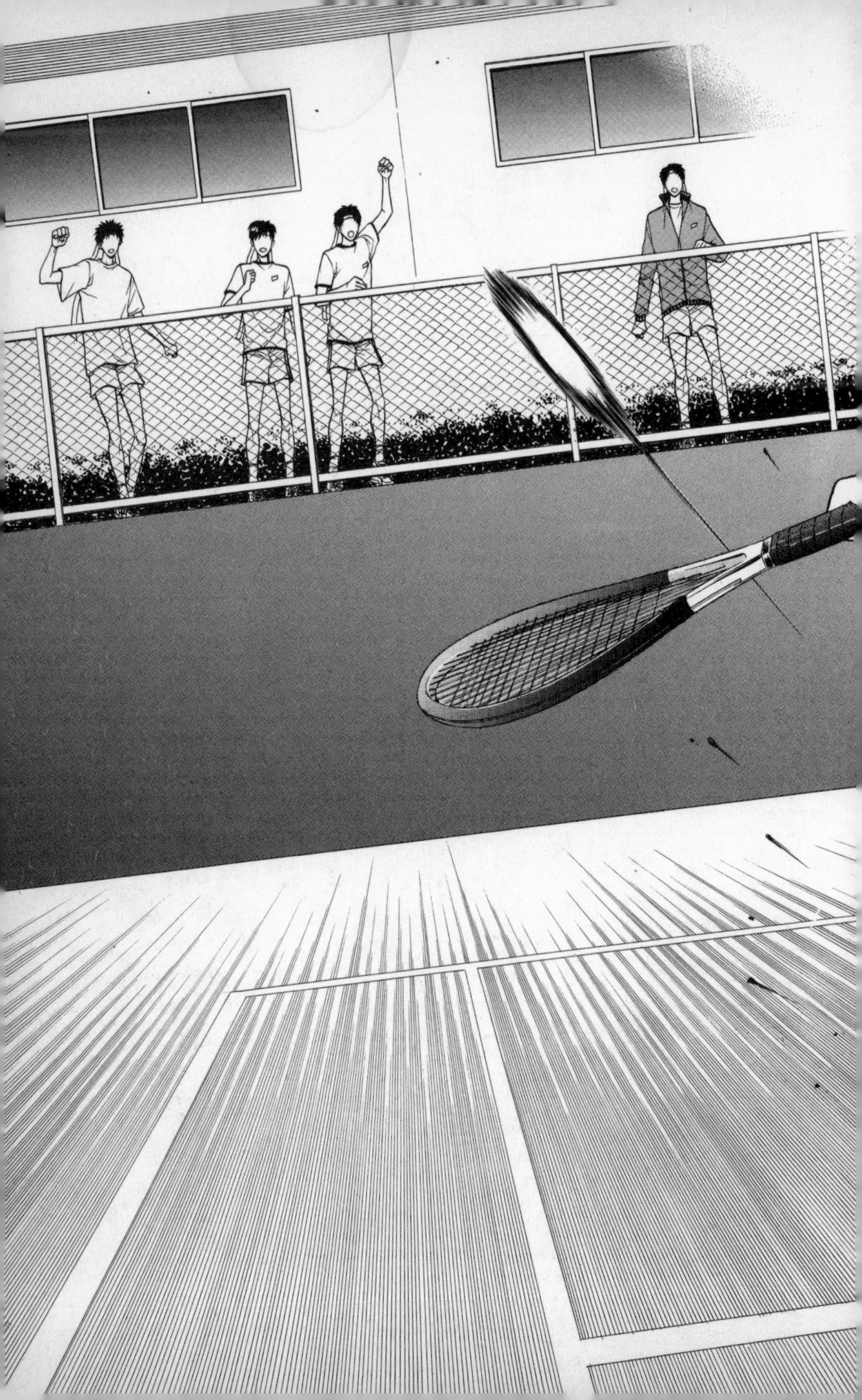

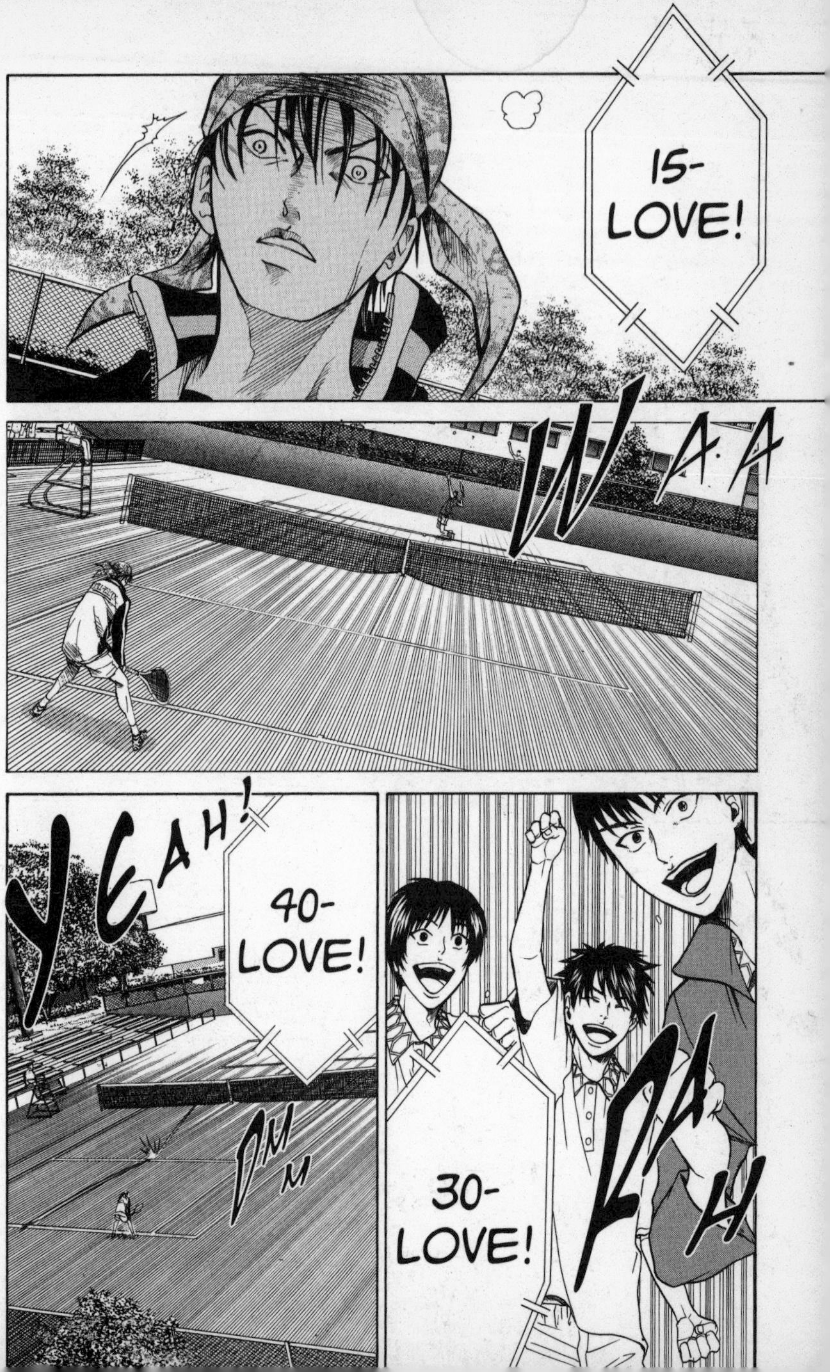
15-LOVE!
WAA
30-LOVE!
YEAH!
40-LOVE!

READ THIS WAY

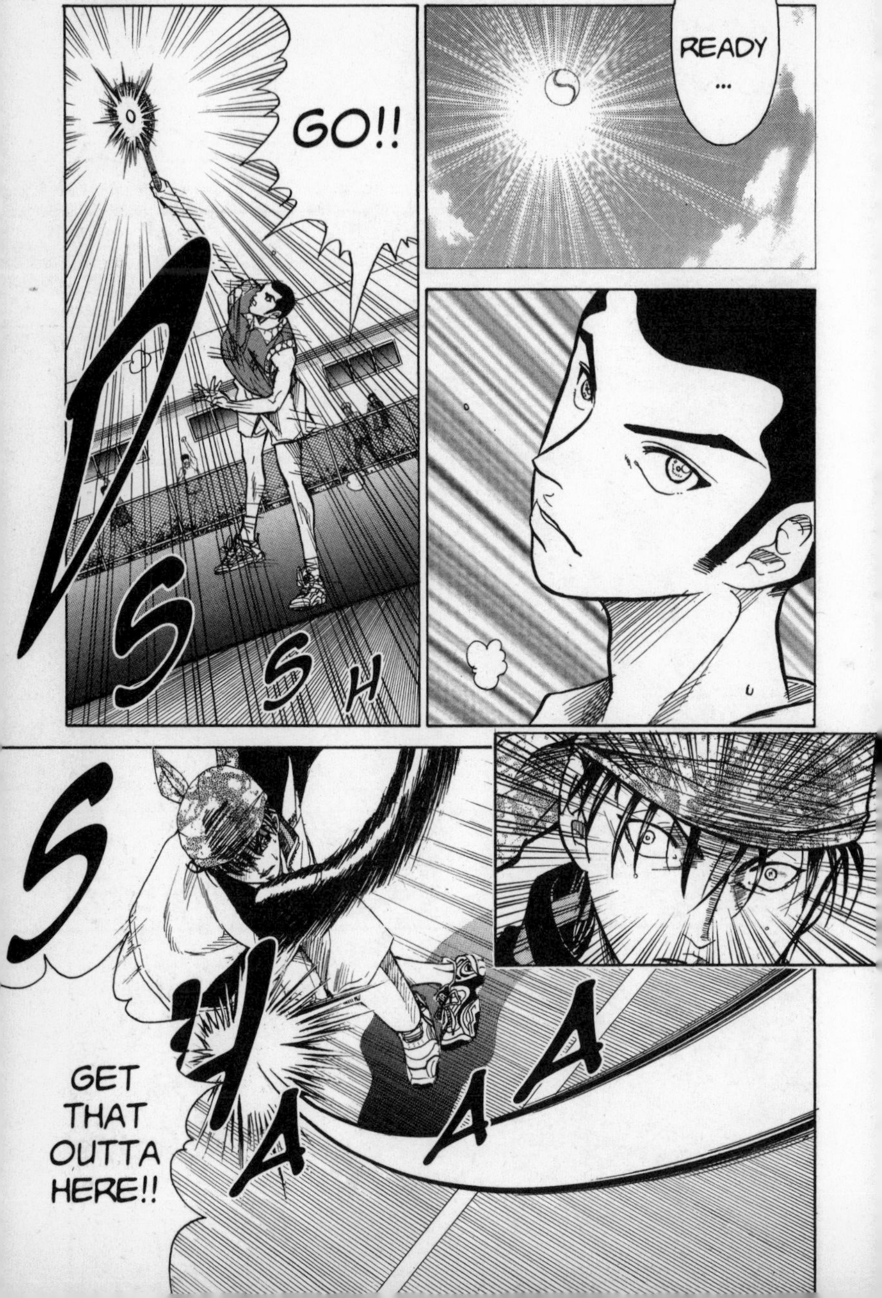
READY ...
GO!!
DSSH
GET THAT OUTTA HERE!!

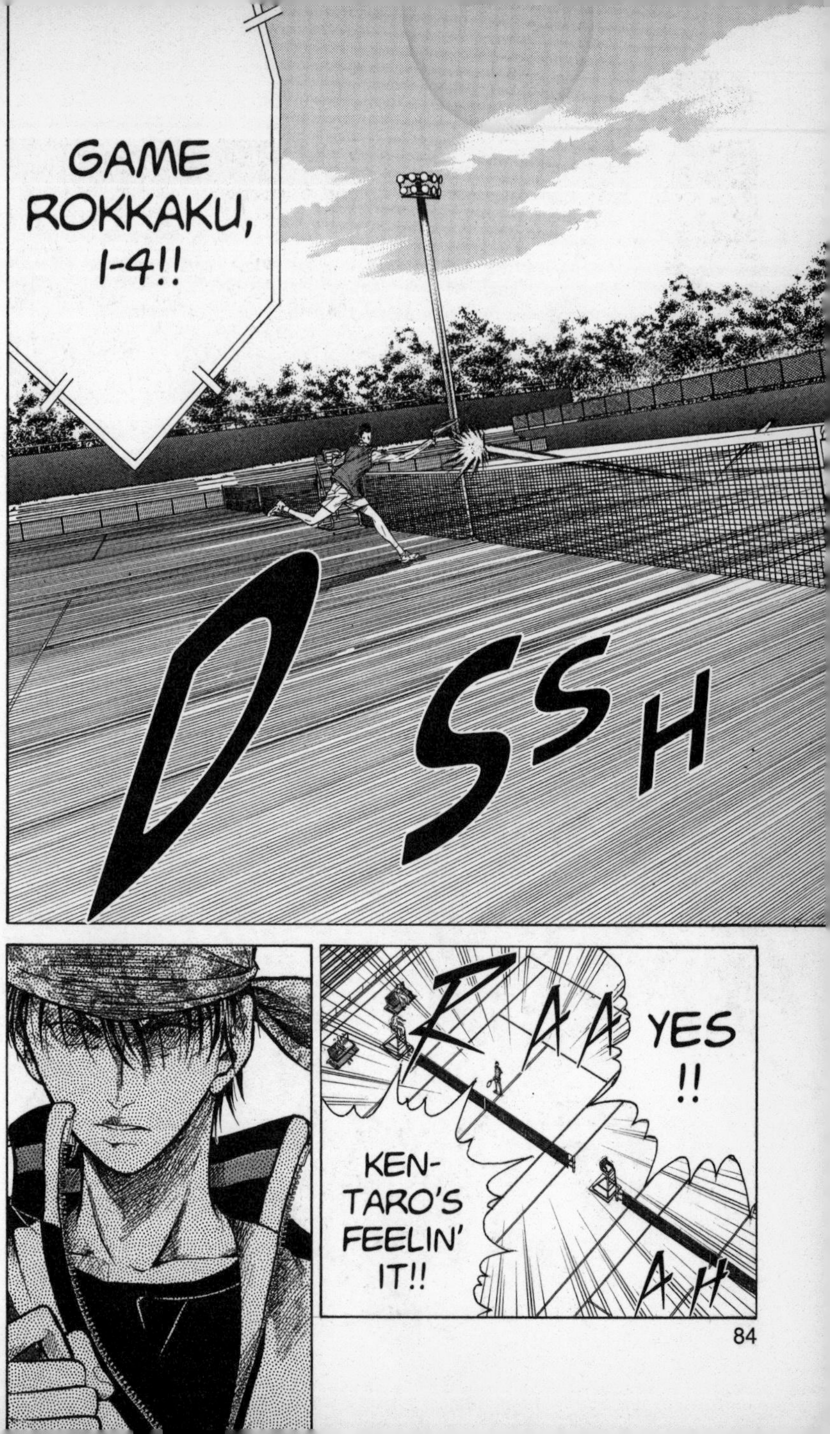
GAME ROKKAKU, 1-4!!
DSSH
YES !!
KEN-TARO'S FEELIN' IT!!
ZRAA AH

READ THIS WAY

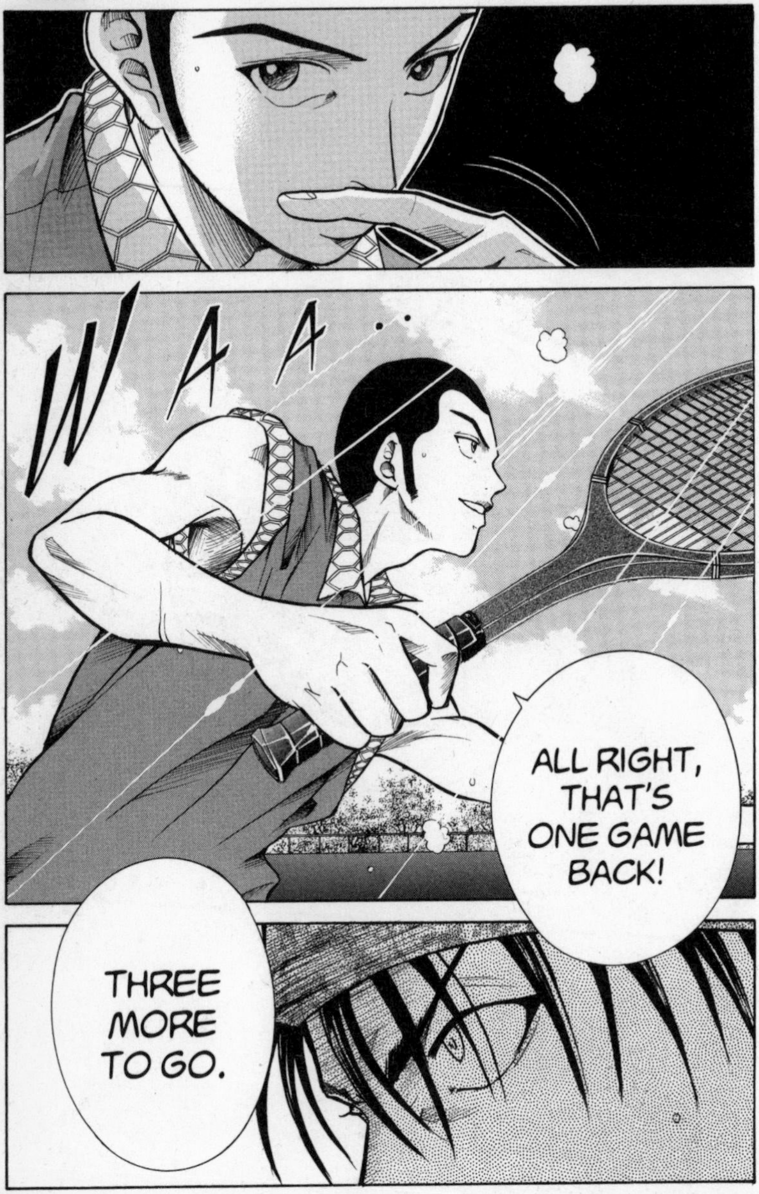
WAA..
ALL RIGHT, THAT'S ONE GAME BACK!
THREE MORE TO GO.

テニスの王子様

THE PRINCE OF TENNIS™

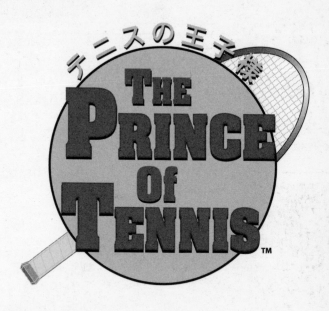

GENIUS 181: KENTARO AOI

FIVE, SIX!

SEVEN, EIGHT!

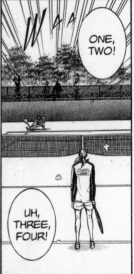

ONE, TWO!

UH, THREE, FOUR!

...

HIS MOVE-MENT'S DIFFERENT ALL OF THE SUDDEN!

GENIUS 181:
KENTARO AOI
MISSION

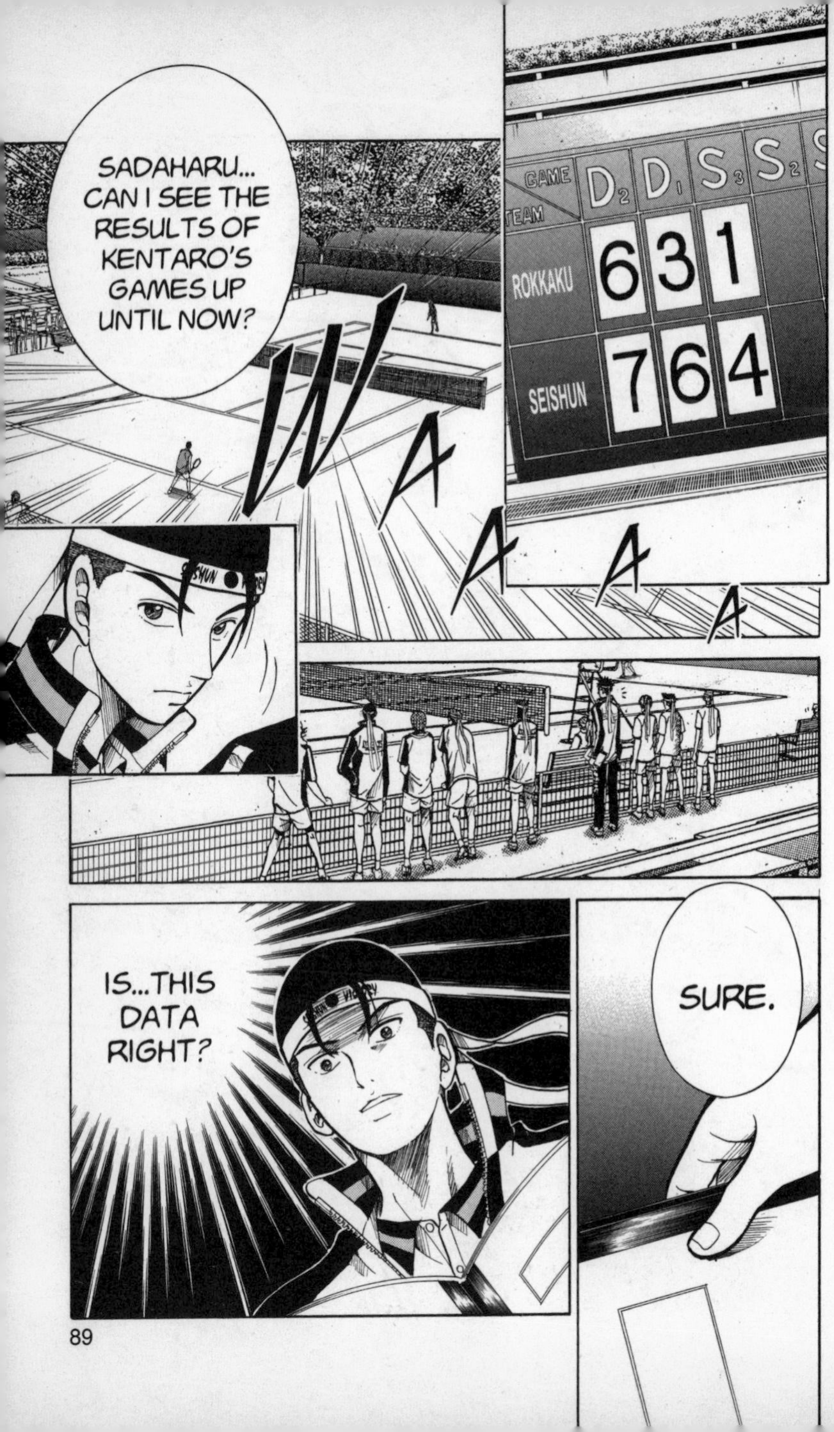
GAME
TEAM
D2 D1 S3 S2
ROKKAKU 6 3 1
SEISHUN 7 6 4
SADAHARU... CAN I SEE THE RESULTS OF KENTARO'S GAMES UP UNTIL NOW?
WAAAA
SURE.
IS...THIS DATA RIGHT?

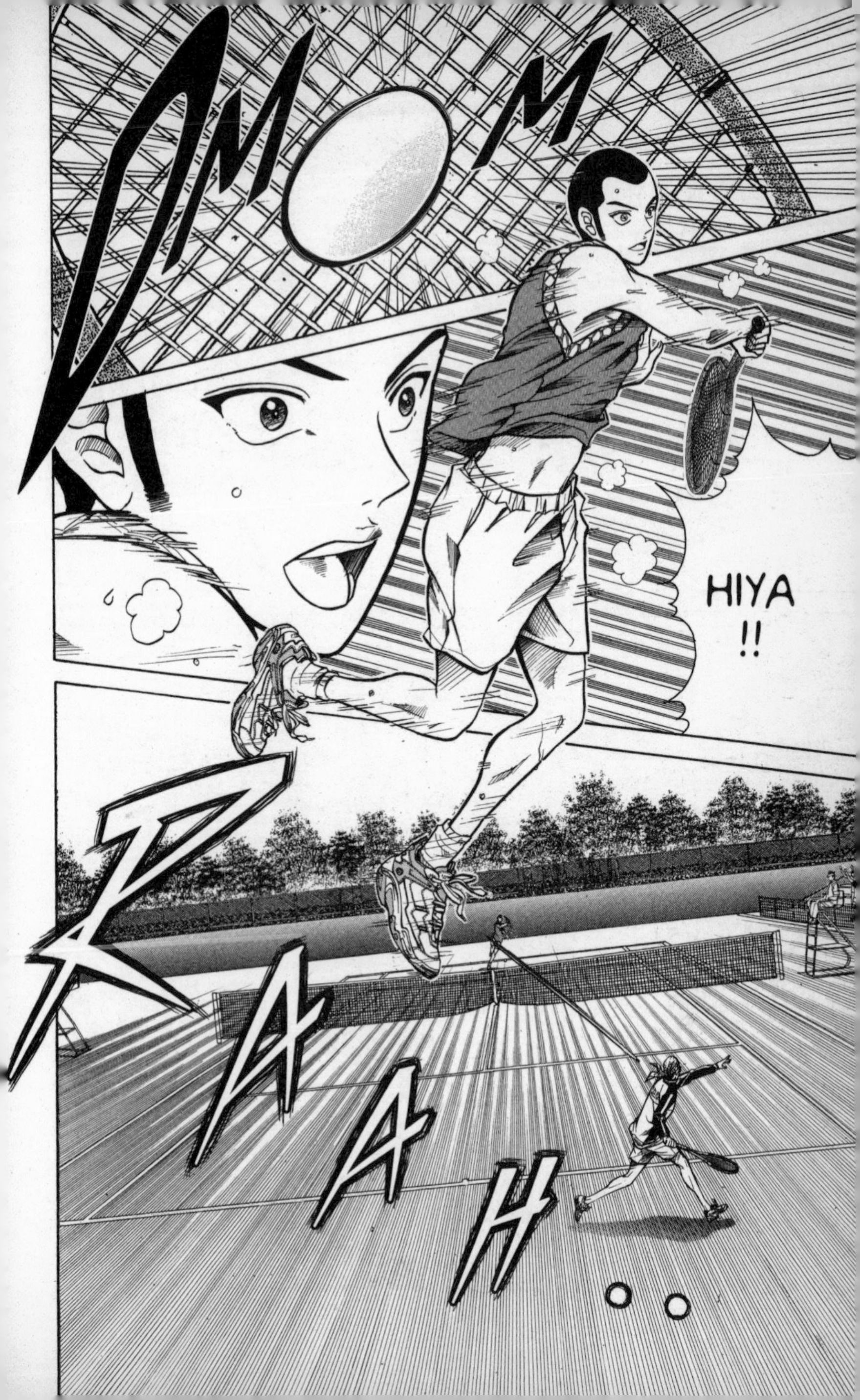
VMOM
HIYA !!
ZAAAH...

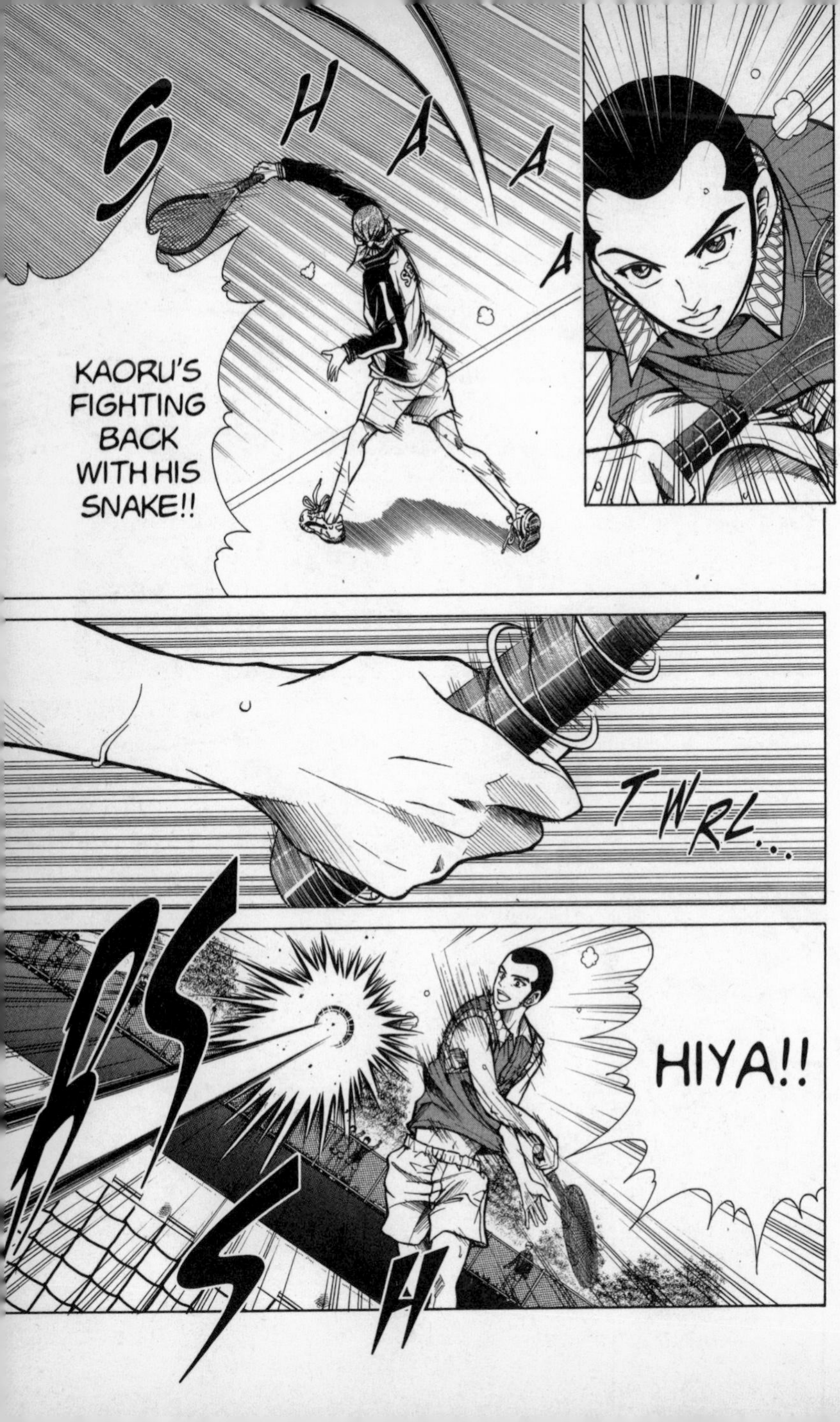
SHAAA
KAORU'S FIGHTING BACK WITH HIS SNAKE!!
TWRL...
HIYA!!

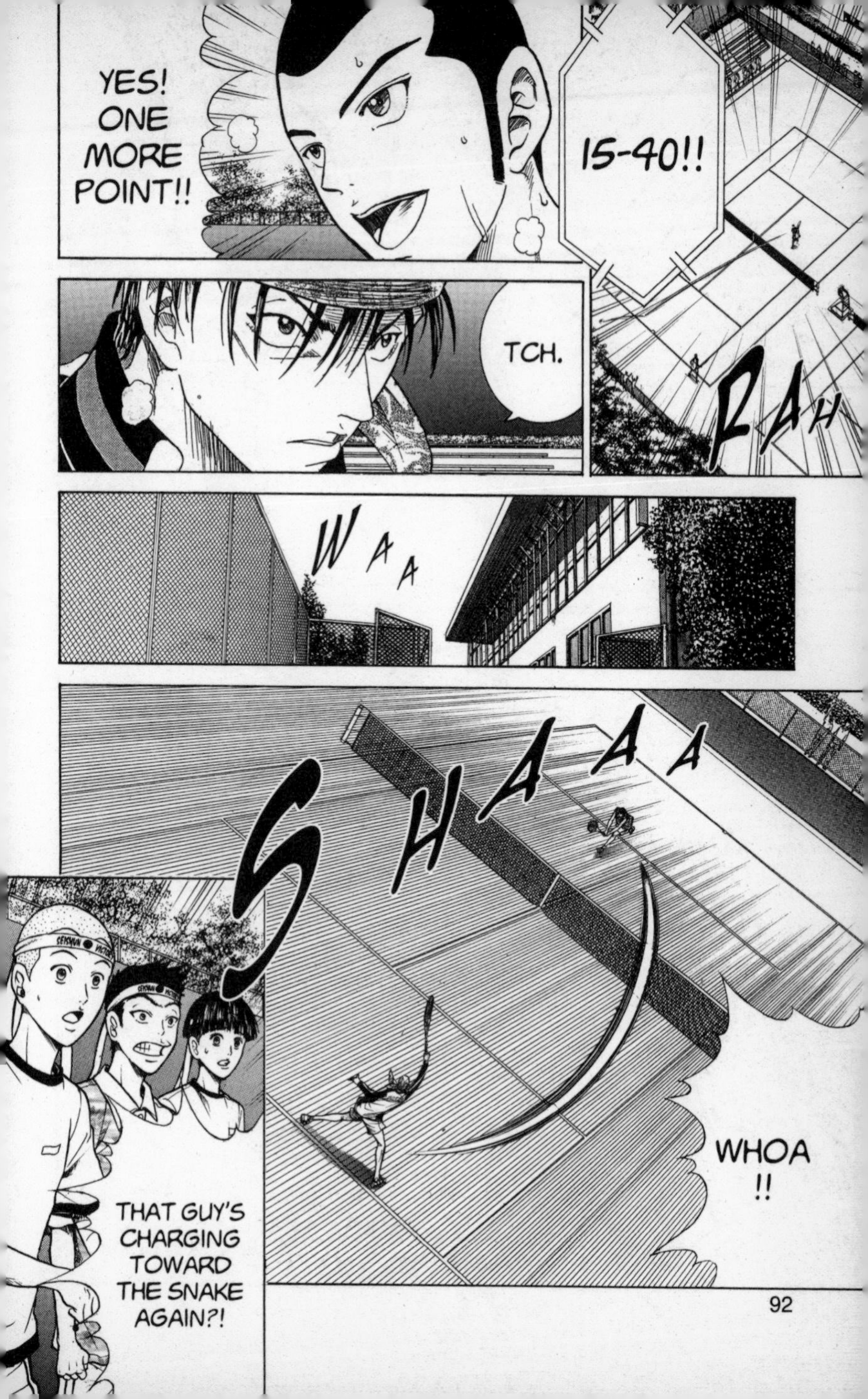
15-40!!
YES! ONE MORE POINT!!
TCH.
PAH
WAA
SHAAAA
WHOA !!
THAT GUY'S CHARGING TOWARD THE SNAKE AGAIN?!

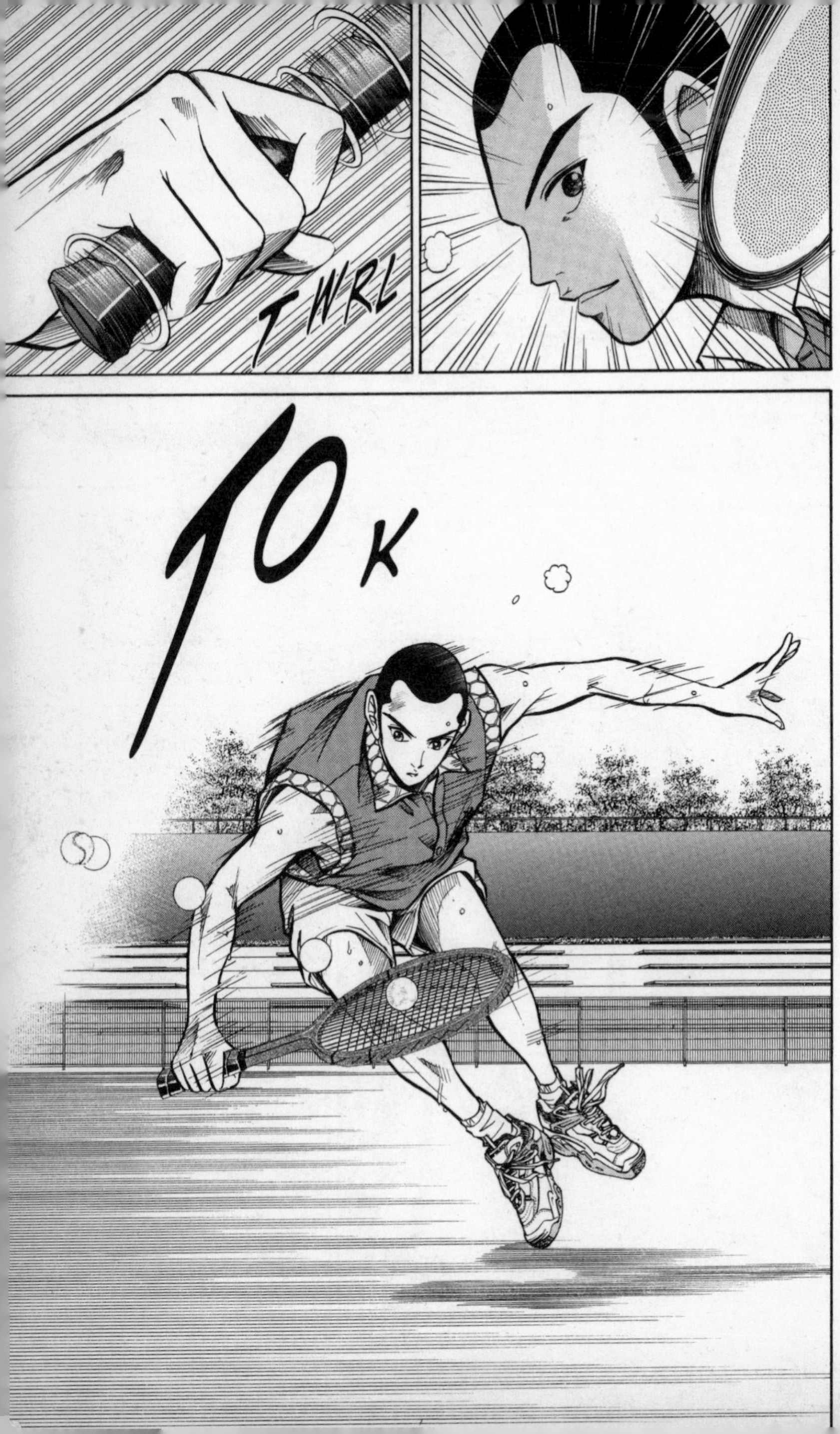
TWRL
TOK

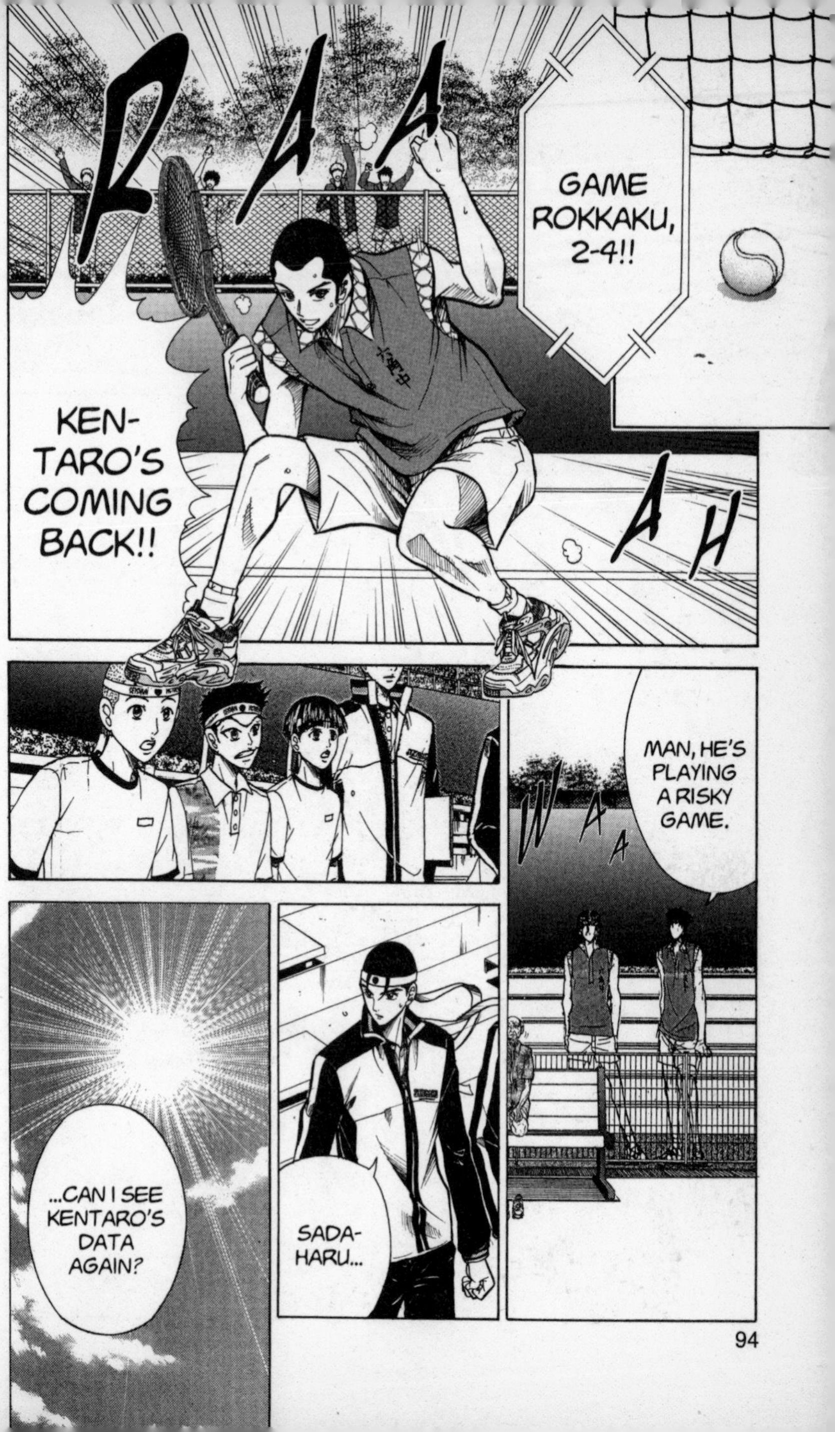

GAME ROKKAKU, 2-4!!
RAA
KEN-TARO'S COMING BACK!!
AH
MAN, HE'S PLAYING A RISKY GAME.
WAA
SADA-HARU...
...CAN I SEE KENTARO'S DATA AGAIN?

READ THIS WAY

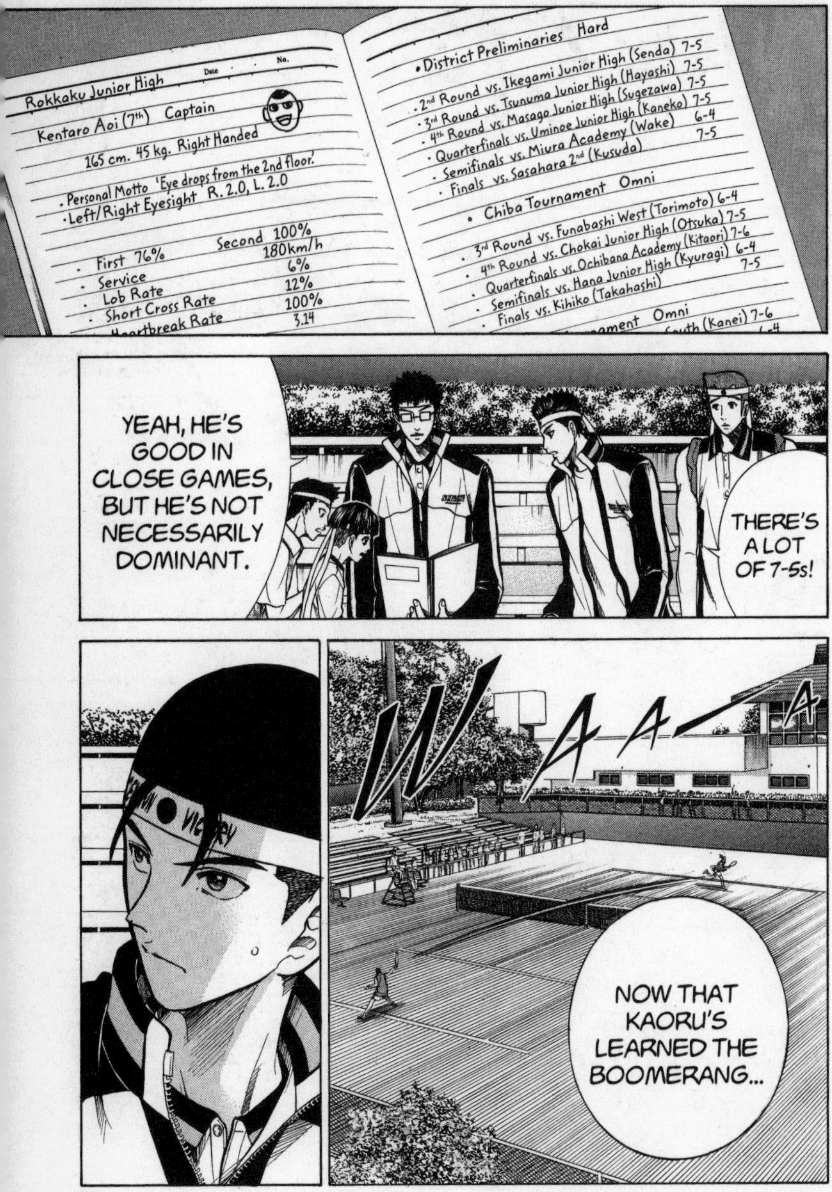
Rokkaku Junior High
Date No.
Kentaro Aoi (7th) Captain
165 cm. 45 kg. Right Handed
· Personal Motto 'Eye drops from the 2nd floor.'
· Left/Right Eyesight R. 2.0, L. 2.0
· First 76% Second 100%
· Service 180km/h
· Lob Rate 6%
· Short Cross Rate 12%
· Heartbreak Rate 100%
3.14
· District Preliminaries Hard
· 2nd Round vs. Ikegami Junior High (Senda) 7-5
· 3rd Round vs. Tsunuma Junior High (Hayashi) 7-5
· 4th Round vs. Masago Junior High (Sugezawa) 7-5
· Quarterfinals vs. Uminoe Junior High (Kaneko) 7-5
· Semifinals vs. Miura Academy (Wake) 6-4
· Finals vs. Sasahara 2nd (Kusuda) 7-5
· Chiba Tournament Omni
· 3rd Round vs. Funabashi West (Torimoto) 6-4
· 4th Round vs. Chokai Junior High (Otsuka) 7-5
· Quarterfinals vs. Ochibana Academy (Kitaori) 7-6
· Semifinals vs. Hana Junior High (Kyuragi) 6-4
· Finals vs. Kihiko (Takahashi) 7-5
THERE'S A LOT OF 7-5s!
YEAH, HE'S GOOD IN CLOSE GAMES, BUT HE'S NOT NECESSARILY DOMINANT.
WAA—A
NOW THAT KAORU'S LEARNED THE BOOMERANG...

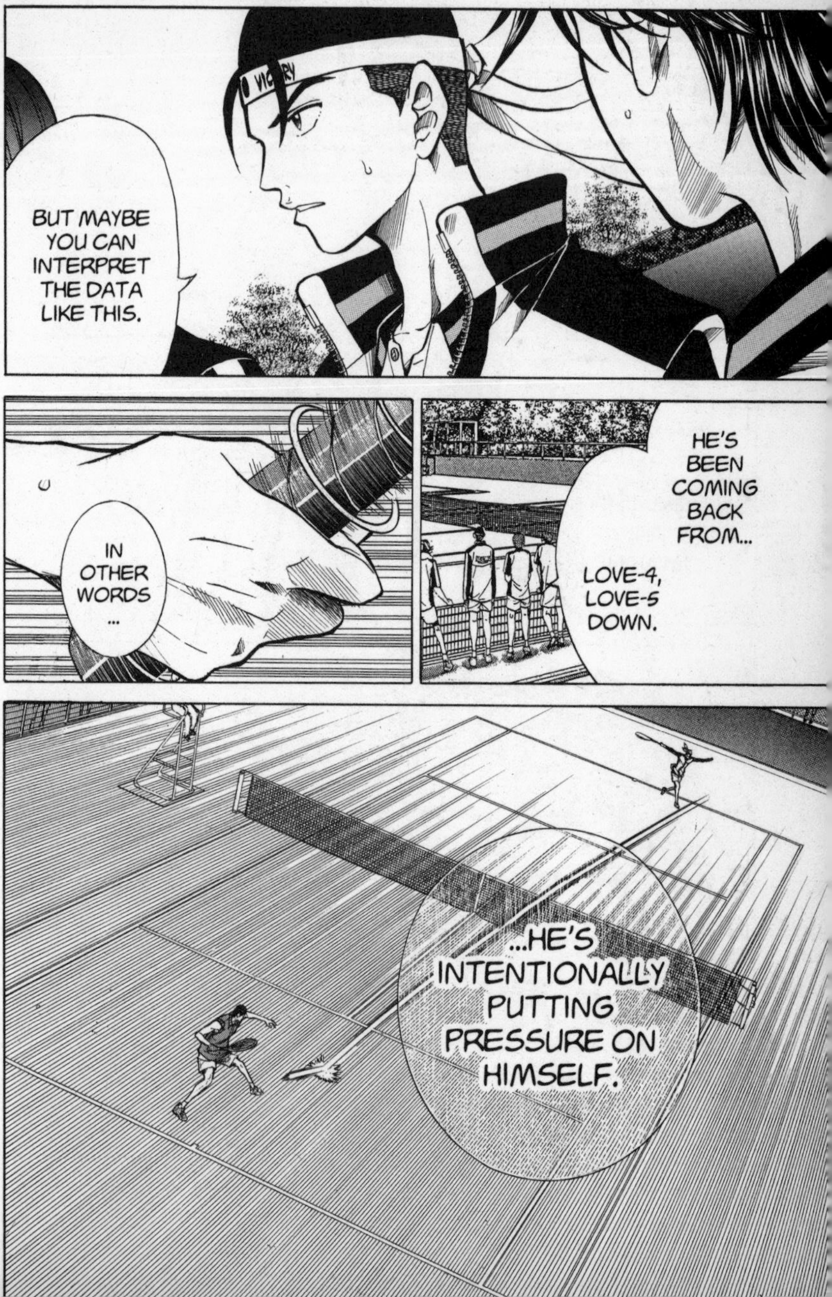
BUT MAYBE YOU CAN INTERPRET THE DATA LIKE THIS.
HE'S BEEN COMING BACK FROM...
LOVE-4, LOVE-5 DOWN.
IN OTHER WORDS ...
...HE'S INTENTIONALLY PUTTING PRESSURE ON HIMSELF.

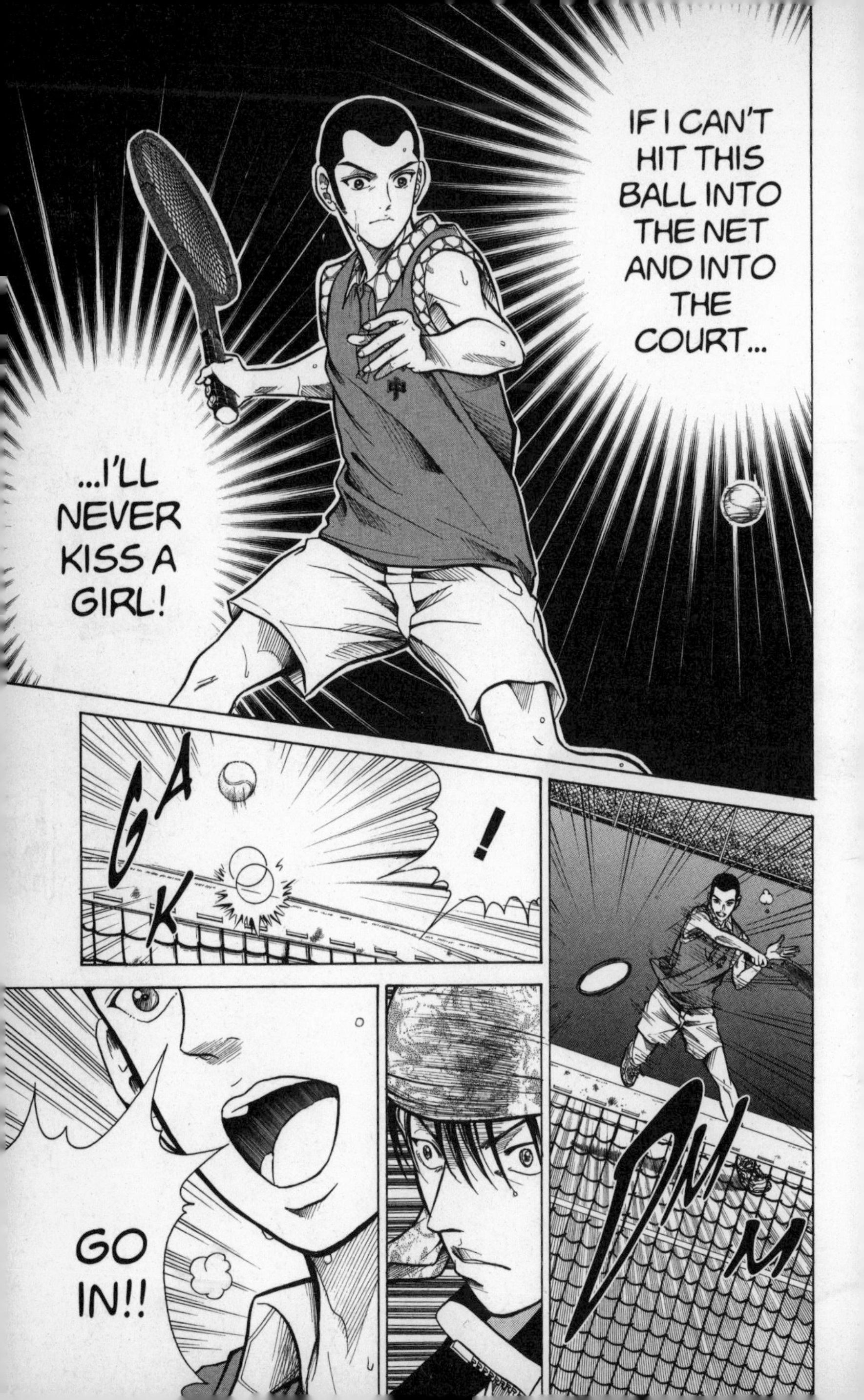
IF I CAN'T HIT THIS BALL INTO THE NET AND INTO THE COURT...
...I'LL NEVER KISS A GIRL!
DMM
GAK
!
GO IN!!

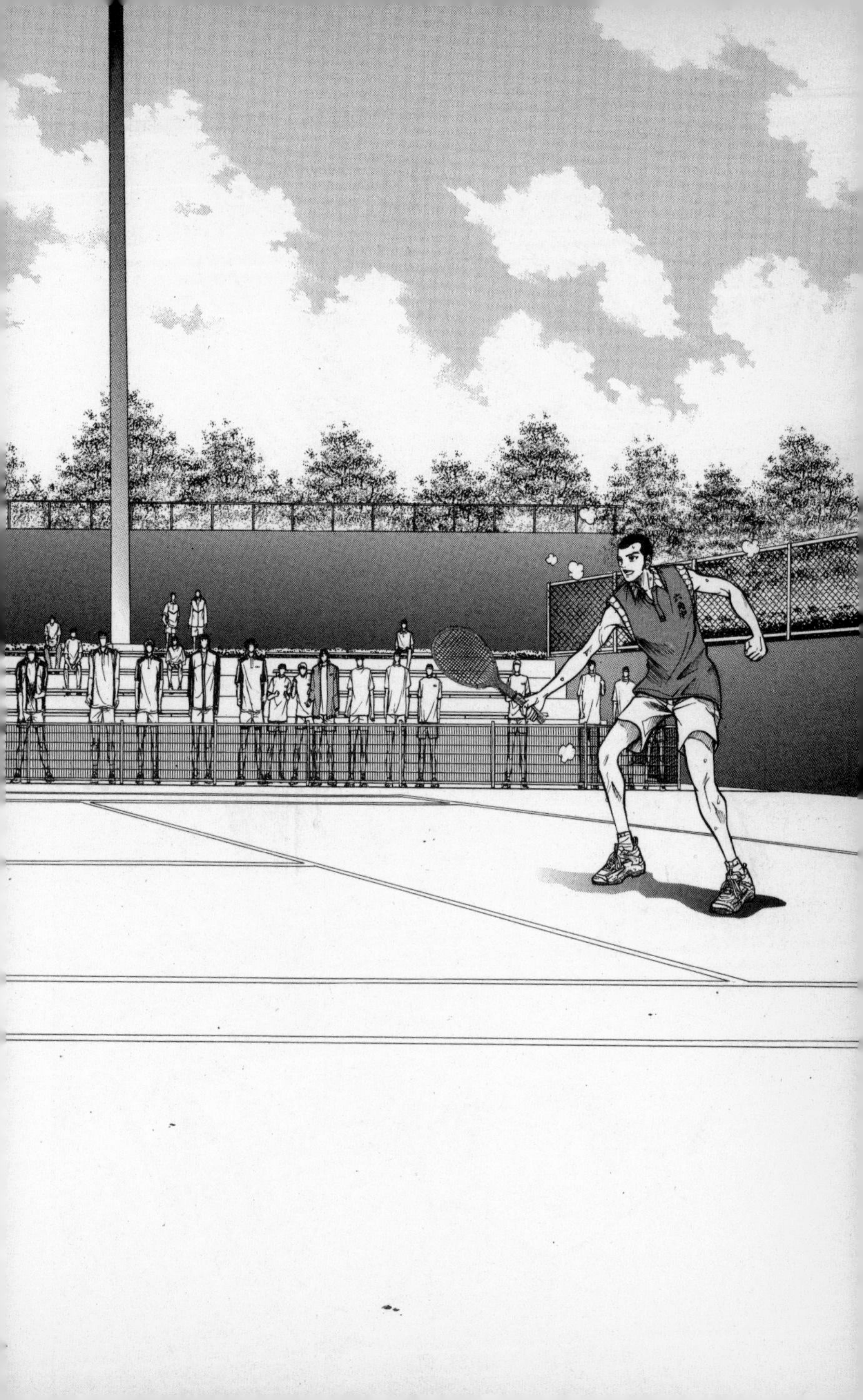

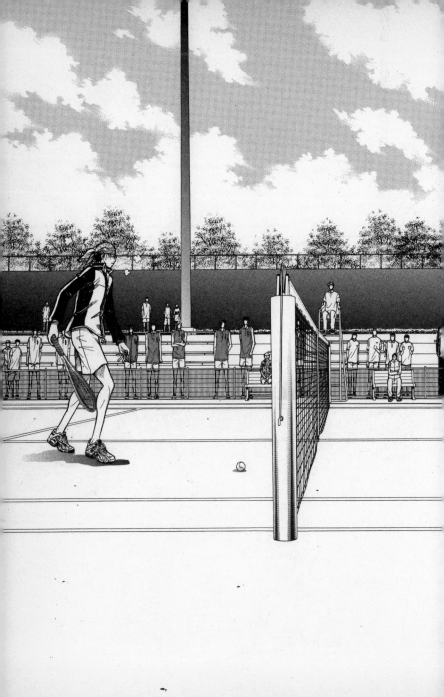

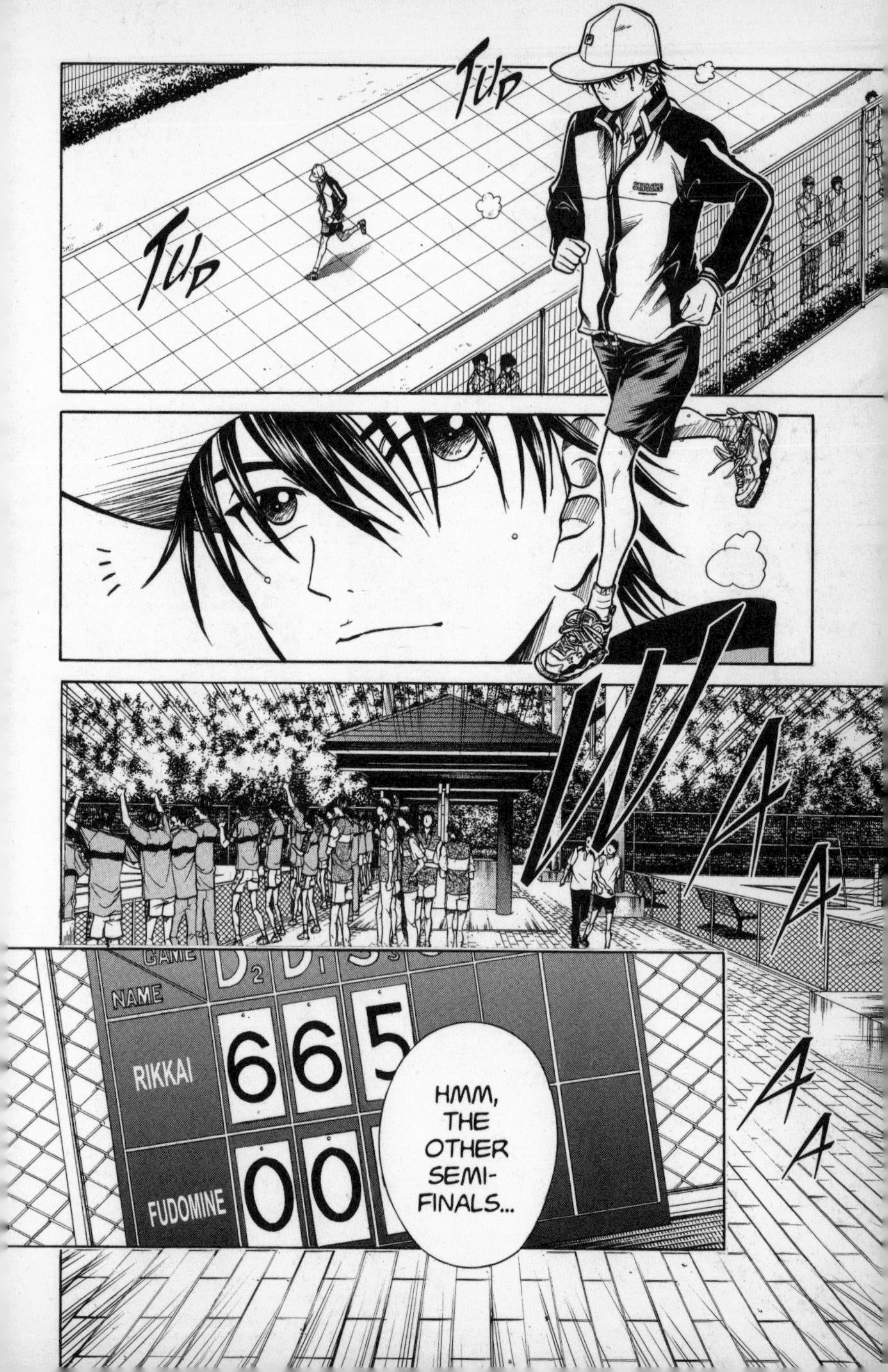
TUP
TUP
WAAAA
GAME
D2 D1 S3
NAME
RIKKAI
6 6 5
FUDOMINE
0 0
HMM, THE OTHER SEMI-FINALS...

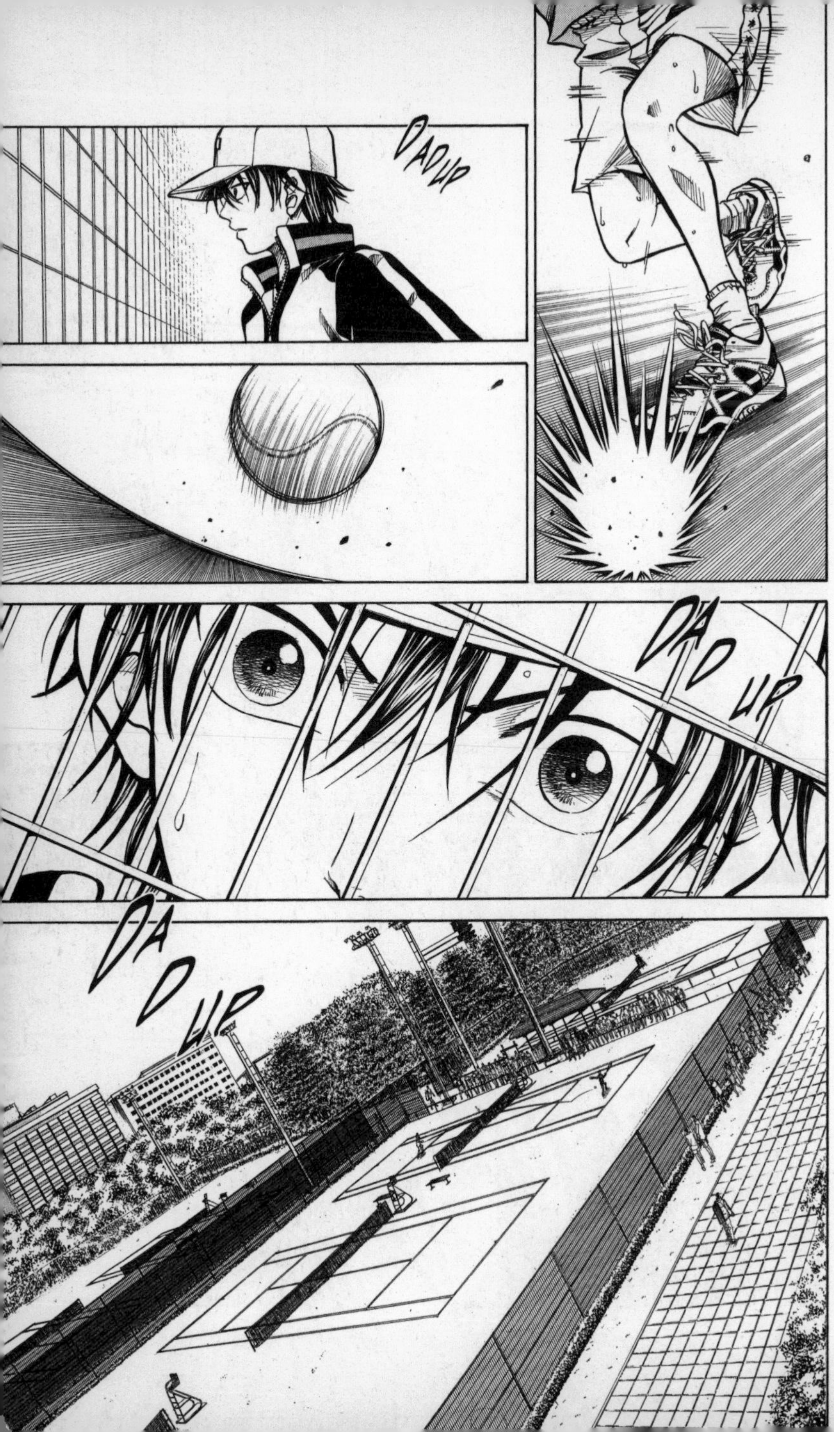
DADUP
DADUP
DADUP

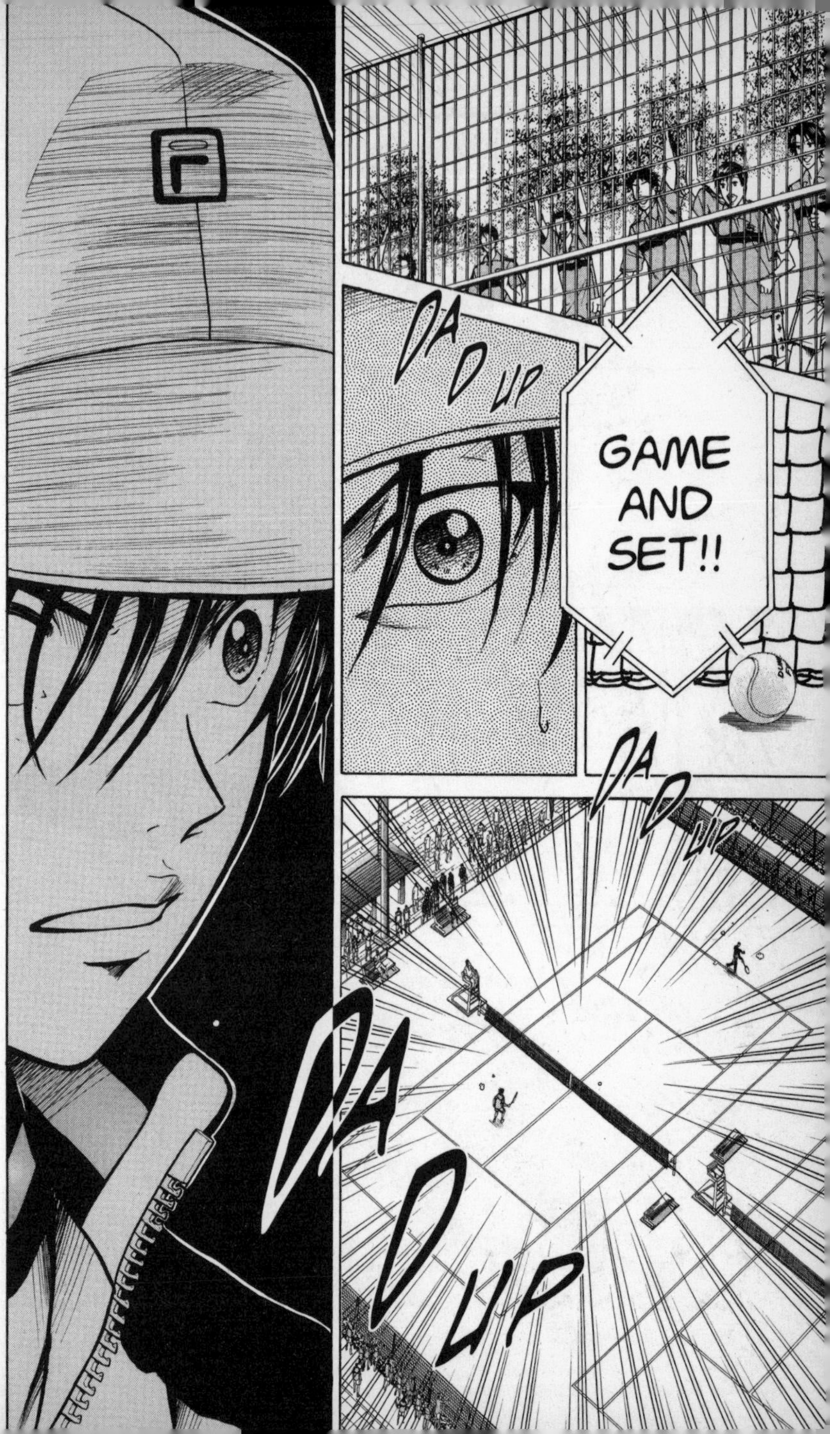
DA D UP
GAME AND SET!!
DA D UP
DA D UP

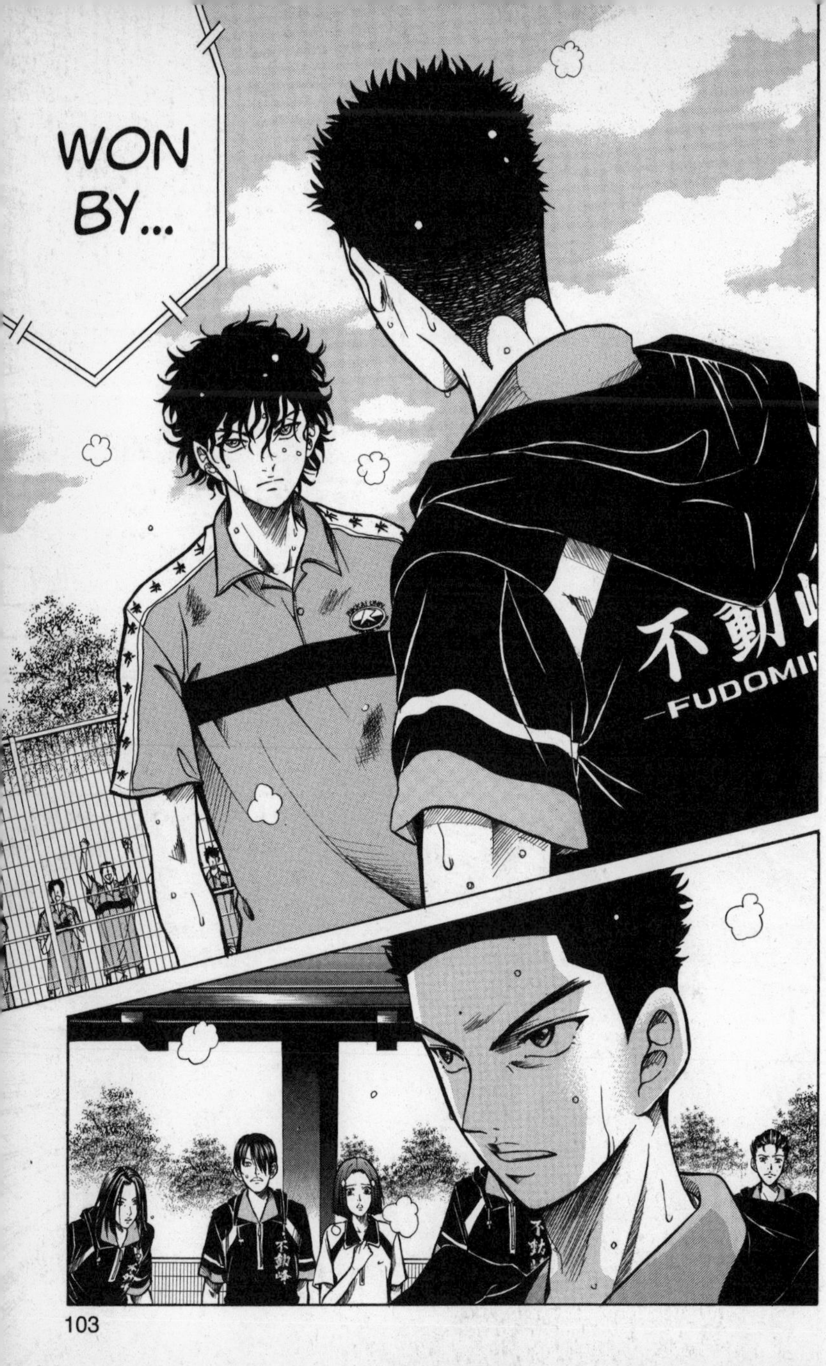
WON BY...
不動峰
FUDOMIN

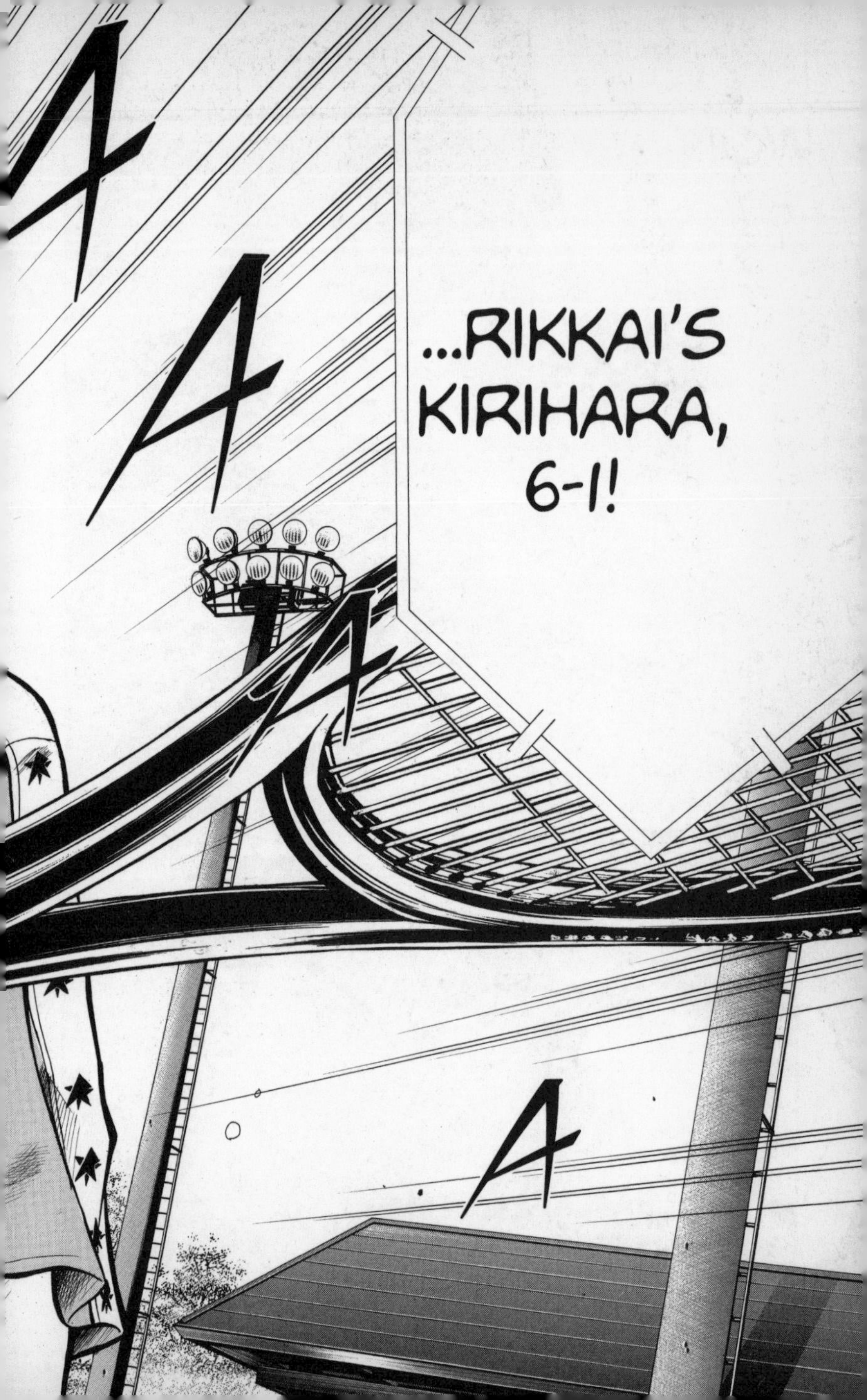
...RIKKAI'S KIRIHARA, 6-1!

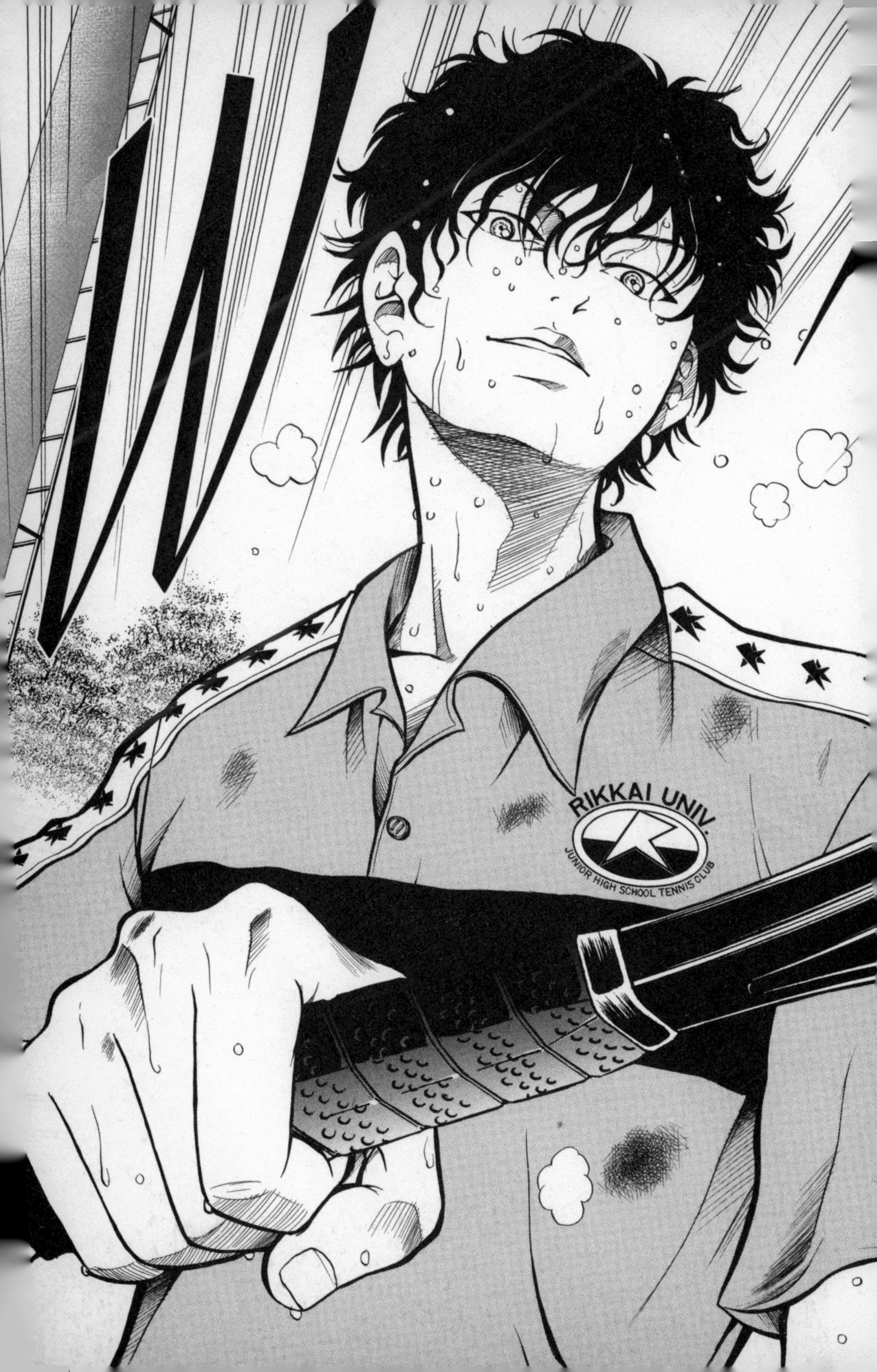
RIKKAI UNIV.
JUNIOR HIGH SCHOOL TENNIS CLUB

テニスの王子様

THE PRINCE OF TENNIS™

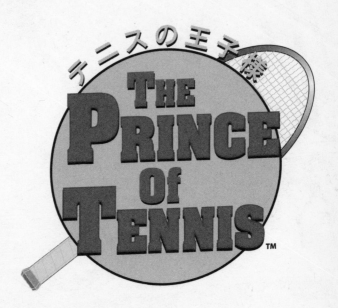

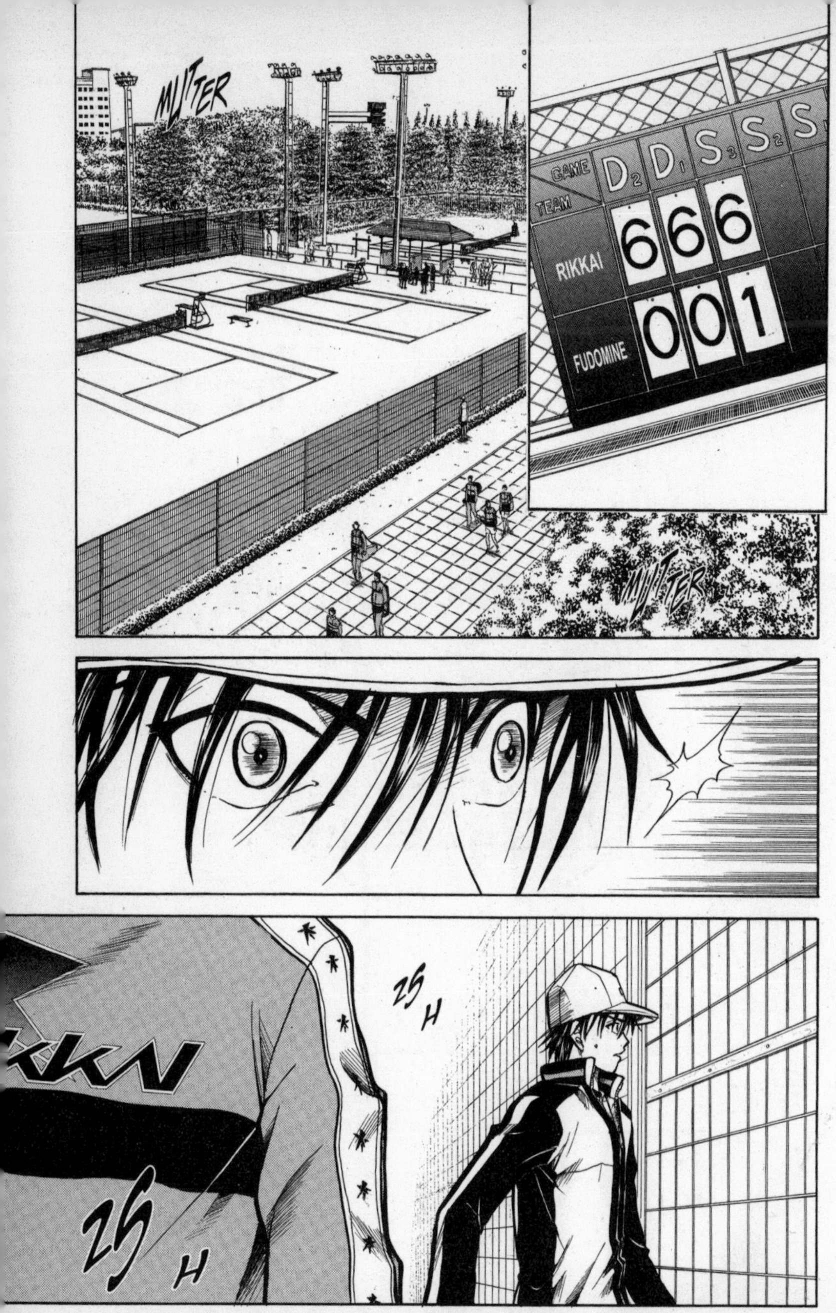
MUTTER
GAME
D2
D1
S3
S2
TEAM
RIKKAI
666
FUDOMINE
001
MUTTER
ZSH
ZSH

GENIUS 182: FIRST CONTACT

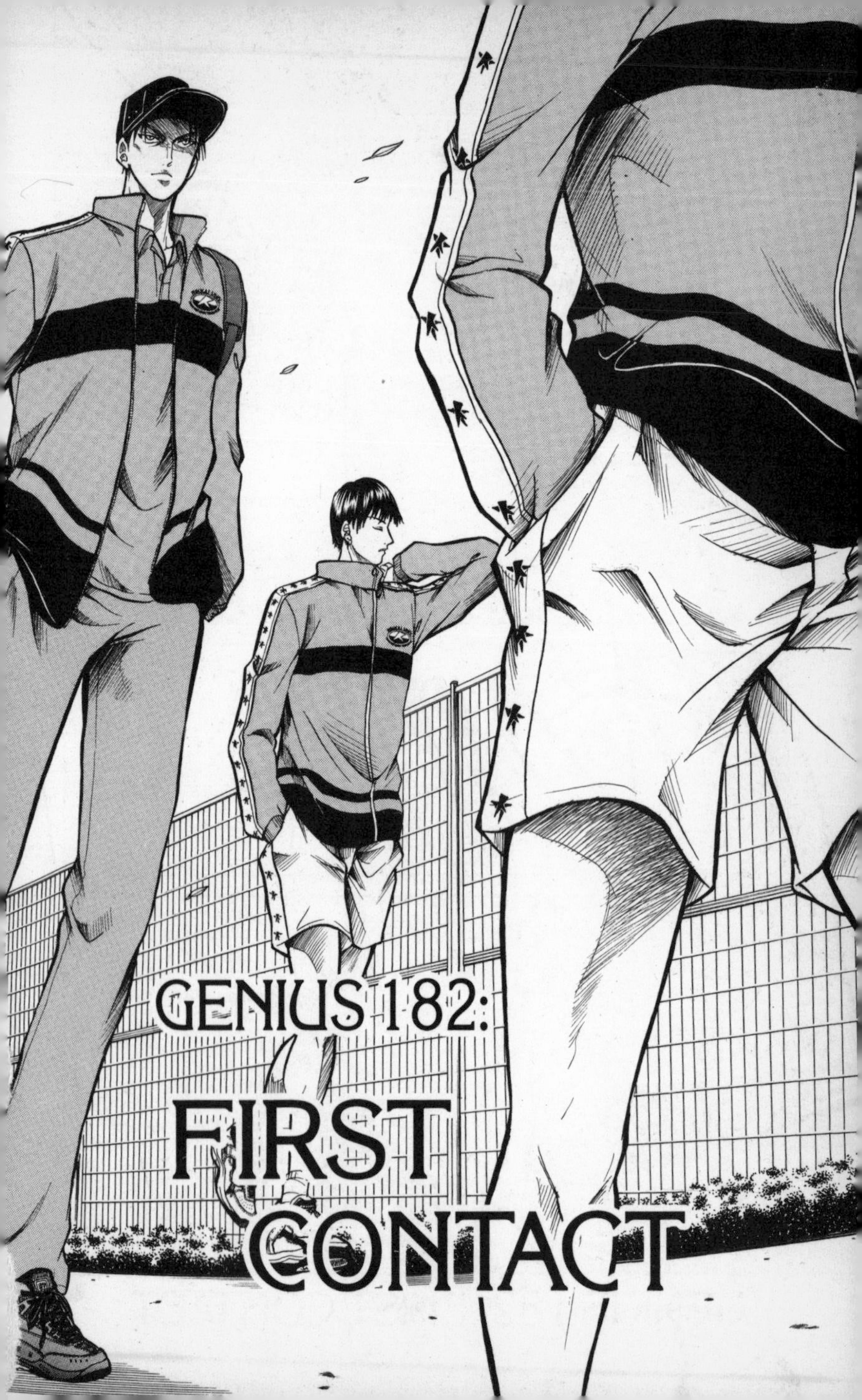
GENIUS 182:
FIRST CONTACT

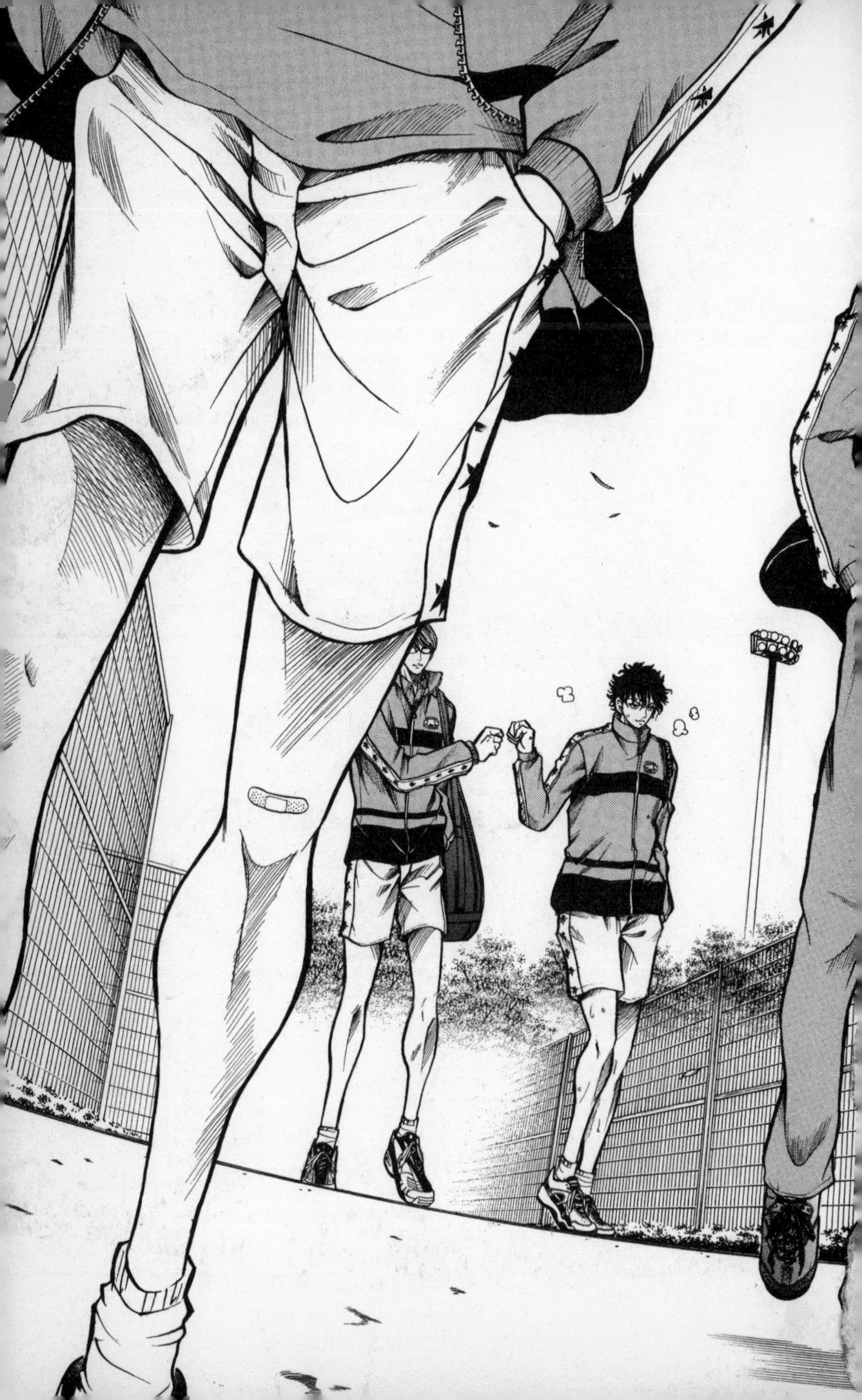

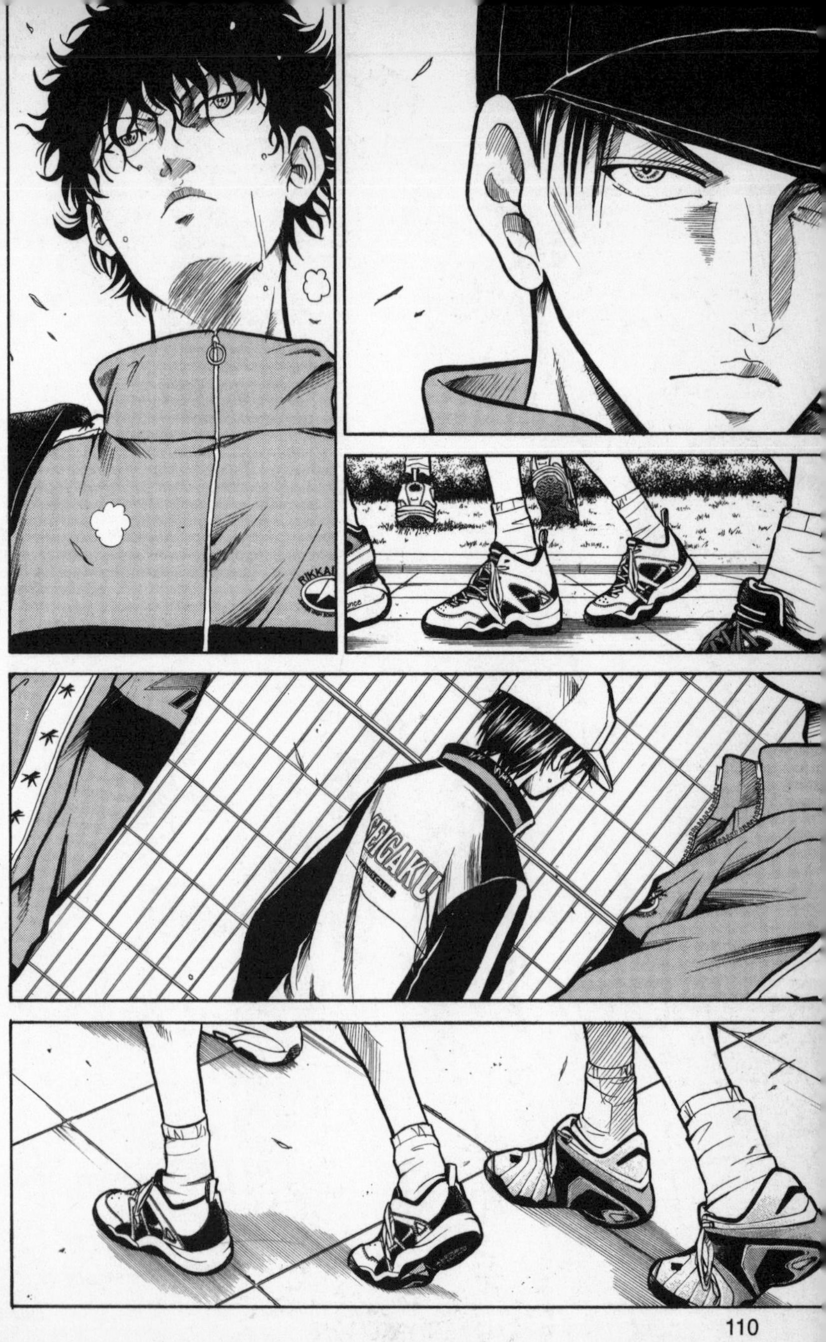

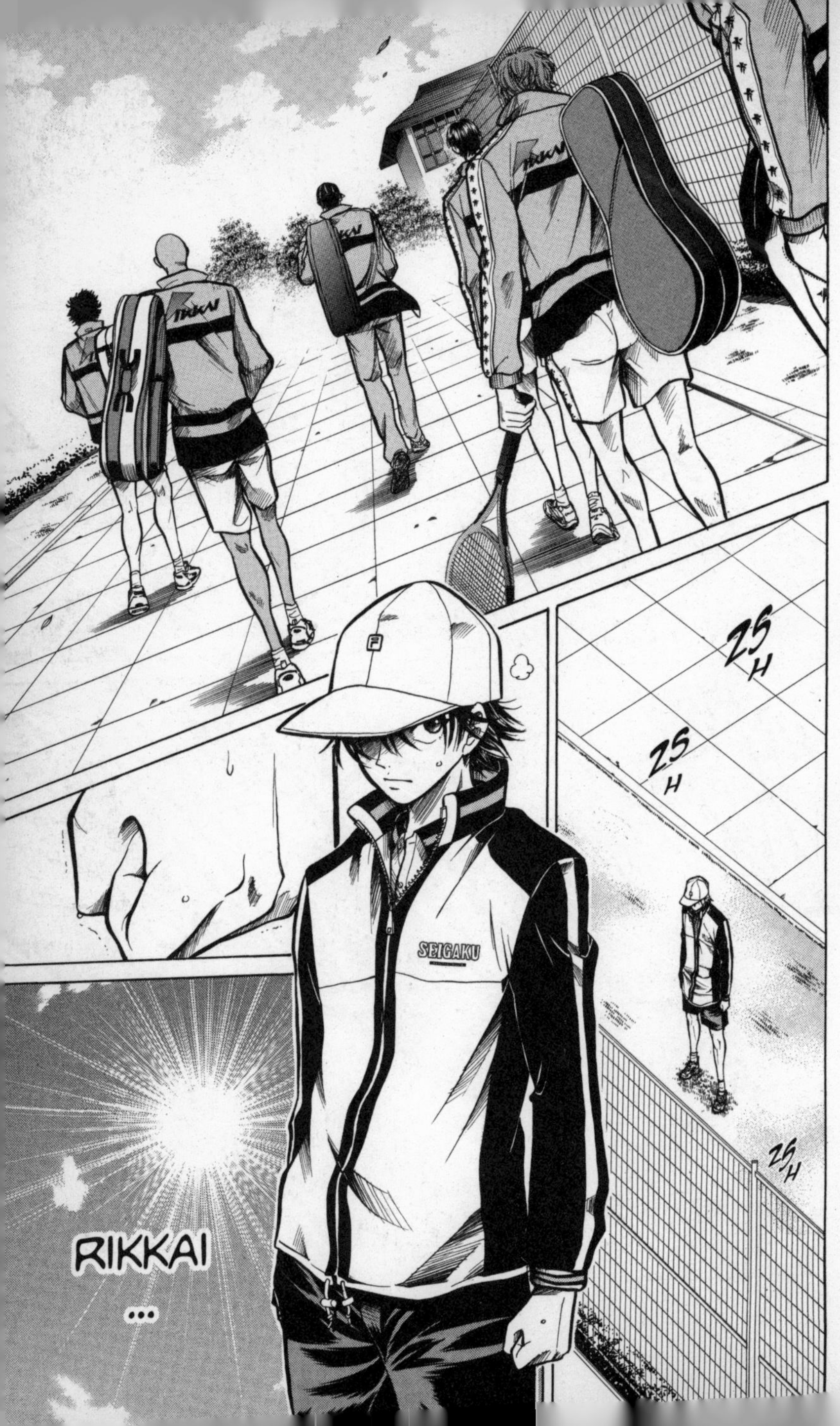

SEIGAKU
ZSH
ZSH
ZSH
RIKKAI
...

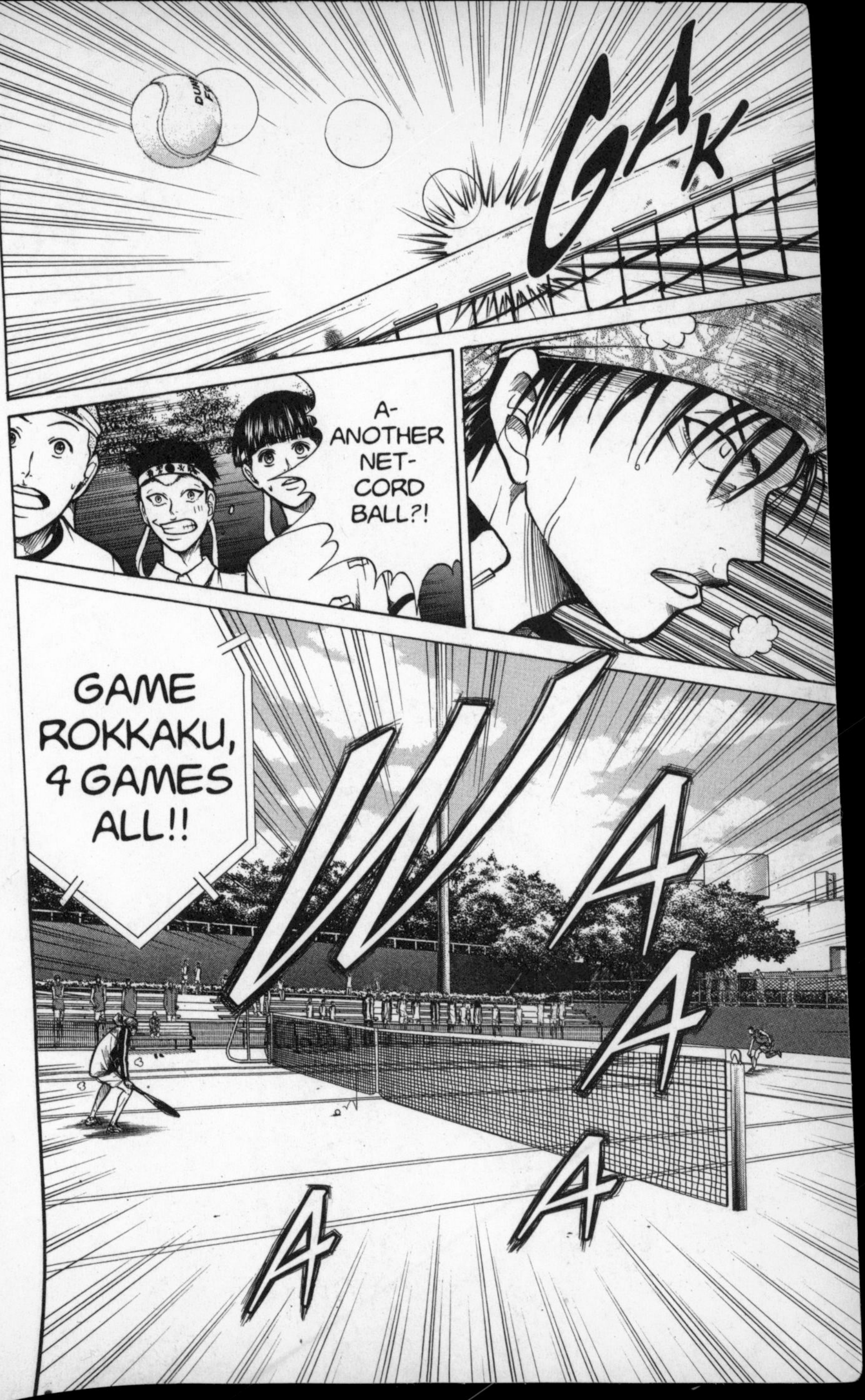
GAK
A- ANOTHER NET-CORD BALL?!
GAME ROKKAKU, 4 GAMES ALL!!
WAAAA

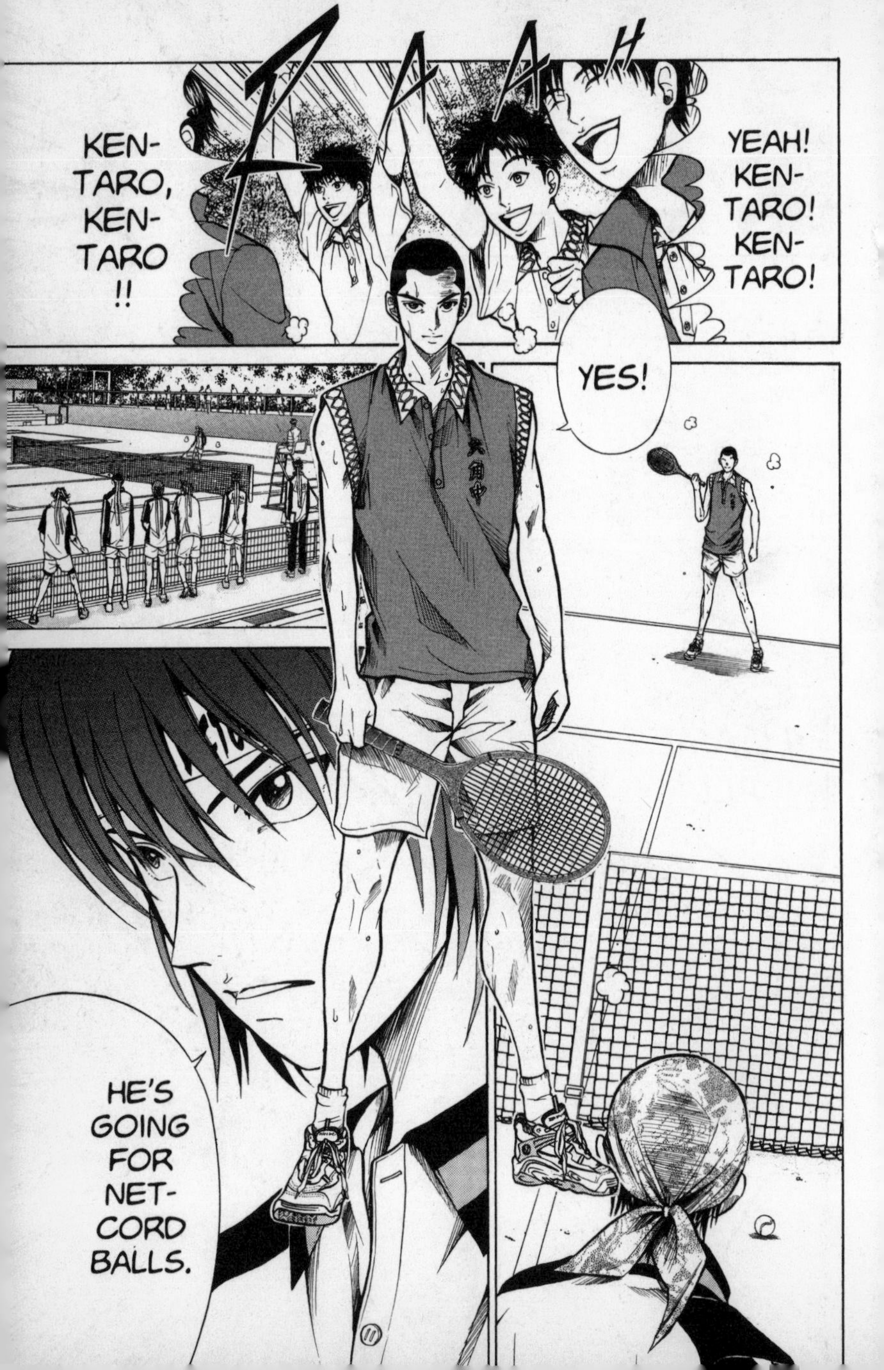
WAAAH
YEAH! KEN-TARO! KEN-TARO!
KEN-TARO, KEN-TARO !!
YES!
HE'S GOING FOR NET-CORD BALLS.

THAT 7TH GRADER'S SHOWING SOME SERIOUS CONCENTRATION.

PURPOSELY LOSING FOUR GAMES TO PUMP HIMSELF UP.

HE'S SO GOOD UNDER PRESSURE...

WHAT?

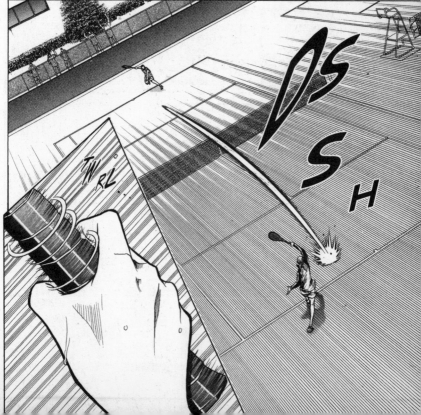

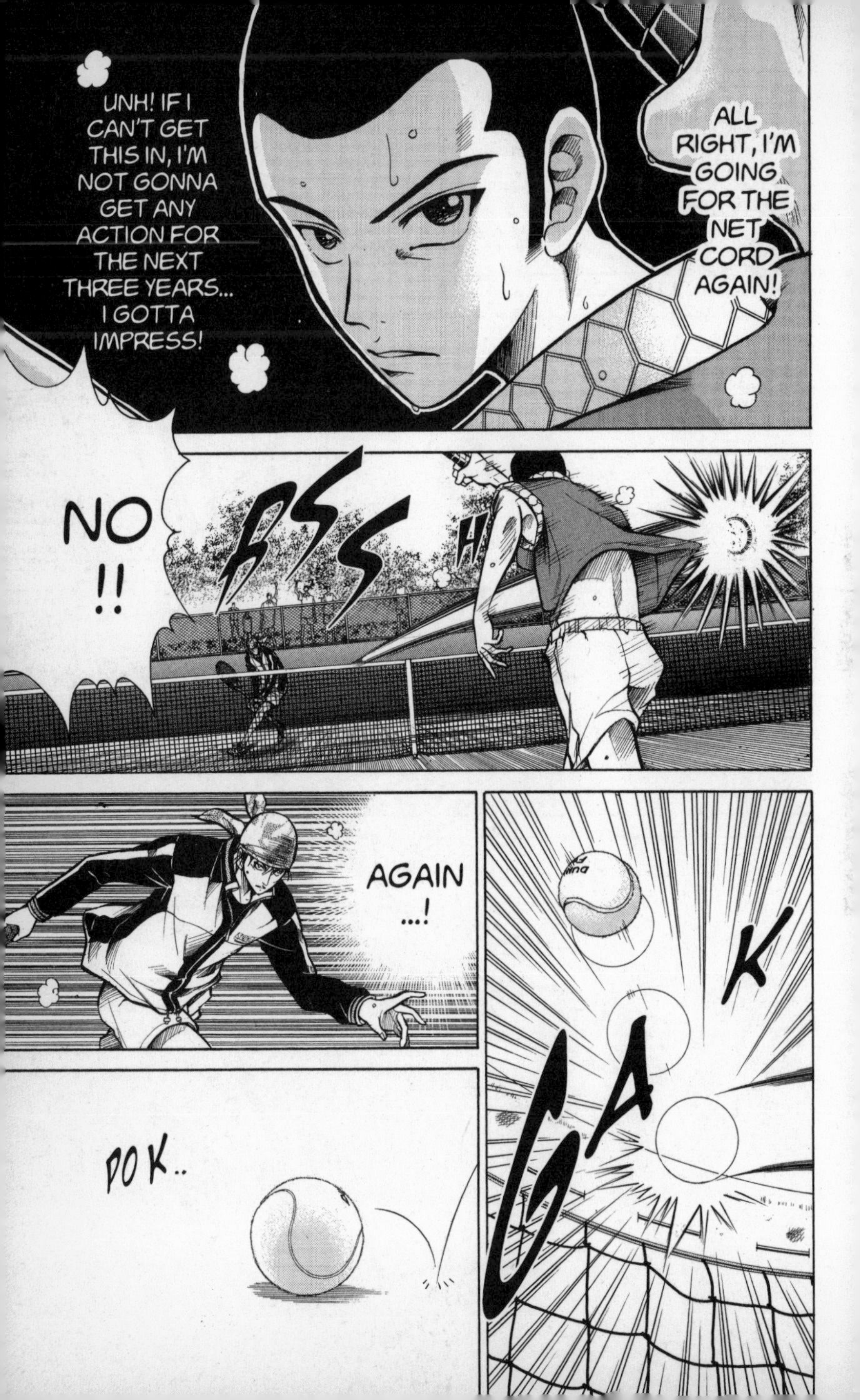
ALL RIGHT, I'M GOING FOR THE NET CORD AGAIN!
UNH! IF I CAN'T GET THIS IN, I'M NOT GONNA GET ANY ACTION FOR THE NEXT THREE YEARS... I GOTTA IMPRESS!
NO !!
GAK
AGAIN ...!
POK..

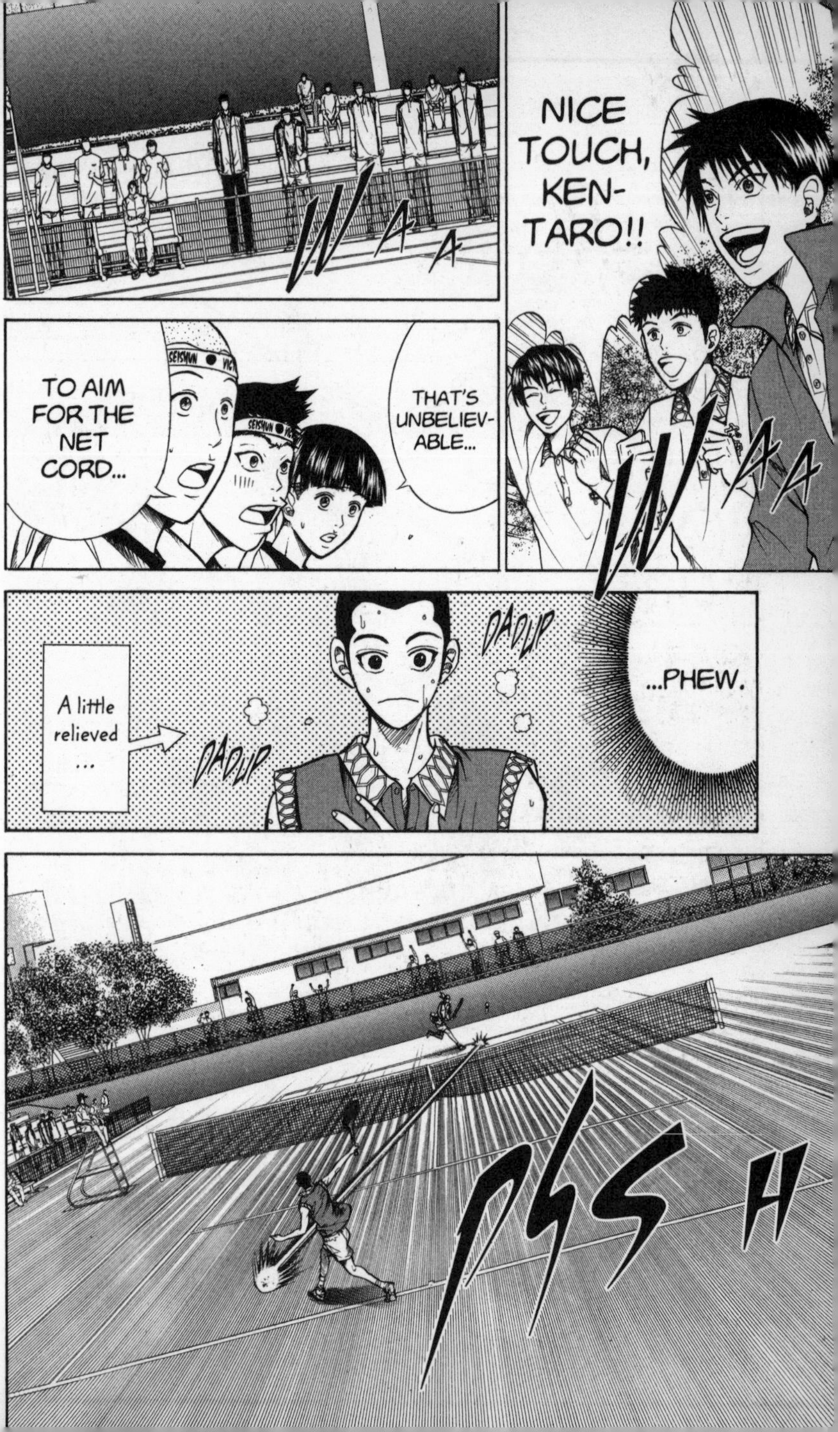
NICE TOUCH, KEN-TARO!!
WAA
WAA
THAT'S UNBELIEV-ABLE...
TO AIM FOR THE NET CORD...
...PHEW.
DADUP
A little relieved ...
DADUP
PSSH

READ THIS WAY

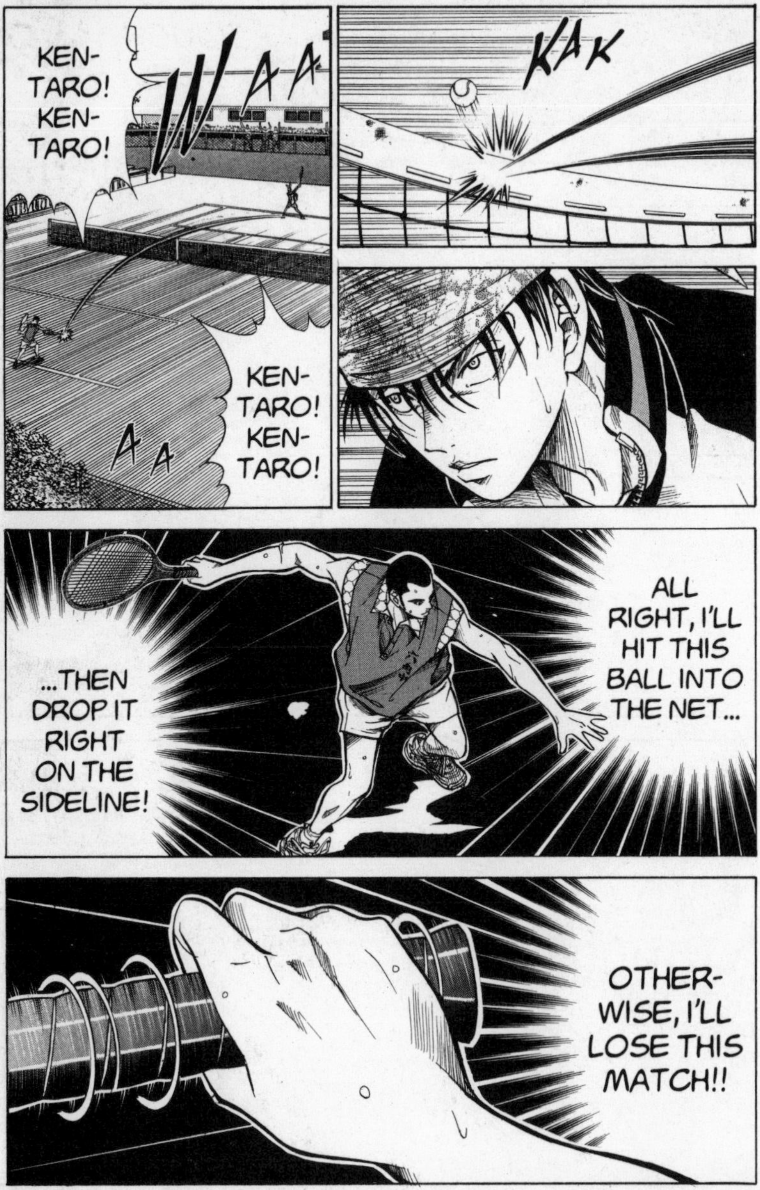

KAK
WAA
KEN-TARO! KEN-TARO!
KEN-TARO! KEN-TARO!
AA
ALL RIGHT, I'LL HIT THIS BALL INTO THE NET...
...THEN DROP IT RIGHT ON THE SIDELINE!
OTHER-WISE, I'LL LOSE THIS MATCH!!

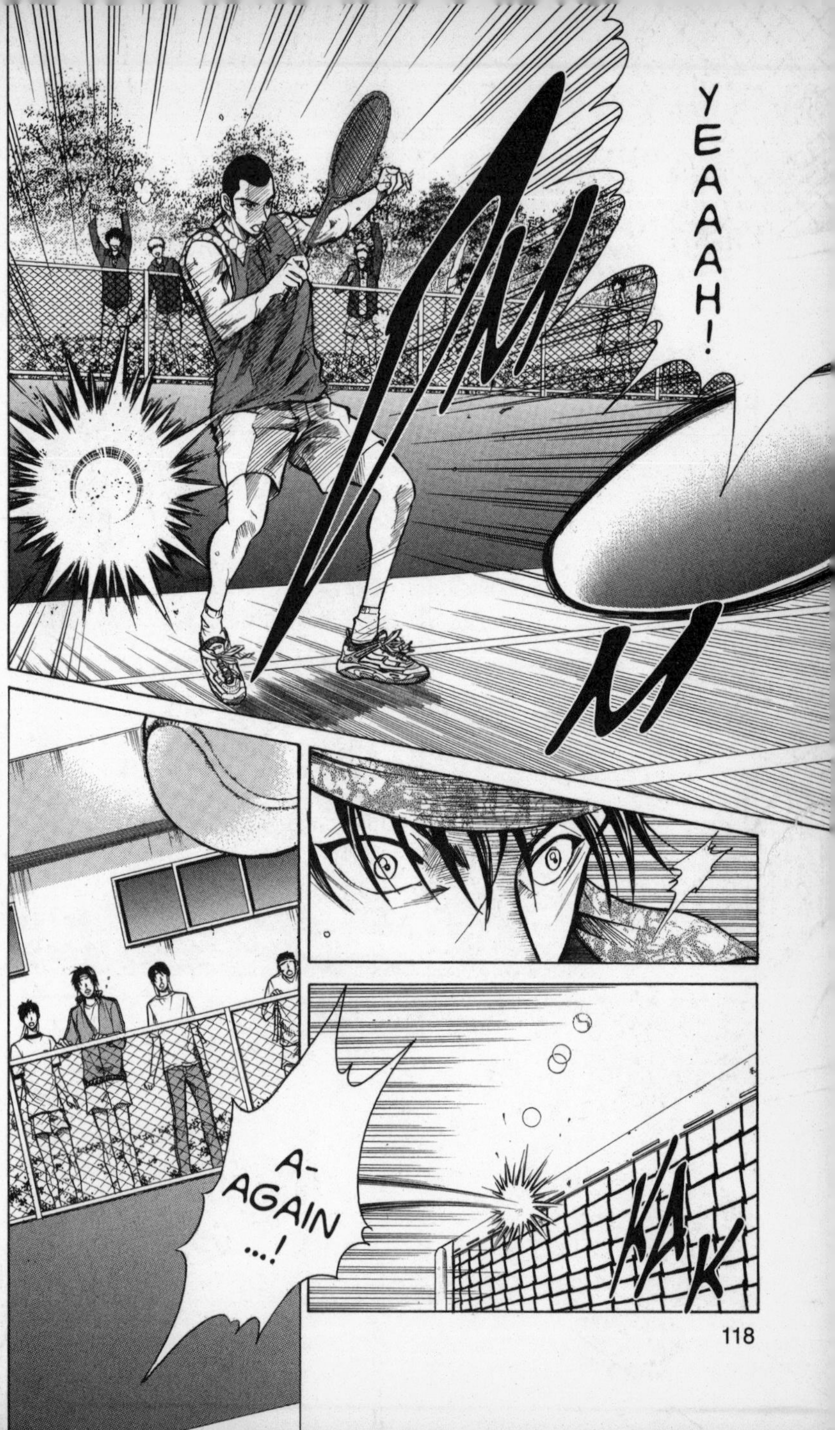
YEAAAAH!
VM
M
A-AGAIN...!
KAK

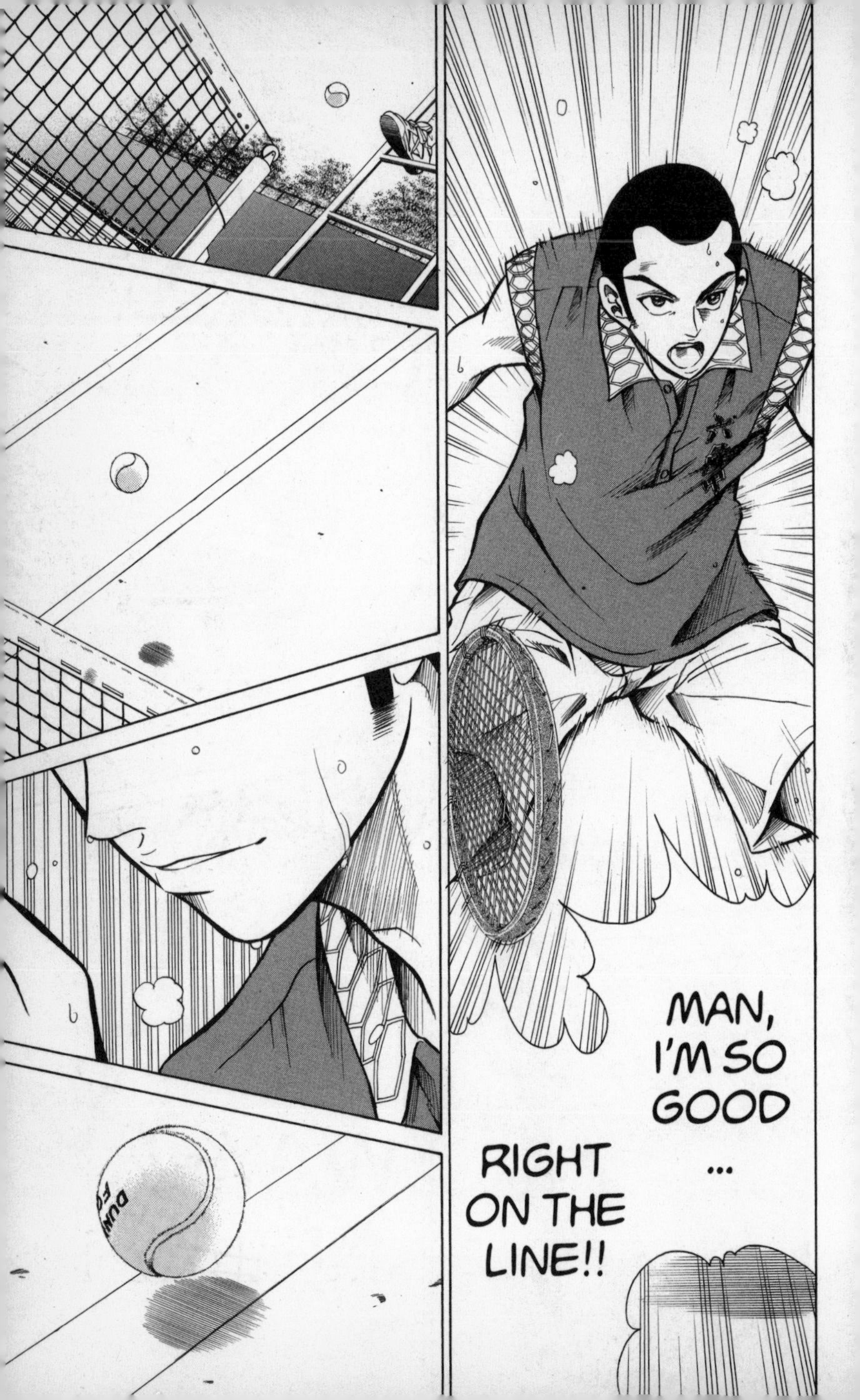
MAN, I'M SO GOOD ...
RIGHT ON THE LINE!!

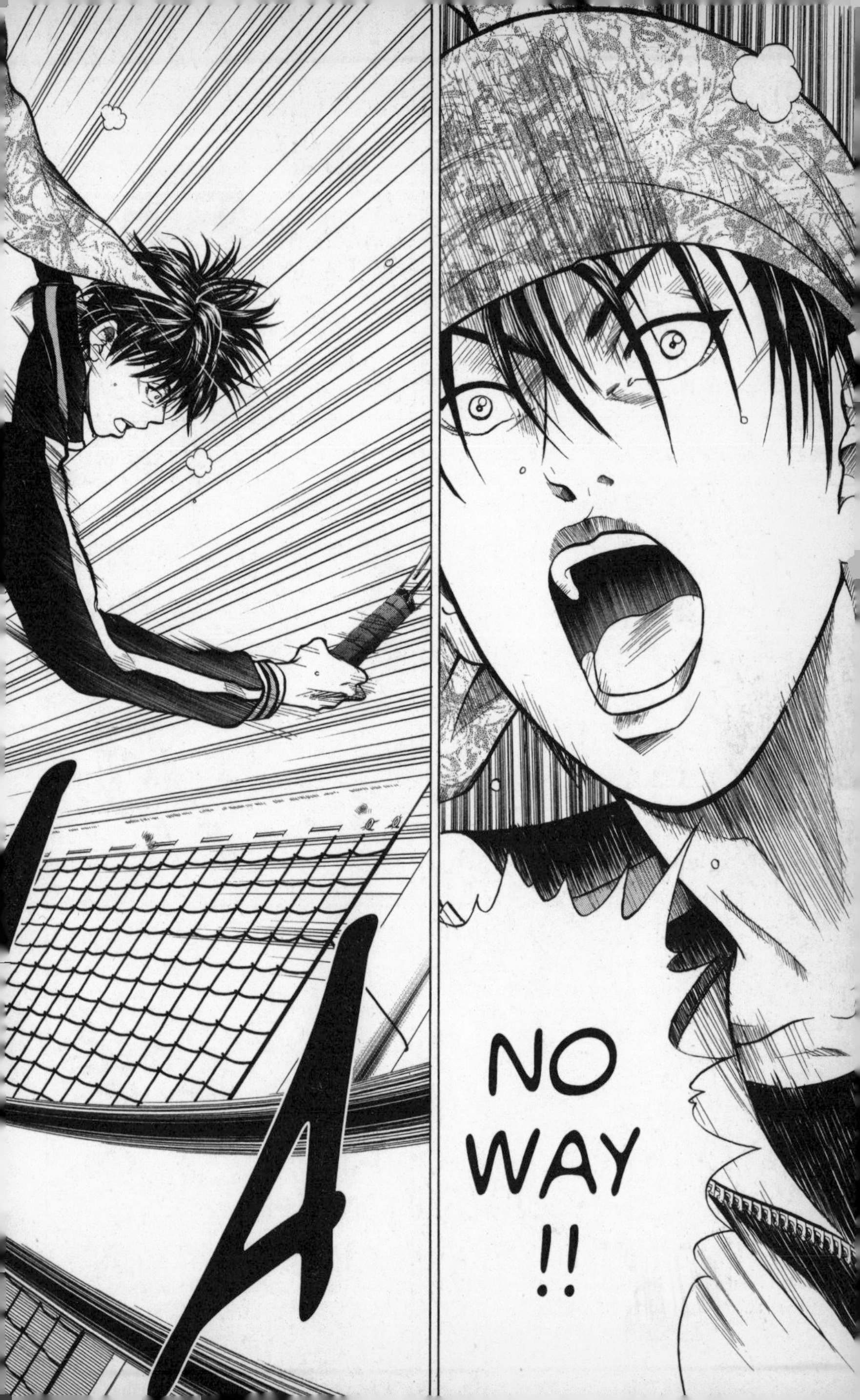
NO WAY !!

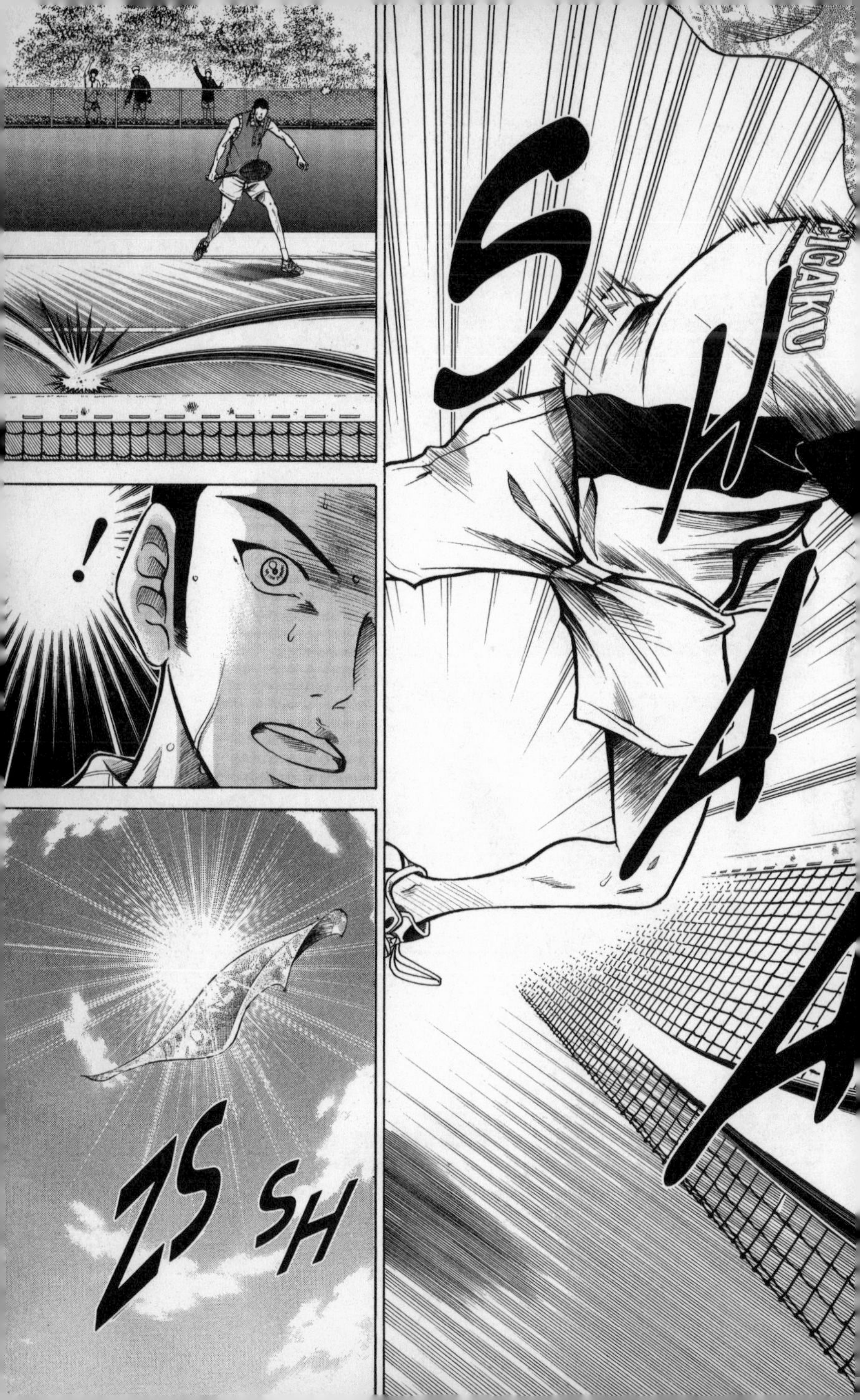
SHAA
!
ZS SH

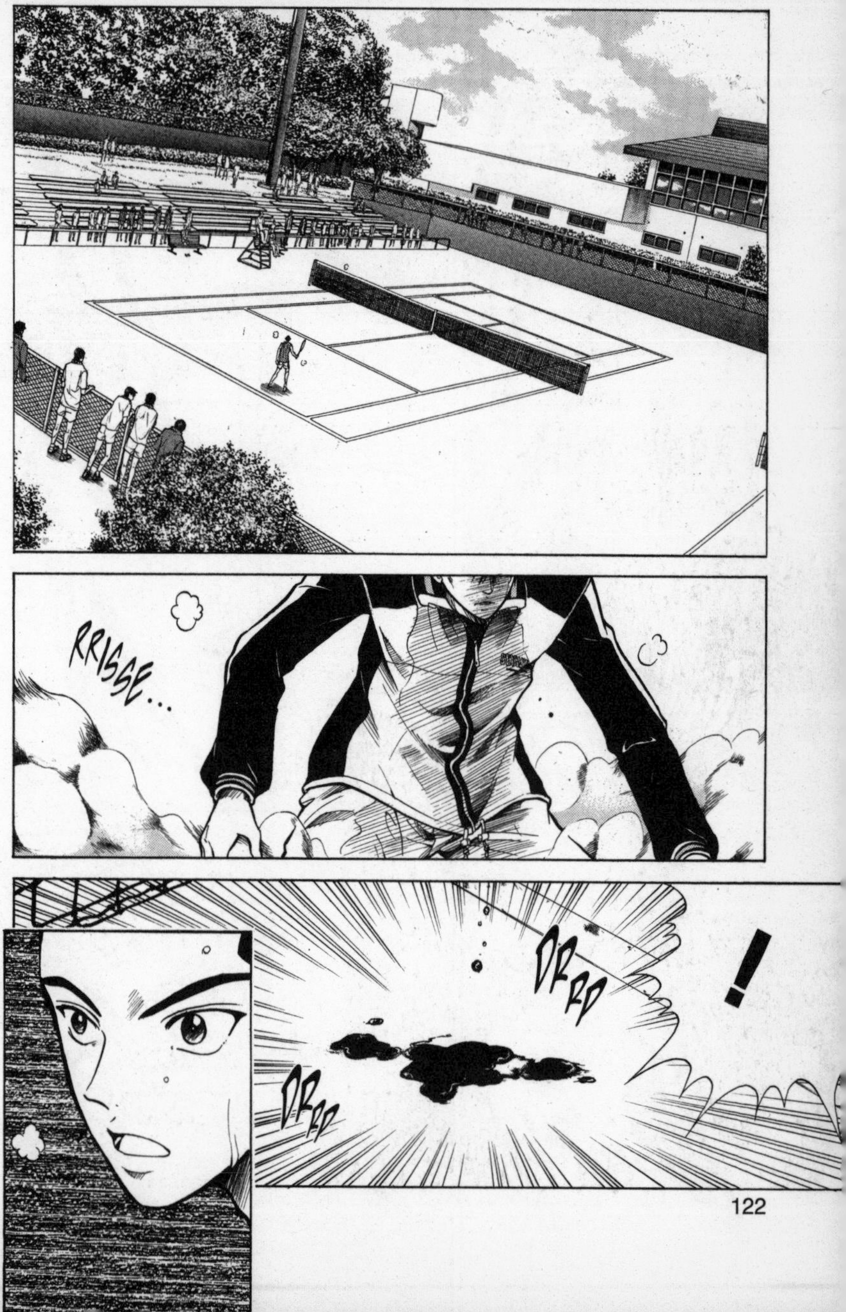
RRISSE...
DRRD
!
DRRD

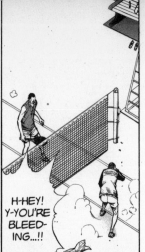

READ THIS WAY

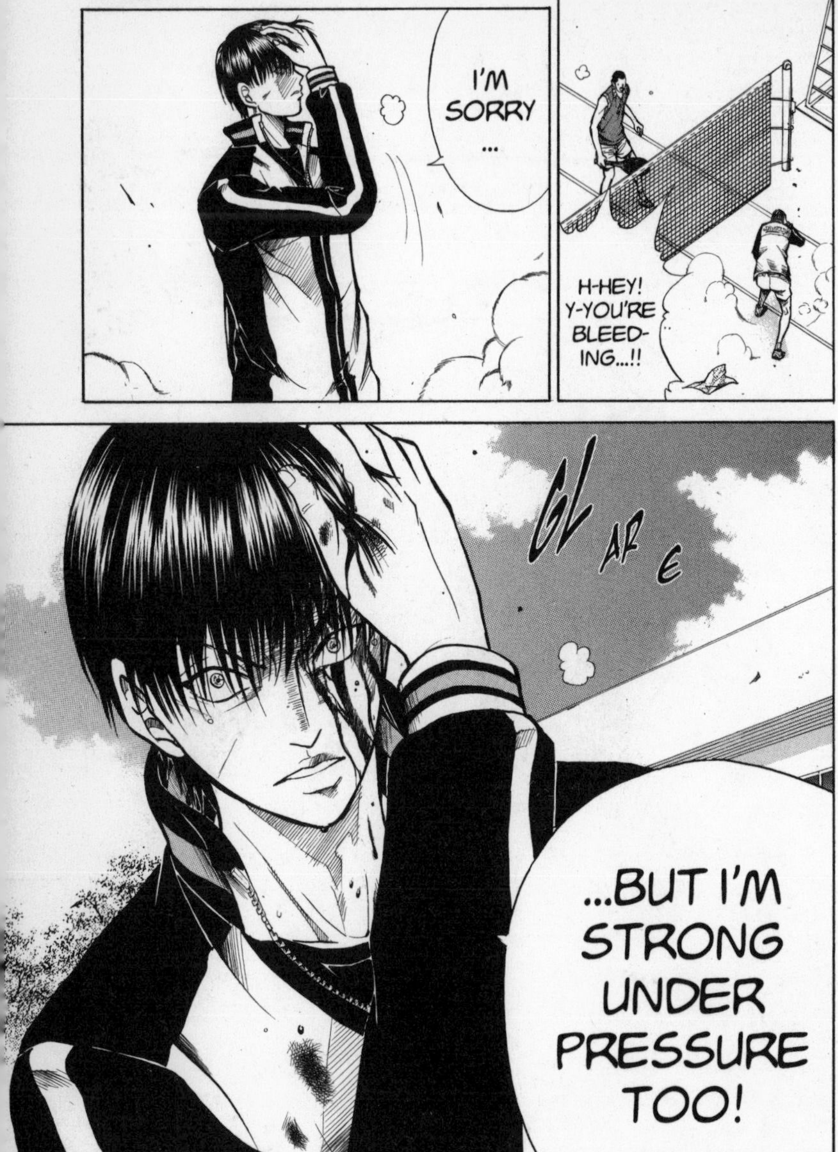
H-HEY! Y-YOU'RE BLEEDING...!!
I'M SORRY ...
GLARE
...BUT I'M STRONG UNDER PRESSURE TOO!

テニスの王子様

THE PRINCE OF TENNIS™

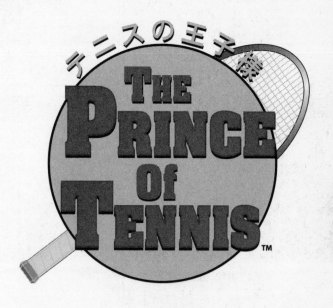

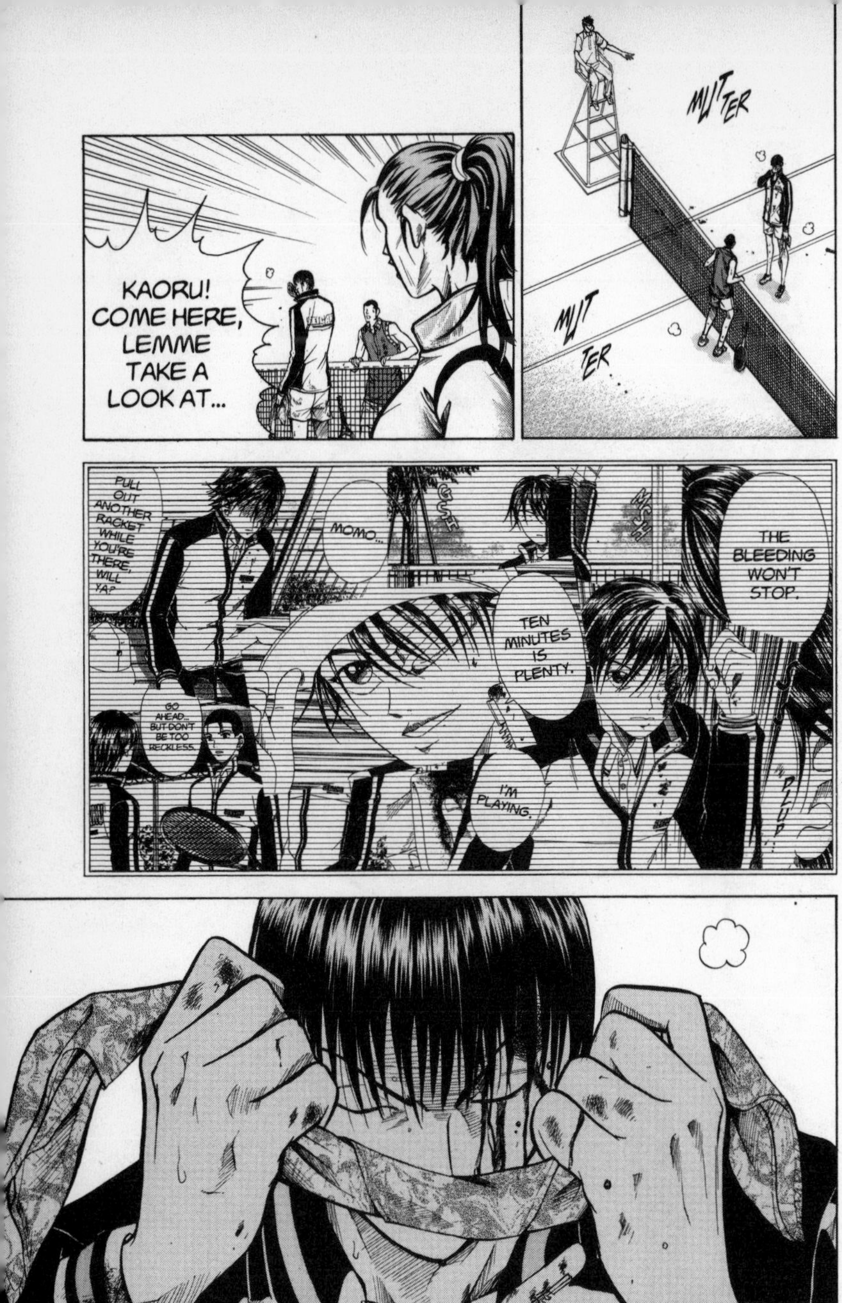
MUTTER
MUTTER
KAORU! COME HERE, LEMME TAKE A LOOK AT...
THE BLEEDING WON'T STOP.
PLUP
TEN MINUTES IS PLENTY.
I'M PLAYING.
MOMO...
PULL OUT ANOTHER RACKET WHILE YOU'RE THERE, WILL YA?
GO AHEAD... BUT DON'T BE TOO RECKLESS.

GENIUS 183: KAORU KAIDO'S GAME

GENIUS 183: KAORU KAIDO'S GAME

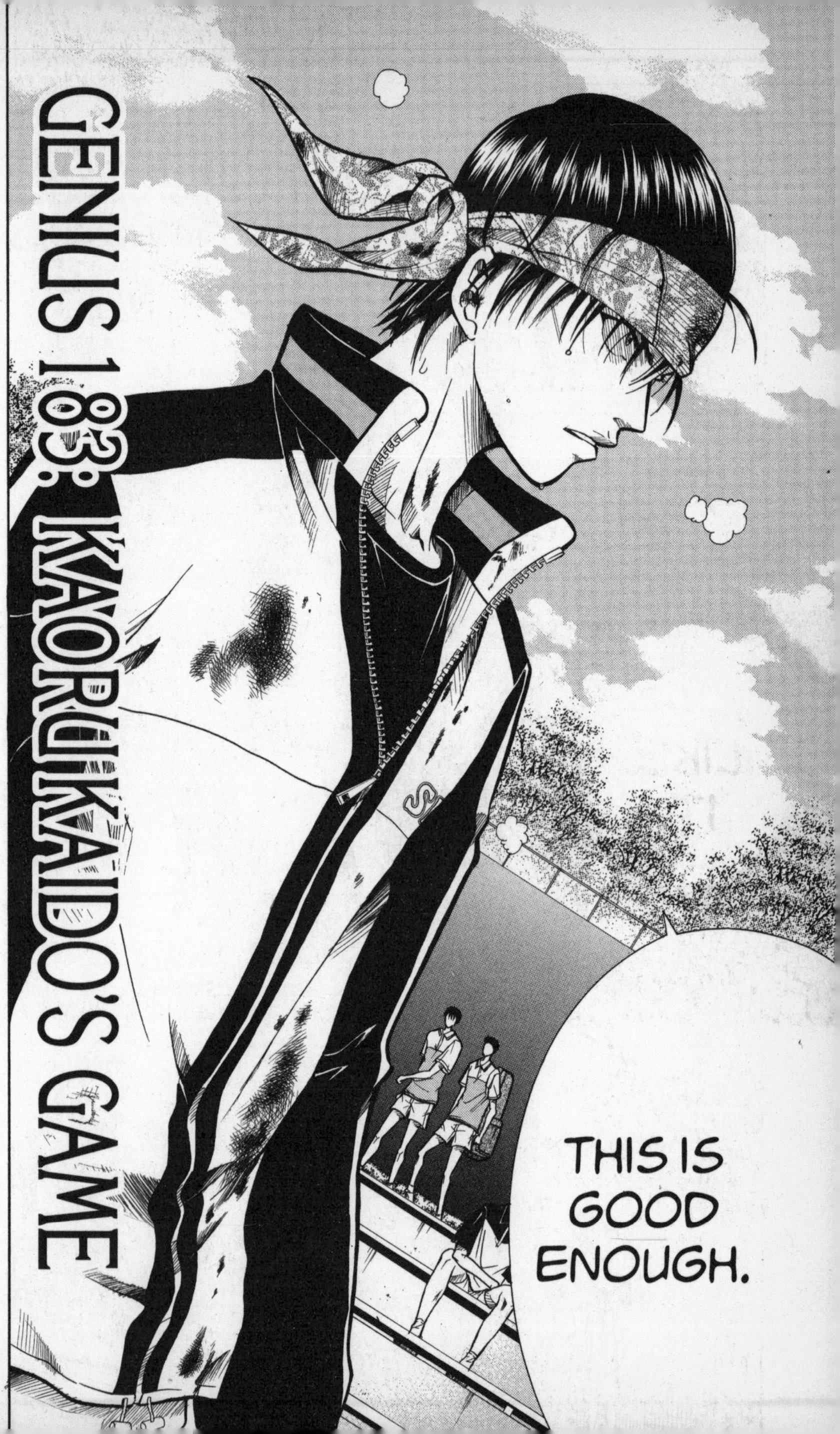
THIS IS GOOD ENOUGH.

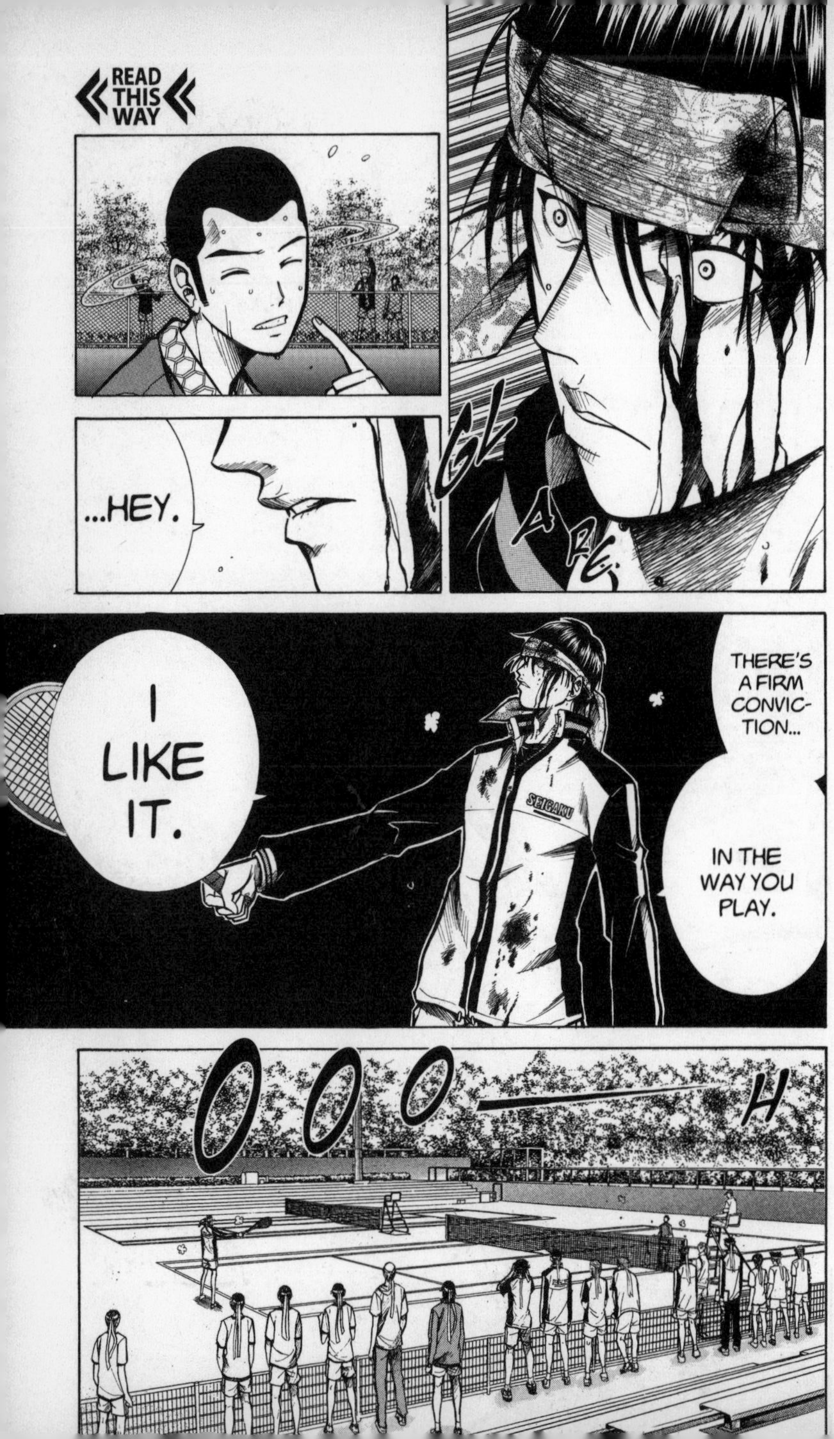
READ THIS WAY
GLARE
...HEY.
THERE'S A FIRM CONVICTION...
IN THE WAY YOU PLAY.
I LIKE IT.
OOOH

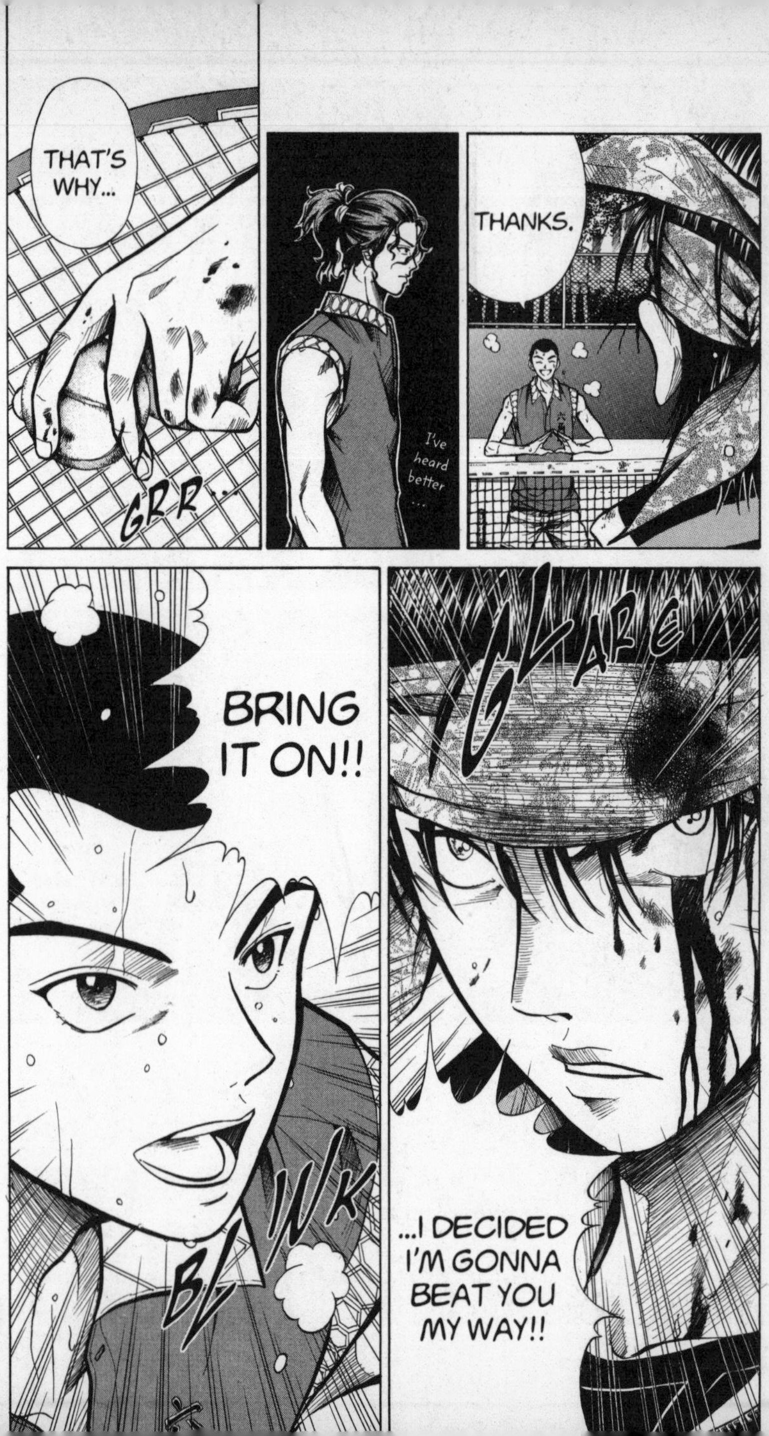
THANKS.
I've heard better...
THAT'S WHY...
GRR...
GLARE
...I DECIDED I'M GONNA BEAT YOU MY WAY!!
BLINK
BRING IT ON!!

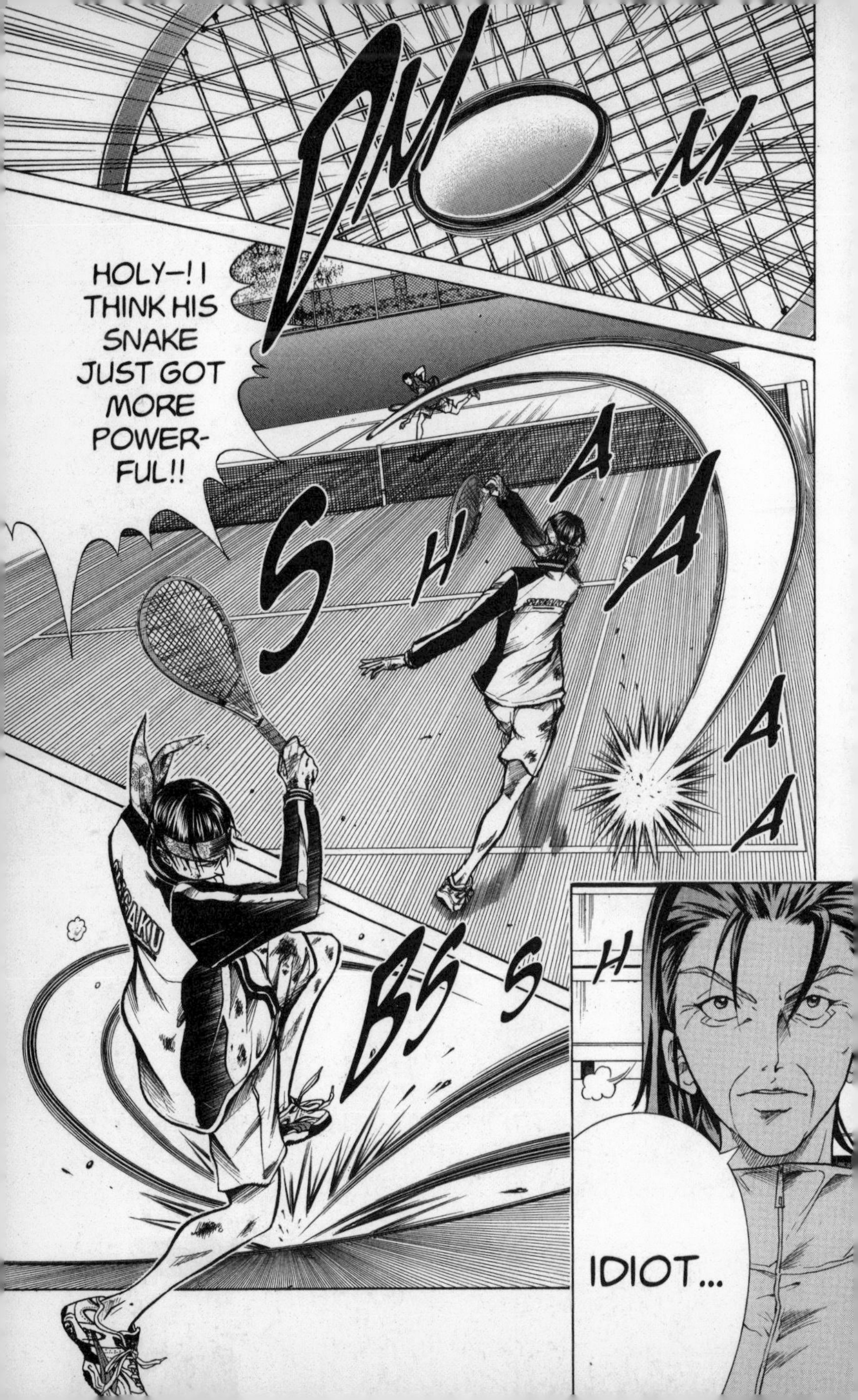
DMOM
HOLY—! I THINK HIS SNAKE JUST GOT MORE POWER-FUL!!
SHAAAAAA
BSSSH
IDIOT...

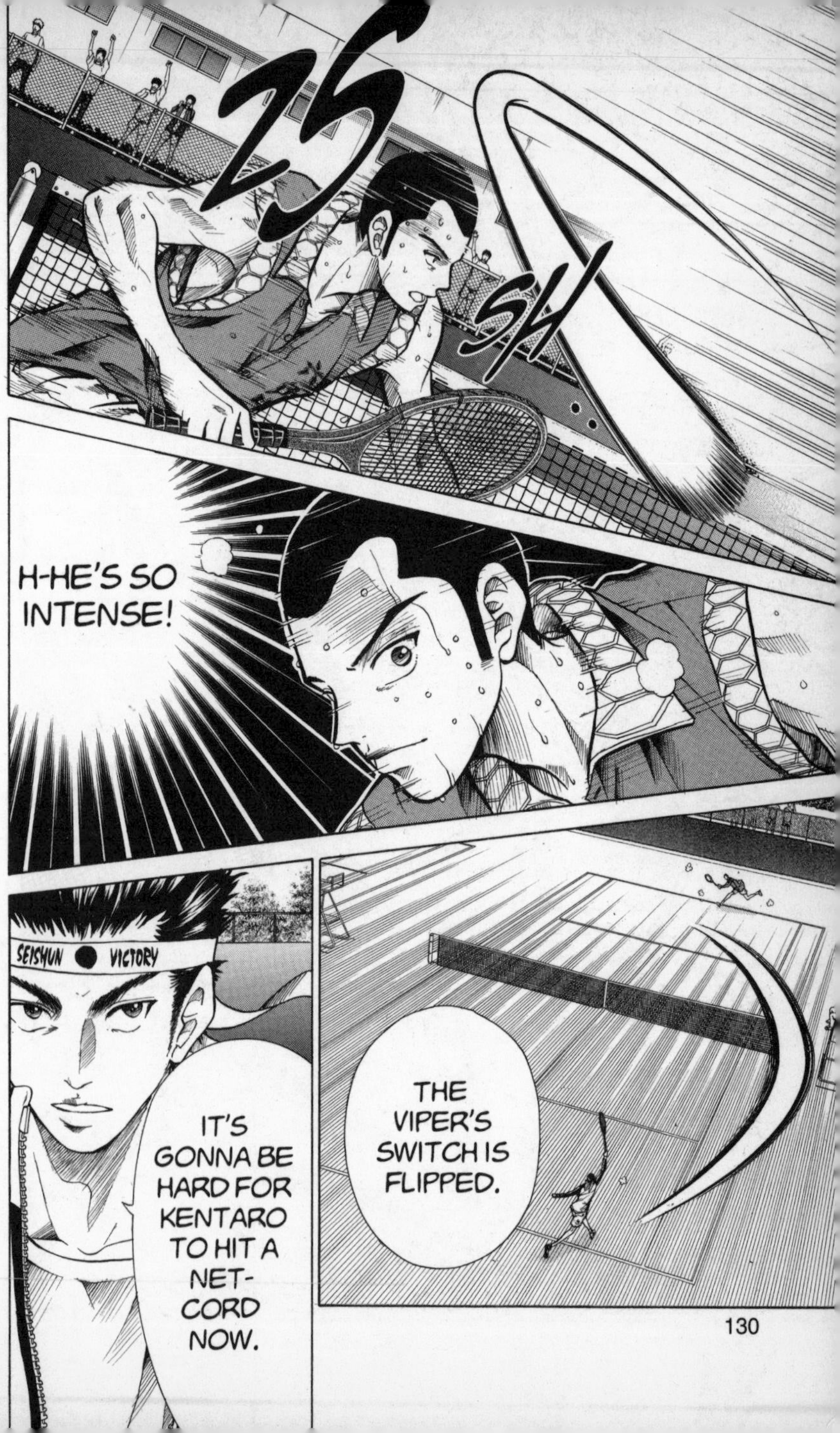
ZS
SH
H-HE'S SO INTENSE!
THE VIPER'S SWITCH IS FLIPPED.
SEISHUN VICTORY
IT'S GONNA BE HARD FOR KENTARO TO HIT A NET-CORD NOW.

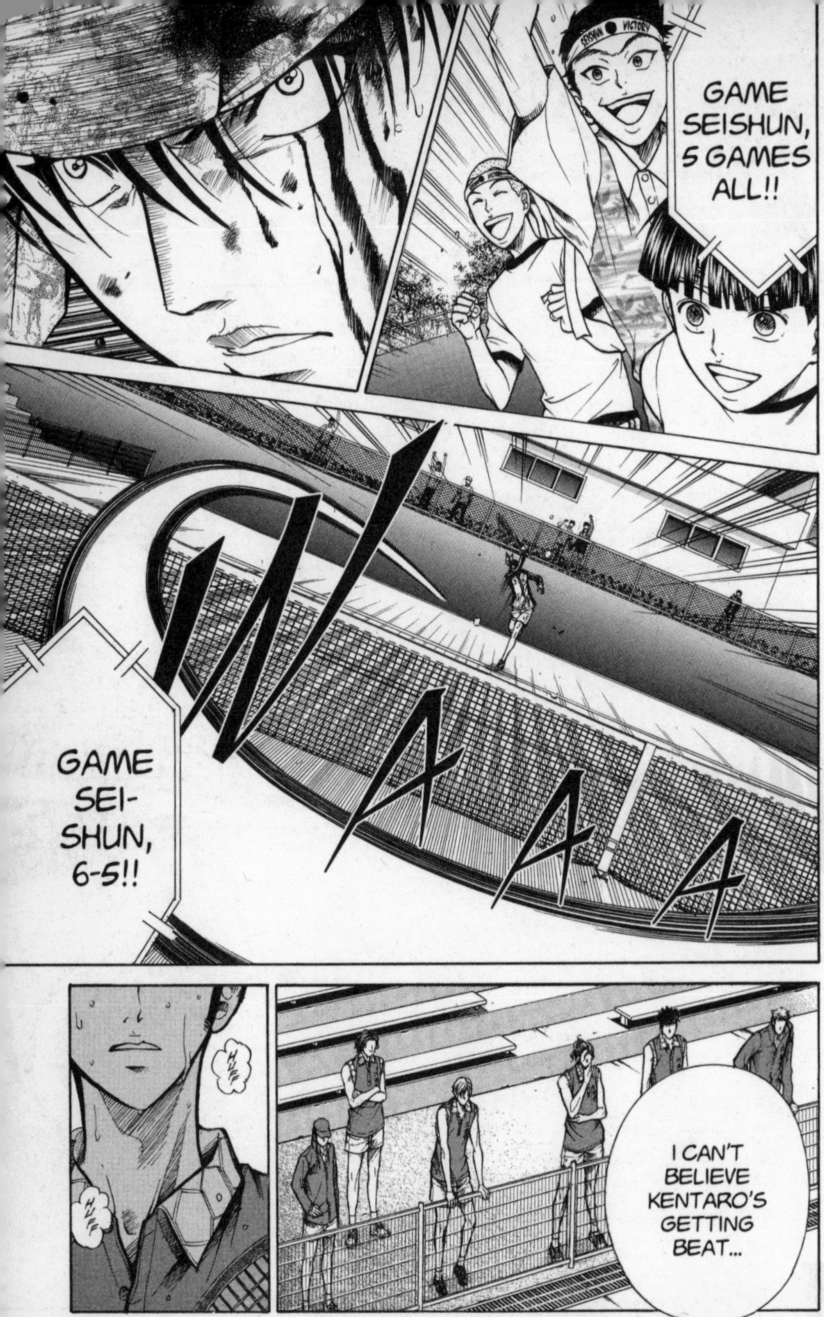
GAME SEISHUN, 5 GAMES ALL!!
GAME SEI-SHUN, 6-5!!
WAAAA
HUFF
HUFF
I CAN'T BELIEVE KENTARO'S GETTING BEAT...

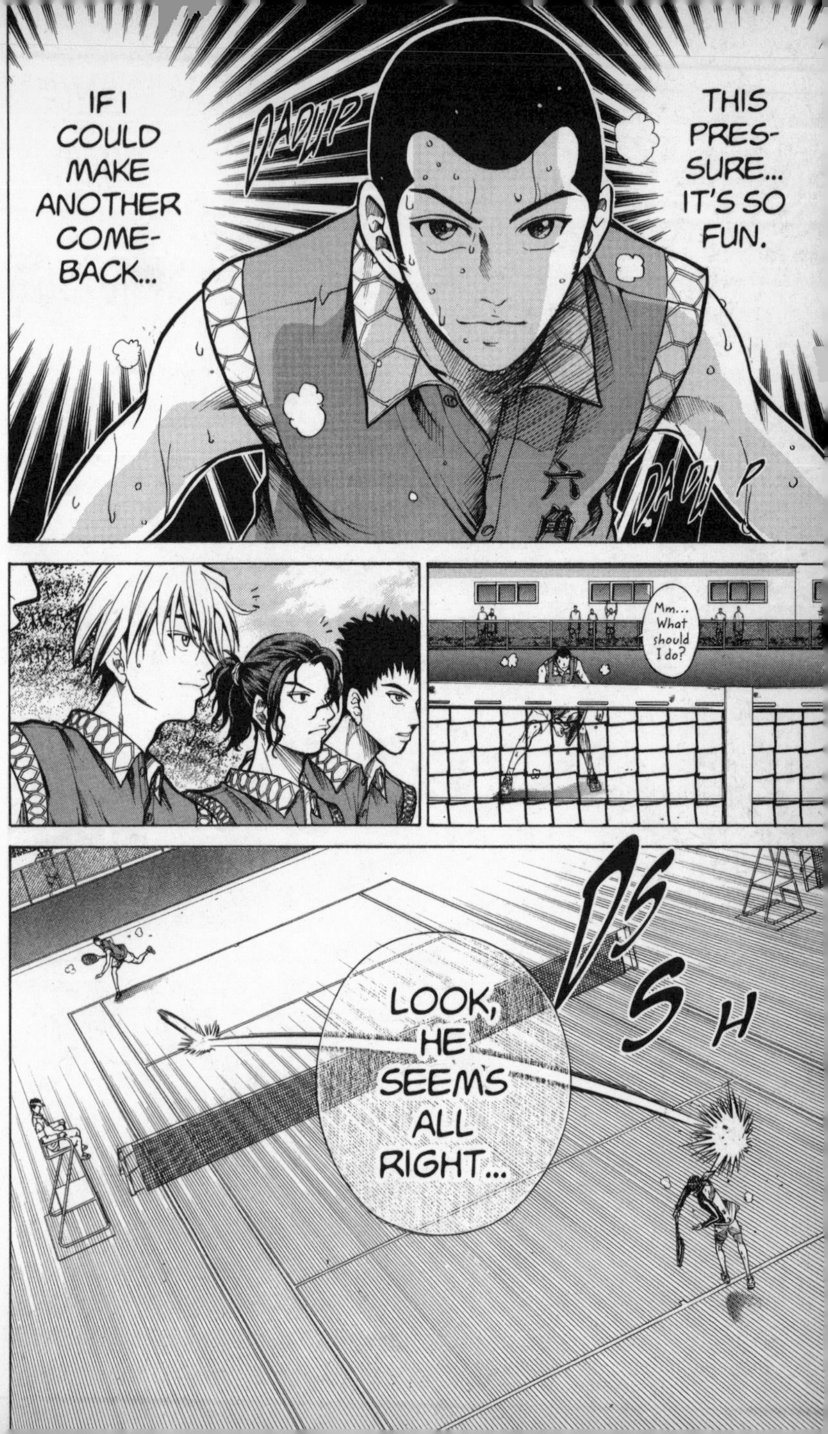
THIS PRES-SURE... IT'S SO FUN.
IF I COULD MAKE ANOTHER COME-BACK...
DADUP
DADUP
Mm... What should I do?
DSSH
LOOK, HE SEEMS ALL RIGHT...

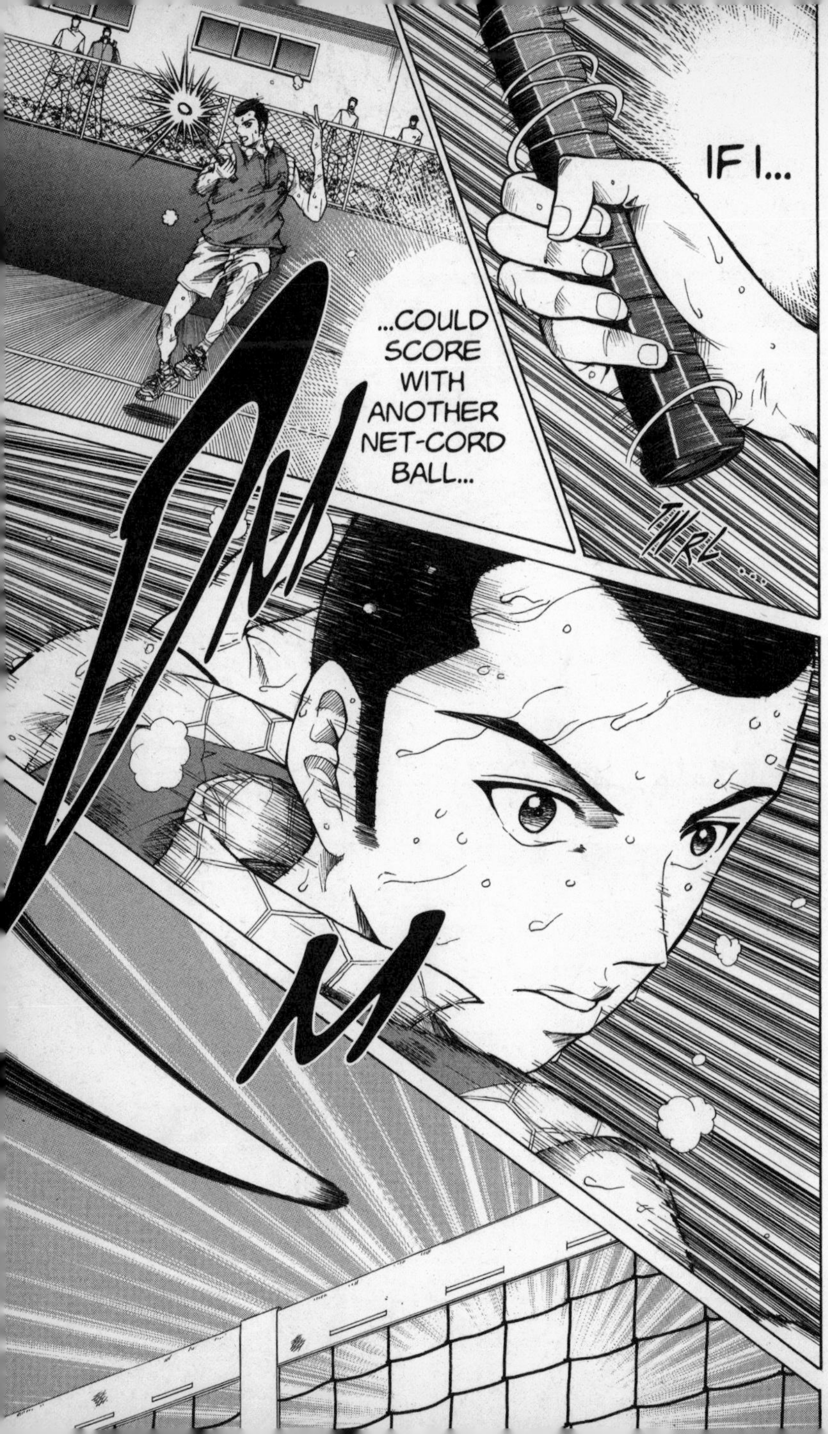
IF I...
...COULD SCORE WITH ANOTHER NET-CORD BALL...

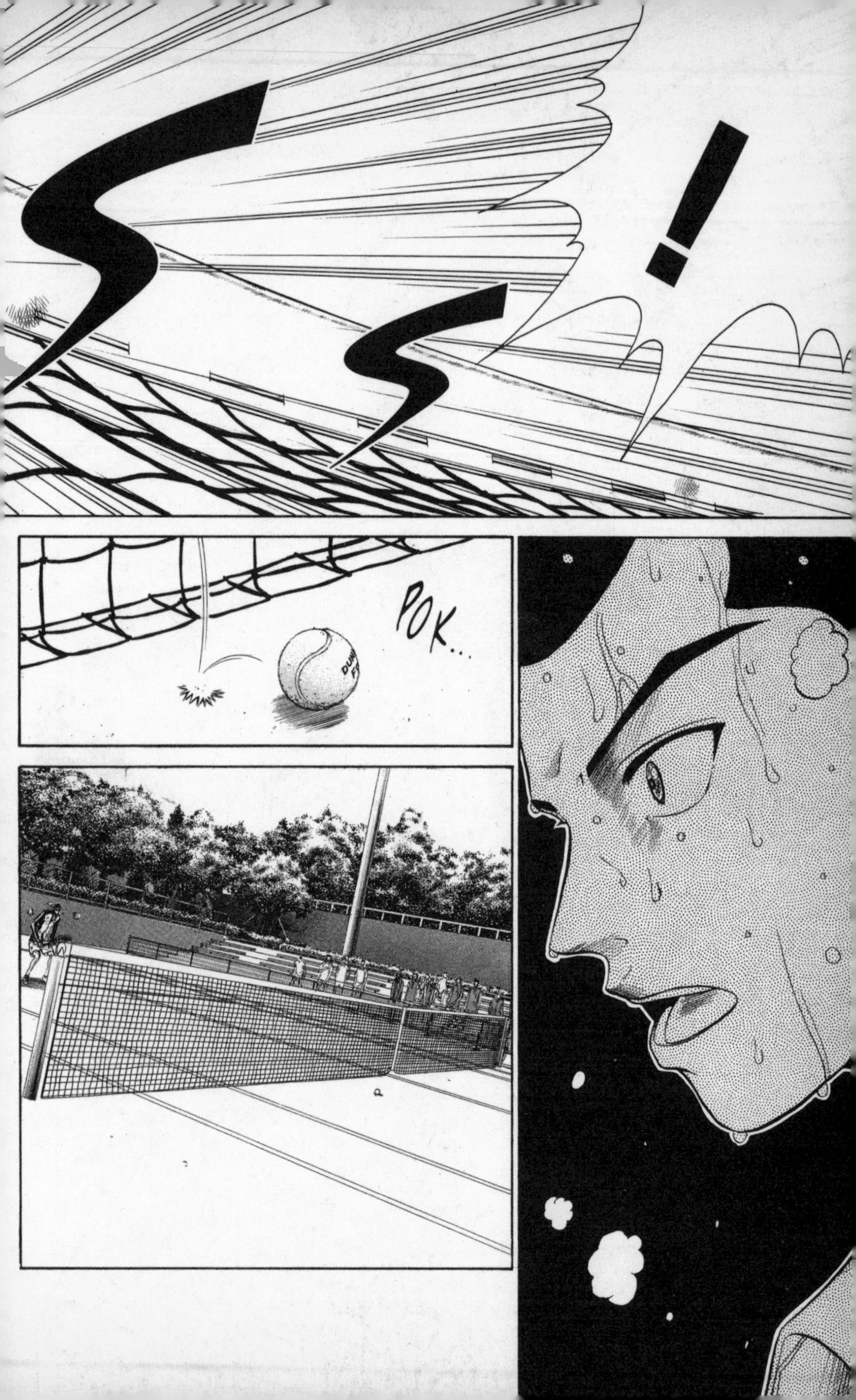
SS!
POK...

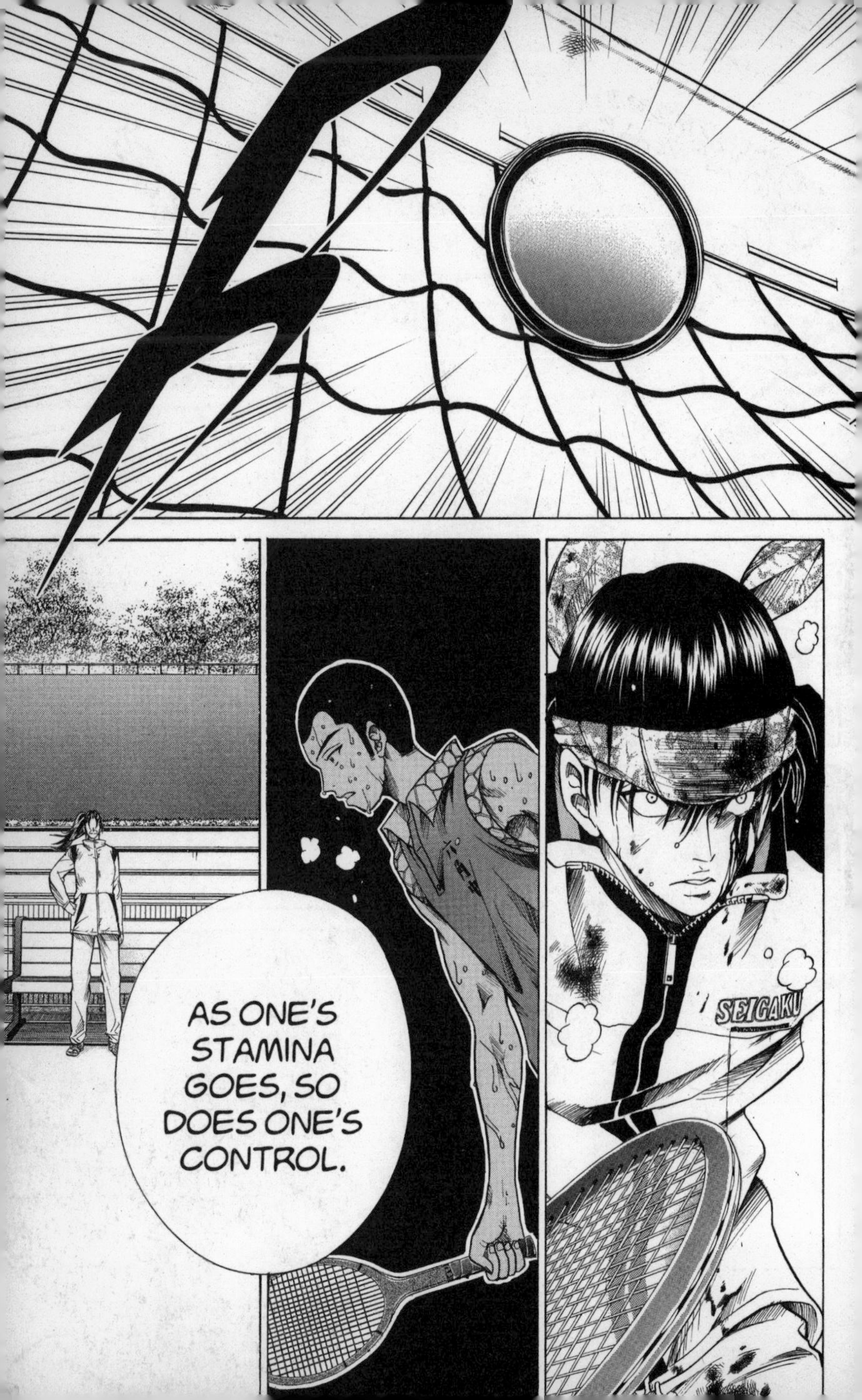
AS ONE'S STAMINA GOES, SO DOES ONE'S CONTROL.

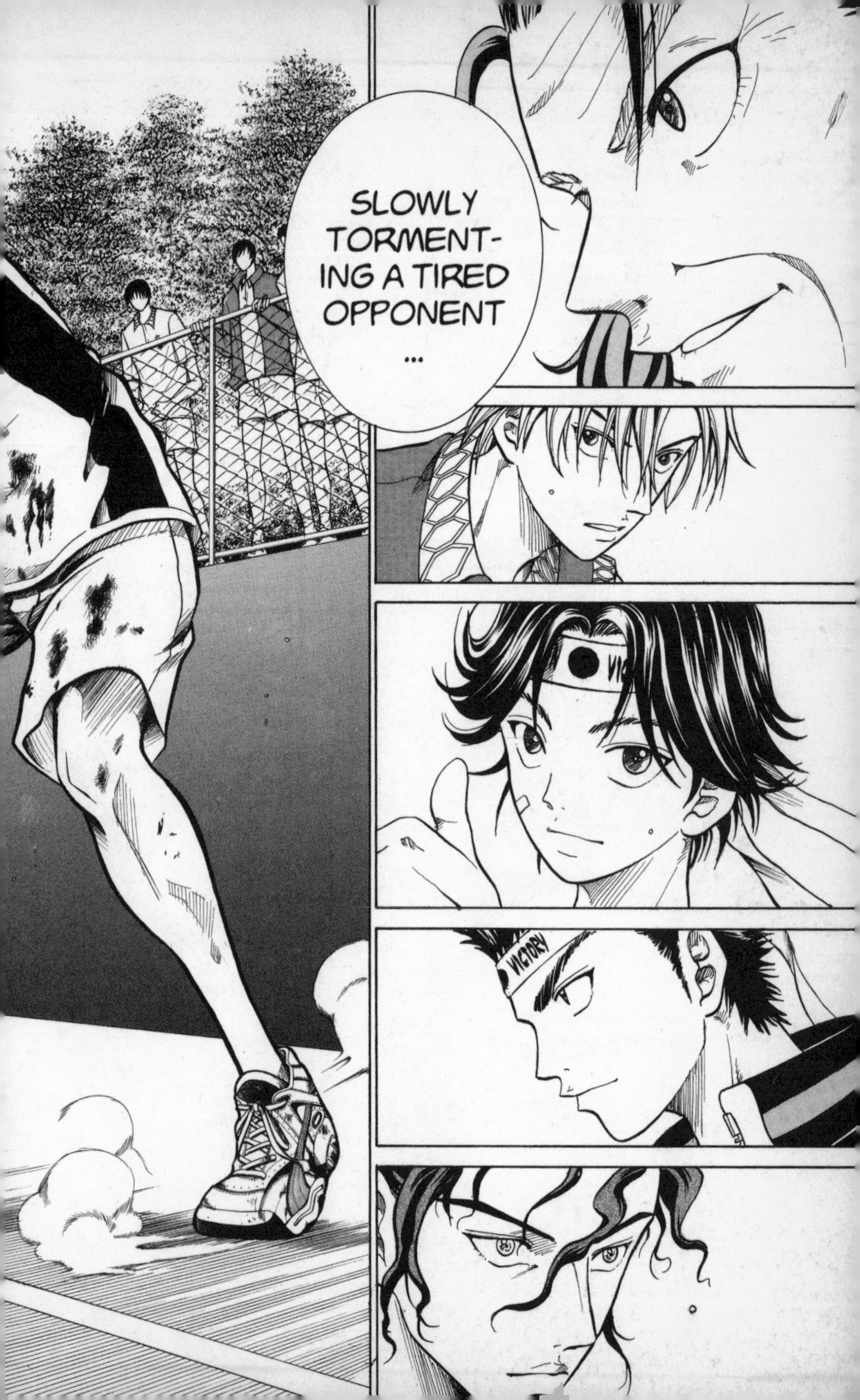
SLOWLY TORMENT-ING A TIRED OPPONENT ...
VICTORY

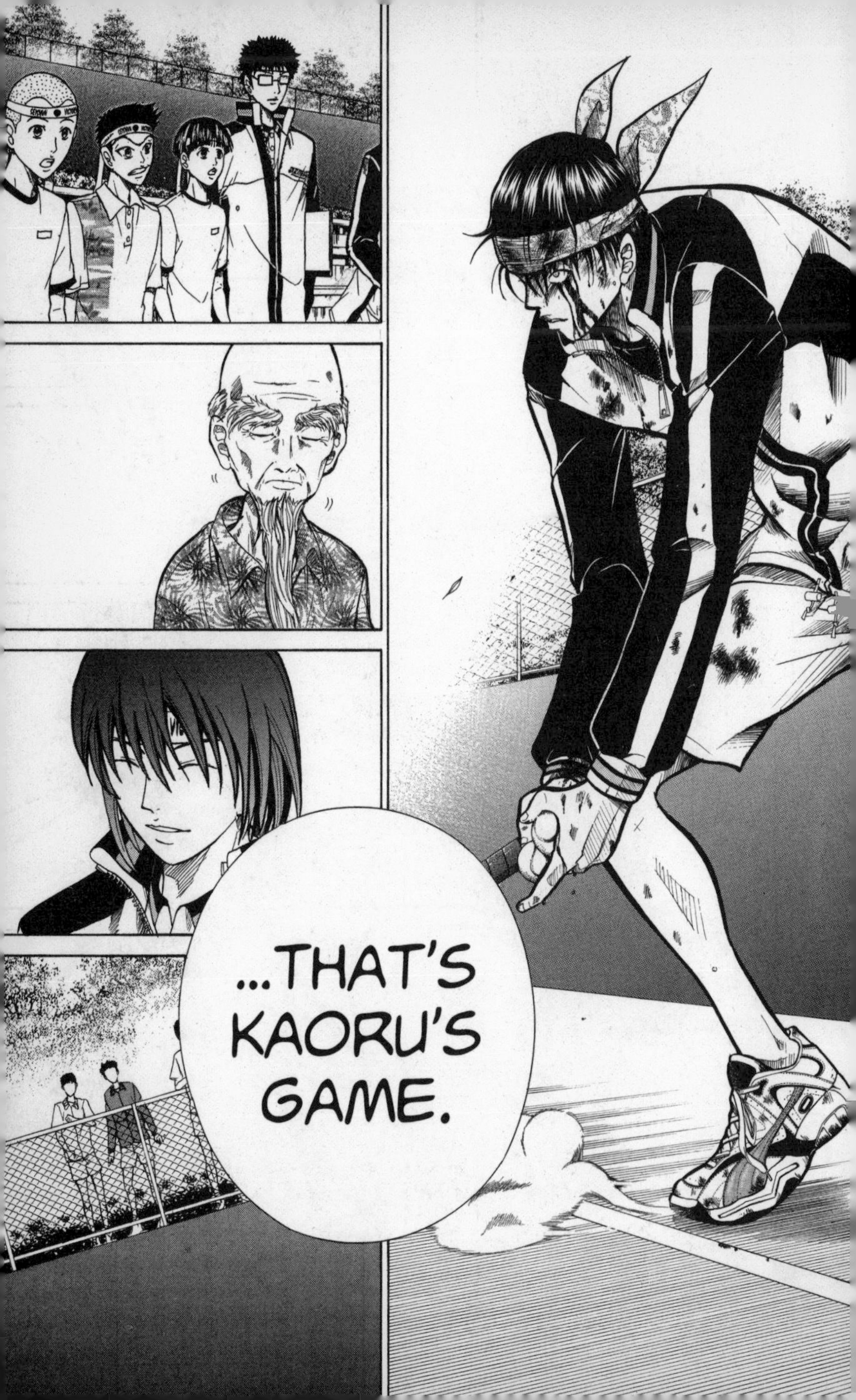
...THAT'S KAORU'S GAME.

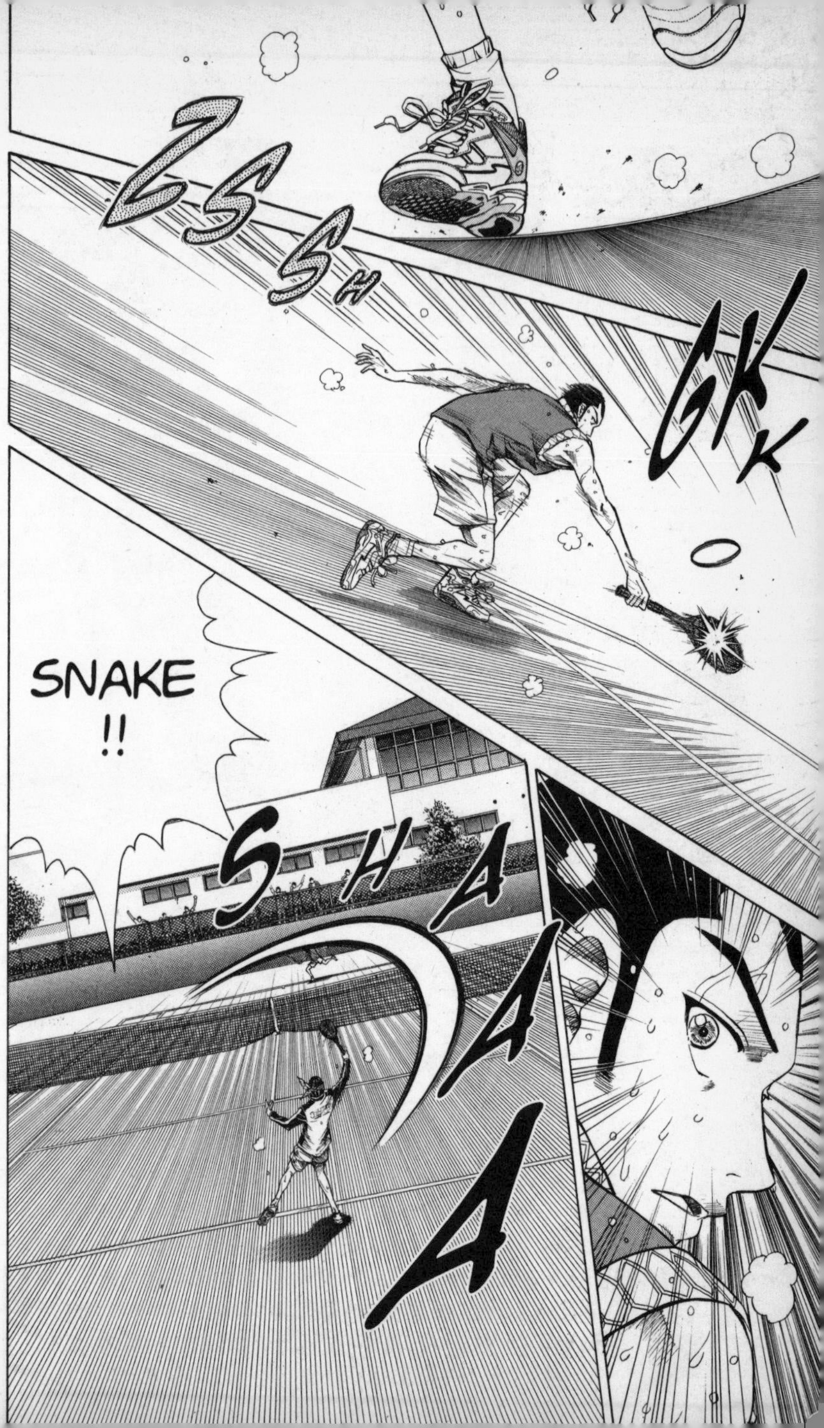
ZSSSH
GKK
SNAKE !!
SHAAAA

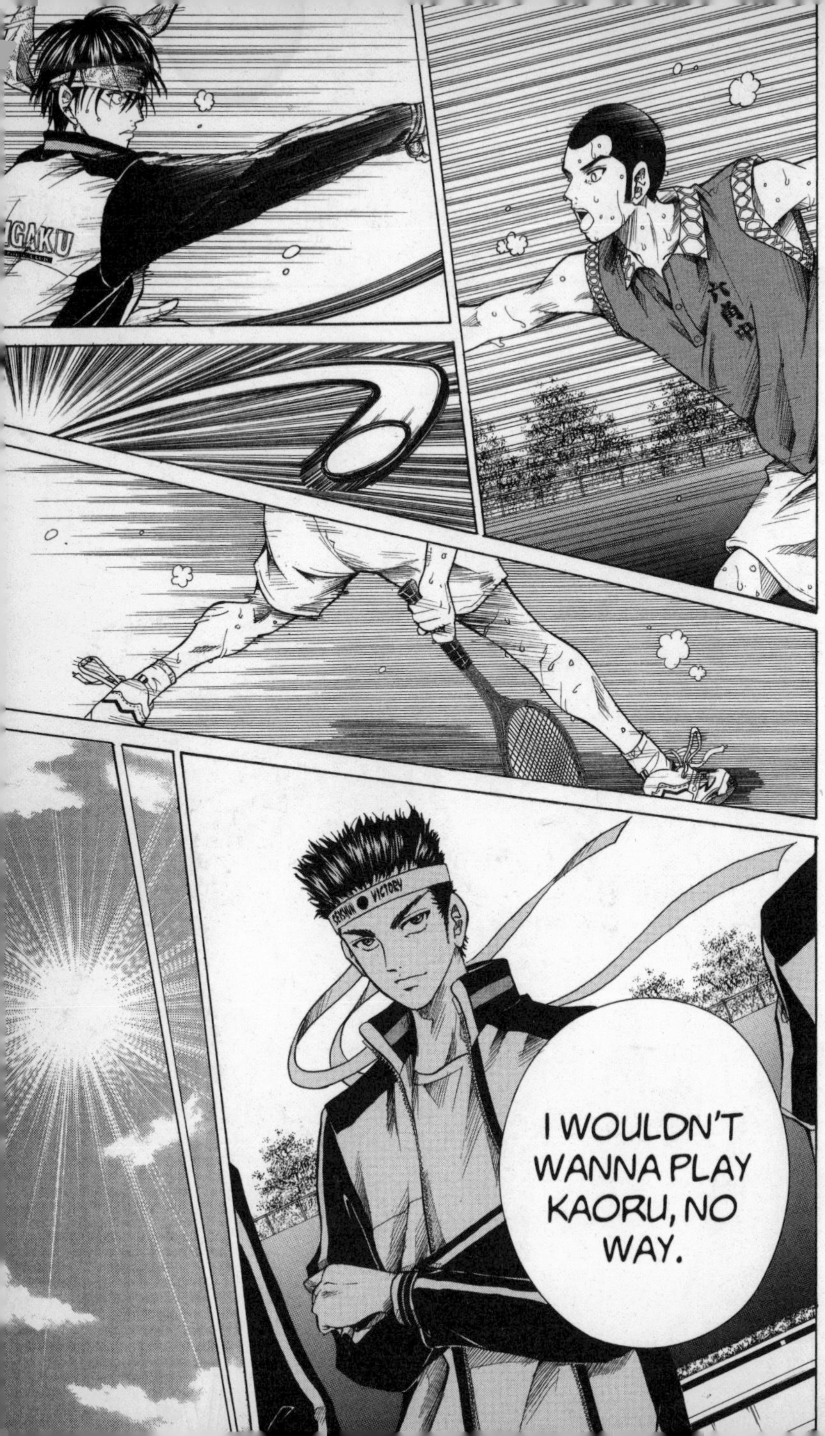
I WOULDN'T WANNA PLAY KAORU, NO WAY.

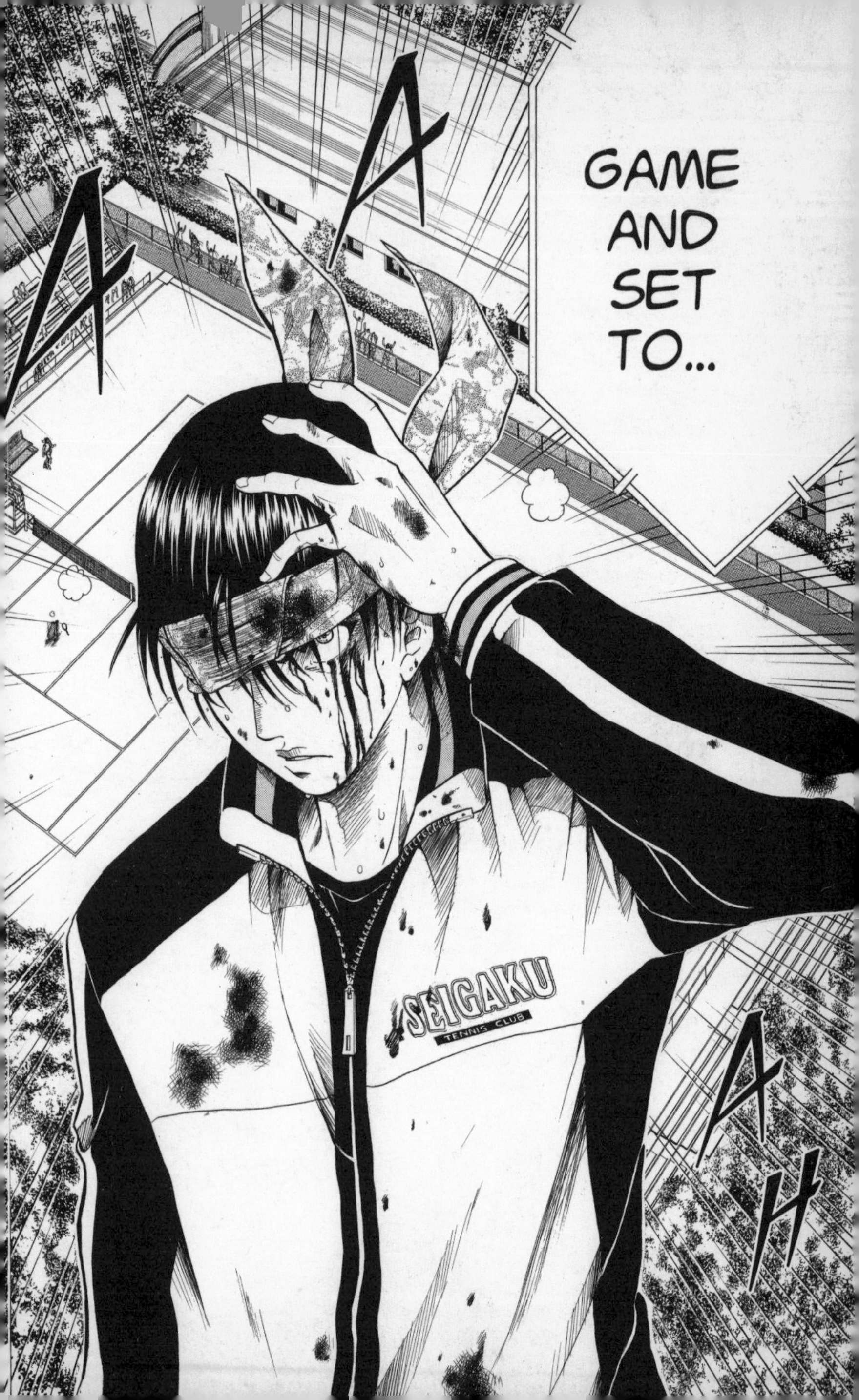
GAME AND SET TO...
AAAAH
SEIGAKU
TENNIS CLUB

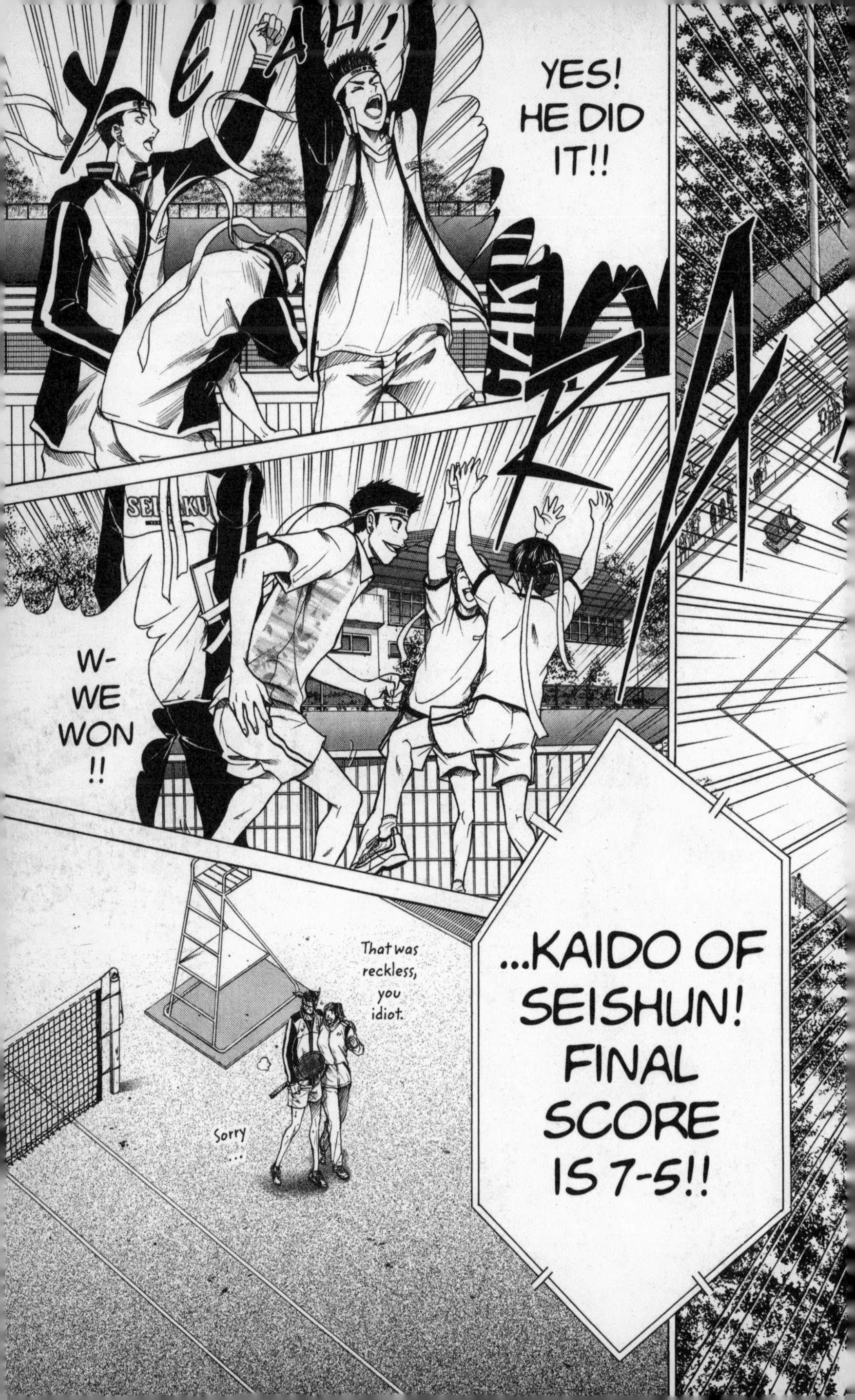
YES! HE DID IT!!
YEAH!
W-WE WON!!
...KAIDO OF SEISHUN! FINAL SCORE IS 7-5!!
That was reckless, you idiot.
Sorry...

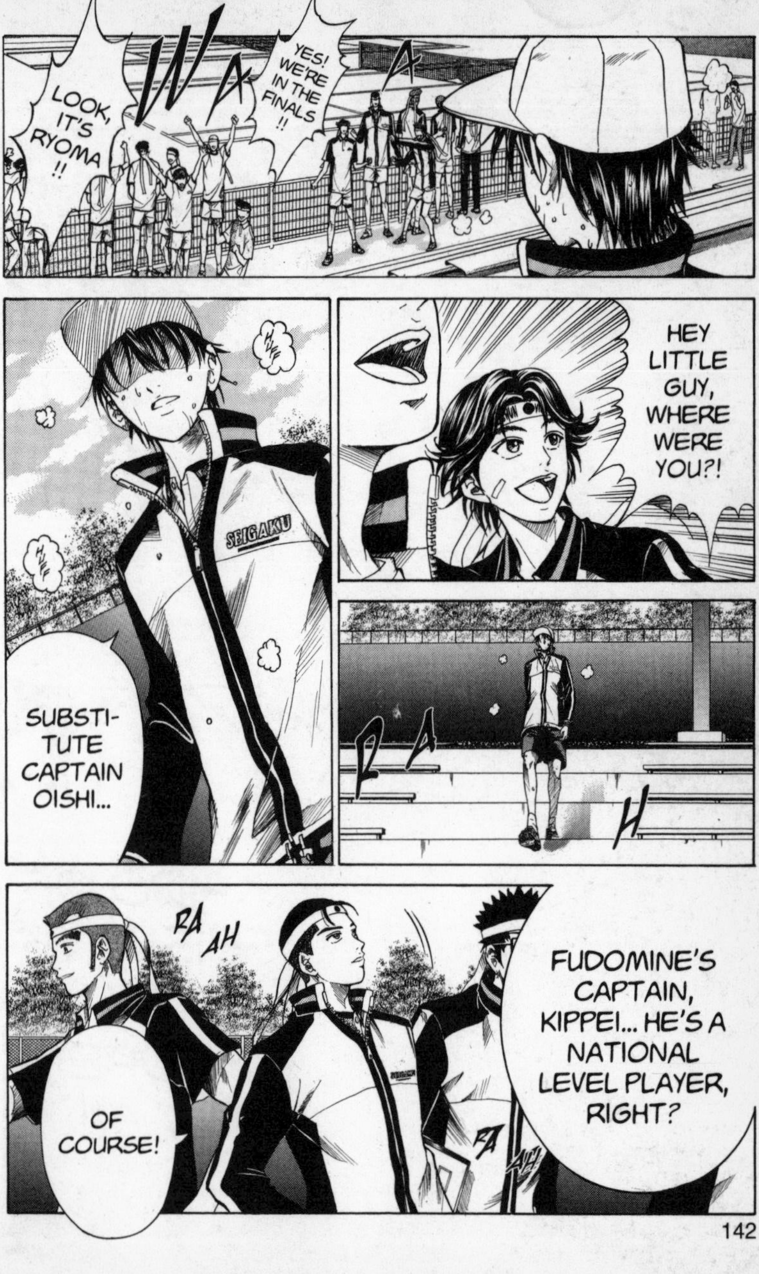
YES! WE'RE IN THE FINALS!!
WA
A
LOOK, IT'S RYOMA!!
HEY LITTLE GUY, WHERE WERE YOU?!
SUBSTI-TUTE CAPTAIN OISHI...
RA
H
FUDOMINE'S CAPTAIN, KIPPEI... HE'S A NATIONAL LEVEL PLAYER, RIGHT?
RA
AH
OF COURSE!

READ THIS WAY

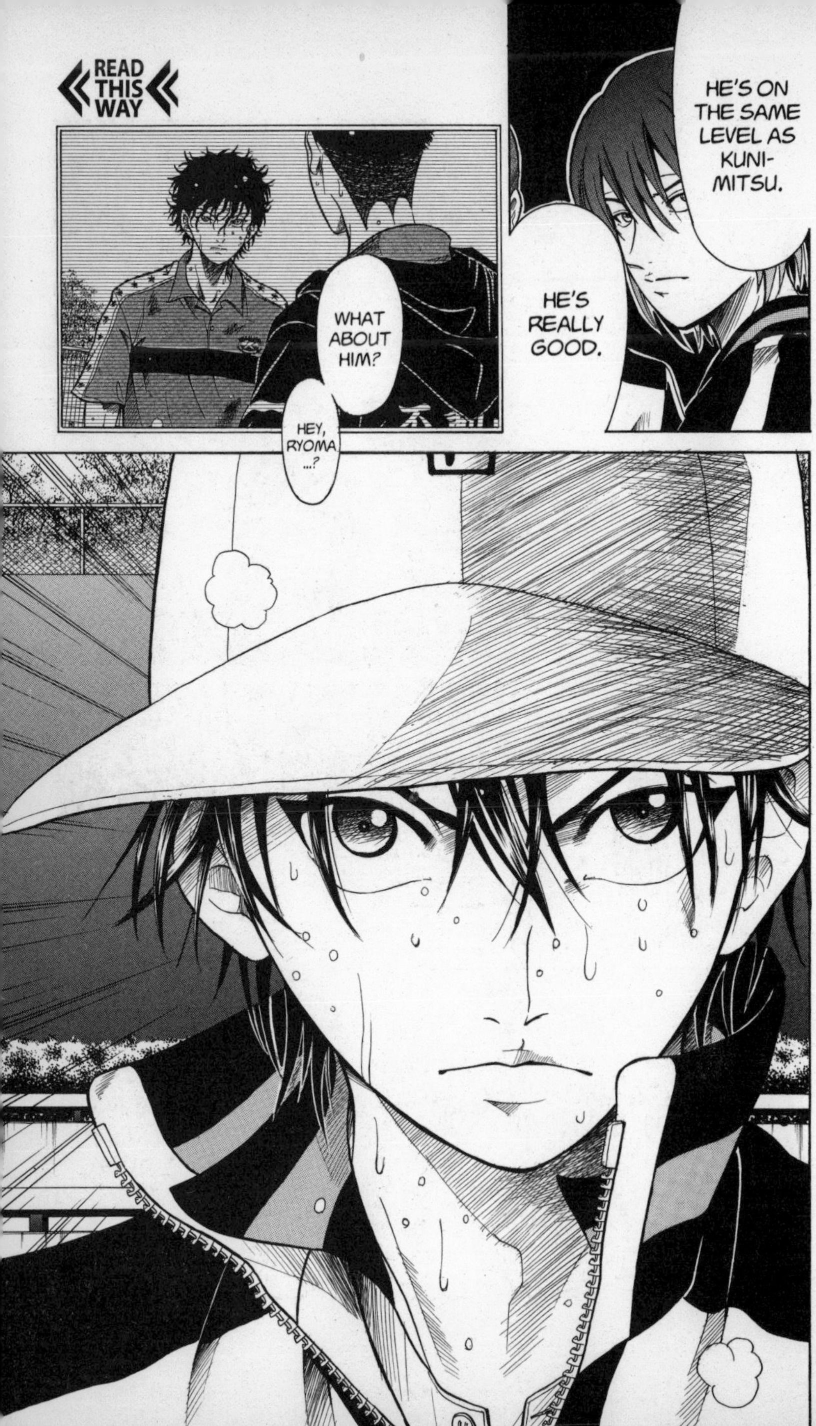
HE'S ON THE SAME LEVEL AS KUNI-MITSU.
HE'S REALLY GOOD.
WHAT ABOUT HIM?
HEY, RYOMA ...?

テニスの王子様

THE PRINCE OF TENNIS™

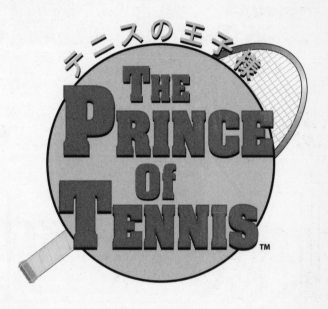

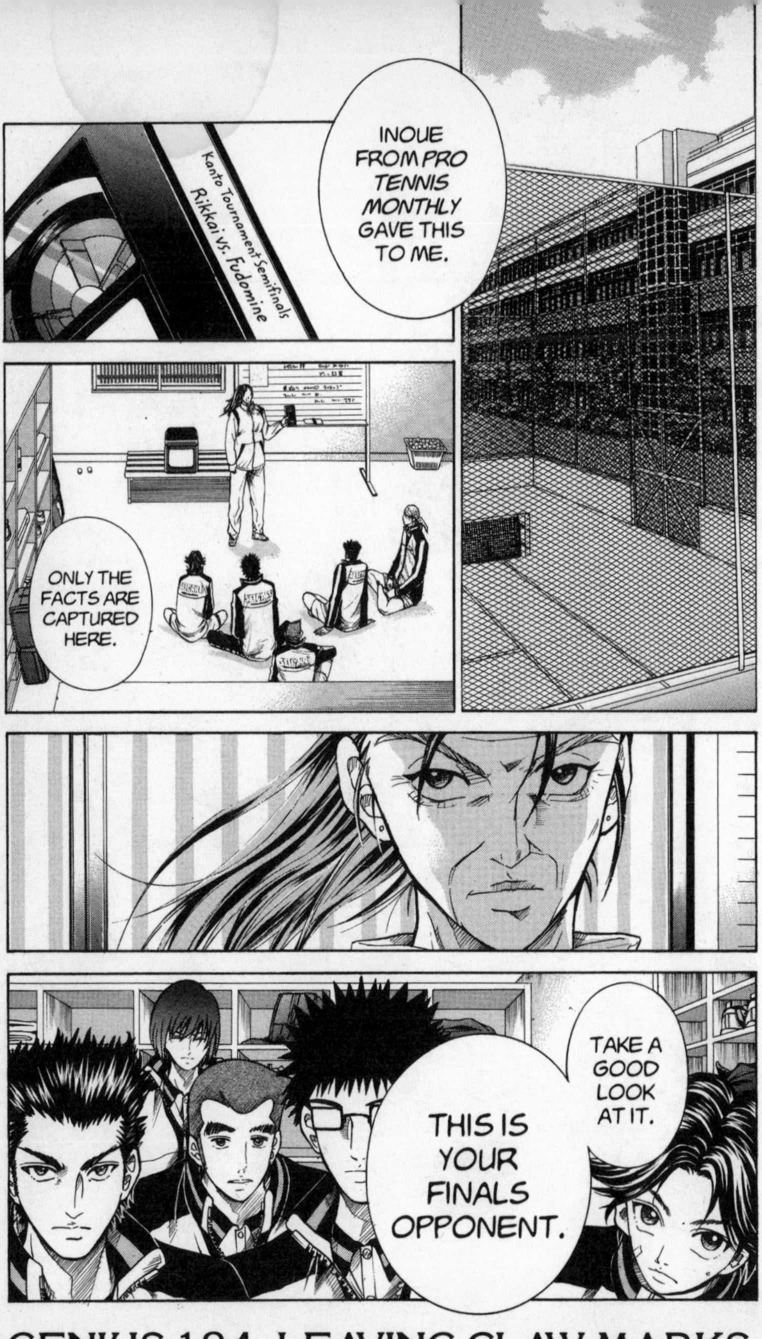
Kanto Tournament Semifinals
Rikkai vs. Fudomine
INOUE FROM PRO TENNIS MONTHLY GAVE THIS TO ME.
ONLY THE FACTS ARE CAPTURED HERE.
TAKE A GOOD LOOK AT IT.
THIS IS YOUR FINALS OPPONENT.

GENIUS 184: LEAVING CLAW MARKS

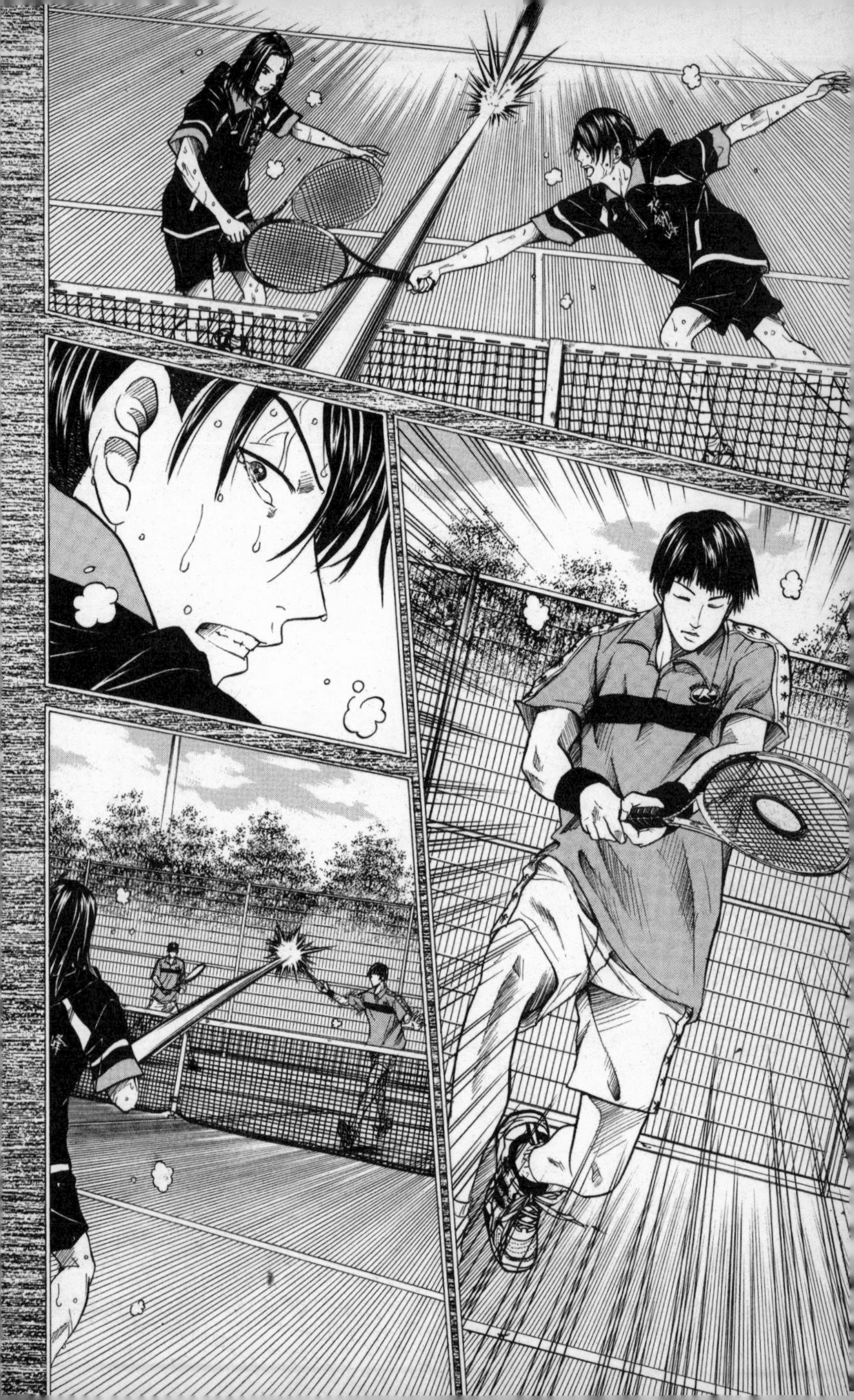

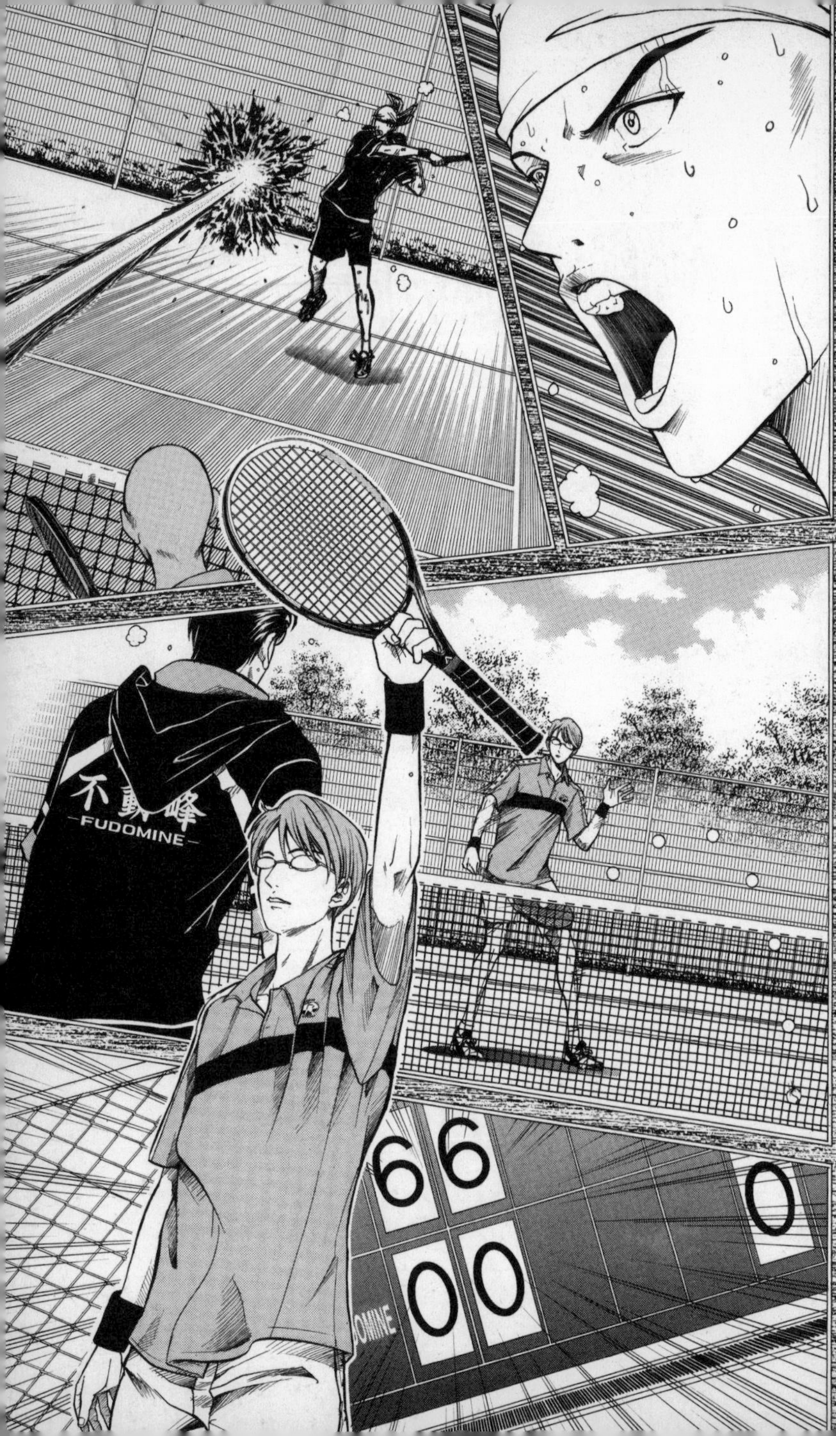
不動峰
-FUDOMINE-
66
0
00

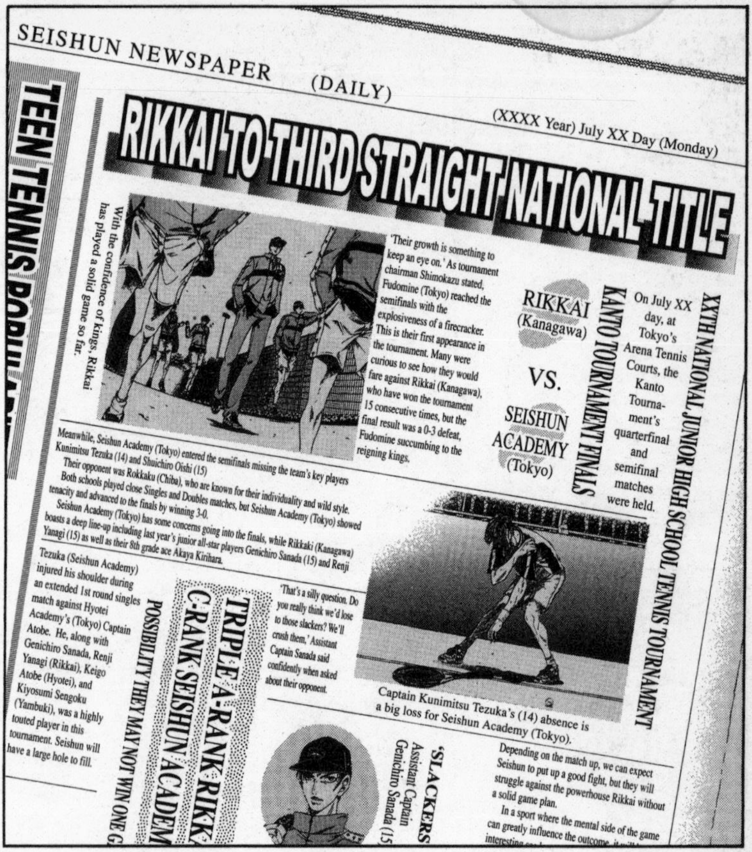

SEISHUN NEWSPAPER (DAILY)

(XXXX Year) July XX Day (Monday)

TEEN TENNIS POPULAR

RIKKAI TO THIRD STRAIGHT NATIONAL TITLE

XXTH NATIONAL JUNIOR HIGH SCHOOL TENNIS TOURNAMENT

KANTO TOURNAMENT FINALS

RIKKAI (Kanagawa) VS. SEISHUN ACADEMY (Tokyo)

On July XX day, at Tokyo's Arena Tennis Courts, the Kanto Tournament's quarterfinal and semifinal matches were held.

'Their growth is something to keep an eye on.' As tournament chairman Shimokazu stated, Fudomine (Tokyo) reached the semifinals with the explosiveness of a firecracker. This is their first appearance in the tournament. Many were curious to see how they would fare against Rikkai (Kanagawa), who have won the tournament 15 consecutive times, but the final result was a 0-3 defeat, Fudomine succumbing to the reigning kings.

With the confidence of kings, Rikkai has played a solid game so far.

Meanwhile, Seishun Academy (Tokyo) entered the semifinals missing the team's key players Kunimitsu Tezuka (14) and Shuichiro Oishi (15).

Their opponent was Rokkaku (Chiba), who are known for their individuality and wild style.

Both schools played close Singles and Doubles matches, but Seishun Academy (Tokyo) showed tenacity and advanced to the finals by winning 3-0.

Seishun Academy (Tokyo) has some concerns going into the finals, while Rikkaki (Kanagawa) boasts a deep line-up including last year's junior all-star players Genichiro Sanada (15) and Renji Yanagi (15) as well as their 8th grade ace Akaya Kirihara.

Captain Kunimitsu Tezuka's (14) absence is a big loss for Seishun Academy (Tokyo).

TRIPLE A-RANK RIKKA

C-RANK SEISHUN ACADEM

POSSIBILITY THEY MAY NOT WIN ONE G

Tezuka (Seishun Academy) injured his shoulder during an extended 1st round singles match against Hyotei Academy's (Tokyo) Captain Atobe. He, along with Genichiro Sanada, Renji Yanagi (Rikkai), Keigo Atobe (Hyotei), and Kiyosumi Sengoku (Yambuki), was a highly touted player in this tournament. Seishun will have a large hole to fill.

'That's a silly question. Do you really think we'd lose to those slackers? We'll crush them,' Assistant Captain Sanada said confidently when asked about their opponent.

'SLACKERS

Assistant Captain Genichiro Sanada (15

Depending on the match up, we can expect Seishun to put up a good fight, but they will struggle against the powerhouse Rikkai without a solid game plan.

In a sport where the mental side of the game can greatly influence the outcome, it will

GENIUS 184: LEAVING CLAW MARKS

BUT...

THE GAME DIDN'T GET AROUND TO THEIR ONLY NATIONAL LEVEL PLAYER, KIPPEI, RIGHT?

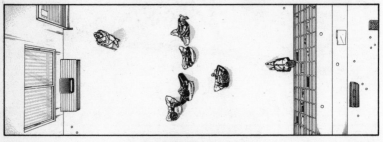

R-RIGHT ...?

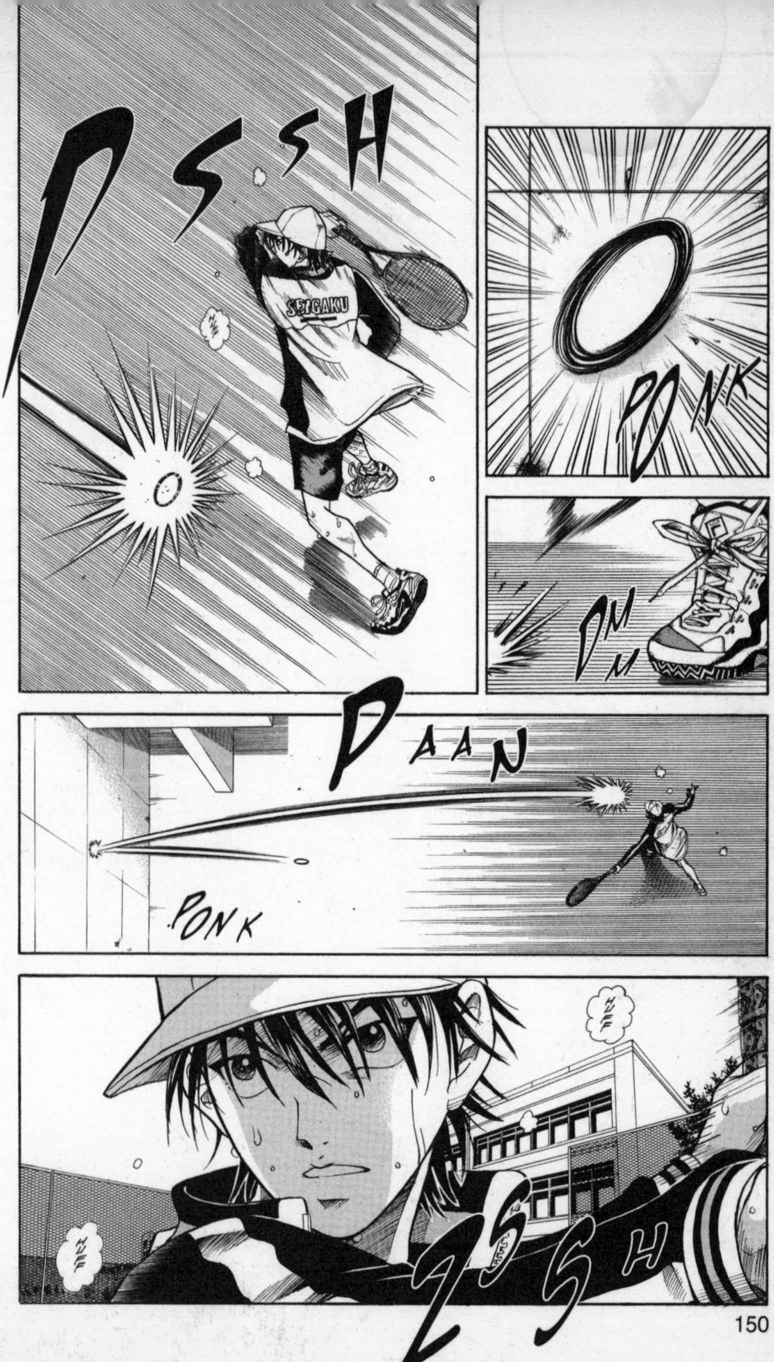
PONK
DMM
DSSH
HUFF
SEIGAKU
DAAN
PONK
HUFF
ZSSH
HUFF

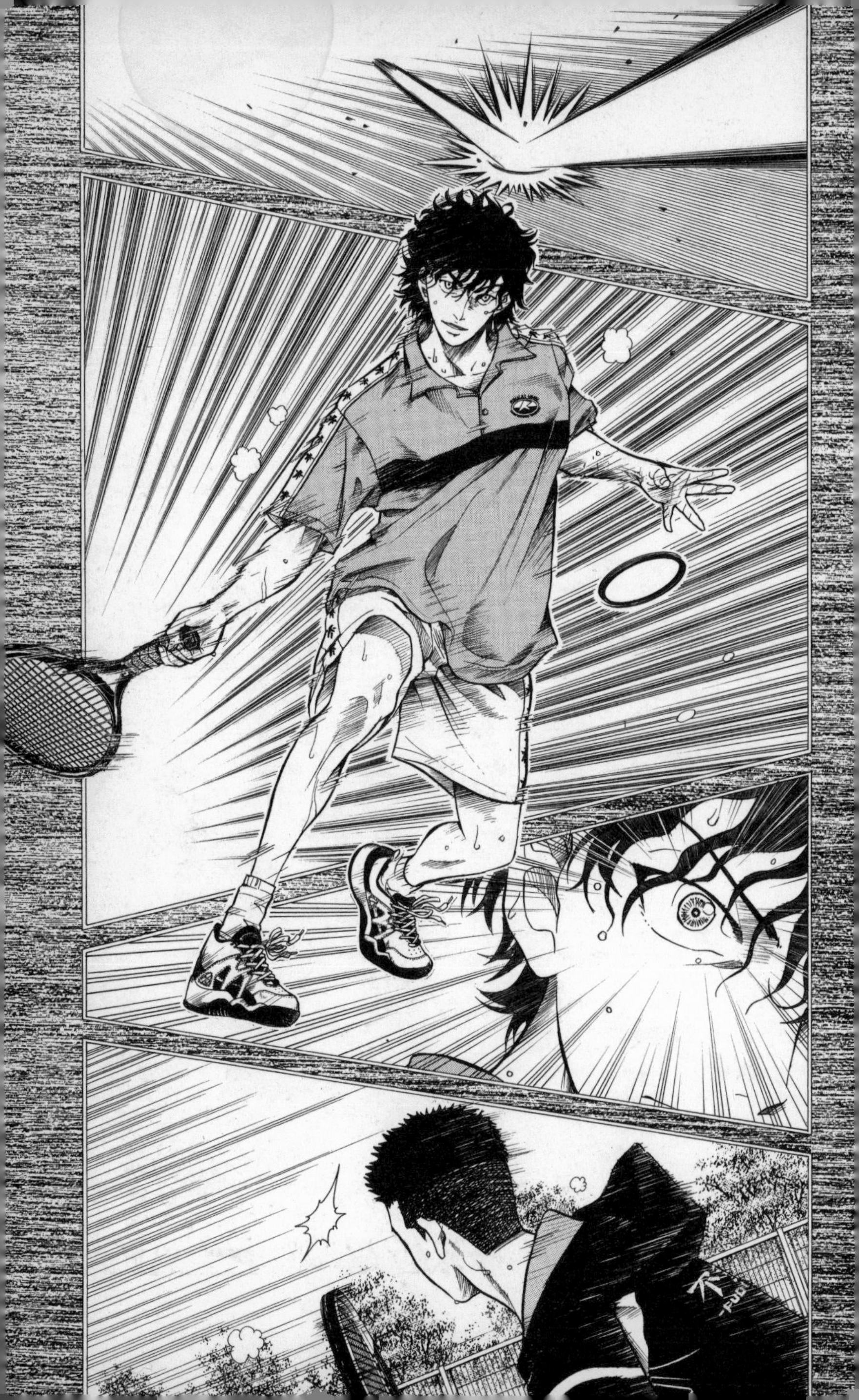

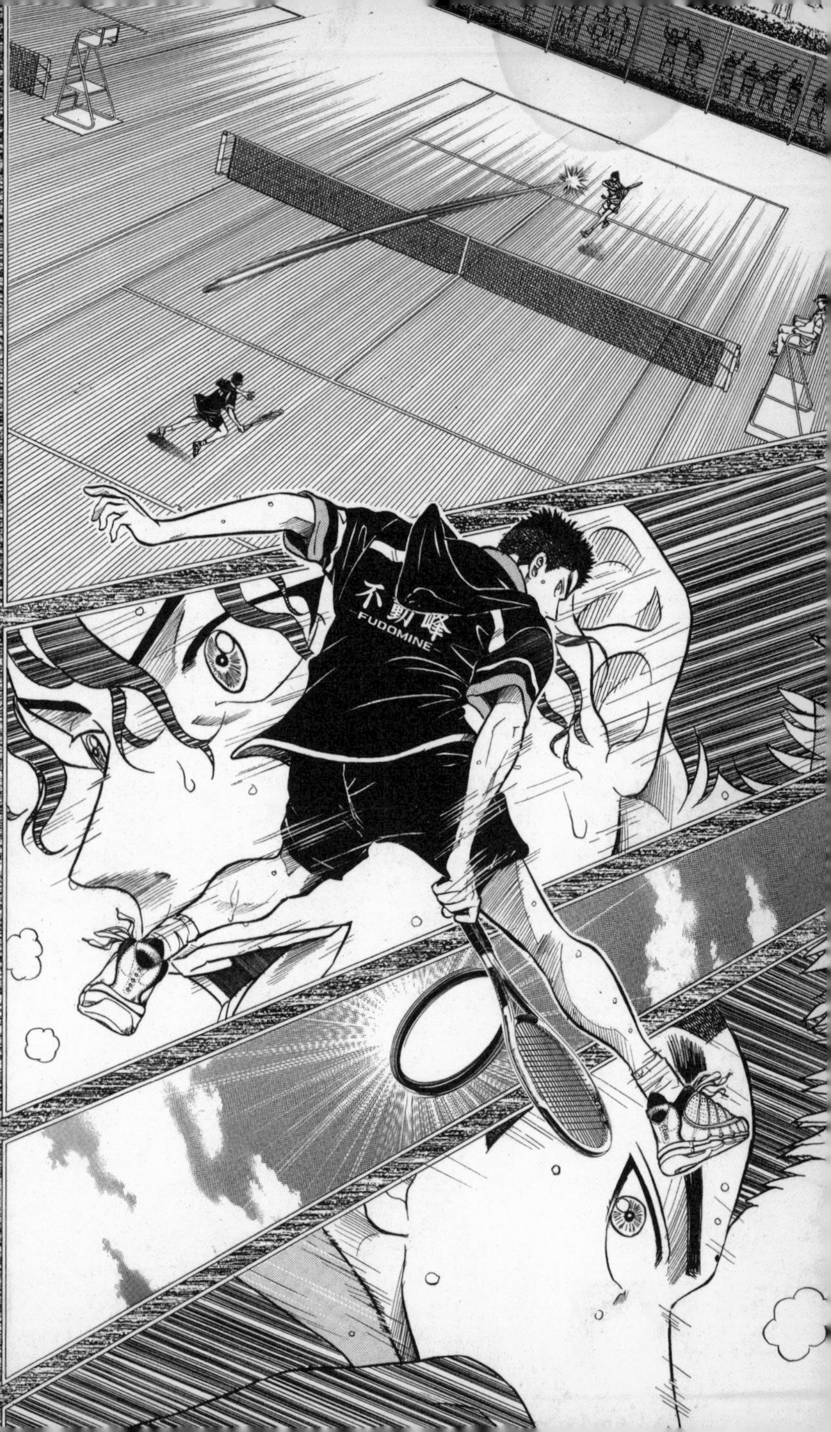
不動峰
FUDOMINE

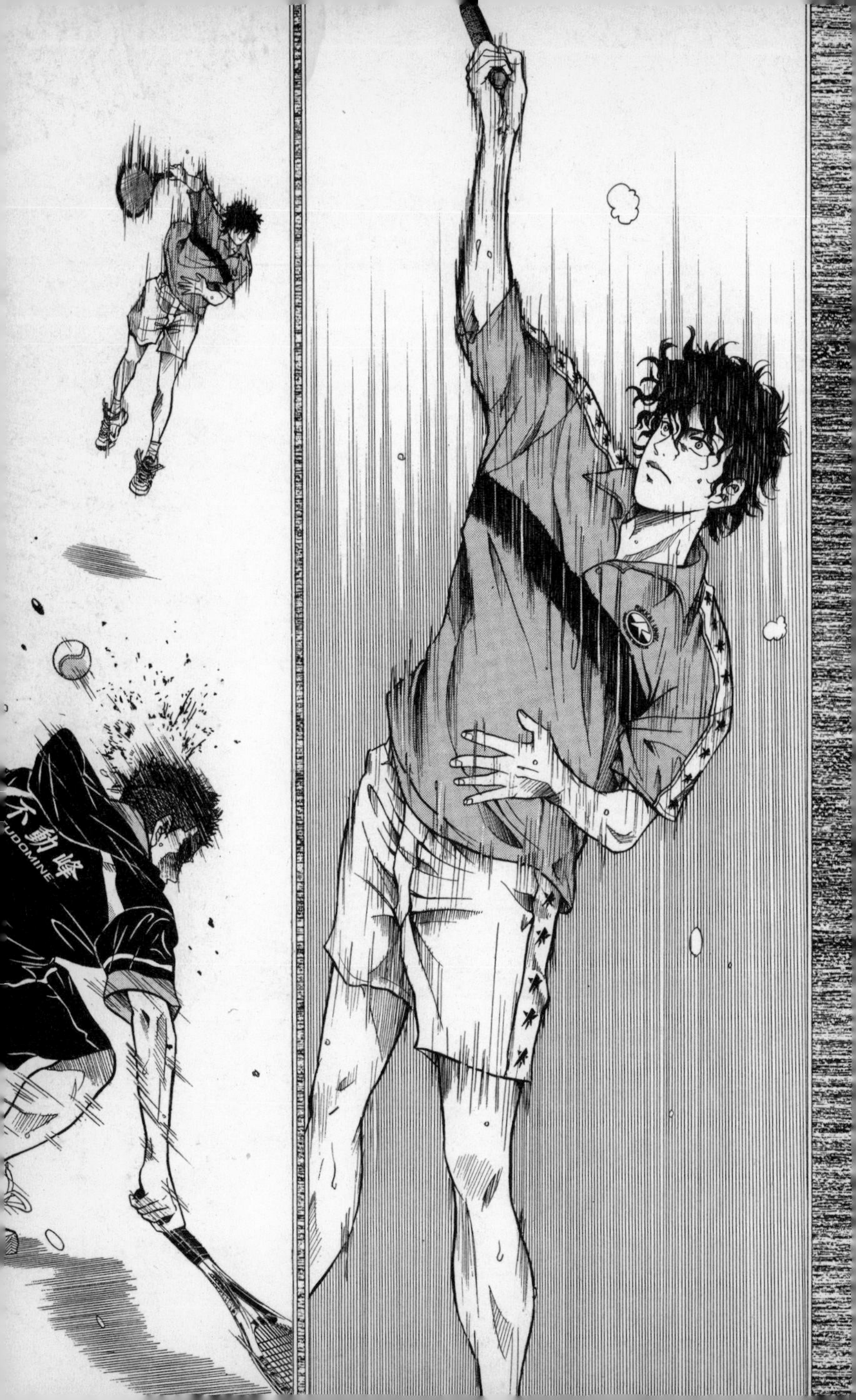
不動峰
UDOMINE

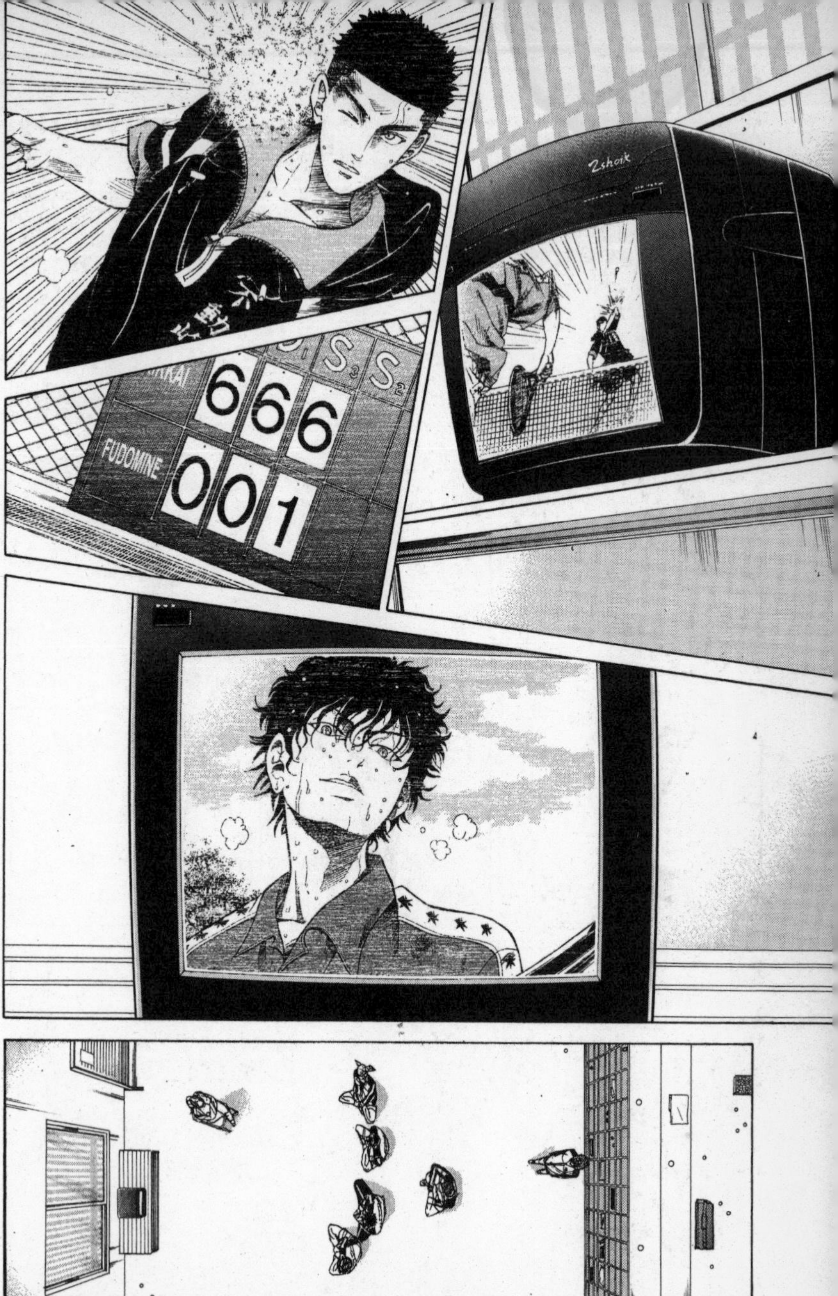
FUDOMINE
666
001

READ THIS WAY

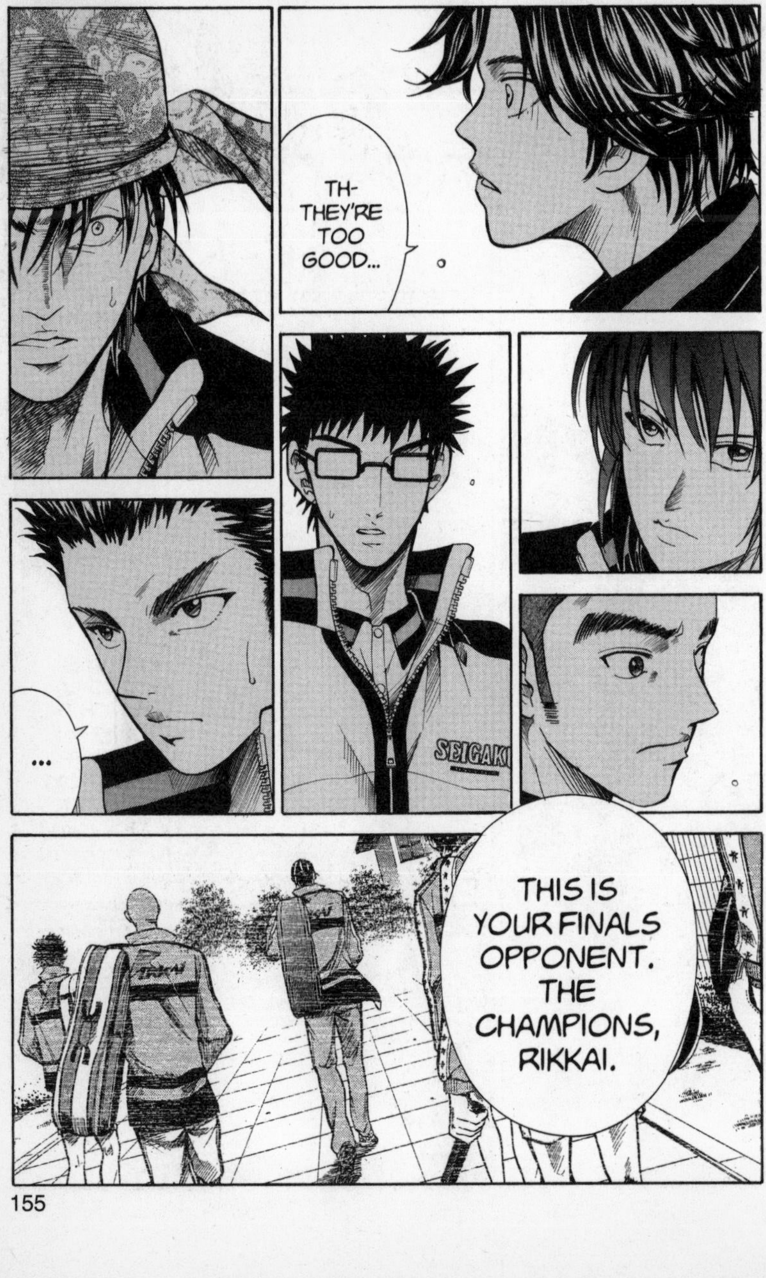
TH- THEY'RE TOO GOOD...
...
THIS IS YOUR FINALS OPPONENT. THE CHAMPIONS, RIKKAI.
SEIGAKU

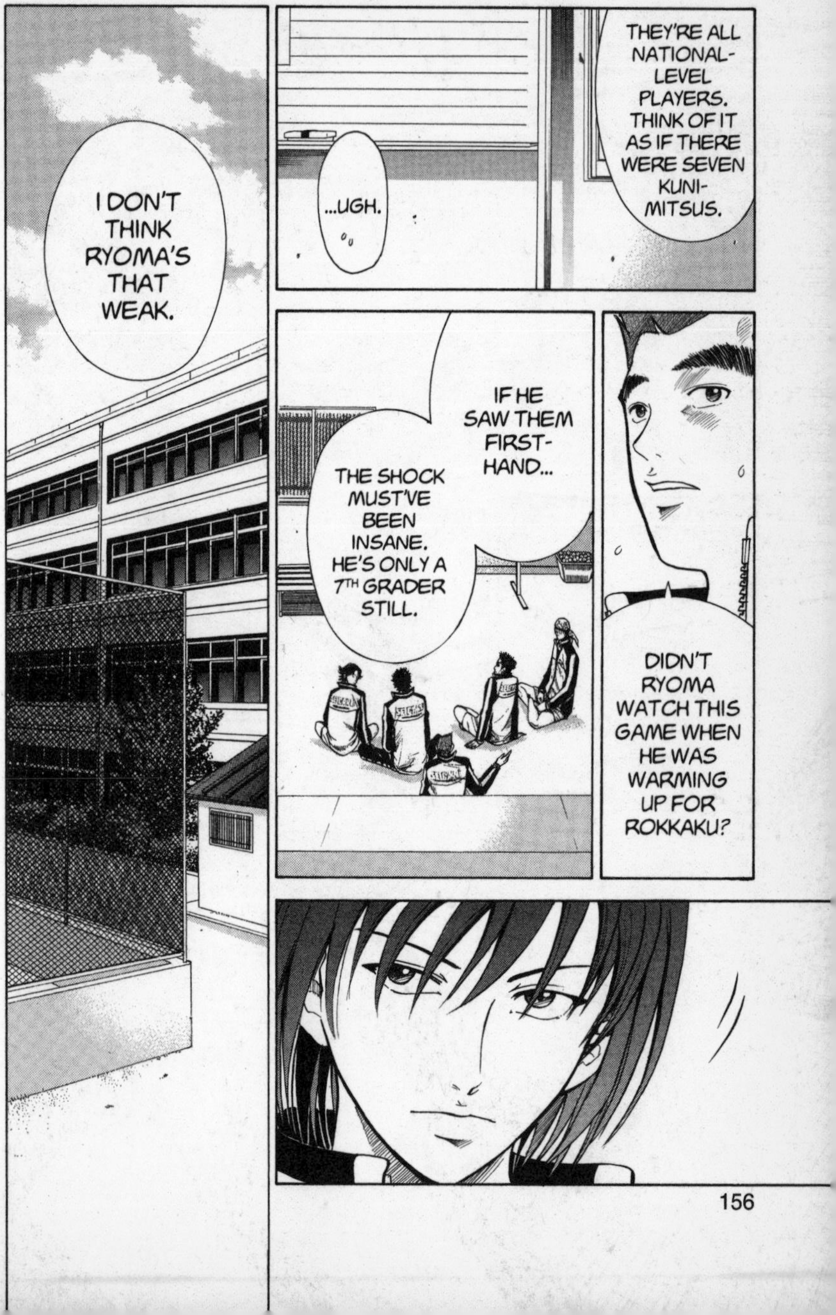
THEY'RE ALL NATIONAL-LEVEL PLAYERS. THINK OF IT AS IF THERE WERE SEVEN KUNI-MITSUS.
...UGH.
DIDN'T RYOMA WATCH THIS GAME WHEN HE WAS WARMING UP FOR ROKKAKU?
IF HE SAW THEM FIRST-HAND...
THE SHOCK MUST'VE BEEN INSANE. HE'S ONLY A 7TH GRADER STILL.
I DON'T THINK RYOMA'S THAT WEAK.

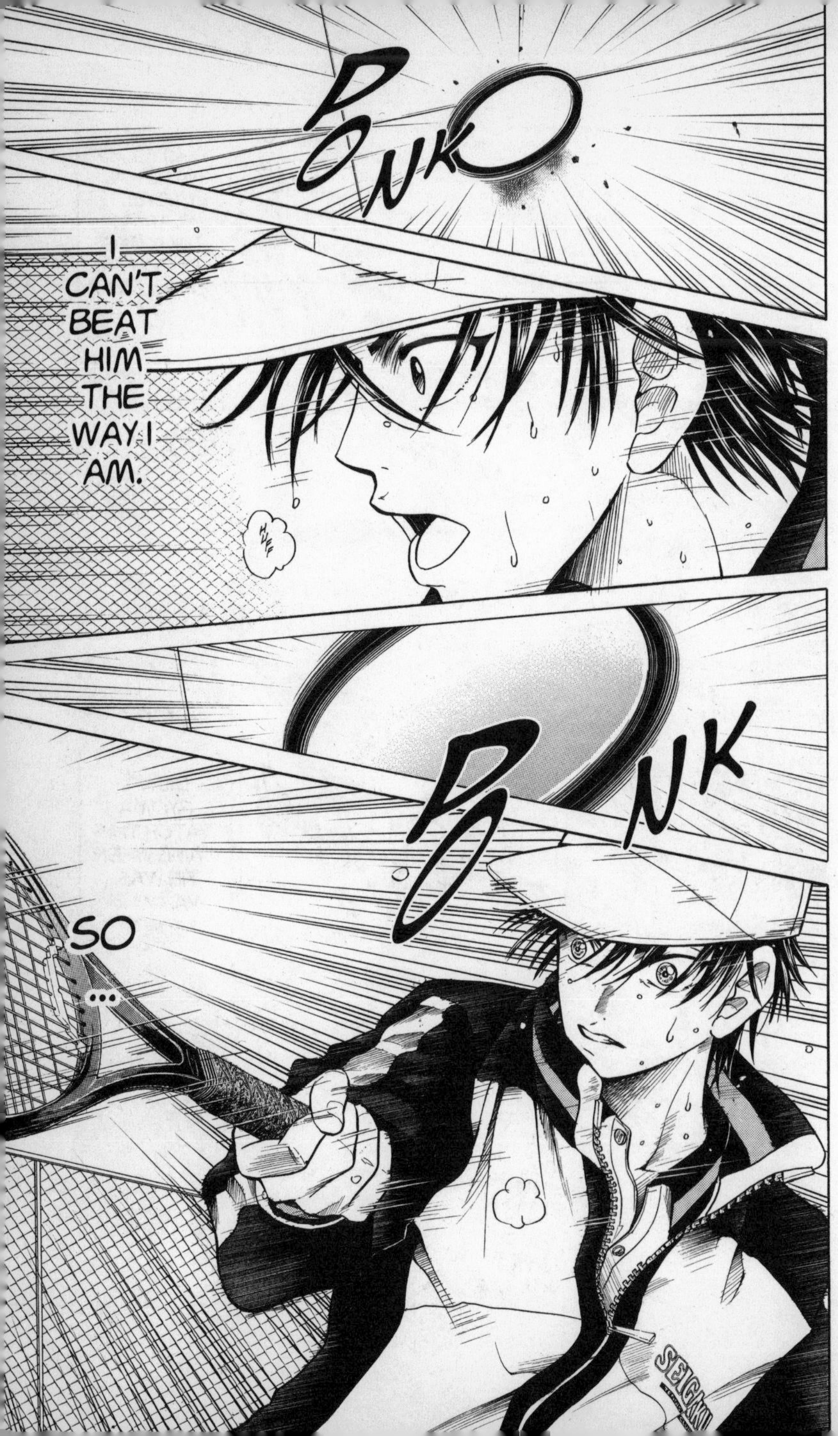
DONK
I CAN'T BEAT HIM THE WAY I AM.
HUFF
BONK
SO...

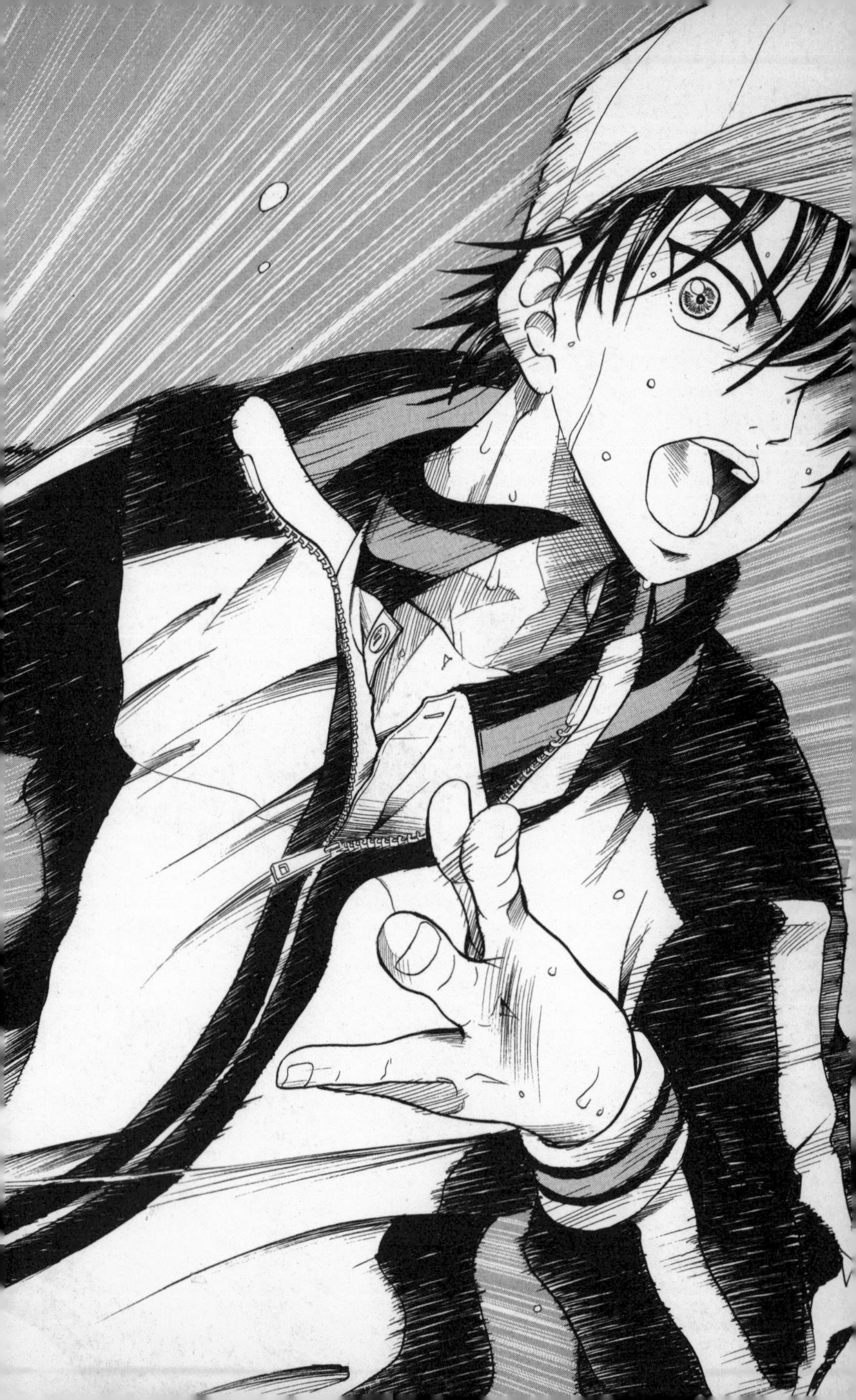

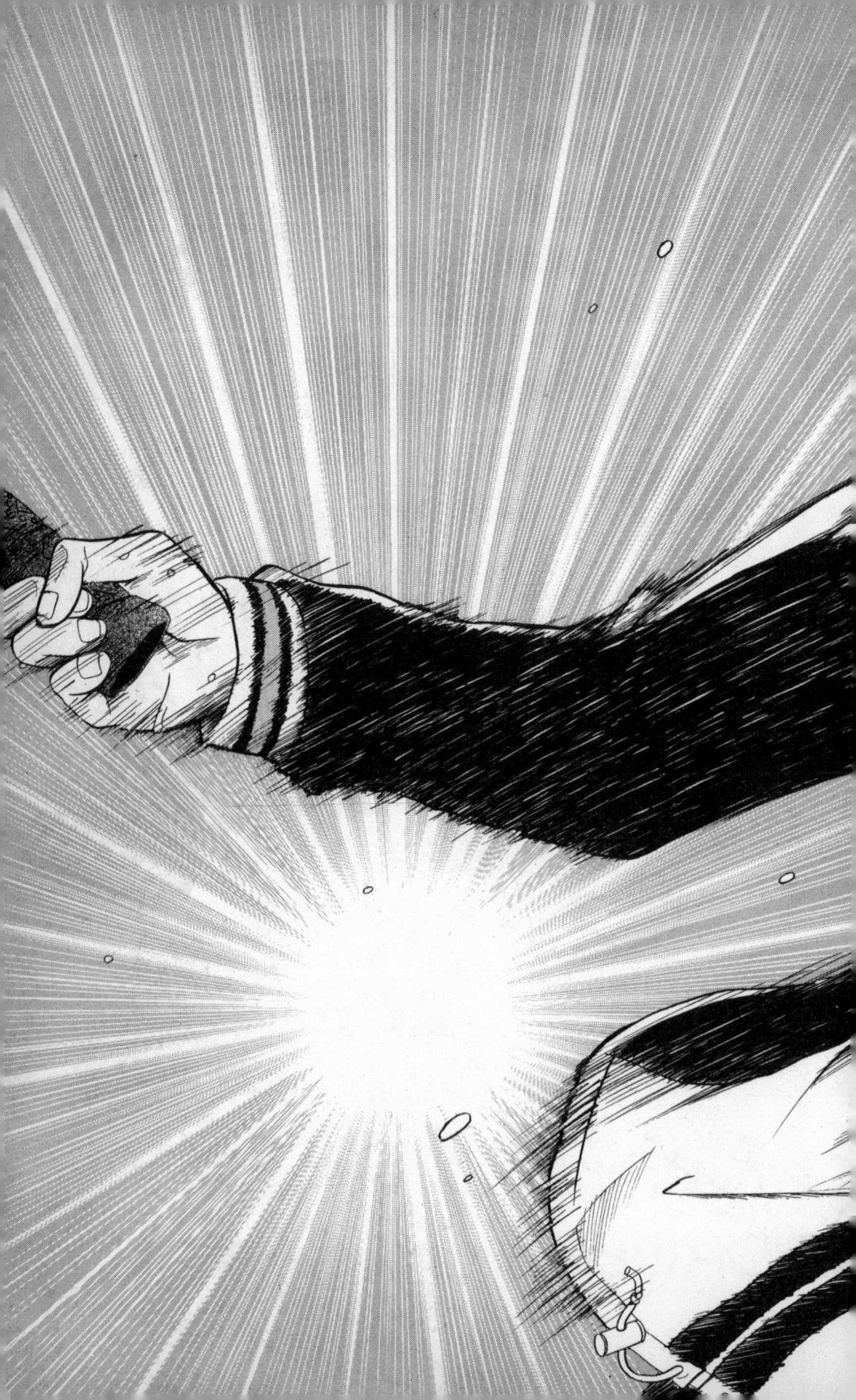

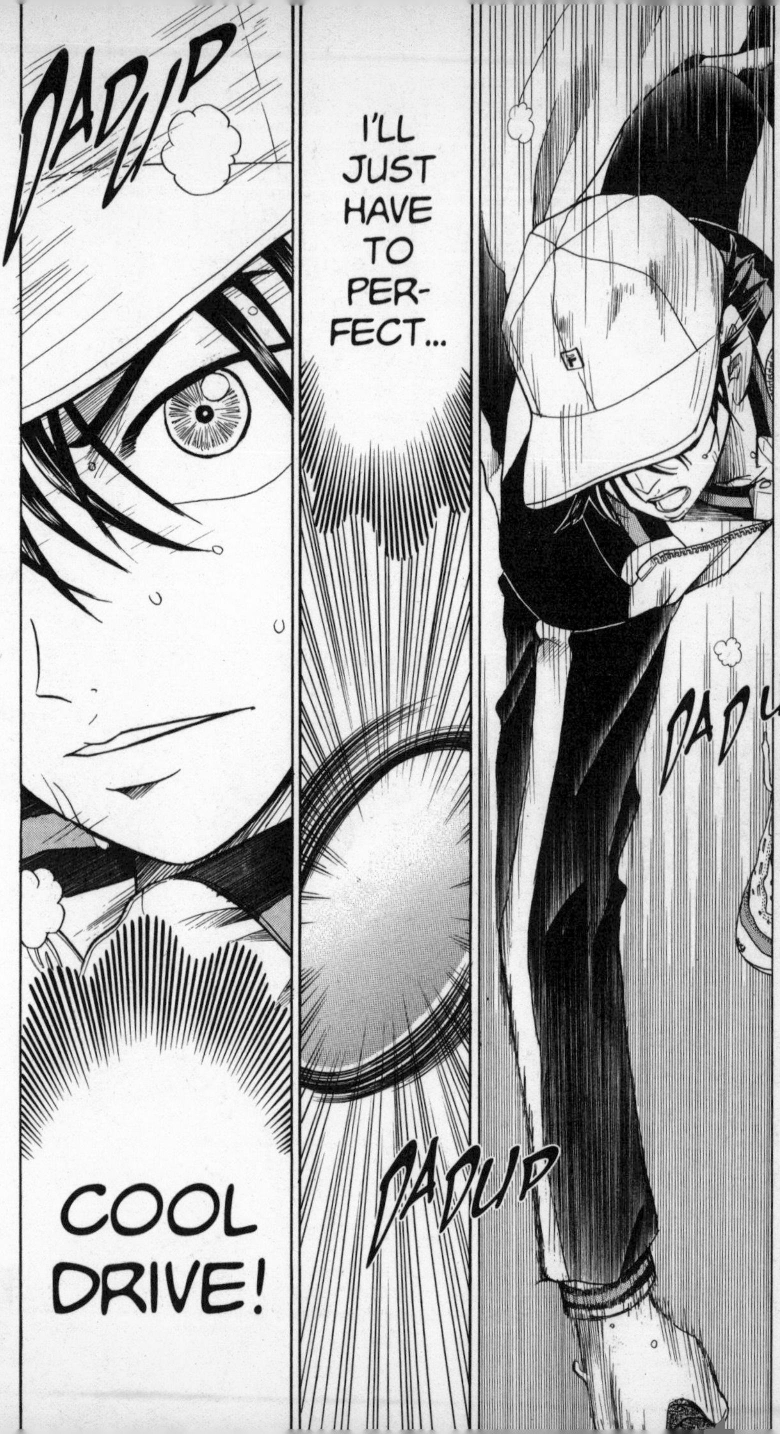
DADUP
I'LL JUST HAVE TO PERFECT...
DADUP
DADUP
COOL DRIVE!

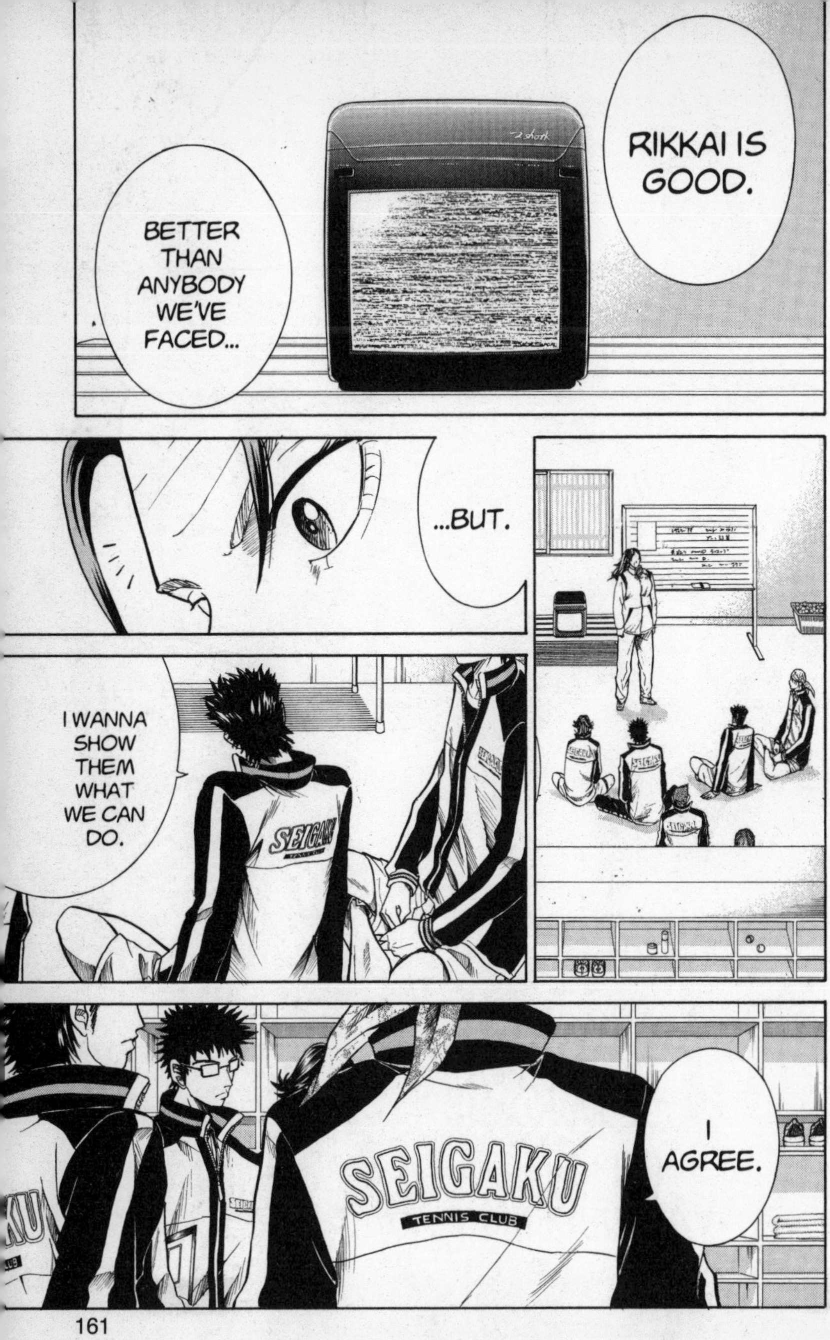
RIKKAI IS GOOD.
BETTER THAN ANYBODY WE'VE FACED...
...BUT.
I WANNA SHOW THEM WHAT WE CAN DO.
I AGREE.
SEIGAKU
TENNIS CLUB

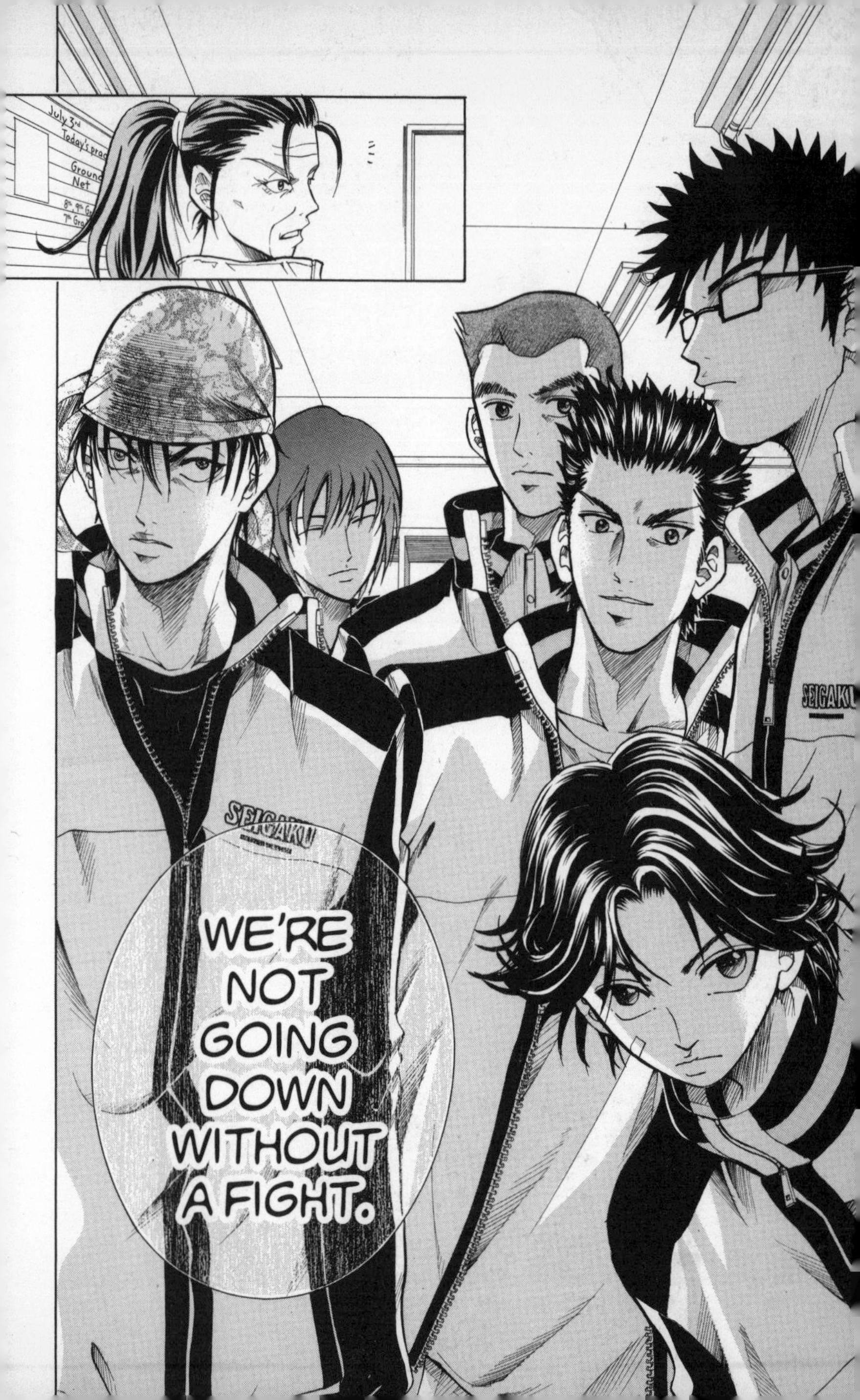
July 3rd
WE'RE NOT GOING DOWN WITHOUT A FIGHT.

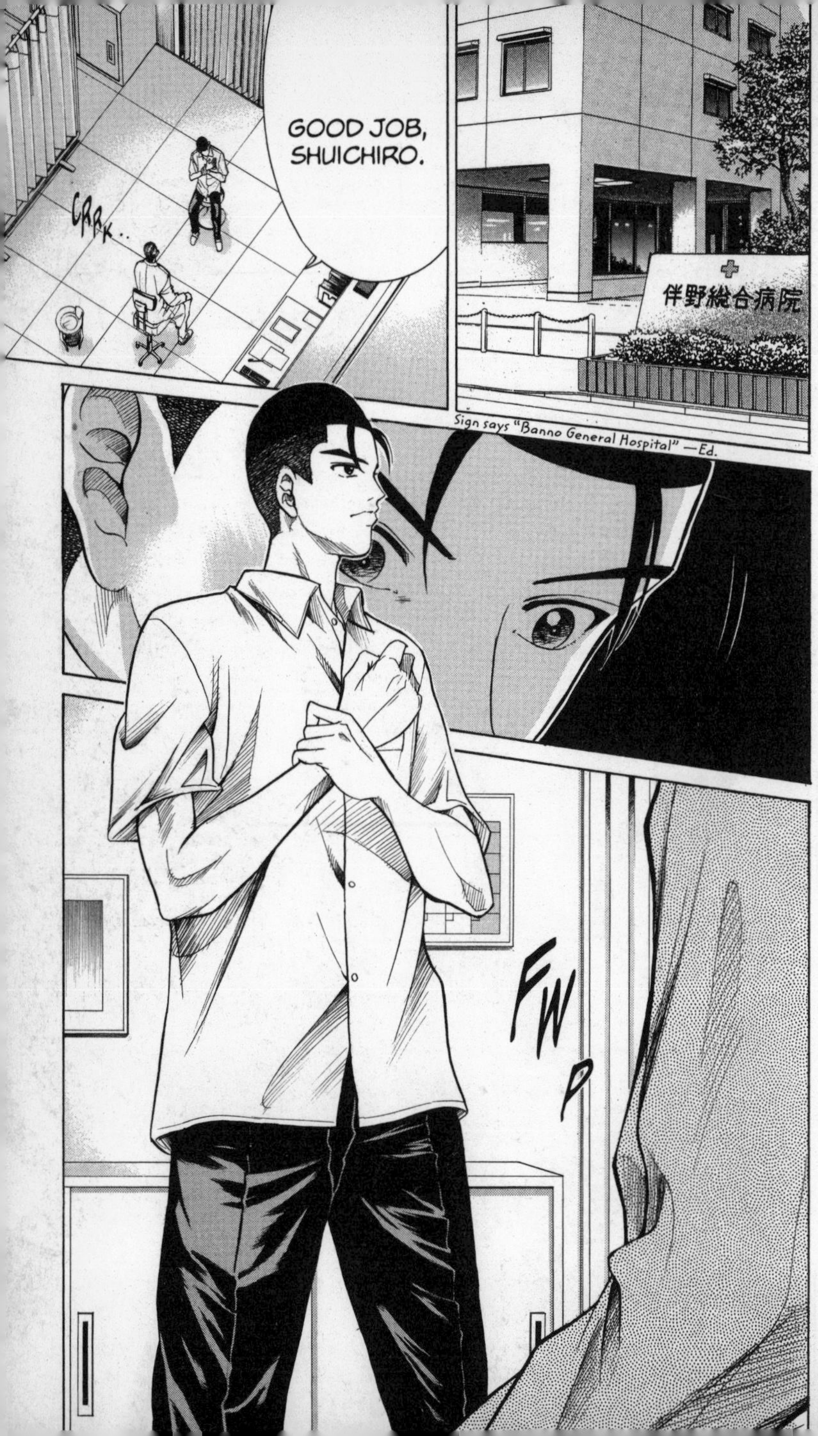
GOOD JOB, SHUICHIRO.
CRRK...
伴野総合病院
FWP
Sign says "Banno General Hospital" —Ed.

テニスの王子様
THE PRINCE OF TENNIS
™

Thank you for reading *The Prince of Tennis* volume 21.

The second fan-book, volume 20.5, is finally out!!
So what'd you think?

Anyways, I had a real hectic schedule working on both this volume and the opening color pages. Starting in the spring, I had to tighten up my schedule to fit in a one-shot story for the four-year anniversary and another one for the summer. I've come this far without a single day off. I turned down most offers for work on anything besides the magazine this year to concentrate on the games against Rokkaku and Rikkai while writing Nanjiro's story, and to release an all-new illustration collection. The illustration collection turned into the fan-book, which I mentioned during March's tennis festival. I plan to take a nice, peaceful break from the end of this year to next year. To those waiting for the illustration collection, I'm sorry! I promise to release one next year. I think you guys will all be surprised by it, so stay with me.

And so, as usual... Keep supporting *The Prince of Tennis* and Ryoma.

T. Konomi
2003.10.28

Send fan letters to: Takeshi Konomi c/o VIZ Media LLC, P.O. Box 77010, San Francisco, CA 94107

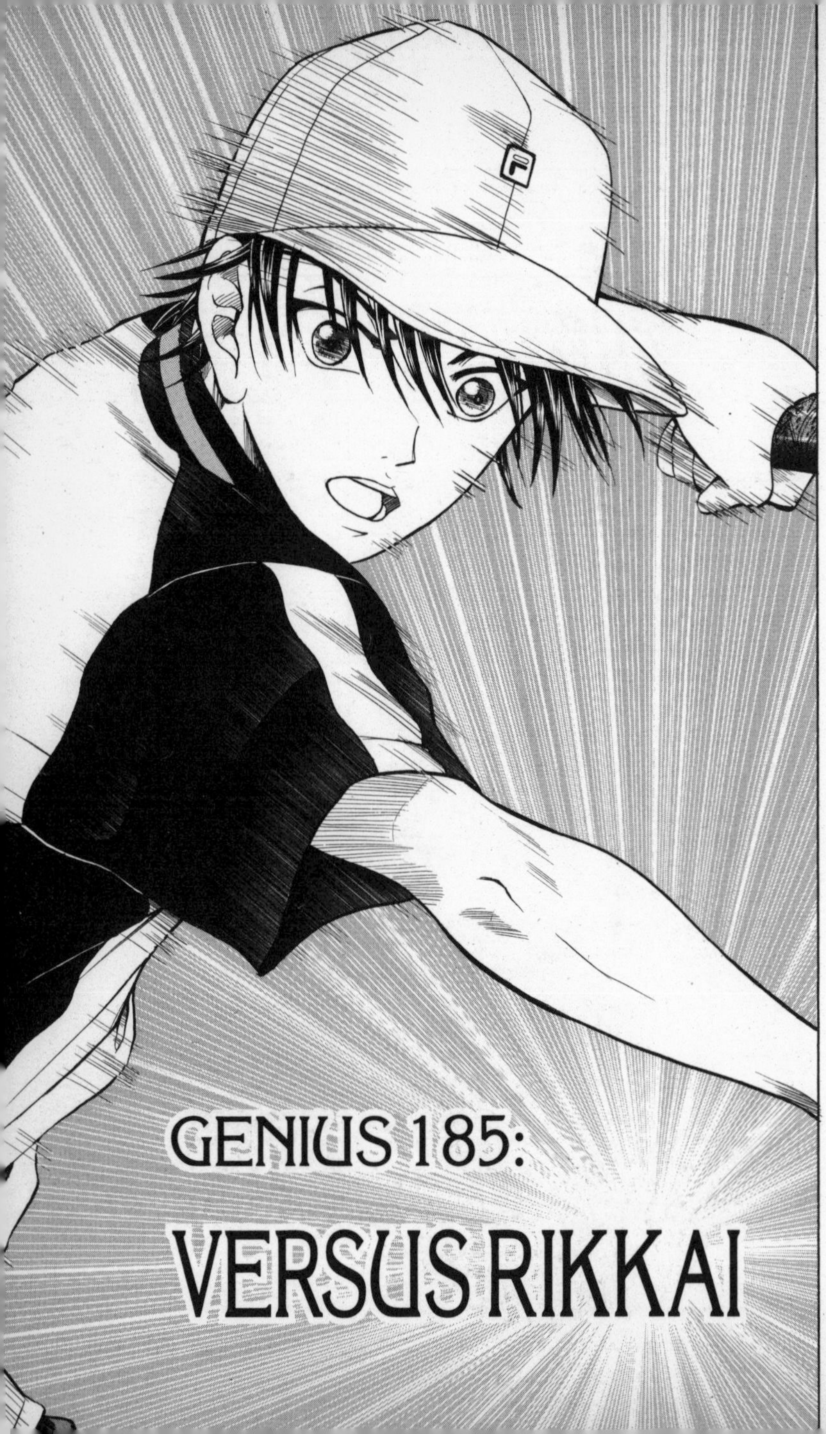
GENIUS 185:
VERSUS RIKKAI

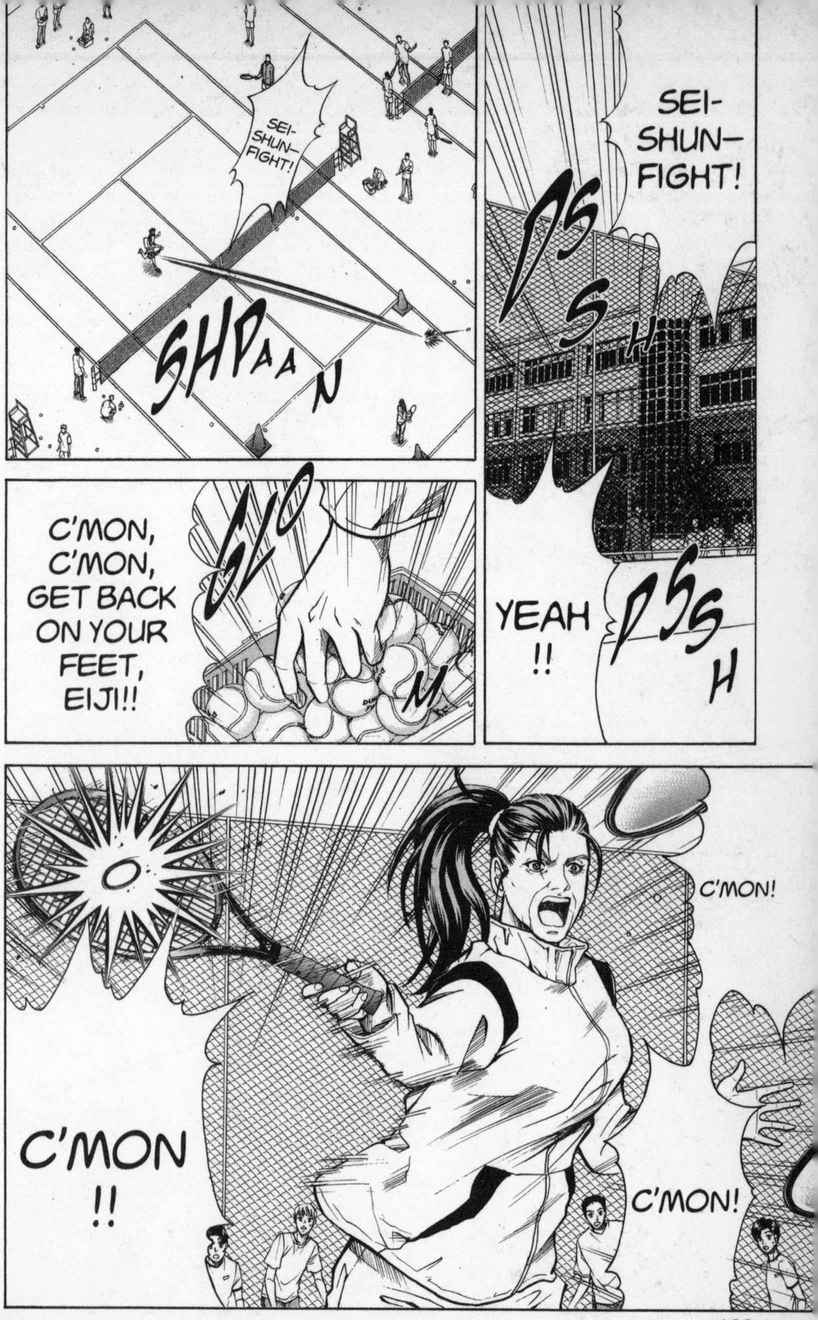
SEI-SHUN-FIGHT!
DSSH
YEAH!!
DSSH
SEI-SHUN-FIGHT!
SHPAAN
C'MON, C'MON, GET BACK ON YOUR FEET, EIJI!!
C'MON!
C'MON!!
C'MON!

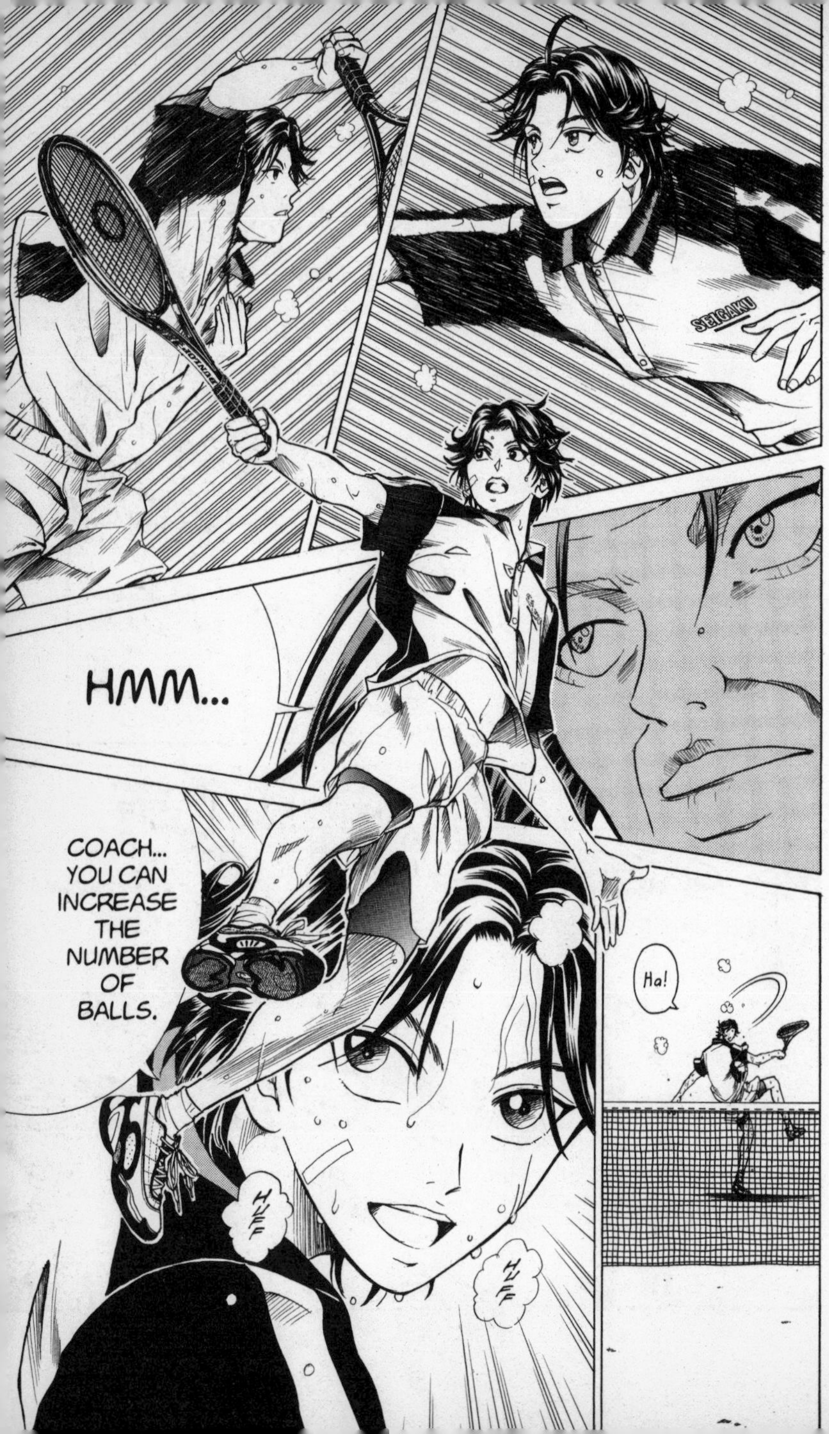
HMM...
COACH... YOU CAN INCREASE THE NUMBER OF BALLS.
Ha!
HUFF
HUFF
SEIGAKU

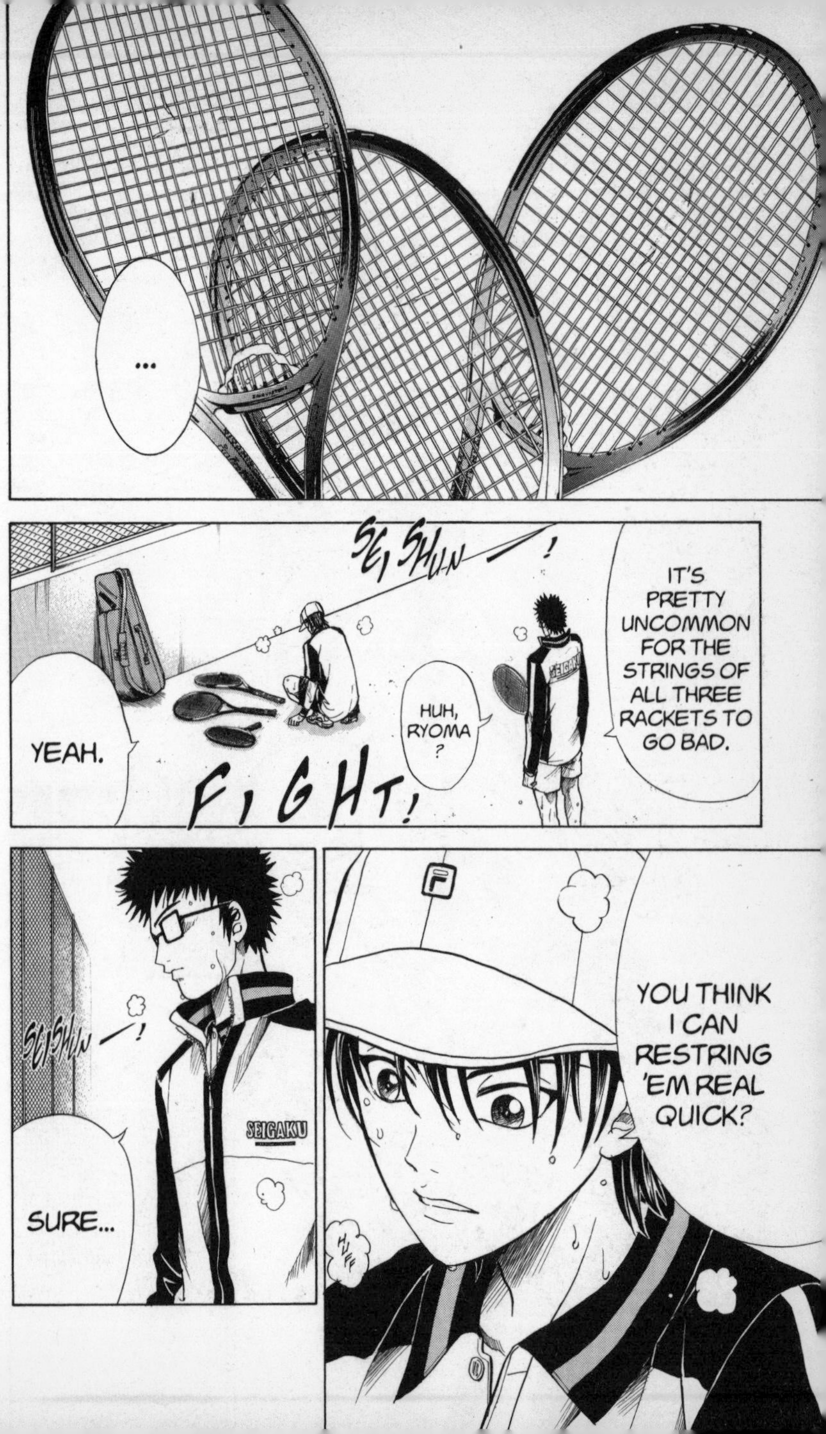
...
SEI SHUN—!
IT'S PRETTY UNCOMMON FOR THE STRINGS OF ALL THREE RACKETS TO GO BAD.
HUH, RYOMA?
YEAH.
FIGHT!
YOU THINK I CAN RESTRING 'EM REAL QUICK?
HUFF
SEISHUN—!
SURE...

READ THIS WAY

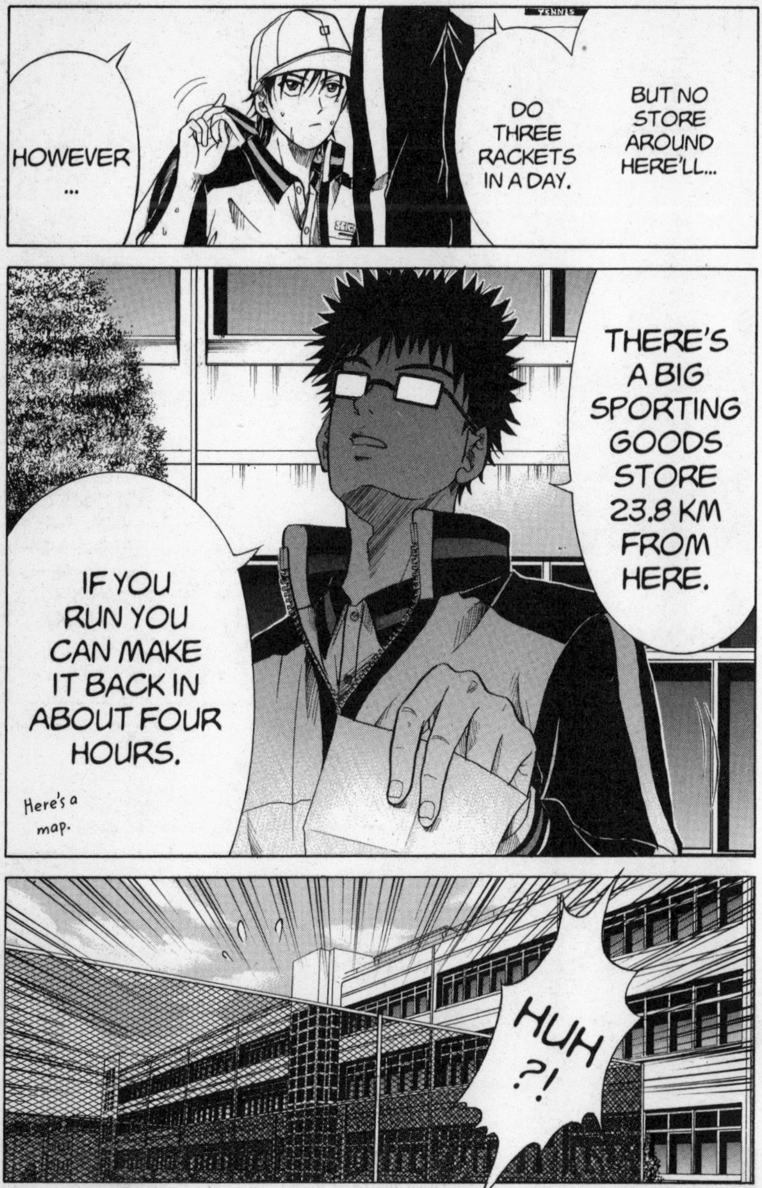

BUT NO STORE AROUND HERE'LL...
DO THREE RACKETS IN A DAY.
HOWEVER ...
THERE'S A BIG SPORTING GOODS STORE 23.8 KM FROM HERE.
IF YOU RUN YOU CAN MAKE IT BACK IN ABOUT FOUR HOURS.
Here's a map.
HUH ?!

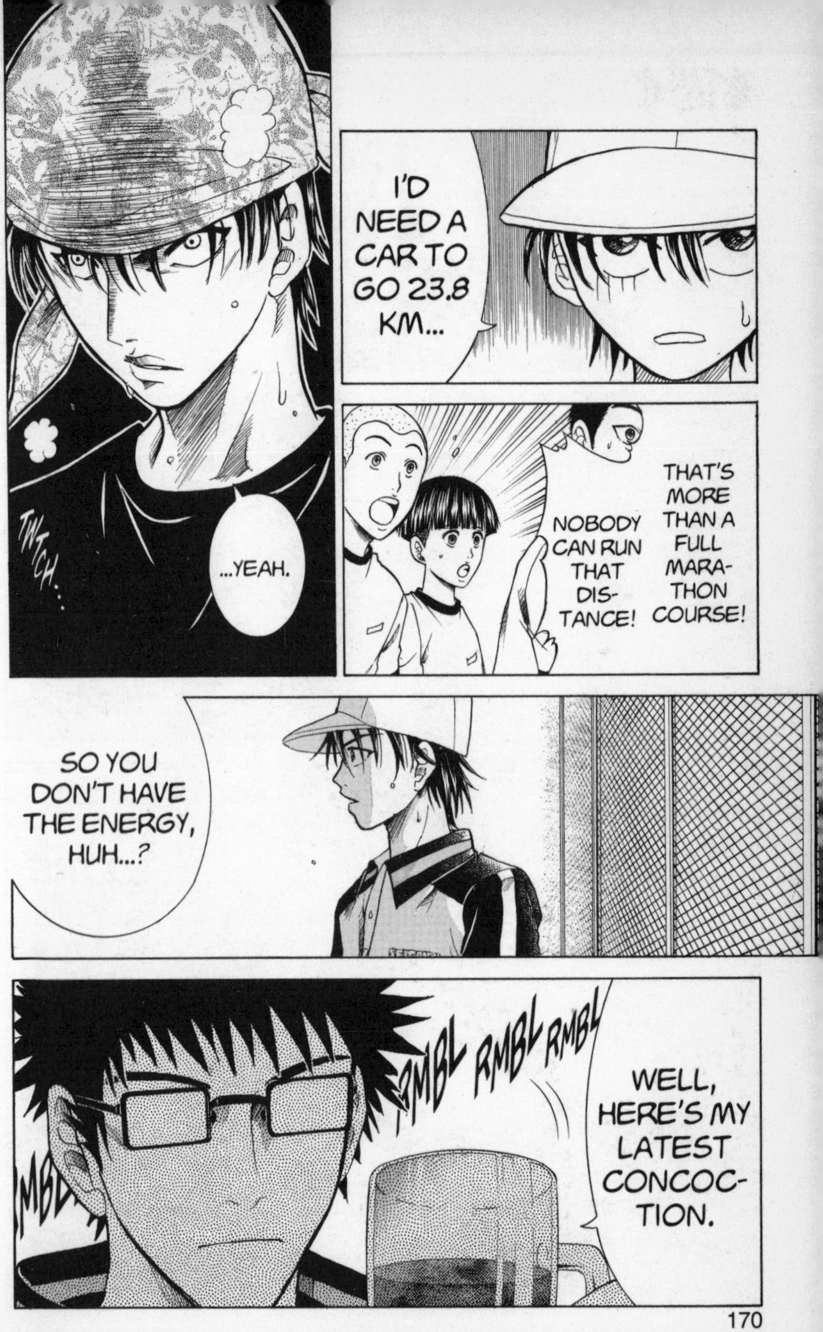
I'D NEED A CAR TO GO 23.8 KM...
THAT'S MORE THAN A FULL MARATHON COURSE!
NOBODY CAN RUN THAT DISTANCE!
TWITCH...
...YEAH.
SO YOU DON'T HAVE THE ENERGY, HUH...?
RMBL RMBL RMBL
RMBL
WELL, HERE'S MY LATEST CONCOCTION.

READ THIS WAY

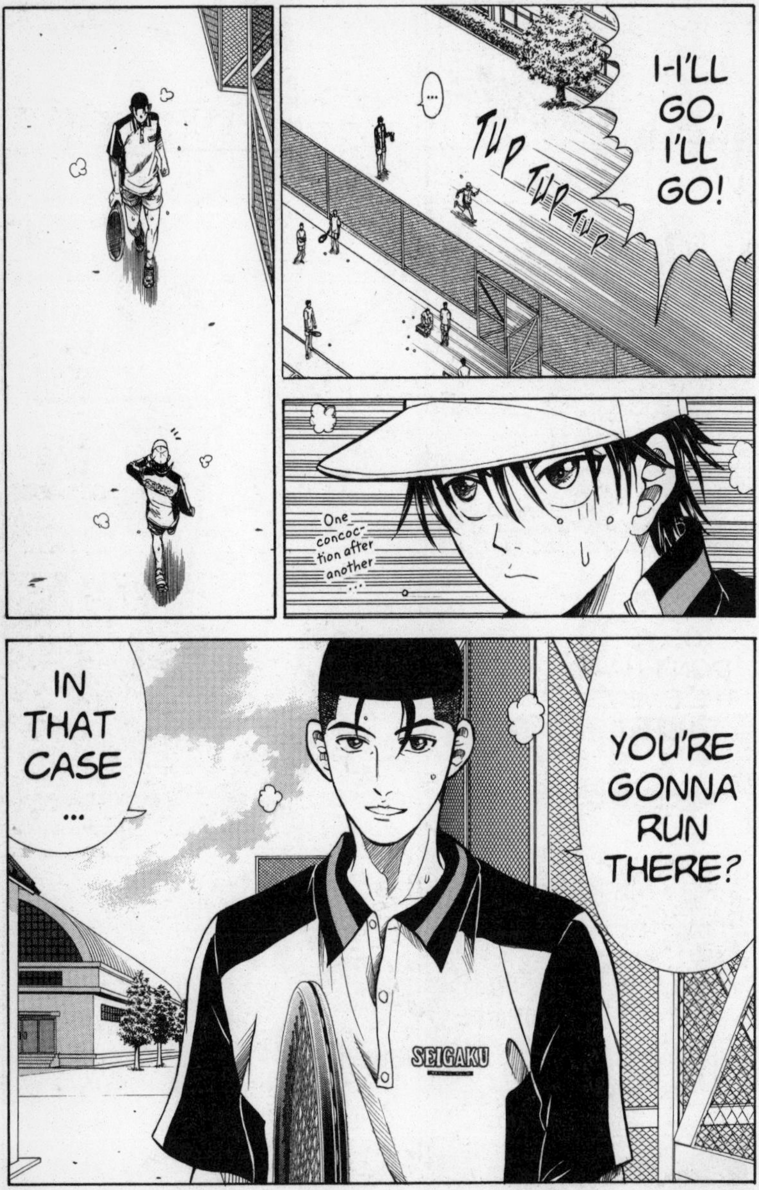
...
TUP TUP TUP TUP
I-I'LL GO, I'LL GO!
One concoction after another...
YOU'RE GONNA RUN THERE?
IN THAT CASE ...
SEIGAKU

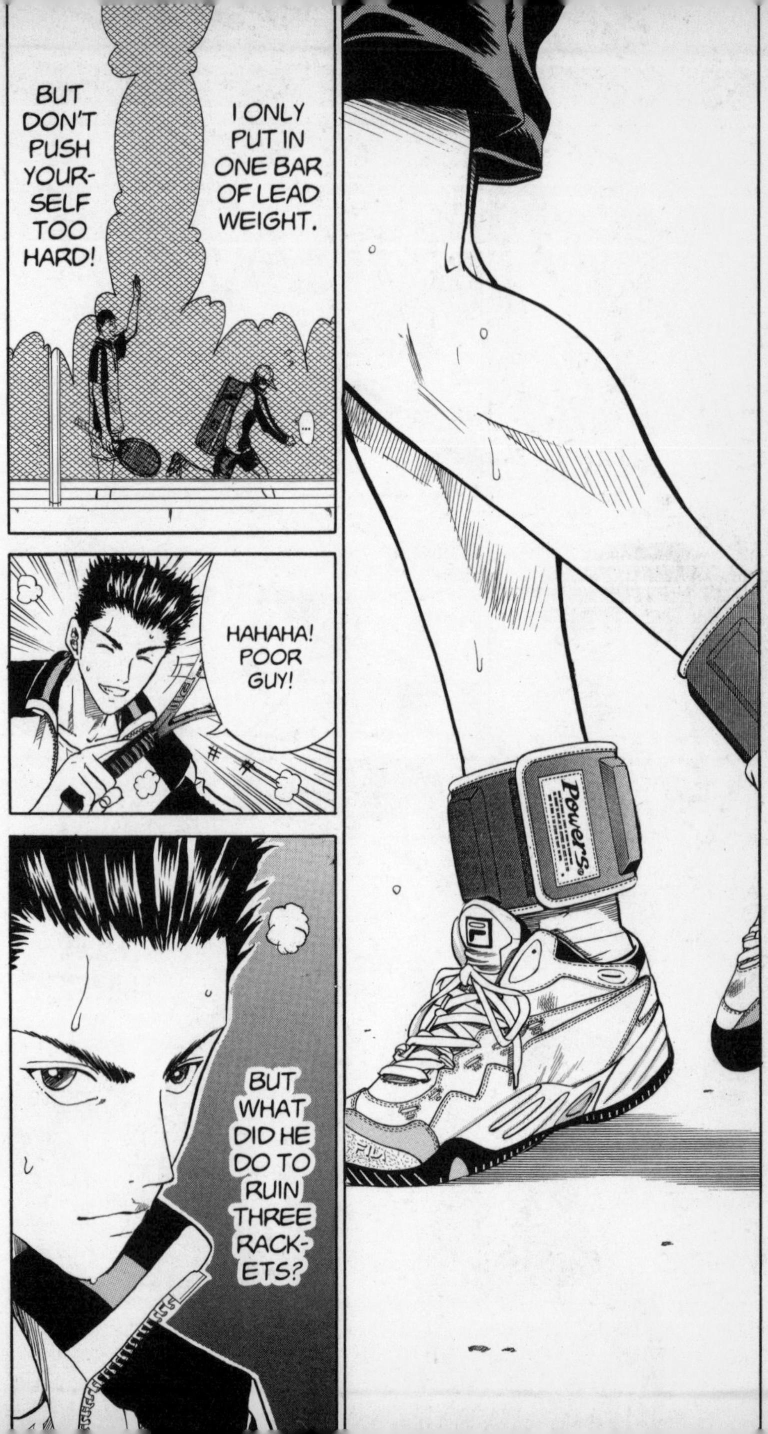
I ONLY PUT IN ONE BAR OF LEAD WEIGHT.
BUT DON'T PUSH YOUR-SELF TOO HARD!
...
HAHAHA! POOR GUY!
BUT WHAT DID HE DO TO RUIN THREE RACK-ETS?

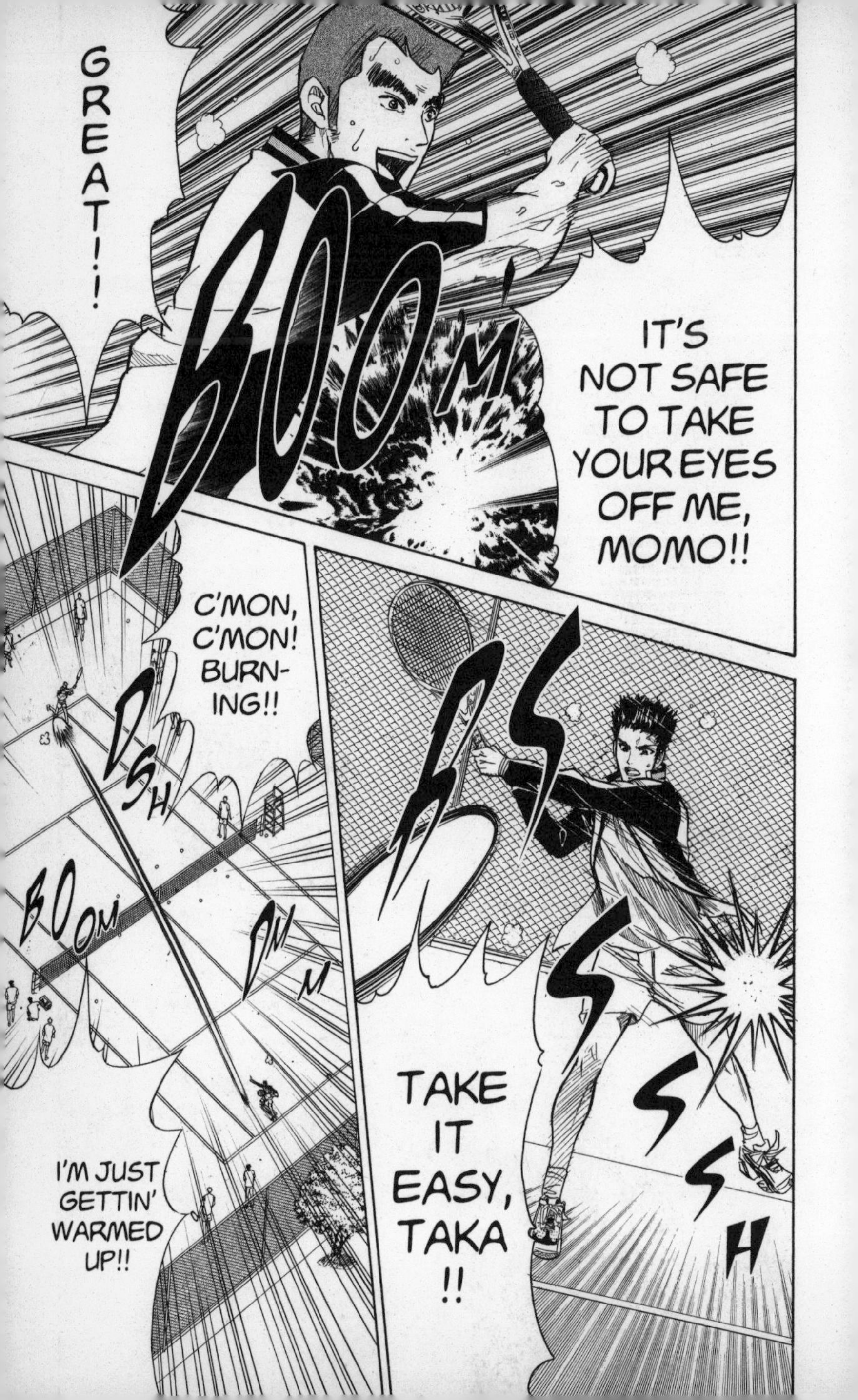
GREAT!!!
BOOM
IT'S NOT SAFE TO TAKE YOUR EYES OFF ME, MOMO!!
C'MON, C'MON! BURN-ING!!
DSH
BOOM
DMM
FSSSSH
TAKE IT EASY, TAKA !!
I'M JUST GETTIN' WARMED UP!!

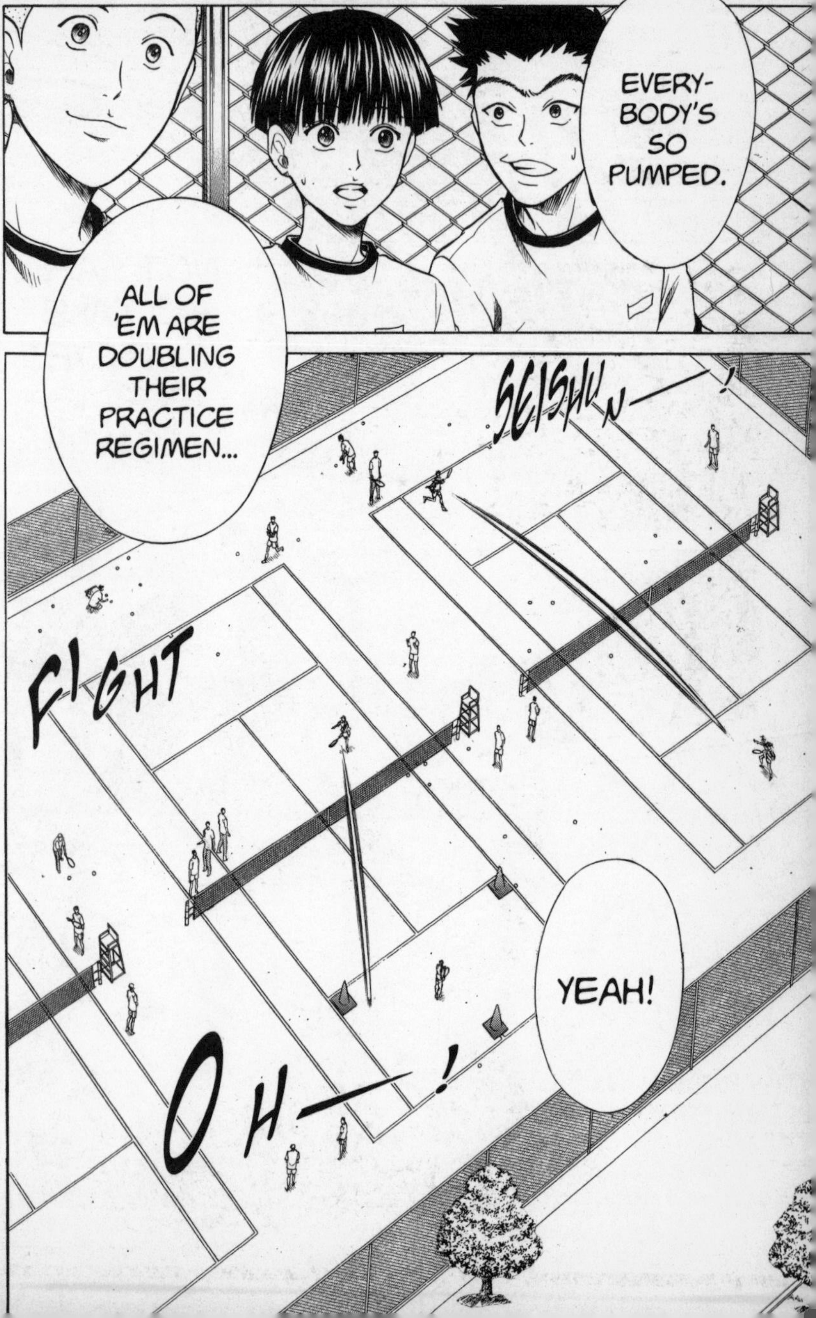
EVERY-BODY'S SO PUMPED.
ALL OF 'EM ARE DOUBLING THEIR PRACTICE REGIMEN...
SEISHUN—!
FIGHT
OH—!
YEAH!

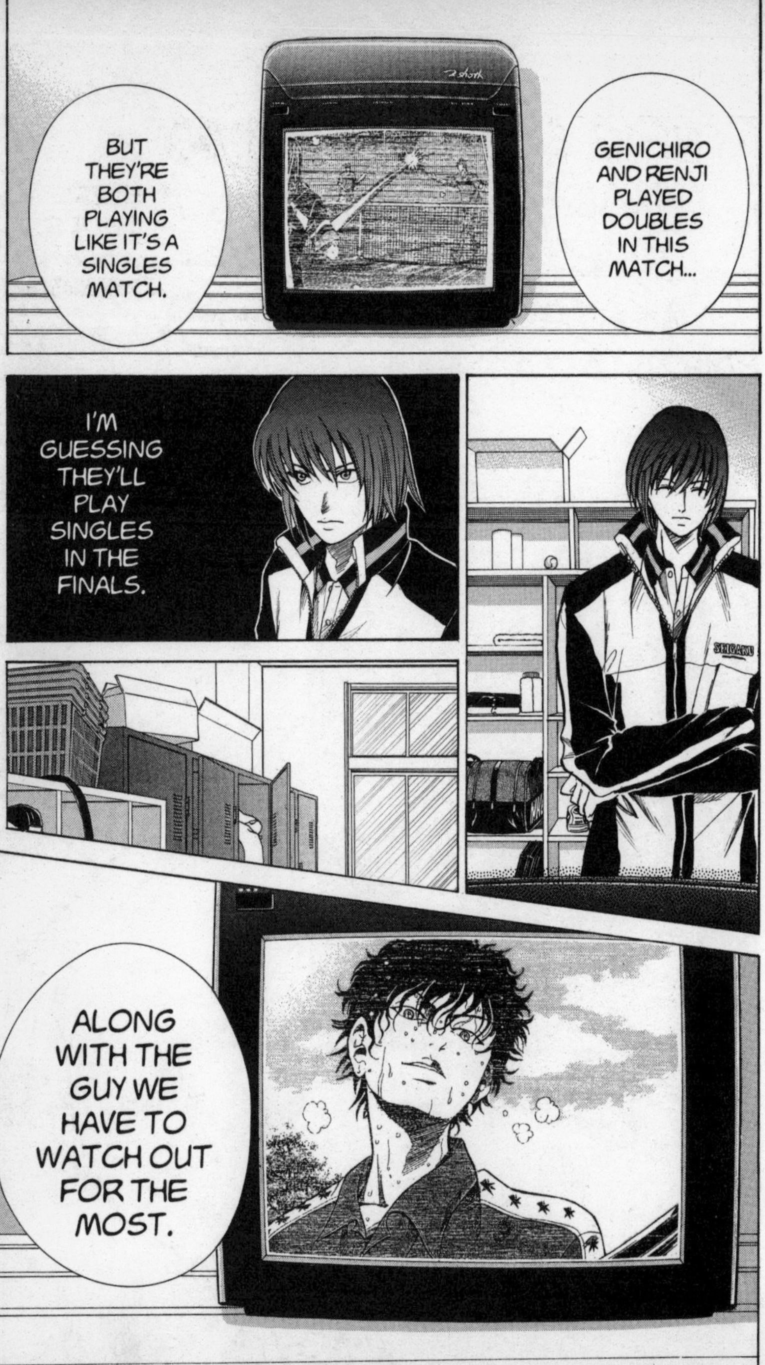
GENICHIRO AND RENJI PLAYED DOUBLES IN THIS MATCH...
BUT THEY'RE BOTH PLAYING LIKE IT'S A SINGLES MATCH.
I'M GUESSING THEY'LL PLAY SINGLES IN THE FINALS.
SEIGAKU
ALONG WITH THE GUY WE HAVE TO WATCH OUT FOR THE MOST.

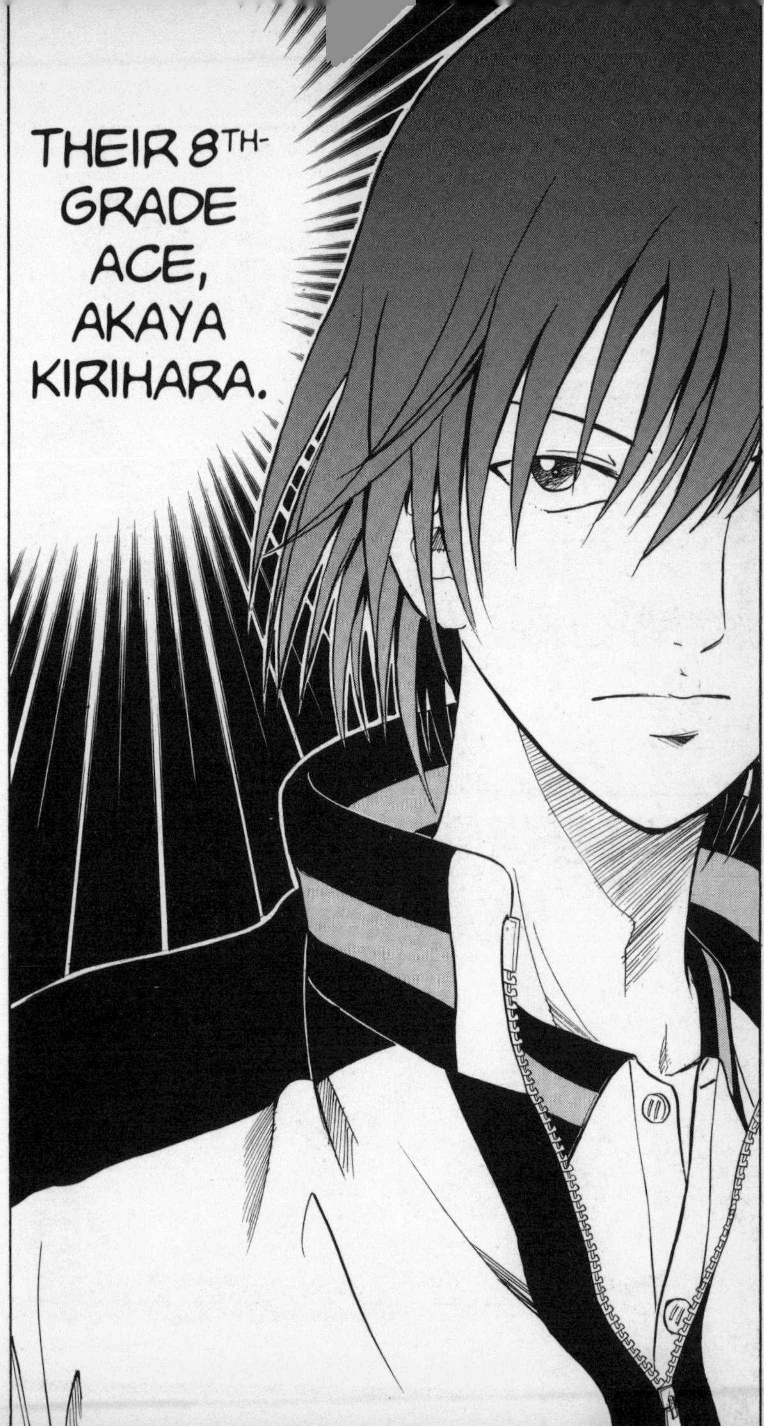
THEIR 8TH-GRADE ACE, AKAYA KIRIHARA.

READ THIS WAY

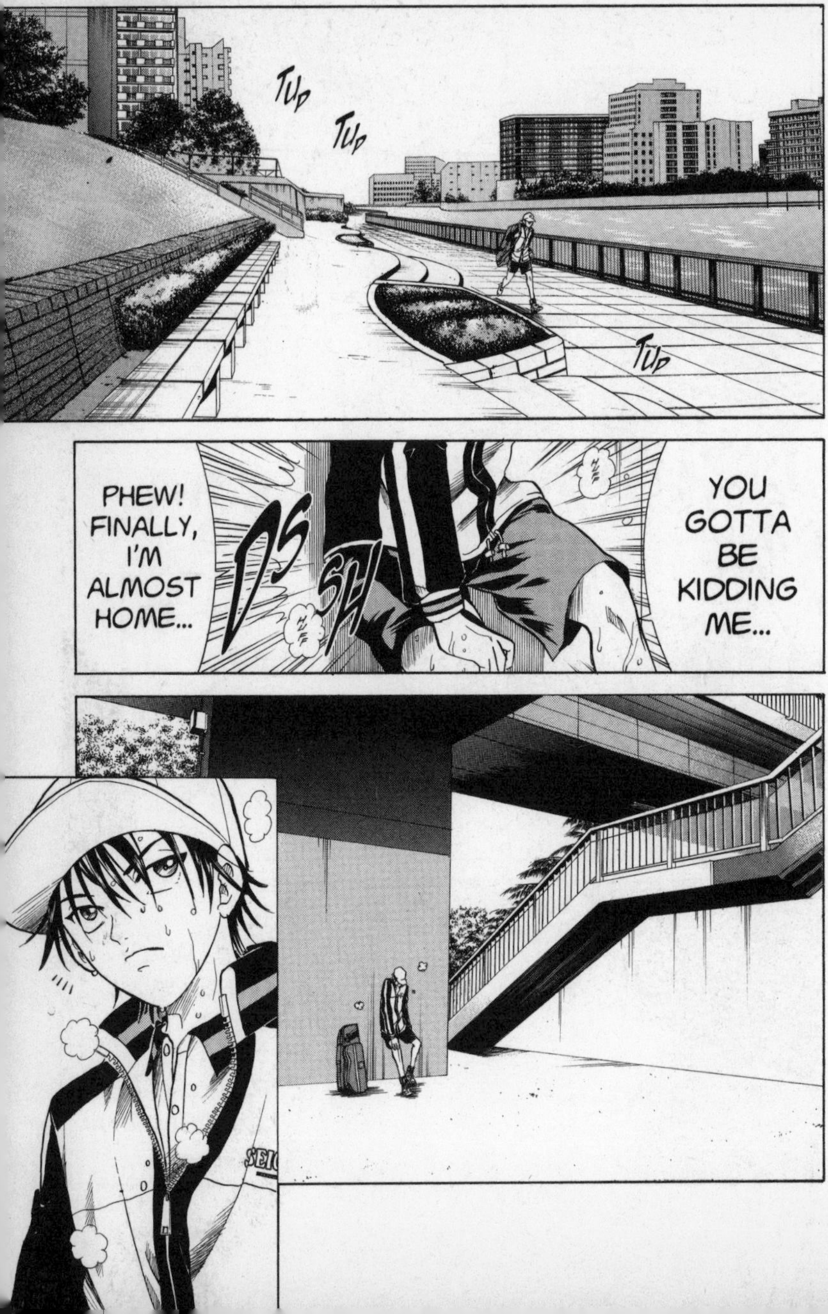
TUP
TUP
TUP
YOU GOTTA BE KIDDING ME...
DSSH
PHEW! FINALLY, I'M ALMOST HOME...
SEIG

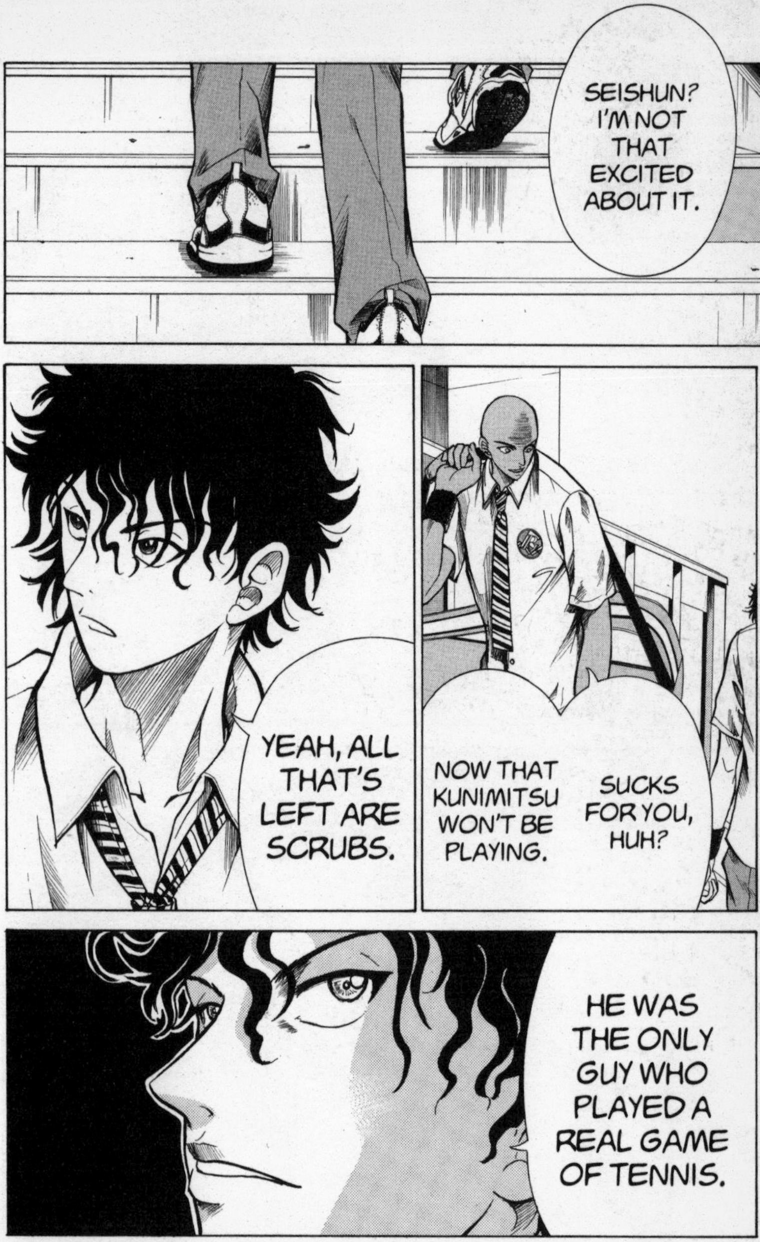
SEISHUN? I'M NOT THAT EXCITED ABOUT IT.
SUCKS FOR YOU, HUH?
NOW THAT KUNIMITSU WON'T BE PLAYING.
YEAH, ALL THAT'S LEFT ARE SCRUBS.
HE WAS THE ONLY GUY WHO PLAYED A REAL GAME OF TENNIS.

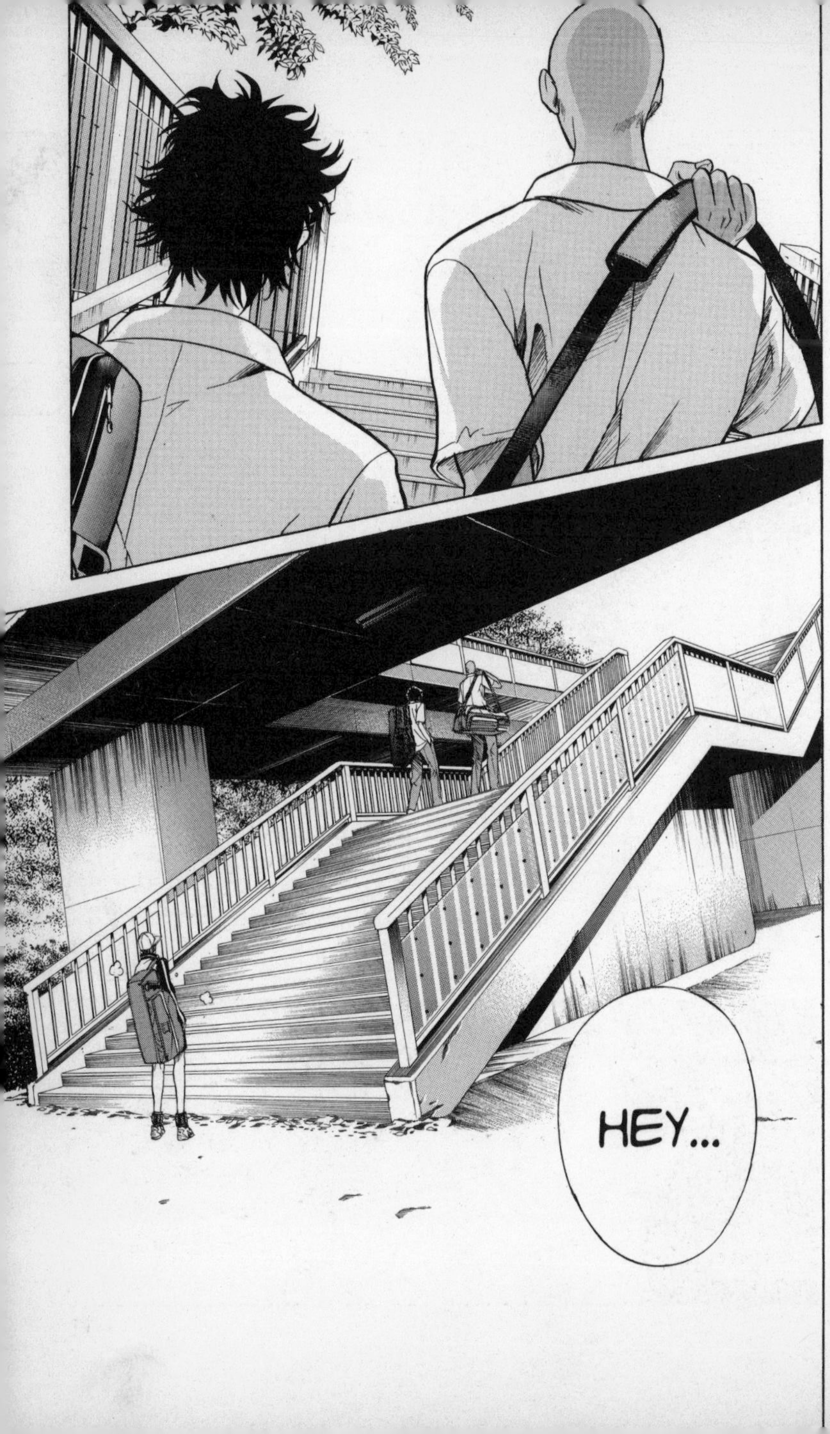
HEY...

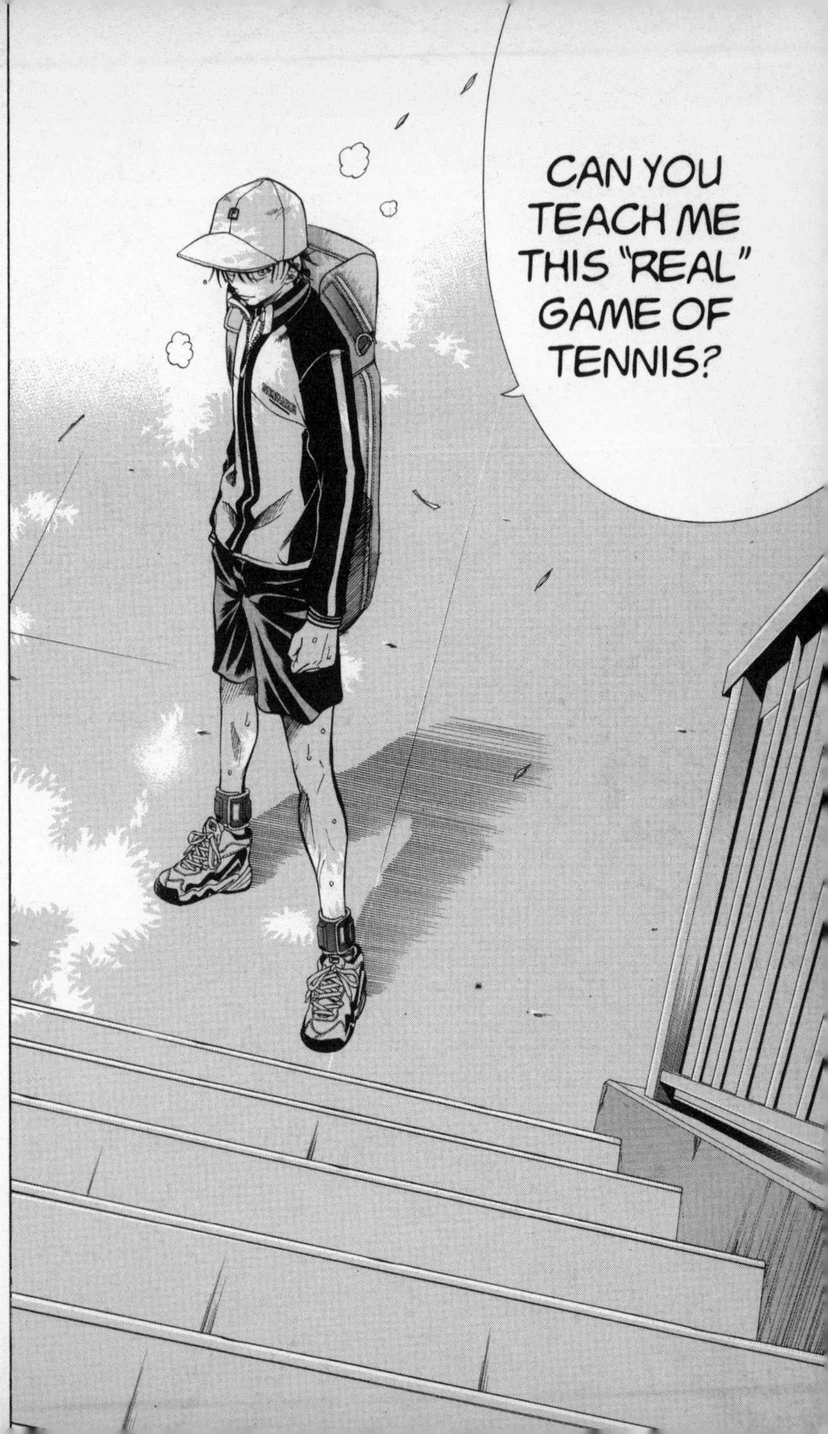
CAN YOU TEACH ME THIS "REAL" GAME OF TENNIS?

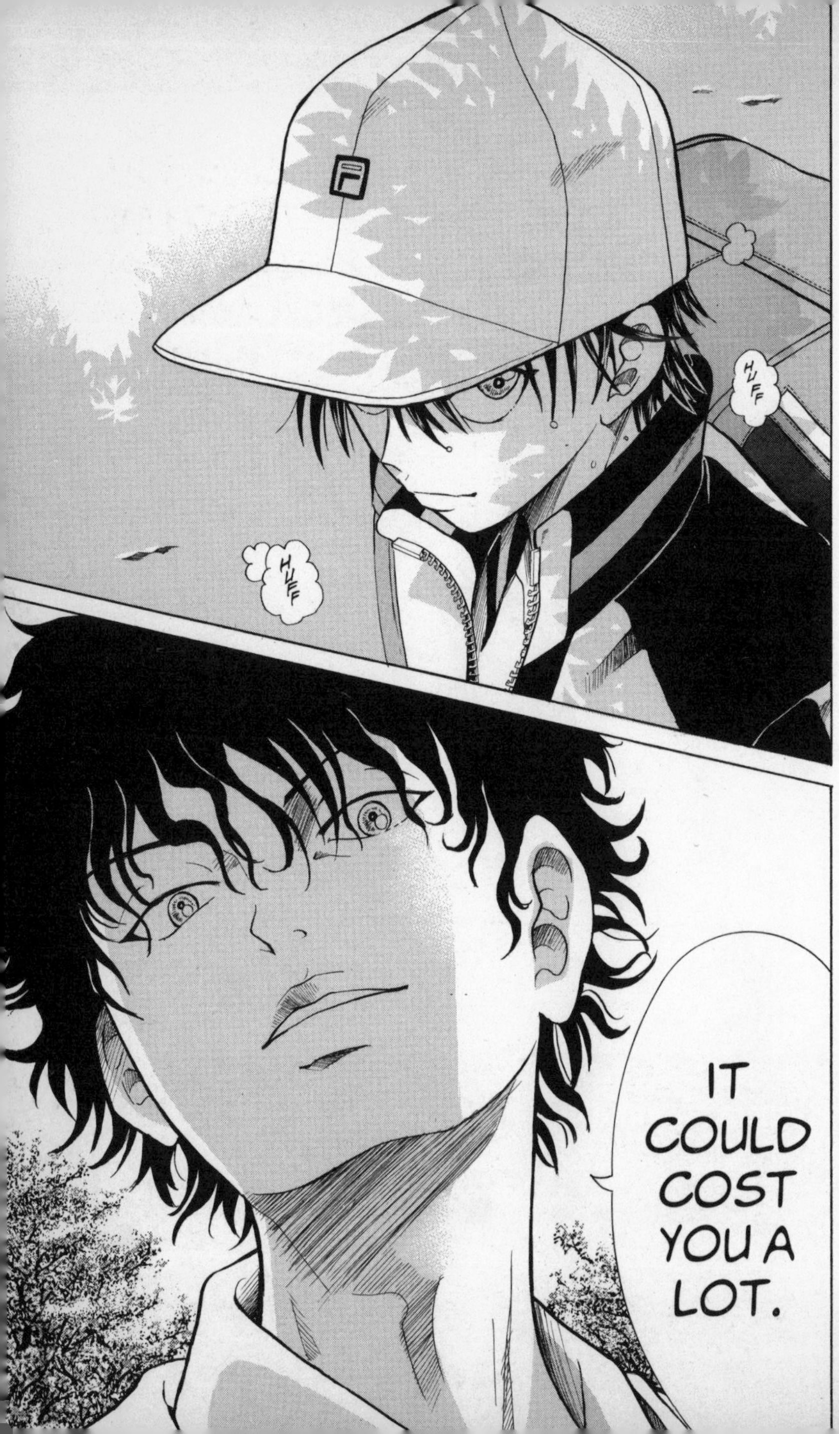
HUFF
HUFF
IT COULD COST YOU A LOT.

Ryoma, Awake!

As if taking on a totally new personality, Ryoma plays an unpredictable match, switching to his left hand and winning point after point. Where does his intensity come from? A bonus story about an entirely different player may shed some light on The Prince of Tennis's skills!

Available November 2007!

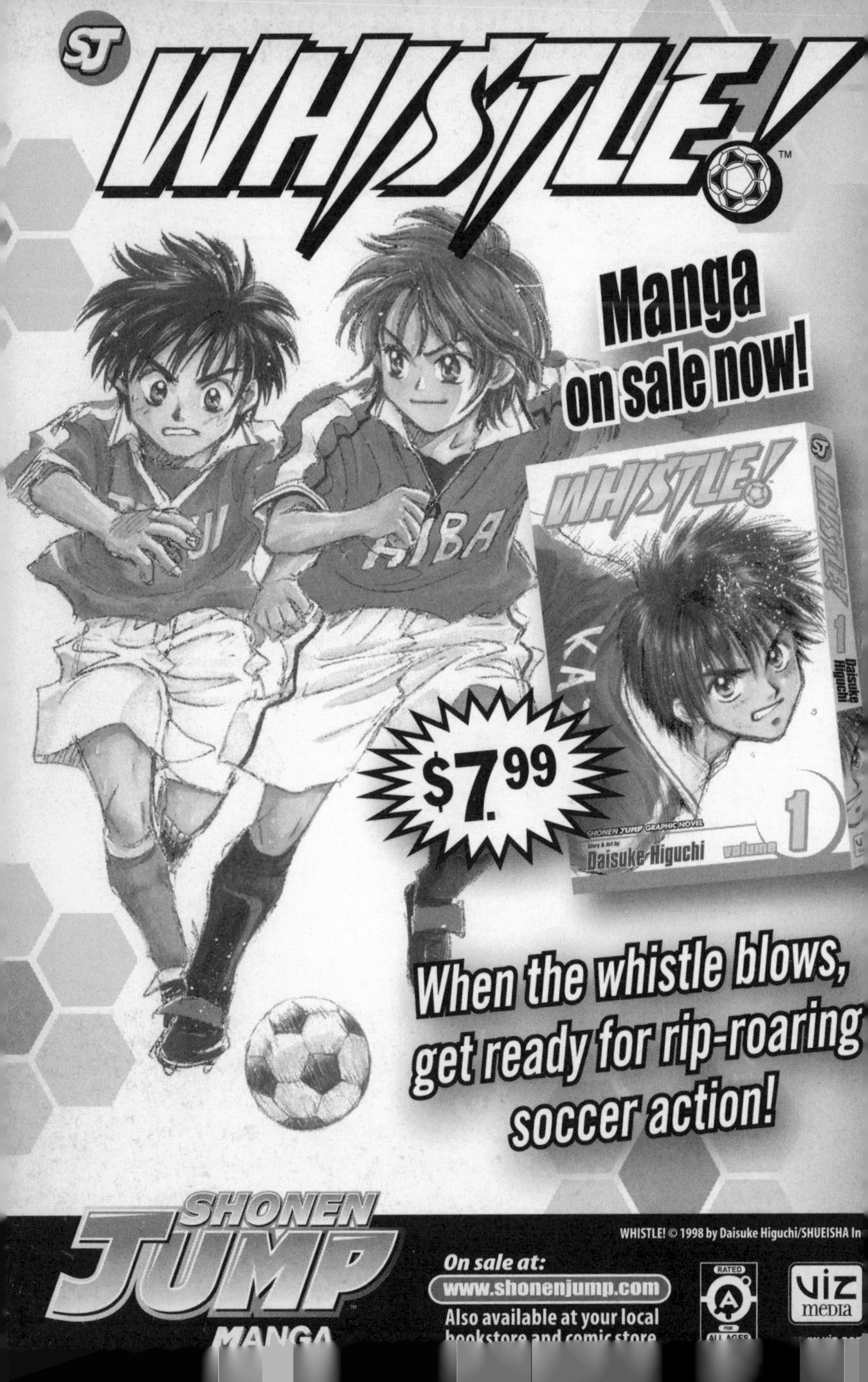
SJ
WHISTLE!
Manga
on sale now!
WHISTLE!
SHONEN JUMP GRAPHIC NOVEL
Daisuke Higuchi
volume 1
$7.99
When the whistle blows,
get ready for rip-roaring
soccer action!
SHONEN JUMP MANGA
WHISTLE! © 1998 by Daisuke Higuchi/SHUEISHA In
On sale at:
www.shonenjump.com
Also available at your local
bookstore and comic store
RATED A FOR ALL AGES
VIZ media

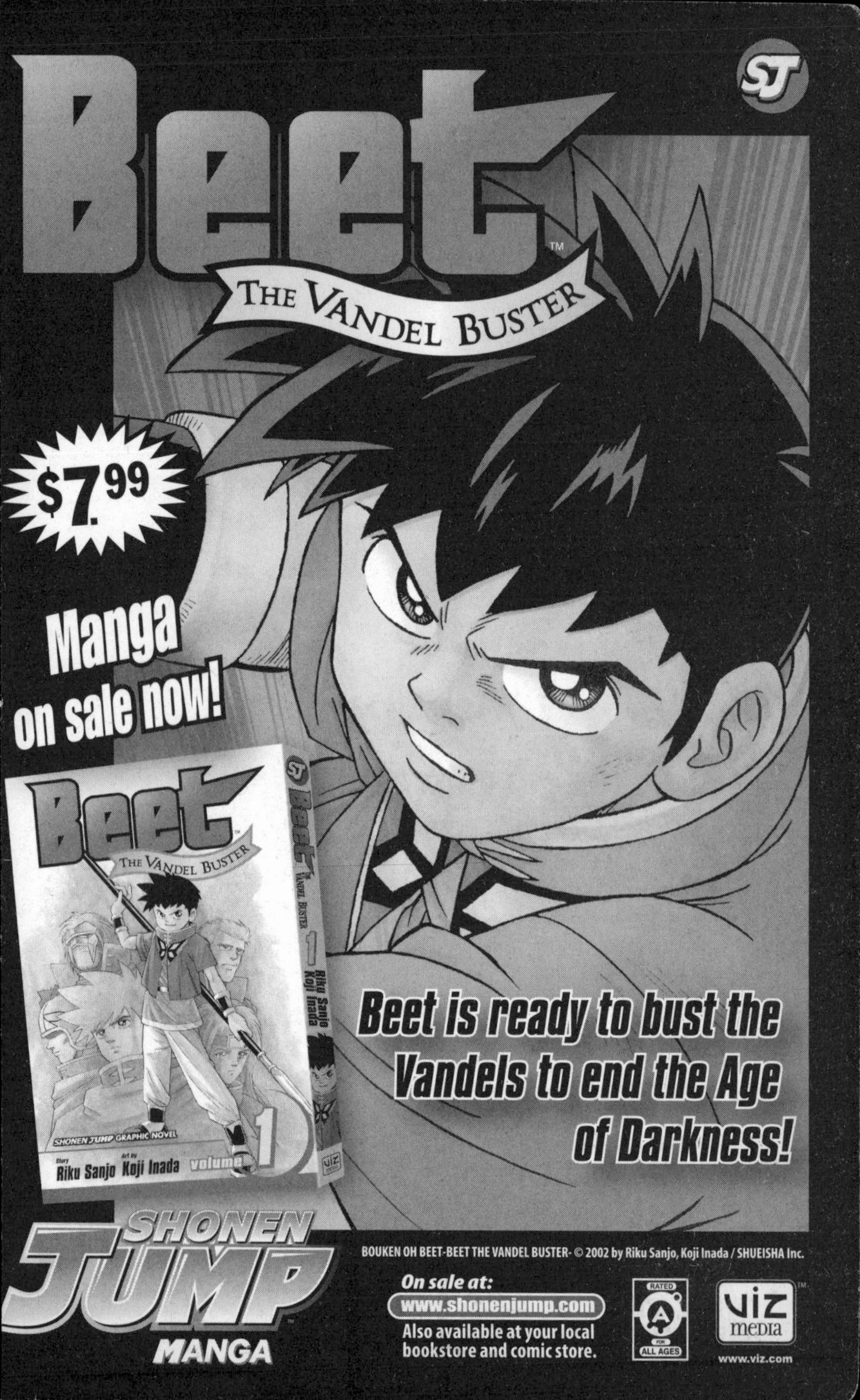
SJ
Beet™
THE VANDEL BUSTER
$7.99
Manga on sale now!
Beet™ THE VANDEL BUSTER
SHONEN JUMP GRAPHIC NOVEL
Story Riku Sanjo Art by Koji Inada volume 1
Beet is ready to bust the Vandels to end the Age of Darkness!
SHONEN JUMP MANGA
BOUKEN OH BEET-BEET THE VANDEL BUSTER- © 2002 by Riku Sanjo, Koji Inada / SHUEISHA Inc.
On sale at:
www.shonenjump.com
Also available at your local bookstore and comic store.
RATED A FOR ALL AGES
viz media
www.viz.com

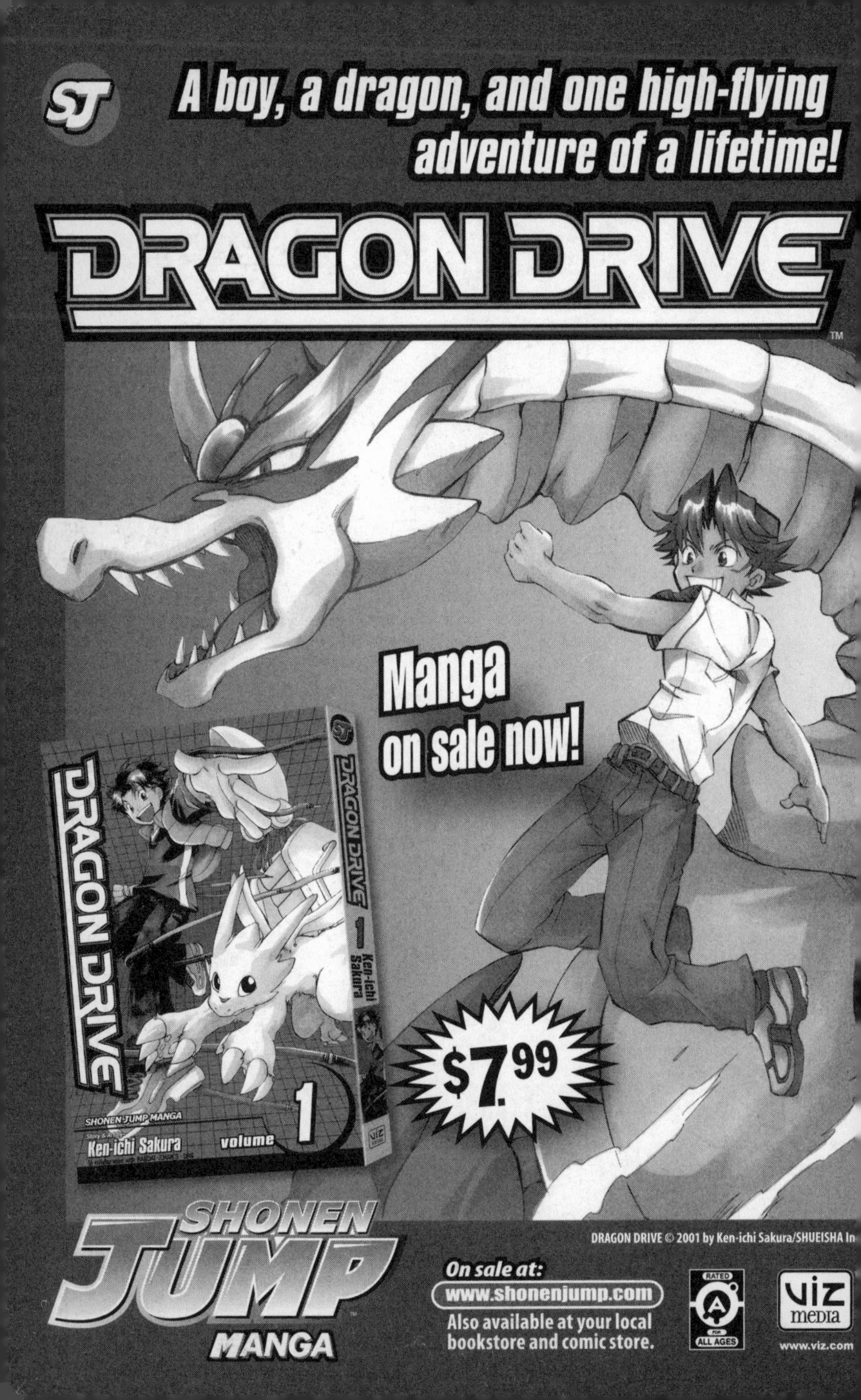
SJ
A boy, a dragon, and one high-flying adventure of a lifetime!
DRAGON DRIVE™
Manga on sale now!
DRAGON DRIVE
1 Ken-ichi Sakura
SHONEN JUMP MANGA
Ken-ichi Sakura
volume 1
$7.99
SHONEN JUMP MANGA
DRAGON DRIVE © 2001 by Ken-ichi Sakura/SHUEISHA In
On sale at:
www.shonenjump.com
Also available at your local bookstore and comic store.
RATED A FOR ALL AGES
viz media
www.viz.com

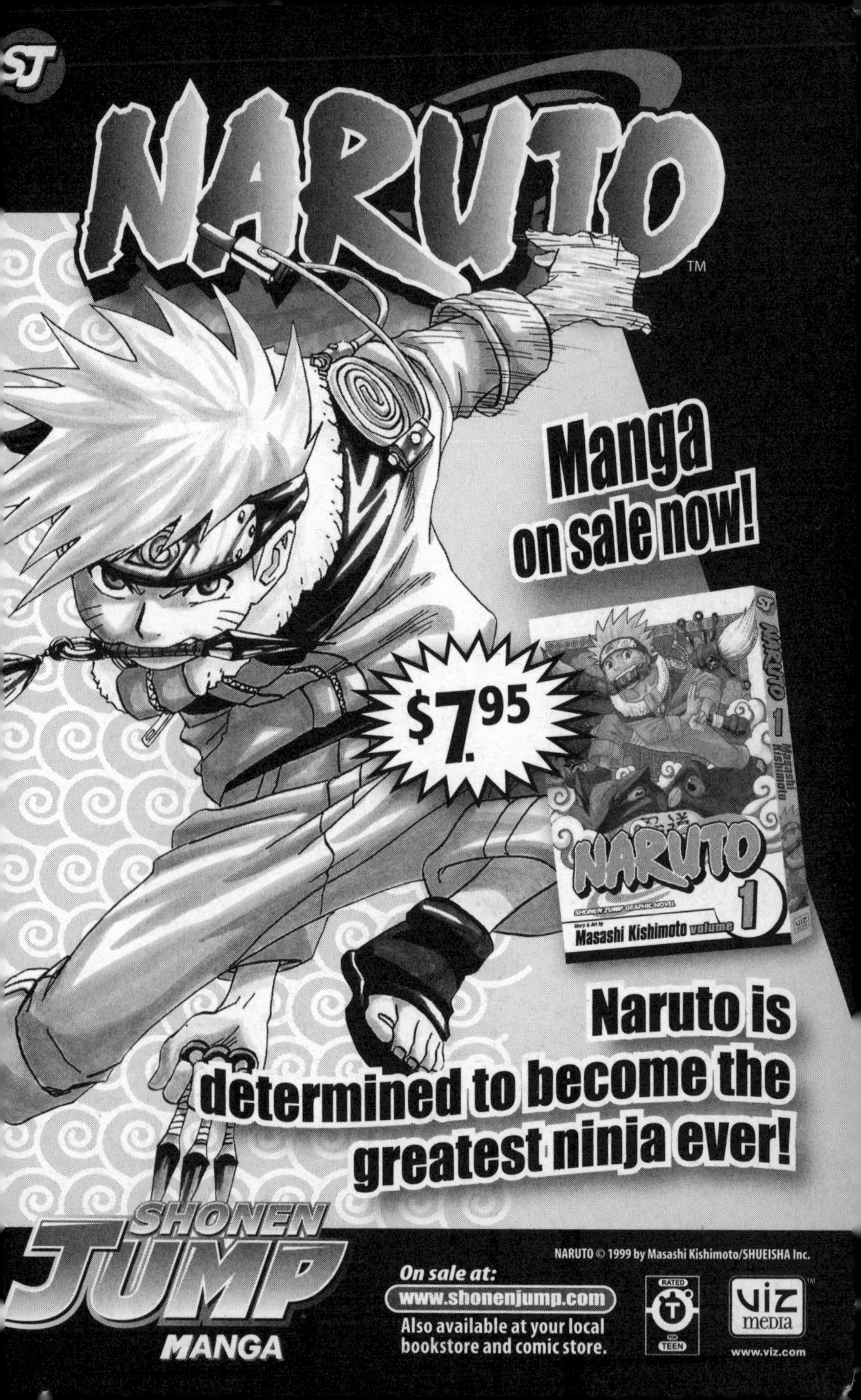

NARUTO™
Manga on sale now!
$7.95
NARUTO 1
Masashi Kishimoto volume 1
Naruto is determined to become the greatest ninja ever!
SHONEN JUMP MANGA
NARUTO © 1999 by Masashi Kishimoto/SHUEISHA Inc.
On sale at:
www.shonenjump.com
Also available at your local bookstore and comic store.
RATED T TEEN
VIZ media
www.viz.com

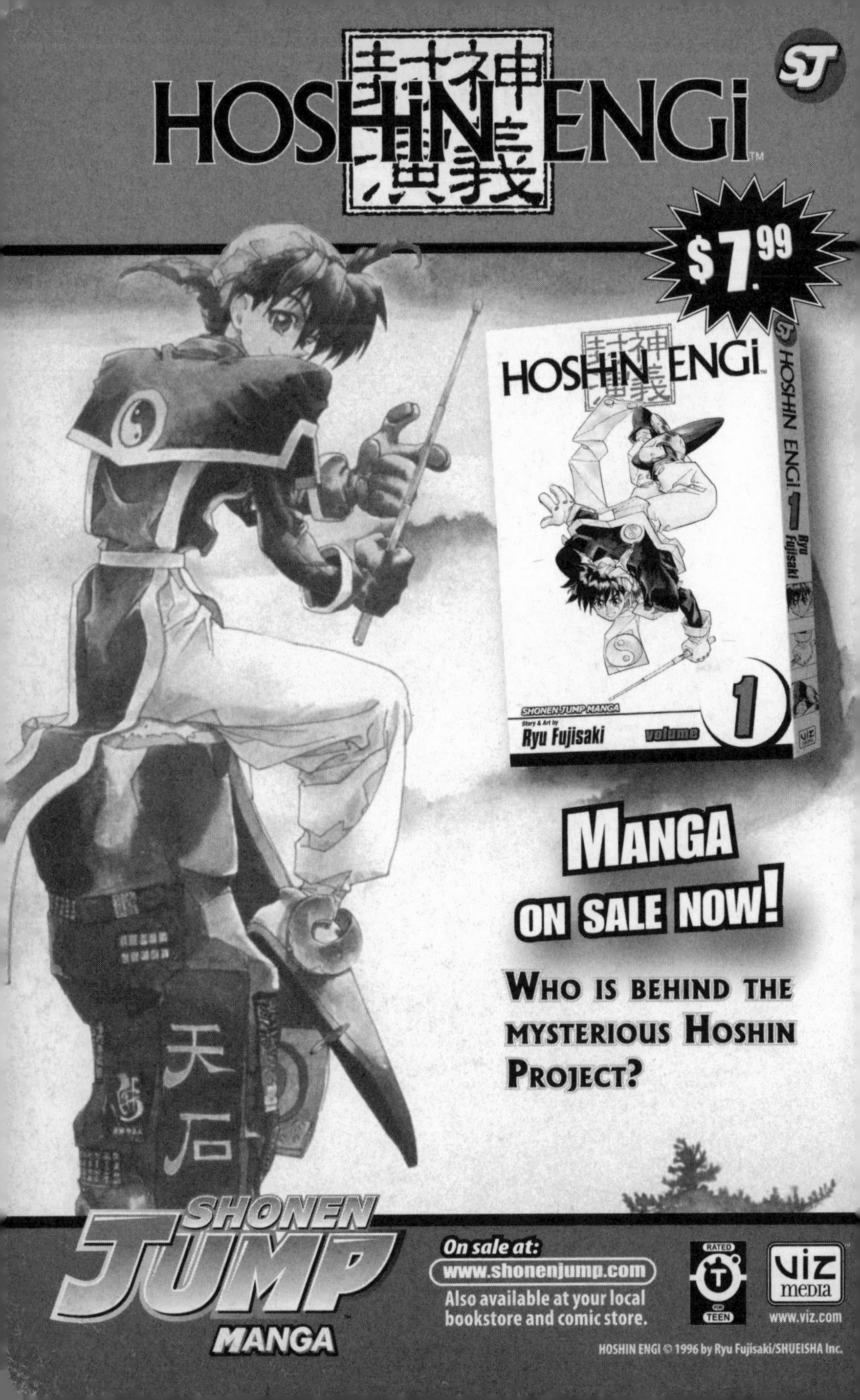
HOSHIN ENGI™
封神演義
SJ
$7.99
HOSHIN ENGI
SHONEN JUMP MANGA
Story & Art by
Ryu Fujisaki
volume 1
MANGA
ON SALE NOW!
WHO IS BEHIND THE MYSTERIOUS HOSHIN PROJECT?
SHONEN JUMP MANGA
On sale at:
www.shonenjump.com
Also available at your local bookstore and comic store.
RATED T FOR TEEN
viz media
www.viz.com
HOSHIN ENGI © 1996 by Ryu Fujisaki/SHUEISHA Inc.

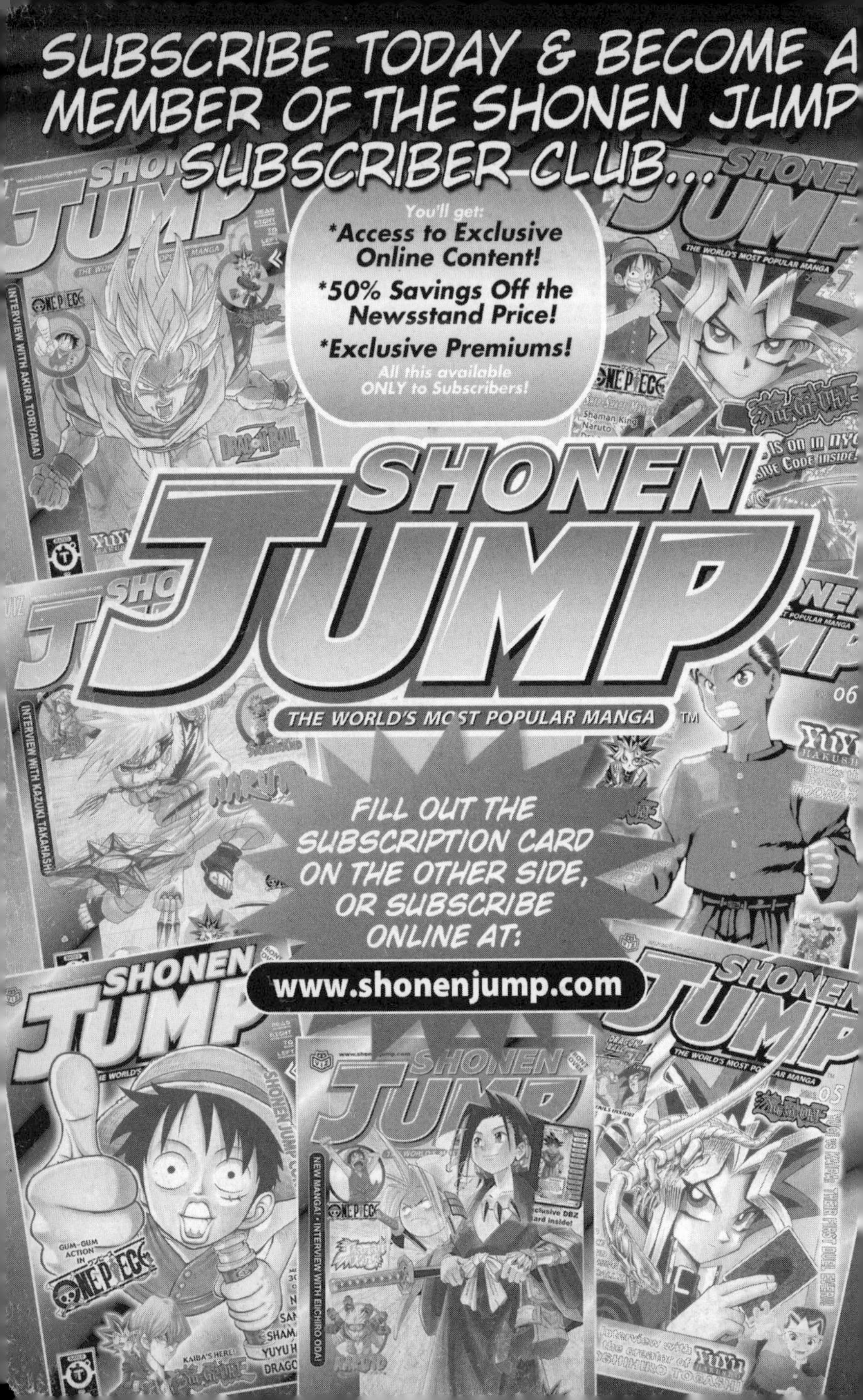
SUBSCRIBE TODAY & BECOME A MEMBER OF THE SHONEN JUMP SUBSCRIBER CLUB...
You'll get:
*Access to Exclusive Online Content!
*50% Savings Off the Newsstand Price!
*Exclusive Premiums!
All this available ONLY to Subscribers!
SHONEN JUMP
THE WORLD'S MOST POPULAR MANGA ™
FILL OUT THE SUBSCRIPTION CARD ON THE OTHER SIDE, OR SUBSCRIBE ONLINE AT:
www.shonenjump.com